D1578047

Praise for *The Humane Hoax*

"Amidst the marketing claims of 'happy' and 'humane,' this anthology provides the truth that sets free consumers who want to live ethically and eat honestly. Concurrently, it seeks to set free those animals trapped in the agricultural system, of which 'small,' 'family' and 'organic' farms are all a part"—**Victoria Moran**, author of *Main Street Vegan* and host of The Victoria Moran Podcast

"We live in an era of a catastrophic and rapid ecological genocide, and concurrently increasing human poverty and exploitation. We live in an era of massive exploitation and suffering of animals on a scale beyond imagining. These calamities are intertwined. Biophysically, we cannot resolve the ecological crisis or achieve global food security without transitioning towards plant foods. Mentally, we cannot relinquish our tendency to rationalize our exploitation of humans, animals or the environment without a universal and encompassing empathy. Never before has the confluence of science, rationality, ethics and compassion been more important. As such I hope this anthology reaches far and wide."
—**Dr. Tushar Mehta**, creator of PlantBasedData.org

"*The Humane Hoax* shines an important and necessary bright light on the many myths and marketing lies surrounding animal agriculture. Violence, exploitation, commodification, and killing sentient beings to satisfy our desires can never be made ethical by adding the word 'humane' to it. Humane animal farming is, and always will be, an oxymoron."—**Charles Horn**, Ph.D., author of *Meat Logic: Why Do We Eat Animals?*

"Animal advocacy is working—more dairy, egg, and meat producers tout 'humanely raised' or 'carbon-friendly' than ever before. Yet *The Humane Hoax* reveals that these glitzy, hollow labels hide the real and significant harms that animal agriculture continues to wreak. This anthology is a necessary, complete rejoinder to the recent locavore, femivore, and meat apologist movements. *The Humane Hoax*'s highly-educated authors show us in entertaining, diverse ways—supported with thorough research and approachable explanation—that a path to a better world cannot include animal agriculture."—**Karthik Sekar**, author of *After Meat*

"Hope Bohanec, and her brilliant team of essayists, expose the meat industry's cynical greenwashing and mislabeling for what it is: Orwellian double-speak. Read this book, learn the truth, and take the power back with your food choices."—**Jane Velez-Mitchell**, TV Journalist, NYTimes bestselling author, UnchainedTV founder

"This book expresses a fiercely compassionate worldview. It refuses to shy away from suffering—and inspires us to do something. Often, food labels and ads mislead consumers and don't tell the whole truth. *The Humane Hoax* will open your mind."—**Alene Anello**, Legal Impact for Chickens

"This collection of thought-provoking essays from a wide variety of voices exposes a truth that the animal agriculture industry works hard to conceal. *The Humane Hoax* is a wake-up call to every consumer who believes that labels such as 'cage-free,' 'pasture-raised,' or 'responsibly sourced' are anything but a marketing ploy."—**Mark Hawthorne**, author of *Bleating Hearts: The Hidden World of Animal Suffering*

"Consumers want to believe that the animals they eat are well-treated. However, humane labels and regulation bring comfort *only* to consumers, while the animals remain just as—if not more—exploited. This anthology helps shine a much-needed light on what 'humane' concepts *actually* mean for the beings they are designed to protect. In order to make informed decisions, to look ourselves in the mirror and ask if we are truly living the values we purport to have, we must know the truth. Consumers deserve to know the reality behind the labels. They deserve to know what they are paying others to do to animals in their name. I urge you to read this book and ask yourself: if you personally had to do to animals what humane labels allow, would you?"—**Emily Moran Barwick**, Activist, Educator, Speaker, and Writer at BiteSizeVegan.org

"As you step into the world of *The Humane Hoax*, you will be instantly transported into the reality of the cruel and harsh world that innocent farm animals endure second by second until they are violently killed for their meat, dairy and eggs. The so called 'humane meat' racket is visually exposed word by word, sentence by sentence in this collection of powerful essays. This book's immersion into the truth behind the lies and deception of humane labeling will leave you ready to ditch any notion that animals are treated any better on so called 'humane meat farms.'

The editor of *The Humane Hoax*, Hope Bohanec, has a depth of compassion for the sentience of all life combined with lifelong knowledge and experience of the issue. The fact that she's seen and documented first-hand these horrors make her an excellent eye-witness. A staunch advocate for revealing the unbridled truth behind the fabricated labels and lies, I highly recommend her work."—**Renee King-Sonnen**, Founder & Executive Director, Rowdy Girl Sanctuary & The Rancher Advocacy Program

"What would the world look like if we were all willing to live a life of empathy based on the truth? Witnessing the truth through this book is so powerful. I want to get a copy into the hands of every human on earth. A perfect eye-opening, heart-opening look at the reality of the myths behind humanewashing labels. A true wake-up call."—**Rae Sikora**, Co-founder Institute for Humane Education, Vegfund and Plant Peace Daily

"*The Humane Hoax* makes clear the depravity of the myth of 'humanely raised' animal foods. The claim to being in any way 'humane' is simply false; the claim to being more healthful is a lie; the cost to the environment is often even worse than from conventional animal farming; and there is the added insult of duplicity."—**Glen Merzer**, author, *Food Is Climate* and *Own Your Health*

"Lies poison everything. Humane hype not only injures animals by hiding the harms they suffer but also hurts people by tricking them into betraying their own ethical commitments. Coming at the problem from every angle, the diverse contributors to this essential volume not only expose the lies but also explain why they have been so persuasive. Read this book to make sure you haven't been hoodwinked and to learn what you need to know to refute the fictions that coax so many people who care about animals into literally buying into cruelty."—**pattrice Jones**, author of *Oxen at the Intersection* and founder of VINE Sanctuary

The
HUMANE
HOAX

Essays Exposing the Myth of Happy Meat,
Humane Dairy, and Ethical Eggs

Edited by Hope Bohanec

Lantern Publishing & Media ● Woodstock and Brooklyn, NY

2023
Lantern Publishing & Media
PO Box 1350
Woodstock, NY 12498
www.lanternpm.org

Copyright © 2023 Hope Bohanec

All rights reserved. No part of this book may be reproduced, stored in a retrieval system, or transmitted in any form or by any means, electronic, mechanical, photocopying, recording, or otherwise, without the written permission of Lantern Publishing & Media.

Cover Design by Rebecca Moore

Printed in the United States of America

Library of Congress Cataloging-in-Publication Data

Names: Bohanec, Hope, editor.
Title: The humane hoax : essays exposing the myth of happy meat, humane dairy, and ethical eggs / edited by Hope Bohanec.
Description: Woodstock, NY : Lantern Publishing & Media, 2023. | Includes bibliographical references.
Identifiers: LCCN 2022031480 (print) | LCCN 2022031481 (ebook) | ISBN 9781590566886 (paperback) | ISBN 9781590566893 (epub)
Subjects: LCSH: Food animals—Moral and ethical aspects. | Animal industry—Moral and ethical aspects. | Animal industry—Marketing. | Animal welfare. | Consumer behavior—Moral and ethical aspects.
Classification: LCC HV4757 .H86 2023 (print) | LCC HV4757 (ebook) | DDC 179/3—dc23/eng/20220818
LC record available at https://lccn.loc.gov/2022031480
LC ebook record available at https://lccn.loc.gov/2022031481

This book is dedicated to Kukkuta the Rooster,
who helped me to discover a new level of love.

TABLE OF CONTENTS

About the Author
About the Publisher

INTRODUCTION

The Humane Hoax: Animal Industry's Labels and Lies

by Hope Bohanec

I had just walked by half a dozen signs announcing that this farm was "Certified Organic" and "Environmentally Certified" and made "Real California Milk" when I saw a newborn calf, no more than a few hours old, curled up in a murky puddle of mud. Still wet with birth fluid, his tiny body was shivering, his eyes wide with fear and confusion looking for his mother. Giving up the search, he woefully bowed his chin to rest on his tucked legs. I knew that he was a little boy because the female calves, who were also dragged from their mothers, were taken to the other side of the dairy farm. They were confined, and sometimes chained, to "calf hutches"—white plastic boxes lined up like milk cartons where the baby girls are separated from their moms and from one another. But this little guy shivering in the mud is a byproduct of the dairy industry and considered worthless because he would never produce milk. A transport truck would soon arrive to take him and the other male calves to be sold at auction and killed for veal or beef.

Despite what the industry would have consumers believe, the fundamental nature of animal agriculture doesn't magically change with a smaller venture, organic certification, or deceptive "humane" label. There are countless inherent cruelties that are ubiquitous in the production of meat, milk, and eggs—no matter the label or size of the farm.

It has been a decade since I wrote the first book on the subject of the humane hoax called *The Ultimate Betrayal: Is There Happy Meat?* In that time, consumer awareness of the suffering of farmed animals in animal agriculture has grown and so has the misleading "alternative" animal product offerings. Euphemistic labels like "cage-free" and "certified humane" are not as rare as they used to be when they were seen only in the dusty back corners of health food stores. These deceptive marketing schemes are now as common and numerous as cows in a feedlot. They can be found in ordinary places like mainstream grocery stores, TV advertisements, social media, and even your local coffee shop. For example, in 2010 eggs labeled "cage-free" were a mere 4% of the market. That had risen to 16% by 2017 and the industry predicts that to meet consumer demand, cage-free production will rise to 71% of the market by 2026.[1]

Animal advocacy organizations, individual investigators, and academics alike have successfully exposed and publicized the animal agriculture industry for its cruelty and devastating environmental impacts, yet the clever industry marketers counter with so-called humane labels, small-scale tall tales, and feel-good falsehoods. It has never been more important to educate consumers about the truth behind the industry's lies. And people are hungry for the truth.

In animal rights forums, conferences, online, and other venues, the term "humane hoax" has been gaining currency since the expression was first coined in 2015 at the Animal Rights National Conference.[*] The "humane hoax" refers to the animal agriculture industry's marketing efforts that employ euphemistic rhetoric conveying a fraudulent narrative of the purported "humane" treatment and "sustainable" management of farmed animal operations. With the exploitation and abuse of animal agriculture effectively exposed, to obscure the blemishes, marketers are wrapping a cloak of deceiving euphemisms, serene stories, and sanguine descriptions around their industry in nearly all sectors. The increasing popularity of these misleading labels manifests across industry lines, from smaller farming operations to the much larger Concentrated Animal Feeding Operations (CAFOs) of industrial farming.

---

[*] The term "humane hoax" was first used as the title of a panel discussion on the subject at the 2015 Animal Rights National Conference hosted by Farm Animal Rights Movement (FARM).

Also tied to the humane hoax are small, noncommercial, "backyard" farms operated by people attempting to "do-it-yourself" (DIY) by raising and slaughtering farmed animals, generally motivated by good intentions, but the consequences are often no less cruel. Clearly, the need for the domination and exploitation of animals to be obscured and concealed in the innocuous, reassuring stories of peaceful pastures and happy animals is being felt by nearly all animal farming sectors, commercial or otherwise, that participate in violence against animals. This book seeks to engage in a thorough analysis regarding the ramifications of this widespread industry shift.

It is a hopeful sign that consumers are demanding better treatment for animals, but the actual difference with humane labeling in the life and death experience for a farmed animal is sadly minimal. I have done extensive research on this issue, interviewed numerous stakeholders, and personally visited multiple animal operations and have concluded that these unregulated labels mean very little, if anything at all, for the animal's experience. I have found, for example, that comparing hens confined in battery cages to those in cage-free floor systems bodes only slight improvements, and those can vary widely from operation to operation. Animal activists have time and again exposed the horrors of hens bred to lay eggs for human consumption crammed tightly in industry standard battery cages. The experience is equivalent to living in a crowded elevator. In response, the clever marketers representing the egg industry distorted the story, altered the labels, and changed consumers' conceptions. Instead of rejecting the inherent cruelty of commercial egg production, shoppers have been offered the false choice of the seemingly humane alternative of "cage-free"—but the reality for the birds, however, is bleak.

The difference in the experience of a bird in a conventionally managed operation versus a cage-free one is negligible. Despite the feel-good label, most chickens in cage-free egg facilities still live in miserable overcrowded conditions in massive windowless buildings. Their eyes and throats burn from the ammonia gas released from their accumulated waste. They never feel the sun on their wings or experience a simple satisfying dust bath. Irrespective of any label, all the birds still go to a brutal slaughter at a very young age. We must not let the deception of "new" marketing eclipse the fundamental cruelty of animal agriculture.

Confinement to a conventional battery cage is certainly tortuous for the hens. Most people would agree that it is beneficial to get the hens out of the cages. This instinctual kindness, however, is exactly what the marketing efforts of the industry seek to exploit. The perception invoked by the "cage-free" label—that the birds are now living a good life—is a decidedly false one, a mirage created by the interaction of euphemisms and consumer hopes in the absence of accurate information.

The multifarious distresses that chickens face in egg production— the horrors of the hatcheries, debeaking, overcrowding, reproductive manipulation, mind-numbing monotony, the terror of transport, a violent slaughter, etc.—are concealed by a rhetorical sleight of hand. All welfare considerations for the hens are funneled through the single lens of the size of their confinement, which is now seemingly resolved by cage-free eggs. The truth is hidden, and the solution is a false promise, a pattern that is all too familiar in the history of human dominance and oppression. The label, though accurate in that they are no longer in small cages, belies a false impression.

These cage-free chickens, *these sentient beings,* are *not* living a good life. On the contrary, they still live miserable, short lives in turmoil and fear in overcrowded conditions.

Slow Growth

The growth of the number of people identifying as vegetarian or vegan is on a steady rise.[2] The latest assessments estimate that 10% of people in the United States are vegetarians or vegan, that's about one in ten U.S. citizens (up from half a percent three decades ago).[3] This is an incredible amount of growth in a relatively short period of time. However, could the increase have been even faster if all the agents of animal product marketing didn't counter-match the critiques at every turn? If consumers didn't have the choice of cage-free eggs, might they not buy eggs at all? This is hard to determine. Nonetheless, it is more critical than ever to expand the public's knowledge of the ugly truth behind alternative labeling of meat, eggs, and dairy. We must remain ever vigilant to spotlight how little difference there truly is between conventional and alternative animal products. As we will explore in this book, these new labels can sometimes be *even worse* for the animals and the environment.

It is interesting to note that 58% of people surveyed in 2017 by the Sentience Institute believed that farmed animals were treated well, and 75% assumed that the products that they purchased came from "animals that are treated humanely."[4]

Unfortunately, we don't have historical data to compare to years past, but I would argue that recent marketing efforts may play a part in manufacturing the misinformation that such statistics represents. Perhaps it is because people are now seeing labels like "certified humane" and "grass-fed," they assume that humane treatment for animals is a trend throughout the animal farming industry. Some consumers may think that even if they are not buying these higher-priced alternative items, all animal farming is reforming, and animals are being given more space and better lives across the board. If that is the case, it is certainly a false assumption as very little has improved in the last five decades for farmed animals. If anything, conditions for farmed animals have gotten substantially worse. As the Sentience Institute proposes, "This suggests a *psychological refuge* effect where people justify their animal product consumption by incorrectly assuming they are eating ethically produced food."[5]

The presence of alternative and "humane" labels in the market exacerbates this effect, appeasing consumers with a false sense that there is an industry-wide movement toward better conditions for farmed animals, when no such trend actually exists. It is therefore the genius of the industry's marketing efforts that while conditions are actually getting worse, consumers believe they are getting better—a situation of true Orwellian doublespeak.

From the extensive research that we will discuss in this book, the reader will become aware of our collective conclusion that there are unavoidable and inherent cruelties in the breeding, raising, and killing of animals to produce meat, dairy, and eggs—and no label can change that. Only very minimal "improvements" are possible if the industry is to maintain an adequate profit margin.

One of our expert authors, Robert Grillo, sums it up nicely in his book *Farm to Fable* by saying:

> Many of the worst cruelties inflicted on animals in large industrial farms are also routine practices in small free-range farms. These include sexual violations and the exploitation of the reproductive systems; the destruction of motherhood and families, routine mutilations without anesthetic; denial of the most fundamental behaviors and preferences; and brutal transport and slaughter conditions.[6]

INDUSTRY FRIENDLY LABELS

One distressing example is the "American Certified Humane" label on Butterball turkeys. Butterball produces more than 1.5 billion pounds of turkey meat a year and is the largest producer of turkey products in the United States.[7] For this "certified humane" label, there is no requirement for outdoor access, and the birds are debeaked[*] and detoed[†], the same as in conventional operations. Unnatural genetic manipulation causes these unfortunate birds to grow to be impossibly overweight, becoming so heavy that their bones are often too weak to support their bulk and their legs simply snap, leaving the bird crippled and in chronic pain. They also suffer from leg deformities or develop arthritis and joint pain just in their first few months of life. Contrary to the labeling, these birds still meet the same horrifying end in a slaughterhouse, as do all of the other non-certified turkeys.

The only tangible difference required to award this label is a few meager inches more of living space than their non-certified counterparts. While this may be slightly better than nothing at all, there is no justification for such a derisory change to be all that is needed to meet

---

[*] Debeaking, referred to by the industry as beak-trimming, is when the tip of the bird's beak is cut off with a heated blade. Debeaking has been scientifically proven to cause acute and chronic pain.

[†] Detoeing is the removal of the first or sometimes first and second section of the toe of a turkey. Workers use any number of different implements, including scissors and branch trimmers, without anesthesia. Detoeing can inflict lifelong pain and debilitation so severe they are unable to walk properly, using their wings as crutches to help them reach food and water.

requirements for a "humane" label. Clearly this is deceiving customers into believing that there are significant differences experienced by the turkeys sold with this label, when indeed there are not. "Consumer fraud" is not an inappropriate label to attach to this willful deception.

It is significant to note that in some counties and states, if the cruel and routine "standard practices" of farming without anesthesia—castration, tail cutting, horn cauterization, branding, tooth filing, toe extraction, etc.—were inflicted on a dog or a cat, the perpetrator could face felony animal cruelty charges. But there are exemptions to animal cruelty laws for agricultural farming practices. Any practice deemed necessary for the efficiency of the operation, by the industry itself, regardless of how cruel or merciless, is defined legally as "standard agricultural practices." These heartless daily procedures are allowed even in so-called humane animal farming.

Other forms of blatantly brutal conduct are routine as well. Just because it may be a "small family farm," or there is a "humane" label, or even if you have personally met the owner or rancher, it does not mean that the animals are not punched, prodded, kicked, poked, shouted at or otherwise tormented. I have interviewed numerous former animal agricultural workers who witnessed this abuse on small farms, on family farms, and on farms with a host of feel-good product labels, as I documented in my book *The Ultimate Betrayal*. Flagrant animal abuse is common practice in *all* animal agriculture.

A "Fair Life"?

Another example of how cruel practices are universal in any animal farming operation, irrespective of scale, came to the public's attention in June of 2019 when an undercover video circulated on social media. The video exposed unimaginably cruel acts committed against calves and cows at Fair Oaks Farms, a supplier for Fairlife Dairy products. It showed workers forcefully dragging, throwing, kicking, and punching calves who were just days old. Calves were body-slammed to the ground, thrown off the sides of trucks, dragged with a tractor by their ears, and some left to die in heat that exceeded one hundred degrees Fahrenheit. The footage is heartbreaking and extremely difficult to watch.

Fairlife was founded in 2012 as a supposed ethical alternative to conventional dairy and, as the name implies, to ostensibly give a "fair life" to the animals. Fairlife's website states that it is "committed to the humane and compassionate care of animals" and that it offers "extraordinary care and comfort" to their cows and calves.

The outrage over the video was so passionate that several workers were charged with animal cruelty and some grocery stores pulled Fairlife products from their shelves. Lawsuits were filed by consumers claiming that Fairlife committed fraud by lying about their standards of care for the animals. For weeks, Fairlife focused much of their energy on damage control with numerous press releases and blog posts denouncing the actions of the employees involved.

Not surprisingly, they blamed the individual workers and condemned their actions as isolated. This is the standard procedure every time a whistleblower comes forward with painful and damaging video evidence. What the public doesn't know, however, is that there have now been hundreds of undercover investigations of numerous dairies, hog farms, chicken meat and egg faculties, and slaughterhouses—both conventional and with humane certifications and labels—and *not once* did the investigator come out empty-handed. Every time, the courageous activists would emerge with damning evidence of animal abuse after just a few days or weeks of working at the farms. They bravely captured videos and photos of horrific violence. The logical conclusion is that mistreatment and cruelty is both common and standard practice in animal agriculture. No advertising efforts designed to develop a niche market will stop the cruelty. Abuse is the nature of commodification and exploitation of sensitive, sentient animals.

Profit Is the Driving Motivation

The profitability of animal agribusiness is the key factor in all of this. Most of the "standard practice" cruelties of animal agriculture came about in the last few decades and were developed for the sake of efficiency and productivity to increase the industry's bottom line. The confinement, family separation, body mutilations, short lives, etc., all make the products more abundant, consistent, and affordable. To meet consumers' more recent demand for better treatment for animals, the industry can only do so much before the product is too expensive and the business is compromised. They rely on keeping consumers blind to the truth and on the deceiving spin of a narrative of something "new," something "better." Perpetuating the "humane hoax" is their only hope of survival. They are paying slick advertisers billions of dollars to craft a sympathetic and benevolent fiction of a new method of farming that exists only on the websites and in the misleading images and phrases on milk and egg cartons and other packaging. In reality, they *cannot* change the nature of their business without the collapse of the system itself.

To the industry, animals are nothing more than commodities; their lives are not important except for making a profit on a product. In any and all animal farming, commodifying the bodies of animals by making consumer products of their body parts and secretions denies their agency. This can never be ethical, no matter how much humanewashing is printed on the label or carton. The fables of caring farmers are for the consumer's benefit only and do nothing for the animals themselves. As author and activist Jacy Reese describes in his book *The End of Animal Farming*, "Importantly, belief in ethical animal farming also reinforces the notion that animals are mere property, inanimate beings that exist only as means to human ends. So long as other animals are considered our property, even their most desperate needs come second to our most trivial wants."[8]

GOOD INTENTIONS, CRUEL CONSEQUENCES

Beyond marketing and labels, there is another emerging aspect of the "humane hoax" phenomenon that is happening right in our backyard. Rejecting industrial animal agribusiness, people with the space, means, time, and resources are buying chickens and other small farmed animals for backyard eggs and DIY slaughter for meat. The intention to "do it yourself," instead of supporting a massive industry that has been repeatedly exposed for its carelessness and cruelty, is a good one. But good intentions are not good enough to avoid the harmful downsides of this seemingly benevolent new fad. This issue is thoroughly explored in Alastor Van Kleeck's poignant chapter in this anthology.

I am so often asked, "What could be so bad about having a few chickens in the backyard and eating their eggs, or eating a neighbor's chickens' eggs?" Most people don't realize how this idealistic hobby can contribute to a malicious industry.

It starts at the very beginning with the initial acquisition of the chickens. Chicks or chickens sold from a feed store or off the internet likely came from industrial hatcheries. Chicks in hatcheries are not born in a warm nest with a doting mother hen. They emerge from their shells in metal incubator drawers and are immediately thrown into a nightmare of conveyer belts, metal machinery, and workers tossing them about like packaged goods. Every year, millions of baby chicks don't survive their first hours or days of life. They are either caught and crushed in the machinery or die from the lack of proper initial care from a mother hen.

Chickens bred for egg laying do not grow as large or as fast as the chickens bred for meat, so the males, unable to lay eggs, are considered a waste product. In their first hours of life, males are separated from the profitable females and are killed straightaway. They are thrown away by the hundreds of millions, stuffed into plastic garbage bags and left to suffer and suffocate, dehydrate, and starve in trash dumpsters in the back of the hatcheries. Other male chicks are whisked down conveyer belts to a grinder with metal blades that chops them up alive for use in fertilizer and other products. Still others are sent to a dark metal box for painful electrocution or gassing.

Some baby roosters are used as "packers" when the company is shipping females in the mail to egg-laying facilities and feed stores. During transport, the newborns will be without food or water for days in all extremes of temperature, roughly handled, and thrown about by the postal workers. The hatcheries know that some will likely die in transport. Adding a few "useless" males in the box with the order of chicks increases the chances of the survival of the desired females. Karen Davis, founder and president of United Poultry Concerns and an expert on the poultry industry, wrote, "People ordering chickens through the mail are often surprised at how sickly the birds are, not realizing that the hatchery experience plus the shipping ordeal weakens the birds' immunity, predisposing them to illness and early death."

From the initial stages of these backyard, DIY endeavors, it matters where the chickens come from and if one is paying for a chick or a chicken. Supporting the hatcheries upholds the same brutal industry that hobbyists are trying to circumvent by "doing it themselves." Davis also says of chicken hatcheries, "Since there are no welfare laws regulating these operations, suppliers provide website images of green grass, sunny skies, and happy chickens, but this is more fiction than truth."

But even if aware of this issue, and conscientious enough to never pay for a bird and acquire one or more "rescued" hens, people are often not prepared for the level of care required to keep these birds. Chickens require a predator-proof coop to be secured in at night. Many people learn the hard way when unprotected birds are terrorized and killed by foxes, coyotes, and other predators. Coops require daily cleaning, as well as regular maintenance and upkeep. The coop needs straw nests and high roosts. Chickens need access to a yard, preferably with both grass and dirt areas, natural sunlight, shaded areas, enrichments, clean straw, a proper diet, treats, and friends. Importantly, the birds need the time and attention of their caregivers.[9]

It is also critical to have a compassionate and sympathetic veterinarian who is educated in treating domestic fowl, ideally a short distance away for emergencies. Chickens bred for laying eggs are so genetically compromised that they are vulnerable to a number of illnesses and get sick easily. Many rescued hens, given the opportunity to live their natural lifespan, die of complications to their reproductive systems. There are numerous illnesses and ailments that afflict chickens, including external and internal parasites, Marek's disease (a highly contagious viral neoplastic disease), Avian influenza, Newcastle disease (a viral avian disease, transmittable to humans), respiratory disease, nutritional problems, reproductive diseases, lice, fleas, tapeworms, and fowl pox.[10] Due to decades of the manipulation of egg-laying cycles, reproductive disorders, including uterine and vent prolapse and egg binding or impacting, are common and painful.* Most people don't foresee the veterinary care and costly bills that can come with keeping chickens and unfortunately, many don't bother to save a bird in distress

---

* A hen having discomfort or pain straining to lay an egg is possibly egg-bound or impacted. Prolapse is when a hen's oviduct, which normally is in her abdomen, pushes out through her vent (the opening to pass waste and eggs).

and will either slaughter her for meat or have her euthanized, even though comprehensive vet care could extend her life.

The side effect of unwanted roosters is another dilemma that is a function of the humane hoax as it manifests in non-industrial, "do it yourself" endeavors. Often, in cities and counties that do allow a certain number of chickens, only hens are allowed. Even though boisterous barking dogs can be even more thunderous, not to mention lawn care and carpentry equipment more an assault on the ears, roosters are not welcome in most neighborhoods because of their fondness for announcing the break of day.

When a backyard enthusiast discovers that her "hen" is actually a crowing rooster, her options are limited. Because of the new backyard egg craze, animal shelters and sanctuaries are inundated with roosters, and they often can't accept even one more. Roosters get dumped in parks, open fields, or wilderness areas to fend for themselves. Others are slaughtered for meat or fed to companion animals or other captive animals. Ryan Hill, cofounder of The Sky's the Limit Sanctuary, wrote in his poignant essay *The Boys of the Egg Industry*:

> The overpopulation of roosters created by the egg industry has become a crisis across the country. The biggest hurdle is that there are so few homes for them and so many are abandoned. And while their means of communication may not be the same as those of a furry mammal, their feelings are just as real. They feel loss. They feel pain. They feel love and trust.

My chapter in this book reveals my first-hand experience of the rooster dilemma when we rescued an abandoned rooster whom we named Kakkuta.

Some of these backyard do-it-yourselfers are going beyond eggs and buying, breeding, and raising animals to slaughter for meat. Chickens and rabbits are popular choices for this venture, but some people are raising turkeys, pigs, lambs, and other animals. Problems here range from keeping animals in small, filthy conditions, to a lack of veterinary care, to botched attempts at unskilled slaughters resulting in animals suffering terribly. I go into detail about gruesome backyard slaughter mishaps and blunders in my book *The Ultimate Betrayal*. Suffice it to say, it is not as easy as one would think to "humanely" kill an animal who does not want to die. We will investigate the issue of backyard slaughter further in this book with John Sanbonmatsu's brilliant exploration of the femivore.

GREENWASHING ANIMAL PRODUCTS

Since writing my first book on the subject of the humane hoax, there has been even more compelling studies of the environmental impacts of alternative animal farming systems. A plethora of such studies are finding that new methods of farming animals that are purported to be sustainable can actually be more harmful than conventional systems. A prime example is pastured, grass-fed beef and dairy. A Harvard Report published in the journal *Environmental Research Letters* found that a shift in the United States from feedlot cattle to grass-fed beef would *increase* greenhouse gas emissions by 43% and would require increasing the number of cows from 77 million to 100 million, as grass-fed cattle go to slaughter at a lower body weight and therefore feed fewer people.[11]

Certainly, some advocates of grass-fed animal products would contest that one cannot just throw the cows out in the pasture and expect environmental improvements; there are methods that must be implemented to make it work. Regenerative grazing (also called holistic management, short-duration grazing, controlled rotation, etc.), for example, involves taking a small herd of cows destined to be slaughtered for beef and moving them periodically from one fenced pasture to another so as to not "overgraze" a given area. However, after four decades of trials and studies, there has been no peer-reviewed scientific evidence showing this management approach is in any way better than conventional grazing systems. This system also requires extensive fencing, which disrupts wildlife migration and movement patterns within habitats.[12]

There have been numerous trials and it has been concluded by reputable scientists that short-duration grazing systems differ little in their effect upon range conditions. The evidence simply does not support the claims of enhanced ecological benefits, despite being rigorously evaluated by numerous investigators at multiple locations and in a wide range of precipitation zones over a period of several decades.[13] These methods simply do not increase soil carbon sequestering, they do not increase plant or animal production, and neither do they improve surface-water hydrology conditions.[14] One issue, of many, is that these systems required many acres more land for fewer animals. A 2014 study in the *International Journal of Biodiversity* stated that their research "could find no peer-reviewed studies that show that this management approach is superior to conventional grazing systems in outcomes."

In a thorough debunking of regenerative grazing systems, YouTube personality Mic the Vegan said, "Holistic management is something that people emotionally want to be true, but it just does not hold water scientifically."[15]

Thus, this new labeling hides an eco-hoax as well. These "humane" labels are lulling buyers into a bogus impression of environmental improvements. As we will see in the coming Greenwashing section, producing animal products, no matter the scale of the operation or the method, is almost always more energy- and resource-intensive, as well as polluting, than farming plants. According to the environmental research organization Worldwatch Institute:

> It has become apparent that the human appetite for animal flesh is the driving force behind virtually every major category or environmental damage now threatening the future—deforestation, erosion, fresh water scarcity, air and water pollution, climate change, biodiversity loss, social injustice, the destabilization of communities and the spread of diseases.[16]

DELVING DEEP

As animal agribusiness attempts to wash the blood off its hands with a new fabrication of fresh farming methods, consumers, activists, and other caring people must keep abreast of the new narratives that the industry continually weaves. As you can see, the challenges and impacts of the "humane hoax" are complex and multifaceted, and there is a lot to unpack.

This anthology features a range of knowledgeable authors who are at the forefront of this marketing shift, chronicling every aspect with in-depth analyses and intellectual rigor. We will explore how so-called alternative animal agriculture intersects with feminism, affects the environment, intertwines with human oppression, is presented in the media, and impacts all human and nonhuman communities.

These trailblazing authors range from academics to organizational leaders to grassroots activists, delving into every dark corner of the humane hoax to reveal the truth behind the labels and lies. Some have done extensive peer-reviewed research on the subject; others have been working in farmed animal advocacy for decades and thinking deeply about this issue. Still others are rescuing farmed animals directly from local and small-scale farms, witnessing first-hand the undeniable suffering that is commonplace in all animal farming.

Compassion Will Win

I have always believed that we will see a just, compassionate, vegan world one day. Why am I so hopeful (beside it being my namesake)? *Because most people love animals.* It is inherent and instinctual. Killing and eating animals may have once been a necessary adaptation for human survival as our early ancestors migrated across the globe and settled in inhospitable lands. Over millennia, animal confinement and killing has become normalized as a tradition and part of our worldview and ingrained as an unexamined paradigm. But when we are confronted with the suffering of an individual animal, our instinct is to protect animals and care for them. When a mother duck attempts to lead her ducklings across a hectic road with cars whizzing dangerously close, courageous and compassionate people will stop traffic and help guide the family to safety. Social media provides an endless stream of video evidence of this type of human kindness toward animals. If we encounter an injured animal on the side of a road, our impulse is to offer assistance. A true carnivore would see an opportunity for dinner. I believe it is in our nature to nurture.

A recent survey by Faunalytics found that a majority of people (68%) support efforts "to minimize and eventually eliminate all forms of animal cruelty and suffering." And 80% feel that animal welfare is very or somewhat important.[17]

A common reaction to someone hearing about veganism or cruelty in animal agriculture is, "I don't want to hear it!" Why? Because they love animals and don't want to see or hear about someone being hurt. They know that something is not right in animal farming and they don't want to see animals suffer. Of course, they also don't want to acknowledge that their own behavior as consumers contributes to the suffering and systematic violence of the animal agriculture industry. Some may even elect for willful ignorance because the truth would result in cognitive dissonance. Acknowledging the truth would require them to either change their behavior or live with the guilt of continuing engagement in and support of something they feel is wrong.

But the evidence that farmed animals suffer in the production of meat, dairy, and egg products is now overwhelming. People are finding it increasingly difficult to ignore it and look away. So, the animal products industries are offering an appeasement, "We will treat the animals humanely before we kill them." This concession has placated many consumers who are now seeking out these "humanely" labeled products. Unfortunately, the industries' promises are hollow and there is very little, if any, difference in the farming methods. The contradiction is that people are pacified with humane treatment for the short duration of the animals' lives, but still accept killing a young healthy cow, pig, turkey, or chicken. How is this justified? The killing itself must be at least as bad as any other violent treatment. Undercover investigations of slaughterhouses reveal terrified animals slaughtered without effective stunning and still-conscious animals left to agonize for minutes after their throats are slit.

It is certainly not necessary to eat animals as the millions of vigorous vegans can attest to. Yet we feel that we must justify slaughter, so a compromise is offered; we will at least treat animals well while they are alive. But how can killing an innocent animal who wants desperately to live, as all animals do, be acceptable? As Robert Grillo states in his excellent book *Farm to Fable*, "Our . . . confusion stems from the startling hypocrisy of this message: We must respect animals during the short time they are allowed to stay alive, but we don't need to respect their very lives." As I explore in my first book, *The Ultimate Betrayal*, animals want to live, and we have no right to kill young, innocent animals simply for the pleasure of eating their flesh.

A Humane World Without the Hoax

Numerous forward-thinking animal advocacy organizations now have educational materials addressing the fictions of free-range eggs, grass-fed beef, and "humane" dairy. More recently, the Humane Hoax Project has stepped up the education and outreach with online conferences, webinars, and full educational booklets on the issue. This is going to be a challenging area for 21st-century animal activism, and my hope is that this anthology will be a vital and useful tool in our advocacy.

It doesn't matter what package it is wrapped in or what story is being told, when someone's bodily autonomy is erased and whose destiny is an untimely death, all for a commercial product, it can only be considered oppression and violence. My hope is that this book will help to clarify, document, and detail the insidious nature of this "new method" of animal farming and expose the ruthless commodification and slaughter of sentient beings, no matter the scale or label.

PART 1:
HUMANEWASHING

"Unfortunately, the only comfort humane labels bring is to our conscience."—**Emily Moran Barwick**, *Vegan Voices: Essays by Inspiring Changemakers*

1

A Pig Called Silver

by Ingrid L. Taylor

W e named her Silver. She was a petite pig, pink with dark spots around her eyes and her back feet. My mother always said she looked like she was wearing makeup and heels. Silver was born on the small Minnesota farm where I spent my childhood. She was the runt of the litter, and as such, she was slated to be killed. We raised "feeder" pigs on our farm, and their size mattered—the larger the better, because they were intended to be slaughtered for meat when they reached a certain size. We had around 40 pigs for breeding, mostly females who, because of forced breeding, produced litter after litter. The piglets were weaned at two to three weeks of age. We then sold them to feedlots at a couple of months old, where they would remain until reaching target weights for market. Silver was part of one of these litters, but she was sickly and too small to be profitable. Conditions were hard for the animals on the farm—despite having a barn for shelter, the pigs were often exposed to wind, cold, and heat, as well as food scarcities. Cutting costs on the farm often meant buying cheap, nutritionally poor feed for the pigs and, given the season, there may not have been much for them to eat on pasture. Infant mortality was a regular occurrence on our farm. Those who were unlikely to survive, like Silver, were sometimes killed by violently swinging them by their hind legs and then smashing their skulls on the ground. The industry calls this "thumping." Other times, they were simply left to perish of illness on their own.

Piglets died on our farm, and this was the cost of doing business. But for some reason, my mother took pity on Silver and brought her into our farmhouse. Perhaps it was the piglet's unique markings, or maybe my mother had seen so much death that she wanted to be able to save just one individual from a painful demise. We made Silver a warm, cozy bed in the downstairs bathroom and bottle-fed her on a regular schedule. Silver quickly adapted to living in the house and playing with my brother and me. She followed us around, stole our toys, and instigated games of chase. To me, at the time, she seemed very different from the pigs outside, who were dirty, didn't want to play, and in fact actively tried to avoid us most of the time. Even as a young child, I could sense their unhappiness, but I didn't understand why being around them made me so uncomfortable. Silver, on the other hand, was a happy pig, and I could spend hours with her.

But Silver grew, as pigs do, and became too large to stay in the house. She still had her striking markings, and she was still small compared to the other pigs, but she had far surpassed her predicated size as a once sickly runt. When she was moved to the outside pasture and barn, she became a solitary pig. Dislocated abruptly from her human family, the only family she'd known, Silver had no idea how to interact with other pigs. My father wanted to breed her—she refused to even consider it and would fight off the boars and run from other pigs. If my mother, brother, or I came out to the pasture, she sprinted at breakneck pace to the fence for a glimpse of us, sometimes trying to push her face between the slats, and other times rearing up with her front legs on the fence as she tried to reach us.

Silver never got over thinking we were her family, but it took me years to realize how deep our betrayal had been of her love and trust. Today, it shatters me to think of her so isolated, in a strange and harsh situation outside of the home she'd grown up in, not understanding why we no longer played together or took lazy afternoon naps in the sun on the living room floor.

Pastured Pigs: An Emerging Niche Market

Farmers who raise pastured pigs construct an idyllic vision of blissful, healthy pigs that contrasts with the abuses of industrial agriculture.

Rather than being confined in tortuous farrowing crates[*] and tiny indoor pens with no access to natural light or the outdoors, pigs raised on pasture are presented as happier, stronger, and more fulfilled—which also translates to better "products" for health- and eco-conscious consumers. On first impression, it may appear that raising pigs on pasture is more humane, but pastured pigs are still subjected to many of the same abuses inherent in the agricultural industry. In addition, raising pigs on pasture has unique complications for animal welfare and well-being. But what, exactly, does it mean to raise pigs on pasture?

Simply put, raising pigs on pasture means a farming system where pigs are allowed access to the outdoors, usually in large pens or fenced areas, to graze and forage. It is not a new idea—150 years ago the dominant farming model for pigs was on pasture.[1] But in the United States, growing and slaughtering pigs for food has become a colossal business. Worldwide, the U.S. is the third largest producer and consumer of products made from pigs.[2] In 1995, the U.S. became a leading exporter and has, in the intervening decades, become the second largest global exporter of pigs and the products made from their bodies.[3] This major shift in pork production has its roots in the early 1980s, when animal agriculture business models moved from smaller farms to large industrial operations that hold thousands of pigs in crowded, confined environments.[4] Small family farms that produced more diverse products gave way to monocropping and specialization in single species of animals, as well as selective breeding to create animals who produced more meat. As of June 2021, 75 million pigs were being raised on U.S. farms, of whom around 69 million will be slaughtered at a fraction of their natural lifespan. The remainder are used for breeding.[5] Since 1960, pigs at slaughter have increased in average weight from 200 to 281 pounds.[6] This transition was rapid, and the face of agriculture underwent greater change in the 20th century than it had over thousands of years.[7] Smaller farms were unable to compete with large industrial operations, and our

---

[*]   Farrowing crates are tight pens, only slightly larger than the pig, that prevent
a mother pig from turning around or moving freely. In addition to the severe
restraint of the pens, farrowing crates also disrupt normal interactions between
a pig and her piglets.

family farm was one of the many that did not survive this economic transformation.

However, there is an increasing awareness among consumers about the costs of industrialized agriculture operations, in terms of animal welfare, human health, and damage to the environment. Consumer choices are being actively influenced by considerations of welfare and sustainability, and consumers hold increasingly negative perceptions of industrial animal agriculture.[8] In research compiled by Animal Welfare Institute, Technomic's 2019 Center of the Plate: Beef and Pork Consumer Trend Report revealed that 44% of people who eat pork want it to come from animals treated humanely.[9] In another survey, commissioned by World Animal Protection, 80% of respondents in the U.S. were troubled by the treatment of pigs in industrial agriculture operations, and 89% thought supermarkets should source pork from farms with high welfare standards.[10]

Consumer worries about animal welfare are not the only concerns for today's conscious buyer. Over the past several decades, greenhouse gas emissions and energy use from industrial pig farming have increased by 70%.[11] Intensive pig farms also pollute nearby air and water,[12] and antibiotic-resistant genes have been detected at high levels in pig manure.[13] The consequences of intensive farming on the environment contribute to serious human illness and death,[14] land degradation, fouling of water sources, and detrimental effects on wildlife.[15] Consumers are not only becoming more invested in sustainable farming practices that do not pollute the environment or contribute to global warming, but they also perceive that higher animal welfare, environmental sustainability, and human health are intertwined.[16]

These changing consumer attitudes have created an opportunity for niche markets to emerge that cater to buyers who prioritize health, sustainability, and animal welfare. One such niche market developed for products made from pigs raised on pasture—in other words, pigs who are raised outdoors with continuous access to paddocks or land suitable for grazing.[17]

While there is a diversity of methods used for pastured pig systems, in most cases, pigs on pasture are also provided with fixed or mobile shelters and/or shade. On some farms, pigs may be confined to indoor pens at various life stages, such as when giving birth. This was the practice on our farm, but on other farms, pigs give birth and nurse their piglets outside. Pigs are also provided with supplemental grain and feed, since foraging on pasture generally does not provide for all their nutritional needs. There is a variety of configurations for feeding and watering systems, from automatic to handfeeding. Pastured operations may also practice organic farming methods, which means pigs must be given organic feed and there are restrictions on pharmaceuticals and hormones, often leading to a lack of medical treatment for certain conditions.[18] Most pastured operations are farrow-to-finish, which means the pigs are born on the farm and raised to market weight, or "finished," and then sent to be killed for their meat and other products. Less commonly, farmers will purchase weaned piglets and raise them to slaughter weight.[19]

Farmers using pastured systems sell their products by several methods that market directly to the public. Direct-to-consumer means that the meat and other products are sold directly to buyers at places like farmer's markets, community-supported agriculture organizations, and via online stores. Some may also sell to restaurants and other food services. To do so, farmers must have the pigs slaughtered in U.S. Department of Agriculture (USDA)–certified facilities—either at a fixed facility that may be some distance away from the farm, or in mobile facilities that can come to the property (as of 2017, there were only nine USDA-certified mobile facilities in the United States).[20] Alternatively, smaller farms may be brought under the umbrella of large, commercial operations like Niman Ranch, which then markets their products to the public.[21] In my family's case, we sent our breeding pigs to slaughterhouses when their bodies wore out and their productivity declined.

Years later, after I had become a veterinarian, my mother asked me if I remembered Silver. I told her I did, and then I wanted to know if she recalled what had happened to Silver. After a long pause, she said, "Probably the same thing that happened to all the pigs." I had never wanted to contemplate Silver's ultimate fate or think of her being loaded onto the truck bound for slaughter, shouted at, beaten, and shocked with electric prods. This broke my heart, as I have no doubt it had broken

Silver's heart too. The thought of her throat being slit and her body strung up and dismembered for the parts to end up in someone's freezer made me physically ill. After another few seconds of silence, my mother amended, "You know, I think she was okay. I like to think she never went, and she just lived out her life." Neither of us said anything after that because we both knew it wasn't true. Silver hadn't been allowed to live out her life, to grow old among people who loved her. None of our pigs had been granted that dignity.

THE HUMANE HOAX OF PASTURED PIGS

Products from pastured pigs are aggressively marketed as more humane, healthy, and sustainable. The Rodale Institute, an organic farming advocacy organization that conducts research on pastured pigs, claims that their practices are teaching farmers to raise pigs "the right way," that "benefits the farmers, animals, and the land."[22] The Institute lists four main benefits of pastured pork—enhanced animal welfare, a more diverse diet for pigs, land improvement, and less feed cost for producers.[23] Pastured pig operations frequently assert that the pigs they raise are better for the environment, healthier for human consumption, and experience greater well-being and happiness.

Are Pastured Pigs Environmentally Friendly?

Sustainability, though commonly claimed by pastured pig operations, is an ambiguous term that can have many different meanings. For some consumers, sustainability may simply equate to labels of organic, natural, and antibiotic-free, but these terms do not necessarily mean that the production system is committed to doing what is best for the environment. While pigs grazing on pasture may experience a better approximation of a "natural" pig lifestyle, pigs on organic and antibiotic-free farms also carry high loads of parasites that compromise the integrity of the soil and result in unmanageable levels of pathogens.[24] This can limit any future uses of the land.

Some pastured pig operations claim to support regenerative agriculture, which includes farming and grazing practices that intend to regenerate topsoil and restore degraded soil health. The Rodale Institute asserts that, if managed properly, grazing pigs can benefit pastures by eating or destroying weeds and providing manure as fertilizer,[25] but practically achieving results that mitigate the environmental costs is challenging and yet to be proven within the context of actual farming systems. And being more environmentally friendly can actually mean poor welfare for the pigs. Large groups of pigs can be detrimental to the environment, particularly when held in a contained location. Pigs disrupt soil structure, contribute to air pollution and odor, create damaging ruts and wallows, kill trees and plants, and leave a pasture barren in a short amount of time.[26]

Feeding pigs sustainably on pasture is another issue. Bob Comis, former pastured pig farmer–turned–vegetable farmer, points out that pastured pigs need good sources of high-energy forage, which means annual pasture crops that require plowing and planting rather than permanent fields of mixed grasses. All of that wastes energy and fuel, and plowed land is vulnerable to erosion and topsoil loss.[27] Comis critiques the broad vagueness of the term "sustainability," which can mean whatever the farmer wants it to mean.[28]

Pastured farming also doesn't prevent environmental pollution by waste and runoff, both major issues in all animal agriculture systems. If pastures aren't rotated properly, manure can build up and contribute to the load of harmful pathogens on the land. Pastures are exposed to rain and snow and contribute to runoff and pollution of surrounding water sources for both humans and animals. Research demonstrates that pastured farming operations have a lot of variability in their environmental impacts, and a 2019 study showed that pasture operations still had a moderate impact on climate change, a very low impact on carbon sequestration, and a substantial contribution to acidification,[29] a process that damages rivers, streams, and plants by decreasing soil's pH.[30] The same study identified the feed that pastured pigs are supplemented with as "hotspots" needing improvement in terms of sustainability, as feedstuffs may not be produced in environmentally friendly ways.[31] Another study comparing pastured pig operations with more conventional operations concluded that, "even though the free-range system theoretically has agroecological advantages over the indoor fattening system and the tent system due to a larger grass-clover area, this potential is difficult to implement in practice due to problems with leaching on sandy soil."[32] Taken altogether, the current state of research fails to establish significant environmental benefits from pastured pigs, and the slippery definition of sustainability raises questions about whether farmers can back up their claims of being environmentally friendly.

Are Pastured Pigs Healthier to Eat?

Farmers assert that products from pastured pigs taste better, have higher levels of nutrients, and are better for the environment. Because pastured pigs eat a more varied diet than their intensively farmed counterparts, advocates of consuming pastured meat claim that it tastes better and contains higher levels of beneficial fatty acids, although one frequently cited research study in support of this assertion is a non-peer reviewed publication with a limited pool of eighteen samples. This study was conducted by Singing Prairie Farm and funded by Sustainable Agriculture Research and Education, an outreach organization backed by the USDA, which has a vested interest in promoting animal agriculture.[33] Other research indicates that the nutrient and fat levels in muscle tissue can, not surprisingly, be manipulated by diet, although studies have shown this has equivocal, and even negative, effects on perceived palatability.[34] And it very much depends on how the diet is controlled, what exactly is fed, and how much.[35]

Claims of greater health by proponents of pastured production systems ignore the overwhelming evidence that diets high in meat, regardless of how those animals were raised, have significant negative health impacts[36] and increase the risk of premature death.[37] These negative health effects include a connection to higher incidents of chronic illnesses like heart disease, stroke, diabetes, and certain types of cancer.[38] Nevertheless, this marketing strategy is intricately linked to the image of happy pigs living natural lives, with the implication that the happier the pigs are, the better they are for people to eat.

Are Pastured Pigs Happier?

Proponents of the pastured production model claim that because pigs can express natural behaviors like foraging, nesting, and grazing, they experience less stress brought on by more freedom of activity and a lack of intensive confinement. Overall, pastured pigs are presented as happier and experiencing higher welfare than conventionally raised pigs.

Kentucky's Elmwood Stock Farm, on their website that offers a variety of organic, pasture-raised, and free-range products, paints a serene picture of pigs' lives on the farm: "They have room to roam, root in the dirt for tasty snacks, and build mud holes to express their natural piggy behavior."[39] Niman Ranch advertises "all-natural" pigs raised on pastures with plenty of foraging opportunities who are "raised with care,"[40] and White Oak Pastures, located in Georgia, claims, "Our hogs breed, gestate, farrow, and live under the farm's shade trees. They eat what they find as they forage, plus peanuts that we give them, and cracked eggs from our pasture-raised hens."[41] In New York, Cairncrest Farm promotes "pastured pork from happy, healthy pigs," coupled with cute sketches of pigs snuffling in the grass, and notes, "There's a world of difference between the pigs on my farm and those in conventional hog factories, where they are crammed into huge barns on slatted floors for their entire lives."[42] Cairncrest Farm also includes several engaging and funny portrayals of pig behavior in their descriptions of pastured pork, including pigs jostling each other for food, being quick to forgive, and tossing up large chunks of grass with their strong noses.[43] Descriptions such as these emphasize a close, caring relationship between the farmer and pigs, and obscure the fact that these same pigs appear as cuts of meat or sausage in the farm's catalogue of products.

These are just a few examples of the common marketing techniques for pastured pig farms, which overwhelmingly include descriptions that emphasize the pigs' natural behaviors, overall happiness, and close care and attention paid to them by the farmers. It is not surprising that, given these descriptions, consumers who are concerned about animal welfare find pastured pork an appealing choice. However, there are substantial costs to the welfare and mental well-being of pigs on pasture that may not be immediately evident based on superficial comparisons between conventional and pastured operations.

The Welfare Costs of Pastured Pigs

The intense marketing strategies around pastured pigs beg the question: do they lead better lives than their counterparts confined in more intensive systems? Certainly, having access to the outdoors and freedom of movement is beneficial and conducive to natural behaviors like rooting, grazing, and exploring. However, research indicates that pastured pigs are neither healthier, nor do they lead lives that are significantly more stress-free than pigs on conventional farms.

While it makes intuitive sense that pigs with access to pasture are happier due to their ability to express a greater range of natural behaviors, this issue is more complex. The notion of happiness can be encompassed by an overall definition of welfare, which includes the presence of a positive mental state in relation to the external environment. Physical health and mental well-being are intricately connected, and pigs on pasture being raised for production experience many stressors that impact a positive mental state. Some of these stressors, like husbandry practices causing unrelieved pain or the distress of rapid weaning in piglets, are similar to intensively confined pigs. Others are unique to pastured pigs, and the scientific evidence of enhanced welfare and positive mental states in pigs in different systems often poses more questions than answers. In a study of over 26,000 Iberian pigs that compared intensive and extensive pig-rearing systems, researchers found that pigs in intensive confinement exhibited higher rates of both *negative* and *positive* social behaviors than pigs in pastured systems. The study also found no difference in exploratory behavior and panic reactions to the presence of humans in both systems, which raises concerns about how positive welfare indicators may be misinterpreted within the context of production systems.[44]

Pigs on pasture tend to be more active, which is often cited as support of more positive mental states. However, more active pigs require greater caloric intake. Frustration from underfeeding and lack of access to quality nutrition may significantly impact pastured pigs' mental well-being, and pastured operations have been associated with poor body conditions in pigs.[45] Thirst and access to clean water sources is another concern, as water sources can freeze, dry up, and become contaminated with bird feces, dirt, and dust. Mortality rates in piglets tend to be higher in pigs bred on pasture, and sow mortality is also greater—although they experience less mastitis.* However, outdoor breeding pigs have higher incidences of urinary tract infections, heart failure, and locomotor disorders.[46]

Pigs are natural rooters and use their noses to pull up and destroy vegetation, so some farmers fit metal rings into their noses to prevent pasture damage. These rings are painful and cause ongoing discomfort to the pigs. Pigs with nose rings show disturbed behaviors, like repetitive and stressful movements of the mouth or constantly digging the ground with their front legs, that are suggestive of extreme distress and frustration.[47]

Wide diversity in approaches to pastured systems can lead to vastly different outcomes in pig welfare. Most modern pig breeds, including many classified as heritage (with the exception of Ossabaw and Choctaw pigs who have maintained free-ranging populations), are no longer well-suited to surviving on pasture and have been removed from pastured systems for generations.[48] Pigs who were raised in other systems and then put on pasture may have negative health outcomes.[49] Like their fellow pigs kept in intensive facilities, pastured pigs are subjected to harms that are universally accepted practices in animal agriculture, and they also experience additional negative welfare impacts from being out on pasture.

Inhumane Management Practices

Even though I was told it was necessary and safer for the pigs, as a child I felt a profound discomfort witnessing castrations. My mother and I both hated the days when we rounded up all the new piglets, just a few weeks old, to have their scrotums cut open and their testicles pulled from their bodies—with no pain medication or anesthesia. My mother held each piglet upside down while my father performed the procedures. The piglets screamed, kicked, and struggled while their mothers made low rumbling squeals and paced nervously behind the fence next to the barn. For some unlucky piglets, the agony was prolonged when they slipped free of my mother's grasp, or it took my father a few tries to pull the slick

---

* Mastitis is a painful infection of the udder and teats.

testicles free of the scrotum. After the bleeding and distraught piglets were returned to their pens, my mother emerged from the barn pale and shaking. For me, there was no way to witness the fear and writhing of the piglets and not understand the pain and trauma they experienced. I felt something rupture inside of me every time I heard their cries, but I still accepted this as part of living on the farm. For a very long time, two conflicting ideas existed side-by-side within me—that what we were doing was a deep and fundamental violation of a fellow individual who felt pain and suffering, and that our actions were necessary and justified for our livelihood.

Pigs in farming operations undergo multiple invasive physical mutilations that cause both acute and chronic pain. Male pigs are commonly castrated to avoid aggression and a strong flavor in their flesh called boar taint, and in most cases, castration is performed with no pain medications or anesthesia. These procedures are done by people with little to no training and no medical background, and a quick search of "pig castration" on the internet will bring up a number of do-it-yourself videos and websites. In addition to the pain caused by castration, complications can include bleeding, swelling, fluid accumulation in the area of the incision, immune suppression, and a greater likelihood of pneumonia and other diseases.[50] Pigs are subjected to other invasive procedures like tail docking (amputation of the end of the tail, again with no pain medication or anesthesia), tooth clipping or grinding, and tusk trimming. Tail docking has been shown to be painful, and pigs with docked tails may suffer from infections, neuromas, and heightened sensitivity to pain.[51] Identification measures like ear notching (cutting out sections of the ear flap in a specific pattern), tattooing, and ear tags cause stress and pain in pigs.[52] Farmers also clip the sharp canine teeth of piglets when they are a few days old, a procedure that causes pain and fractures, gum and tongue damage, abscesses, and exposed nerves.[53] Many pig farms in the U.K. and Australia do not castrate piglets,[54] but in the U.S. the vast majority of male pigs are castrated, and it is considered to be a routine procedure on most farms.[55]

Piglets are weaned as early as one to two weeks old on commercial farms and up to five weeks old on pastured farms. In the wild, piglets would gradually transition from their mother's milk to solid food over a period of about 17 weeks, but on farms, weaning happens abruptly over just one or two weeks and causes distress in both piglets and their mothers.[56] The stress of early weaning has negative effects on a piglet's immune system, growth rate, ability to feed, and intestinal structure and function.[57] Research in pastured piglets has shown that the earlier they were weaned, the more likely they were to exhibit stress and fear and have difficulty adapting to their new situation.[58]

TRANSPORT AND SLAUGHTER

One of my worst memories from the farm was the day we slaughtered some of our pigs. My father sold some to a few families in the area, and he agreed to let them come and slaughter the pigs on our property. This only happened one time—after watching how the pigs were killed, no one in my family, my father included, ever wanted to repeat it, even though we continued to send pigs to an out of sight, out of mind slaughterhouse. When the men arrived to claim the pigs, my father helped them chase and corner the ones slated for death that day. It was a chaotic and stressful tactic that left the entire herd fearful. They huddled together afterwards in a corner of the paddock and stared at us with pinched, worried faces.

The men killed the pigs in the open dirt area between the pens and the chicken shed. The selected pigs were driven out, one by one, and someone wrapped chains around their hind legs. Then, together, the men hoisted the pig up, upside down, while she screamed and thrashed. With a large knife, one of the farmers cut the pig's throat.* Her blood sprayed everywhere, soaking the dirt and turning it to a thick, purple sludge. After several moments of agonized writhing, her life finally drained from her body. They then cut her open, removed her internal organs, skinned her, and chopped her body into pieces. I still remember how the pigs' death cries reverberated through my whole body, and how these killing acts left a cloud of sorrow and shock over the farm. Most of all, I think of how the

---

*   The American Veterinary Medical Association's Humane Guidelines recommends that pigs be stunned prior to exsanguination, and farms often use firearms or captive bolt guns to accomplish this, but I don't recall any pigs being stunned on that day. When I spoke with my mother, she thought the pigs may have been hit over the head in an attempt to knock them out.

remaining pigs watching from a distance must have been traumatized by the violence and callousness of our actions.

No matter how they may be presented to the public, pastured pigs are bred and raised for human consumption. Whether they are slaughtered on the farm or at a slaughterhouse, they are all eventually killed for this purpose in ways that are traumatic, frightening, and inhumane. Pigs slaughtered on farms endure prolonged suffering from farmers lacking knowledge and practical experience in "proper" techniques. Shooting pigs in the head with small caliber firearms is often the stunning method of choice for farmers, but it can take multiple attempts before the pig is rendered unconscious or dead. Like castration, a quick search on the internet will bring up multiple instructional websites for do-it-yourself slaughter that fail to account for crucial considerations of humane handling, anatomy, and behavioral knowledge. Pigs are often killed within view or earshot of their fellow pigs, which causes fear and emotional distress in the remaining population.[59]

Pigs who are transported to slaughter face additional abuses. According to the U.S. Pork Checkoff, as of April 2020 there were around 74 slaughter facilities for pigs in the U.S. Depending on a farm's location and proximity to a slaughterhouse, pigs will suffer through long hours of transportation in crowded, poorly ventilated trucks. During this time, they are exposed to extremes of cold and heat, and overcrowding leads to trampling, fighting, and injuries. Only one federal law in the U.S. governs pig transport, called the Twenty-Eight Hour Law, which allows animals to be transported for up to 28 hours without food or water. However, this can be extended to 36 hours if requested by the "owner" of the pigs.[60] While long transport times certainly add to pigs' suffering, research shows that even short trips to slaughter cause significant mental and physiological stress and lead to increased transport deaths.[61] Transport does not stop in freezing or excessively hot weather, and pigs experience fatigue, hunger, dehydration, trauma, bruising, and broken bones from loading and vehicle movement, as well as heat stroke and cold stress.[62]

When the exhausted and physically compromised pigs reach the slaughterhouse, they face a new set of horrors. Pigs unloaded at the slaughterhouse are handled roughly using paddles and electrical prods.[63] They may be housed in barren pens with other pigs for hours awaiting slaughter, fully able to hear and smell the pigs dying in the slaughterhouse.[64] When they enter the slaughter line, pigs are first stunned to render them unconscious, then exsanguinated by cutting the major vessels in their necks, a process that can take several minutes. Then, their bodies are dumped into scalding tanks before being processed into cuts of meat and other products.[65] Pigs are stunned either via electrical currents applied to their heads or by being lowered into a chamber where they are exposed to high levels of carbon dioxide.[66] Both methods are problematic and can cause agony during slaughter—stunning may be ineffective and pigs may regain consciousness before death while bleeding out or be immersed fully awake in boiling water.[67] Carbon dioxide stunning has been linked to intense suffering, including causing "pain, fear, and respiratory distress."[68]

HARMS SPECIFIC TO PASTURED PIGS

Pastured pigs also face environmental, health, and welfare issues that are specifically related to being out on pasture. Silvana Pietrosemoli and Clara Tang conducted a review of scientific literature published on pastured pigs from 2000 to 2020 that revealed numerous welfare issues in pastured production systems, including infectious diseases, parasite infestations, heat stress, hypothermia, sunburn, predator attacks, and challenges in monitoring and treating sick animals.[69] All of these issues compromise welfare and impact the quality of life of pastured pigs. Based on Pietrosemoli and Tang's review, the following four broad categories, though not inclusive of all possible harms, are identified as significantly impacting pastured pig welfare.

Pasture Hazards

Pigs are subjected to hazards on pasture relating to ground conditions, flooding, soil texture, and the number of pigs contained in a given area. Depending on the ground and soil conditions, pigs could remain in wet, dirty, and muddy circumstances for extended periods of time. Pigs naturally cover themselves in mud to regulate their body temperatures and express social behaviors like scent marking, hence the common trope of "wallowing in the mud."[70] However, they will also seek to clean themselves if possible, and prolonged exposure to muddy conditions impacts their health. A perpetually wet and dirty environment creates conditions where slips and falls can occur, leading to injuries, as well as causing skin lesions and infections.[71]

Domesticated pigs rely on humans for their care. They are not wild animals, and they face difficulties acclimating to extensive outdoor environments. Pastured pigs are at risk of injury from holes, stumps, wires, thorns, and other hazards that may be present on pasture. Stony soil causes joint injuries, foot trauma, and eventual lameness. Ingrown claws and toe erosion, both painful issues that impact mobility, are also problems for pastured pigs.[72] These animals are exposed to a variety of toxins on pasture, including mushrooms and toxic plants that can cause illness and death. When pigs graze and forage, they tend to ingest large amounts of soil and, in this way, can be exposed to toxic metals or other contaminants in the soil, which can accumulate in tissues and internal organs and potentially cause health problems.[73]

Because it is difficult to observe pigs directly and consistently on pasture, it may take longer to identify individuals who are injured or ill, resulting in prolonged discomfort and worsening of their conditions before they are discovered. The logistics required to access and confine pigs on pasture also poses challenges to delivering preventive and emergent medical care on a timely basis.[74]

Weather

Rain, wind, humidity, and temperature fluctuations cause physical and physiological stress in pigs that they may not be able to successfully assuage on a confined pasture. They are unable to migrate and seek out trees, shade, and water sources. Exposure to extreme temperatures leads to heat stress, which can lead to life-threatening heatstroke and cause higher numbers of stillbirths and greater piglet mortality.[75] Lactating pigs are particularly susceptible to heat stress.[76] Sunburn, particularly in lighter-skinned pigs, creates discomfort, pain, and blistering. Certain plants pigs may encounter, like parsley, turnips, and clover, can cause photosensitization when ingested, leading to excruciating skin blistering and peeling when exposed to the sun.[77]

Cold stress can progress to hypothermia, which is both immediately life-threatening and leads to an increased vulnerability to infections like *Mycoplasma* pneumonia. Pigs also suffer when they can't find adequate protection from the wind—this has been reflected in slower growth rates and poorer body conditions.[78]

Wild Animals and Pathogens

Pastured pigs have a higher likelihood of close encounters with a variety of wildlife, including predators and animals who serve as reservoirs for diseases. Interactions with coyotes, foxes, raccoons, badgers, dogs, cats, snakes, insects, and birds all risk injury and transmission of illnesses to outdoor pigs. Predators most commonly prey on piglets,[79] but their activities will also scare adult pigs, who may then break down fences in fear for their lives.[80] Piglets who are left behind and not taken by predators are at risk of starving or succumbing to the elements.[81] In addition, pastured farms may have high rates of missing or unaccounted for piglets that are due, in part, to predation. In a study of fox encounters at a pastured operation in Australia, predators accounted for most of the 20% of piglets reported missing on the farm, and cameras recorded foxes stalking and carrying off piglets.[82]

High levels of pathogens, including *Salmonella*, *Campylobacter*, *Toxoplasma*, and *Trichinella*, have been detected in pastured operations.[83] *Salmonella*, depending on the serotype, causes illness ranging from mild diarrhea to serious disease such as hepatitis, septicemia, and pneumonia.[84] *Campylobacter* can cause diarrhea in piglets and young pigs, which can lead to dehydration and poor nutrition.[85] Pigs are exposed to other significant pathogens carried by mice and rats, who will opportunistically gravitate to sources of grain and other food for the pigs. These rodents are reservoirs for diseases including *Leptospira*, *Yersinia pestis*, *Brucella suis*, and *Erysipelothrix rhusiopathiae*. Cats, both feral and domestic, may carry and spread the parasite *Toxoplasma gondii* to pigs. Birds and wild pigs serve as reservoirs for *Streptococcus suis*—a disease that causes meningitis, endocarditis, and septicemia. Contact with feral pigs and wild boars can result in the transmission of pathogens between both wild and domestic swine, which increases the ability and likelihood of a disease to spread widely.[86]

Internal and External Parasites

The high prevalence of parasites in pastured pig operations is an ongoing and intractable problem. Heavy infestations of internal and external parasites can cause significant welfare issues, including poor growth and nutrition. In a study of a population of free-range pigs in Austria, 75% had gastrointestinal parasites and 30% had lice.[87] Common internal parasites include *Ascaris suum* and *Oesophagostomum* spp., both roundworms that dwell in the gastrointestinal tracts of pigs, but other parasites may also be present. The eggs of these parasites are hardy and survive in soil for long periods, making it very difficult to prevent reinfection of pigs on pasture.[88] The Rodale Institute conducted a survey in 2019 of nine pastured pig farms in the Midwestern U.S., and they found that rates of parasite infection ranged from 10% to 100% of all pigs on a given operation.[89] However, in a 2020 webinar that addressed this issue, the Rodale Institute's Farm Director, Rick Carr, made it clear what a farmer's priorities should be in addressing parasites. While admitting they were a problem for pigs and for farmers, Carr stated, "The most important thing about parasites is how it relates to pork production . . . our pigs have parasites and we don't hide that information, but we do seem to be able to finish* our pigs in a similar time based on industry standards."[90] Carr further pointed out that the parasite problem in organic pasture operations hinges on money—farmers want the grain going to feed the pig, not the parasite.[91]

While there is no doubt that pigs in industrial agriculture operations suffer immensely, it cannot be assumed that pastured pigs don't suffer as well. Pastured pigs may have the benefit of greater freedom of movement and more opportunities to express natural behaviors, but they are still commodified, subjected to inhumane practices, exposed to sickness, injury, and other traumas, and killed so their bodies can be consumed. In addition to the harmful management practices that are universally

---

* To grow a pig to slaughter weight.

accepted by farmers, pastured pigs face unique challenges to their health and quality of life from being on pasture, and these challenges significantly impact their well-being and welfare.

HERITAGE PIGS AND THE CONSERVATION QUESTION

Heritage pig breeds are frequently the breeds of choice for pastured farming operations. Unlike the Yorkshire breed commonly used in intensive, commercial production, pastured farming proponents argue that heritage breeds possess the fortitude, conformation, and genetic impulse to thrive in a foraging environment.[92] Popular breeds for pastured operations include the Tamworth, Gloucestershire Old Spots, Red Wattle, and Large Black.[93] Unlike the Yorkshire pigs with their upright ears and heavily muscled bodies, farmers claim that the floppy ears, leaner bodies, and upturned noses of heritage breeds lead to their greater success on pasture.[94] Farmers, and other proponents of animal agriculture, argue that rearing heritage breeds is important for their continued conservation and survival, as the predominance of conventional intensive farming has threatened the viability of these populations.[95] By using the language of conservation, farmers present themselves as helping, not harming, pigs and the ecosystem.

The conservation argument for raising heritage breeds on pasture conflates non-native species with critically threatened native species and obfuscates the fact that the breeding and farming of heritage pigs is a for-profit industry. The ultimate intent is not preservation of a breed, but the marketing and selling of niche pork products. That the pigs themselves are actually harmed in this process becomes lost in the fluid use of terminology like conservation and heritage. Robert Grillo, founder and director of the animal advocacy nonprofit Free From Harm, puts it this way, "By calling this livestock conservation, farmers who buy heritage breed animals are suddenly elevated and likened to the altruistic intentions of true species conservationists, who are driven by their passion for protecting those species rather than making a living off of exploiting them."[96]

Conservation efforts are proportional to the economic benefits that can be gained by farmers for breeding certain pigs. The breeds that bring the greatest financial returns are not necessarily the most endangered. In fact, most of them are not even native North American species. According to the Livestock Conservancy, which tracks endangered pig breeds by gathering data from breed associations and individual farms, there are eleven heritage breeds at varying levels of population threat. However, only six of these are considered native to North America, and among these six, the Choctaw, Mulefoot, and Ossabaw Island are critically threatened. Estimates place the Choctaw pig population at only a few hundred and the Mulefoot at fewer than 200 remaining individuals.[97] Of the most popular heritage breeds used in pastured farming operations, only the Red Wattle is native to North America. Other breeds commonly used in pastured operations were introduced to North America in the past 150–200 years, including the Tamworth, imported before 1900, and the Large Black and Gloucestershire Old Spots, both imported after 1900.[98] These breeds are larger, meaning more meat and other products can be extracted from their bodies. In contrast, the Choctaw pig is small, weighing only around 120 pounds, and does not, as the Livestock Conservancy notes, "produce much of a market carcass."[99] This makes it an unattractive target for "conservation" efforts. As per the Livestock Conservancy, "few commercial opportunities are available for the breed's use, and lacking any economic return to support conservation efforts, the Choctaw faces substantial obstacles to survival."[100]

Attaching the word conservation to heritage pig farming as a marketing ploy is deliberately confusing. It misleads consumers into thinking that farmers are contributing to the preservation of native species and ecosystems, when in fact pastured operations may take land and resources away from native species in favor of grazing for non-native species with commercial appeal. Bringing imported species under the umbrella of heritage breed conservation was not accidental. In a quote appearing in *Food Republic,* a Livestock Conservancy representative stated, "When we created the term 'heritage,' it was intentionally left loosely policed so that raisers of the breeds on our Conservation Priority List could use it for marketing their animals. . . . In recent years, several breeds such as Berkshire, Mangalitsa, and Kunekune have started using the 'heritage breed' term in their marketing, but according to the heritage swine definition, they technically wouldn't be included."[101] The mutability of this definition minimizes the pressing issues that face critically endangered native species, like the Choctaw pig, and it obscures the fact that economic exploitation is a major driver for heritage breed "conservation." Indeed, raising so-called endangered breeds to be slaughtered and eaten runs counter to the premise of conservation.

An Equation that Doesn't Balance

Silver, with her emotional capacity and ability to reciprocate affection, was not unique among pigs—all pigs can express deep, lasting emotions. Although I frequently observed our pigs showing a variety of identifiable emotions on the farm, including distress, sorrow, and contentment, I was conditioned to minimize and discount their feelings. Research on pig cognition and emotional capacity indicate that they possess advanced cognitive skills, including the ability to anticipate and plan for events, understand social cues between other pigs and also humans, and take on the perspective of other pigs and humans.[102] Individual pigs have complex, unique personalities, and they engage in sophisticated systems of social play. Pigs are sensitive to how a person is behaving towards them, know whether someone is paying attention to them, and adjust their behavior accordingly. They also have well-developed memories and will prioritize the important ones.[103] Pigs remember bad experiences, and these can have long-term effects on their behavior and attitudes.[104] Pigs understand empathy—if one pig is experiencing a negative emotional state, the other pigs around them will also exhibit negative emotional states.[105]

I never formed lasting relationships with the other pigs on our farm because of how we used them. Even though they lived outside in a herd, they were still not able to form stable social relationships or fully express their natural behaviors. Being on pasture did not spare them the pain and suffering of being treated as objects in an exploitative system. They were often cold, hungry, sick, parasite-ridden, and forced to produce litter after litter of piglets, whose family units would be broken up when the piglets were taken away and sold. We often used force and punishment to get the pigs to do what we wanted. At just a few weeks of age, they were subjected to painful castrations and tail dockings. They watched as their companions were brutally killed. It's no wonder that they had little interest in interacting with us. Some other farmers may have better rapport with their pigs, but there's no denying the inherent violence and subjugation of that relationship. Comis, who gave up pig farming when he realized how much his pigs suffered, said in a *Modern Farmer* interview quoted in *The American Scholar*: "[L]ivestock farmers lie to their animals. We're kind to them and take good care of them for months, even years. They grow comfortable with our presence, and even begin to like us. But in the end, we take advantage of the animals, using their trust to dupe them into being led to their own deaths."[106] Comis has frequently stated that he is haunted by the ghosts of the 2,000 pigs he sent to slaughter.

I, too, am haunted by these ghosts. When I remember my childhood on the farm, I see Silver trotting toward me with a stuffed toy in her mouth. I see the dozens of pigs, still babies and no different from Silver in their desire to run and play, loaded on the truck to be taken to barren feedlots. They are, in part, the reason I became a vegan—to try to balance the equation for the suffering I'd taken part in. At face value, the notion of keeping pigs on pasture, allowing them to forage and move freely, seems very attractive. They appear to have fulfilled lives, and people still get to eat them. But practically, it can never be an ethical situation. It simply doesn't work. Even with reassuring words and labels like humane and pasture-raised, animal agriculture causes immense suffering, and pastured pig operations are no exception.

Ingrid L. Taylor is a writer, veterinarian, and independent scholar who has worked in veterinary clinical practice, public health, and animal protection. She is an award-winning poet, and her writing has appeared in many journals and magazines. Find out more about her work at ingridltaylor.com.

2

THE TERRIBLE TRUTHS OF BACKYARD CHICKEN FARMING

by Alastor Van Kleeck, Ph.D.

BIBI

In September 2014, my partner and I rescued a little white hen and brought her to our sanctuary to live out her life. This probably doesn't sound like a particularly unique scenario. But the story of this one little hen lays bare many of the terrible truths of backyard chicken keeping, which has grown in recent decades from a quirky fad to a full-blown industry in its own right. In cities small and large, from urban to suburban neighborhoods, chickens are becoming increasingly popular (or I should say hens, and not roosters, both of which are "chickens"— but I'll get to that).

A year or two prior to her rescue, this hen was born as part of a hatching project at a small, home-based school in a nearby city after the teachers got a dozen fertilized eggs from a local farm. Of the twelve eggs, eight of the chicks who hatched were roosters, who were sent back to the farm and likely killed. The four hens who hatched were kept in the backyard of the school in what's commonly referred to as a "chicken tractor"— a moveable cage with an enclosed area inside for the chickens to sleep in. These contraptions are popular among backyard chicken farmers because they're mobile, inexpensive, and easy to set up. Unfortunately, they make poor living spaces for chickens, with too little space, no ability to provide temperature controls, and little protection from predators.

One night, a raccoon broke into the chicken tractor where the four hens were sleeping. The woman who operated the school heard the ruckus of terrified birds fighting for their lives, ran outside, and scared away the raccoon. He had killed three of the hens and was in the process of killing the fourth when he was interrupted. The one surviving hen suffered several injuries, including a broken top beak, a punctured bottom beak, and torn wattles.*

The owner of the school contacted us days after the attack because, as she described it, the surviving hen refused to sleep in the chicken tractor, opting instead to sleep in the branches of a nearby tree. The hen also spent her days standing outside the sliding glass doors that accessed the backyard.

When she came to our sanctuary, we named her Bibi, changed from the name Busy Bee, given to her by a child at the school. Right away, it was clear just how much emotional trauma she had suffered in addition to her physical injuries. She was in shell shock, barely mobile, and only content when sitting on blankets in our bathroom. Although we had been rescuing chickens and other farmed animals since earlier that year, this was our first experience with an attack victim, and we quickly realized that even without physical injuries needing treatment, Bibi had much healing to do.

After her quarantine period was over, Bibi finally started to come out of her shell through something simple and yet powerful: meeting one of our other hens, Hypatia. Introductions are often uncertain affairs. Chickens have big personalities, and sometimes two personalities just don't work out well together. This is as true for hens meeting hens as it is for roosters meeting roosters, also for hens meeting roosters. In this case, Bibi immediately perked up and began interacting with Hypatia, and she never looked back from there. It was not hard to infer that during those hours Bibi spent standing beside the glass doors after the raccoon attack, she was likely seeking the only companion she had left—her reflection.

With time and care, Bibi blossomed into a lively hen who never let her permanently broken beak slow her down. Initially, we weren't sure if she would be able to eat and drink adequately on her own, and we even

---

*   The wattle is one of the flaps of red flesh under a chicken's chin.

made a failed attempt to attach prosthetic tips to her beak, but in the end she adapted without the need of our interventions. While chickens with beak deformities and injuries can find ways to eat on their own, they often require special preparations for their food and/or hand feeding. Bibi, ever the independent one, never needed much help besides a full bowl of food (which she usually managed to scatter about by scratching around with her feet). Bibi's permanently broken beak also limited her ability to preen properly, making her more sensitive to cold—for her comfort, she lived inside for the colder months each year. Most chickens adapt well to being indoors, and Bibi was no exception. Besides bossing around the cats, as chickens almost always do, her favorite thing was to find a warm spot near a heater or in a patch of sunlight. One of my favorite memories was seeing her sprawled out near our woodstove, soaking up the heat from the fire and from the toasty tiles on the floor.

Years go by far too quickly, and yet it often feels like some people never age—until all of a sudden, they do. Bibi certainly exemplified this, her age finally becoming apparent when we rushed her to the emergency vet on New Year's Eve 2020. She was diagnosed with ovarian cancer, one of the most common causes of death for laying hens genetically manipulated so terribly in the egg industry. Despite receiving preventative medical interventions that began shortly after her arrival at our sanctuary, Bibi developed this deadly reproductive disease. She was able to bounce back as a result of treatment, though the diagnosis meant her future was uncertain. We knew the cancer was there, while Bibi seemed much like her usual self—a spunky little white hen, sprawled out in the sunlight with her friend Salamandra.

Bibi's life is more than a tale of survival; it also touches on several of the clearest problems with backyard chicken farming. While using animals for food or other human purposes is inherently unethical, relying as it does on speciesist oppression and millennia of domination, backyard chicken farming also has systemic practical problems that cause suffering and death to untold numbers of individual chickens. In Bibi's case, we can see glimpses of how backyard chicken farming harms and kills chicks, creates an unsolvable problem of unwanted roosters, exposes chickens to danger through improper protection and care standards, and perpetuates suffering caused by (often untreated) medical disorders that result directly from the history of domestication and exploitation.

LIFE'S BEGINNINGS

Much like Bibi's, the story of every single chicken begins at hatching. Similarly, the exploitation of chickens begins at hatching—and more specifically, in most cases, at *hatcheries*. While it might seem logical that the chickens comprising backyard flocks were all born under the warm wings of doting mother hens, the reality is very different. While there aren't reliable statistics on how many chicks are hatched at a hatchery versus "on the farm," for reasons of economics and convenience, most chicks raised in backyards are born in large industrial incubators, entering the world inside a machine. Chicks born to chickens bred for laying eggs will be examined within the first few hours to determine their sex. Males are separated from females by inspecting the wings or vents (the opening where eggs and waste come out), and the males will then be killed as they, of course, don't lay eggs, nor do they grow fast or big enough to be profitable for meat. The methods of killing are brutal. Some chicks are grounded up alive in macerators (large machines with spinning blades), others are electrocuted in metal boxes, and still others die from suffocation, dehydration, and exposure in trash bags and garbage dumpsters.

One important fact about chicken reproduction becomes relevant here: chickens hatch roughly equal numbers of male and female babies.[1] That is, for every hen who breaks out of her shell, statistics predict a baby rooster will break out of another shell. This may come as a surprise to many who have lived around chickens, given the relative dearth of roosters in backyard flocks—but those missing roosters are missing by design. Hatcheries even account for their expected financial losses of unsellable baby roosters by padding the price of sexed female chicks, making them more expensive than both unsexed (or "straight-run") chicks and male chicks. When someone buys sexed chicks from a hatchery or from a farm store, one is paying to have that same number of young roosters killed.

This is true whether those chicks end up on a large egg farm, at a small, local pastured egg operation, or in one's own backyard.

After birth and sexing, chicks who are just hours old will be shipped out to farm supply stores, other businesses, and homes. Some are so young that they still have an egg tooth on the tip of their beak.* When orders are placed for female chicks, baby roosters are sometimes packed in with the hens, being used as a living packaging material to help cushion and warm the baby hens. They travel many hours around the country with the mail and other packages, facing the risk of injury or death en route to egg farms and feed stores.

A particularly striking example of what can happen when fragile, newly hatched chicks are shipped this way came in August 2020, when COVID-19 was wreaking havoc on the U.S. Postal Service and Americans were panic-buying chicks in the nonsensical pursuit of food security.[2] As reported by the Associated Press, "At least 4,800 chicks shipped to Maine farmers through the U.S. Postal Service have arrived dead in recent weeks after rapid cuts hit the federal mail carrier's operations. . . ."[3] The article continues, "Pauline Henderson, who owns Pine Tree Poultry in New Sharon, Maine, told the newspaper she was shocked last week when all of the 800 chicks sent to her from a hatchery in Pennsylvania were dead." The cause of death: lack of food and water due to delays in delivery.

Even if you have never cared for chickens, you may have seen bins of chicks being sold for a few dollars apiece at a local feed store or pet store. I've walked by these bins many times over the years, while children with their parents gawked and chattered and reached in to handle the downy babies. It doesn't take too skilled of an eye or extended periods of observation to discover chicks who are sick or injured in these bins. They may be disabled from injuries sustained during shipping or in the scramble of bodies in the store. Due to congenital problems or inadequate temperature control, they can become ill with respiratory, digestive, or other sicknesses. Sometimes the problem isn't clear and a chick just doesn't thrive.

---

* An egg tooth is a temporary, sharp projection at the end of a chick's beak to help them puncture the eggshell from inside and break free. The egg tooth will fall off after hours or a few days of hatching.

It's heartbreaking to know where they've come from and see what they experience, and we've rescued dozens of sickly chicks from local feed stores. Some of them can bounce back with individualized acute care, but many can't—their young bodies cannot handle the strain. In 2018, I worked with several local feed stores to take in chicks who were surrendered to us because they weren't faring well in the bins. After just a few weeks, we were given over two dozen chicks—some recovered, and some did not. This is an all-too-common situation, repeated wherever chicks are sold, but rarely seen by customers. As a result, "chick days" at farm stores remain popular, hatcheries thus supplying new bodies to the growing backyard chicken trend every spring (and sometimes later as well). It may seem, on the surface, like a relatively benign system. The truth is less visible and can be found in all the suffering of chicks who die or are injured during shipping from hatchery to store, or those who are removed from the selling floor and taken in the back to die, their tiny bodies usually thrown out with the trash.

Hatcheries are a major, largely unseen, component of backyard chicken farming, but some chicks are in fact born more "naturally," when farmers breed and sell them or, intentionally or not, allow their hens to brood on fertilized eggs. It's impossible to put numbers on how many backyard chickens were born in a nest and not in a hatchery incubator, but it's easy to surmise that they are in the vast minority. Some farmers do breed chickens to sell chicks, many (as in the case of Bibi's dozen) sold as unsexed. Much like a hatchery dispatching baby roosters, breeders rarely keep males; roosters who make it to maturity, on or off the farm, quickly become a problem once they reveal themselves to not be hens— as the saying goes: "Once they crow, out they go."

WHERE ARE THEIR BROTHERS?

The problem with eggs is also the concern for roosters. The fate of roosters is intimately and irrevocably intertwined with the experience of hens in backyard flocks—and in egg consumption generally. Please read that again. Read it three times if necessary. The conversation about backyard chickens is almost always about *hens,* but the story is incomplete if we don't also talk about *roosters.*

Because of the egg industry, roosters will likely face death in a number of ways within the first few months of life: first, just after they hatch if they are sexed by a hatchery or farmer, and second, when they show signs of sexual maturity (including unique feathers and, more obviously, crowing). These morbid milestones are faced by *all* roosters, wherever they are born. Thus, it is quite common to find farmers selling baby roosters as "fry-pan" chicks—they're just the right size to fry up in a pan. For older roosters, the method of disposal often transitions from the fry pan to "freezer camp," a backyard chicken keeper's euphemism for killing a chicken and freezing their carcass. "Freezer camp" is a popular point of humor among backyard chicken farmers, wielded as a threat to unwanted or surprise roosters, ornery roosters, noisy roosters, etc.

Killing is a gruesome business, of course, and many backyard farmers choose another method of ridding themselves of unwanted roosters: abandonment. Rooster dumping is another inevitable but largely hidden consequence of backyard chicken farming, growing in frequency as the popularity of backyard chickens grows as well. Indeed, the majority of roosters who live or have lived at our sanctuary were abandoned, usually in some place that seemed somewhat woodsy—including next to an industrial office building, as in the case of a rooster we named Leland after I caught him in the darkness in 2017. Alternately, some roosters are abandoned at animal shelters, who rarely have the resources to manage and adopt chickens. Most are euthanized.

While I have no qualms about blaming backyard farmers for abandoned roosters, the larger problem is driven by more than just individual human whims. In recent years, more towns and cities have been either adding or revising ordinances to allow chickens (and other farmed animals) in not only rural areas, but also suburban and urban neighborhoods. The plight of roosters becomes more complicated because only a tiny fraction of municipalities allow both hens *and* roosters due to concerns about noise nuisance. As Chicken Run Rescue in Minnesota has spelled out on their website, rooster crows usually have a lower decibel level than other common (and legal) parts of a city soundscape—including dogs, mechanical equipment, and traffic.[4] As long as municipalities decide to allow hens but prohibit roosters, they guarantee the deaths of countless roosters by forcing people who might have chosen to keep their roosters to get rid of them. These laws also prohibit people from adopting roosters who need homes. Enforcement of rooster bans is almost always fierce, with no opportunities for exceptions.

Since starting our sanctuary, my partner and I have caught dozens of dumped roosters. While some are dumped as part of a group (be it two, six, or nine), far too many are solo roosters, who are left in an unfamiliar place with no protection from the elements or predators, having lost their home territory and any companions they might have had. Sometimes a rooster is dumped as part of a group and then becomes a lone rooster after his companions are killed. This was the case with Jennifer, a rooster who was living next to a KFC restaurant by himself after his brothers were picked off subsequent to being abandoned there. I can't imagine how terrifying it must be for them, let alone dangerous. They are easy prey for wildlife, and over time can become sick and malnourished as well. Chickens are not wild animals— they are domesticated, farmed birds. Abandoning them in the wild is an almost certain death sentence.

One memorable instance of rooster rescue came for us in the fall of 2017 when we were contacted by local animal control about a group of roosters who had been abandoned in an upscale golf-course neighborhood. Although some animal control officers will catch stray chickens, many will not. After catching one of them, the animal control officer in this case turned the task over to me. Besides the one who had been caught, there turned out to be six other roosters roaming the wooded neighborhood. Two roosters had been killed overnight, shortly after being abandoned, with only trails of feathers revealing their fate. It took two weeks to round up all seven of the roosters, after many late nights wandering with a net and a flashlight, and after such notable experiences as tripping on barbed wire and bashing my knee on a rock; being called "suspicious" and "weird" by a group of kids on bikes; getting yelled at for walking through someone's yard; and being out in the woods near midnight on a Friday the 13th. We called the seven roosters The Alchemists, naming each one after a historical alchemist such as Agrippa, Cagliostro, Trithemius, and Philalethes. Even now, the remaining members of the group are strongly bonded, staying close to each other among the larger rooster flock they belong to.

Without question, roosters are the most common farmed animal in need of homes. Animal sanctuaries around the United States and elsewhere are constantly asked to take in surrendered roosters, but few have spaces for roosters. It's important to recognize that roosters are always a part of the backyard egg industry, but very few people want to acknowledge them. Indeed, "backyard chickens" is its own sort of euphemism, relying on an omission of roosters (*roosters are chickens*) in order to maintain the bucolic image of happy chickens (i.e., hens) and happy eggs. But this is a hoax—it is the humane hoax in practice. It's a lie that makes backyard farmers feel better about the same exploitation of non-consenting bodies, of manipulated reproductive systems, for their human benefit. It's the sort of lie that makes macerating and suffocating chicks at a hatchery, or dumping nine roosters in a strange place at night, or sending Bibi's eight baby brothers back to the farmer—all horrid forms of collateral damage that are necessary to maintain the happy hen and happy egg image.

The "problem" of roosters is thus a problem of humanity, as is always the case in any form of animal farming. A crucial question, then, for anyone proclaiming the joys of keeping and eating the eggs of backyard hens, is: *Where are their brothers?*

IMPROPER PROTECTION AND CARE

Although the prevailing narrative about and among backyard chicken farmers tends to focus on how abundantly happy, healthy, and tasty the birds and their eggs are, the reality is far more troubling. It's easy to focus on the differences between a backyard farm and a massive industrial operation, where tens of thousands of hens are crammed into sheds and into tiny cages, and to believe that a backyard flock is the best life possible for chickens. Over the years, we've consistently encountered a number of serious problems with backyard chicken farming through individual chickens who have come to our sanctuary, including *inadequate protection from predators* and *inadequate medical care*.

Bibi's story displays both of these facts quite well: she and her sisters were locked inside of a predator buffet, and after the attack she was left to recuperate on her own with no medical exam or other care, despite her injuries. Further, Bibi was one of many "sole survivors" of predator attacks whom we have taken in, always a result of improper living spaces and human negligence—trauma often accompanies the physical injuries.

Chickens are especially vulnerable to predation because most domesticated breeds have been robbed of the ability to fly (which isn't particularly desirable to farmers who just want to sell their eggs or their flesh). The necessity of proper predator protection for chickens thus cannot be overstated: a sanctuary must know the predators in their region and take appropriate steps to keep predators out and residents safe.

Aviary netting, metal fencing, digging barriers, and other methods to build fully predator-proof living spaces are not cheap—unlike chickens. Given the time and money required for setup and maintenance, many backyard chicken farmers opt for cheap and easy options. This means chickens frequently free-range in backyards without sufficient fencing and covering to prevent attacks by airborne predators, or the birds are kept in flimsy enclosures like the chicken tractor that Bibi was kept in.

The list of predators varies from place to place but is almost always startlingly long, including dogs, foxes, coyotes, bears, badgers, weasels, raccoons, owls, hawks, and many more. While we should never portray predators as enemies or villains, caregivers bear the obligation to keep animals safe when we have responsibility for them. Unfortunately, far too many people see depredation of chickens as the "circle of life" in action—a natural and thus inevitable occurrence, rather than an utter failure to seriously consider the safety and interests of individual chickens in our care. Sanctuaries should always strive to prevent *any and all* predator attacks. Our genetic manipulation and domestication has made chickens vulnerable; we now have a responsibility to protect them. But for far too many farmers, protecting chickens from predator attacks isn't worth the price of prevention.

We've experienced this countless times over the years. One particularly striking example was a hen we named Bronagh, who survived a fox attack in someone's backyard. Rather than receiving immediate veterinary care, which is critical for bite wounds due to the risk of infection and physical damage, Bronagh was placed in a bathtub to recuperate. Once she was somewhat stable, she was placed back out with her flock who immediately attacked her and caused even more injuries to her head. I picked her up one night, finding a hen whose head was covered in scabs and missing many feathers. It took several days for one of her eyes to finally open, and for months she experienced disorientation resulting from injuries to her inner ear from the fox attack—basically, she spent months with her head upside down. She did recover from her injuries and was able to hold her head high again after a long period and extensive medical care. To most backyard farmers, this sort of intensive, individualized care is ridiculous, and properly preventing this sort of attack is too much work. Predators will always be where chickens are kept, and "circle of life" arguments or shoulder shrugs at suffering individuals contradict the predominant narrative about the humane nature of backyard chicken farming.

A second common problem, inadequate medical care sometimes follows from the first problem, though not always. Even when backyard chicken farmers talk about their birds as "pets" or "my girls" or as members of the family, underlying their proclamations is the fact that chickens are considered farm animals by society at large and by many veterinarians—and why would "food" need medical care?

Chickens are cheap to buy but can be very expensive to care for. Due to the extensive genetic manipulation of the species and complications of domestication, chickens are prone to reproductive disorders and other health problems, ranging from intestinal parasites to heart disease, and providing appropriate care often means seeing a veterinarian several times in a chicken's life. A typical small animal vet or a farm vet may not have the knowledge and experience to treat a chicken, so avian specialists are the best option but usually cost more and are hard to find. It will not make sense to a farmer to spend hundreds or even thousands of dollars on a single bird who only cost them a few dollars to buy.

Complicating matters further, chickens are masters of stoicism and can hide illness or injury as an instinctual strategy to avoid predators. Unfortunately, this means that a health problem may not be recognized until long after it began, making treatment much harder. Identifying health problems early takes an experienced eye, but many backyard chicken farmers never put in the time to gain this set of skills, which requires actually treating sick birds, or they rely on truly horrible advice from online forums.

Let's be generous for the moment and ignore preventative care and comprehensive treatment for subtly sick chickens. Even if we focus on acute injuries, such as predator attacks or other obvious medical issues like a broken bone or a prolapsed vent,* it is not uncommon for backyard farmers to either ignore issues (as was the case with Bibi and Bronagh), kill the chicken themselves, or surrender the one who needs care. It becomes painfully obvious that ignorance and apathy run rampant in the backyard farming community, along with misinformation and shockingly horrible do-it-yourself (DIY) approaches to handling sick and injured chickens. Backyard chicken discussion groups and forums abound with stories of amputations, caponizing (neutering roosters, which most avian vets will not do without medical necessity), and much more. Here you'll find that TUMS, cayenne pepper, Epsom salts, and apple cider vinegar are miracle cures for all that ails chickens. Without any reference to actual research, medicine, or diagnostics, backyard farmers throw cheap ingredients at sick chickens rather than provide well-informed care, frequently misdiagnosing problems (like calling everything "egg binding," when egg binding is actually quite rare in chickens), and forgoing post-mortem exams to find the actual cause(s) of death.

For Althea, the sole survivor of a predator attack at a Montessori school, even blindness due to injury wasn't enough for them to seek veterinary attention. Instead, under the so-called guidance of a teacher who had backyard chickens at home, Althea was given water and yogurt in a tube by the young students. To be clear, administering liquids by mouth to chickens is a delicate affair—aspiration is a serious risk that can lead to respiratory infection. The thought of children handling and attempting to medicate Althea, now blind and in pain, rings all of my alarm bells, and perhaps this is why Althea still prefers not to be handled

---

* A prolapsed vent occurs when the opening that passes waste and eggs, the vent, pushes out of the body causing pain and distress. If left untreated, it can also lead to death.

by humans. It took several hours of negotiation for the teachers to agree to surrender her immediately after they contacted us, but thankfully Althea recovered well. Like most blind chickens, she is independent and requires only modest accommodations in order to eat, drink, and be merry in a protected environment with another blind hen, Helena.

The pervasive problems with predator attacks and inadequate care call into question just how humane backyard chicken farming really is. How humane can something be when individual lives are measured in dollars and cents, and when a culture of ignorance and neglect is accepted as the standard?

EGGS HURT

Eggs hurt hens. Eggs hurt roosters.

Backyard farmers play up the aesthetics of their flocks and pretend that they've created ideal habitats for happy hens to provide them with happy eggs. If everyone's so happy, then it must be humane as well . . . right?

When it comes to consumption of eggs by humans, backyard farmers ignore the realities of the eggs themselves in order to portray their exploitation of chickens as positive. The reasons why egg consumption can never be ethical or humane lie not in the aesthetics of a chicken's living space, but in the very biology of domesticated chickens.

Contrary to popular opinion, the egg laying of modern hens is far, far from "natural." A female red junglefowl, a hen's wild ancestor, on average lays only ten to fifteen eggs per year, usually in clutches of four to six, primarily in the spring, and she will maintain a close relationship with her chicks for weeks after they hatch.[5] Compare that with modern-day chickens, who have been selectively bred to lay eggs unceasingly:

> [In 2004,] an international team of geneticists produced a complete map of the chicken genome [. . .]. Another mutation that resulted from selective breeding is in the TSHR (thyroid-stimulating hormone receptor) gene. In wild animals this gene coordinates reproduction with day length, confining breeding to specific seasons. The mutation disabling this gene enables chickens to breed—and lay eggs—all year long.[6]

All this comes at great cost, of course, to hens' bodies. Whereas their ancestors easily lived 15 years in their natural habitat, or 30 in captivity, modern hens are lucky to live beyond a couple of years. Most hens will die well before they reach middle age (or should it be quarter age?) of any one of numerous reproductive issues, such as impacted egg material, peritonitis, and cancer.[7] Indeed, egg-laying hens are the only animals that "spontaneously" develop cancer at such high rates that they are being used as laboratory models for human ovarian cancer studies.[8] (Of course, calling a direct consequence of selective breeding *for maximum egg production* "spontaneous" is misleading at best.) Additional problems like osteoporosis and fatty liver disease are common and can be connected directly to a hen's domesticated genetics.

One of our former residents, Beatrice the hen, experienced multiple reproductive disorders and related problems. In 2015, she became ill and was diagnosed with peritonitis,* requiring the vet to drain multiple large syringes full of fluid from her abdomen, as well as the need to administer medications and other treatments. Further, she had such severe osteoporosis that her bones looked "moth eaten," in our vet's words, and he recommended we avoid picking her up due to the risk of her bones breaking.

Thankfully, the treatments worked and she was able to recover from peritonitis, as well as rebuild bone mass. She was the picture of health after that and became the alpha hen of her flock before she fell ill again in 2017. She died at the vet's office, and a necropsy revealed numerous egg impactions, including one that was the size of a baseball. Egg impactions occur when egg material gets stuck in the oviduct and cooks from the hen's body heat. As more eggs are produced, the impaction grows. Over time, the cooked egg material can fill up a hen's abdominal cavity and cause serious infection. Our vet suspected that Beatrice had been carrying around the impaction for several years, possibly since before she came to our sanctuary. It is still painful to realize that she died from the equivalent of what many people eat for breakfast: cooked eggs.

---

* Peritonitis occurs in hens when yolk from a developing egg ruptures and is deposited within the body cavity, causing infection. It is one of the most dangerous conditions in hens bred for egg laying.

The biology of modern domesticated laying hens is thus perhaps the strongest argument against seeing backyard eggs as humane. The history of chicken domestication and manipulation has trapped them inside of a body that lays so many eggs it kills them. While it is possible to tweak hens' laying rates, and although laying rates change with age and with the seasons, all breeds of domesticated chickens lay many times more eggs than their wild ancestors—as much as 20–30 times for some breeds. This sort of hyperactive reproductive activity is an evolutionary nightmare, so far from what would be sensible or natural for birds in the wild as to be absurd. In the case of large-scale industrial egg farms, hens are usually only kept in production from around 6 months to the ripe old age of 18–24 months, after which time they are considered "spent" and are sent to the rendering plant or to the landfill if killed onsite. For backyard farms, hens may get to live longer lives (though many backyard farmers also kill hens after that peak performance horizon of 18–24 months old), and they can continue to lay eggs into old age. We have seen laying, and laying-related complications, in older hens like Bibi (who was at least eight years old when diagnosed with ovarian cancer).

There is no such thing as an ethical, humane egg for human consumption. Every egg, whether laid in a battery cage or a backyard coop, is the result of oppressing hens' reproductive systems. Hens suffer immensely as a result of human breeding; every egg is both a testament to this terrible legacy and a potential death sentence.

AN END TO EGGS

The horrors of industrial animal farming are obvious and innumerable, so backyard farming can seem downright bucolic in comparison to sheds filled with tortured animals. Still, we should not ignore the realities of the backyard farming industry. Beneath the surface, we can find scaled-down versions of practices used on industrial farms, along with versions of the same mindset held by industrial farmers. Cruelty, neglect, and entrenched ignorance are widely evident if you know what to look for.

One of the most revealing ways to gain insight into how backyard chicken farmers think about their flocks is to eavesdrop in online groups and discussion forums. I should warn, however, that doing so often means reading about amateur surgeries performed on kitchen tables, botched slaughter attempts, and all manner of neglect in situations requiring actual medical care, but the exercise is enlightening even if deeply depressing.

A common theme is the farmers not getting as many eggs as they want. For example, one post in a backyard chicken group on Facebook included a photograph of a gray and white barred hen seated next to a person's leg. The post read: "I honestly think this brat sees herself on the same boss level as me . . . girlfriend still hasn't given me an egg, but she has the audacity to sit by me with that expression. [. . .] It's like she doesn't even believe that there's a chopping block." Another glimpse into backyard farming can be found on Craigslist, where posts seeking to sell or give away roosters are endless, as are posts about so-called "aging" hens. One post read:

> "I have about five hens that are around three years old. They're past their egg-a-day production and lay maybe one or two eggs a week. [. . .] And while I like chicken stew as much as the next person, killing a bird because it's no longer producing eggs just doesn't seem very enlightened to me. [. . .] But we do need to replace these girls with layers to justify our feed costs, so I'm seeking new homes for these sweet old ladies."

I've heard versions of all this and much worse many times over the years. Nearly every rescue story involves some troubling proof that backyard farming is far from humane, whether or not the humans involved believe that they mean well. Thus, it is crucial that we include backyard farming in our vegan activism, not ignore it entirely for the fight against industrial farming, because suffering and exploitation occur anywhere an animal is being used for human benefit.

Indeed, if we understand the realities of so-called "humane" forms of animal farming, such as backyard chicken keeping, we can confront more directly the issue of exploitation itself, and thus speciesism, rather than deal with the methods of farming. The horrors of industrial farming (i.e., the methods of industrial farming) can often dominate the argument, opening up discussions of welfare reforms that may obfuscate the underlying ethical problems with any form of animal farming. If we can expose that even "humane" backyard farms rely upon oppression, inevitable biological suffering, taking without consent, and treating living beings as objects that exist for our own ends, the ethical case against industrial farming is already made.

Personally, I also feel that addressing "humane" animal farming means confronting exploitation that occurs all around us, be it around our town or in the yard next door. This makes issues like backyard chicken farming excellent opportunities for local activism. Indeed, as citizens of a particular municipality, we have a much more realistic chance to make direct change and be heard by local representatives. I myself have spoken in front of city councils and worked with local animal control numerous times. It is very difficult to have direct influence (however small) in a similar way when it comes to industrial farms. Perhaps this chapter will inspire you to learn more about the chicken ordinances in your city and (if there are any) how they address permitting processes, welfare inspections, onsite slaughtering, roosters, and how we can help to make them more beneficial to animals. As microfarms become more popular in urban and suburban areas, we desperately need advocates to work in their own hometowns on behalf of the animals.

After nearly eight years of rescuing and providing sanctuary to chickens, I cannot help but see the problems of animal farming through the lived experiences of my family members who have shared a home with my partner and me at our sanctuary. So many of them have survived such horror and pain, such injury and loss, and yet here I get to see them thrive, form friendships, enjoy natural behaviors, and live out the fullness of their lives as individuals—as ends in themselves. To pretend that their stories matter less than those of animals trapped in industrial farms (or vice versa) would be to invalidate the truths that their stories bring to light. Our fight must be against all forms of oppression, not simply some forms of it, until we achieve collective liberation for all beings.

In memory of Bibi

Alastor Van Kleeck, Ph.D. is a freelance writer, educator, and community organizer. They spend most of their time working at the Triangle Chickens Advocates sanctuary, which they and their partner founded in 2014, and which inspired them to start The Microsanctuary Movement. Dr. Van Kleeck is co-founder of the Humane Hoax Project and also founded and contributes to the radical vegan blog **Striving with Systems.**

3

MURDER, SHE WROTE

Legitimating the Meat Economy with "Femivorism"

by John Sanbonmatsu, Ph.D.

As the ecological, health, and ethical contradictions of animal agriculture and the fisheries industries worsen, imperiling all life on earth, a "legitimation crisis" has developed around the animal economy.[1] To restore the lost luster of meat, both the meat industry and society at large have sought to find new rationales for our killing of billions of nonhuman animals each year. As part of this effort, movements for locavorism, organic farming, Slow Food*, and regenerative and silvopastoral† agriculture have promoted the idea that smaller-scale, organic animal husbandry offer a solution to the ecological and moral harms of industrial farming. By raising farmed animals more naturally and "sustainably," allowing them to graze or forage outdoors, instead of forcing them to live in cages and feedlots, we might thus create a "humane" animal system that would be a win-win for everyone—for the environment, farmers, consumers, and the animals too. Millions of consumers have responded to this vision, seeking out animal commodities marketed as "welfare-certified," "free-range," and "humane."[2]

---

*   Slow Food is an anti-corporate movement promoting local food, traditional cooking, and the communitarian pleasures of shared meals.

†   Silvopastoralism is a form of agriculture that integrates animal foraging and grazing with forest environments.

One of the most striking things about this new carnivory is that it is being promoted with the greatest enthusiasm and moxie not by men, as one might expect, but by women. For centuries in Western culture, killing and eating animals was closely associated with masculine virility and power through the myth of "Man the hunter."[3] Though it is still overwhelmingly men who run the cattle, dairy, and meat industries—and who hunt, fish, and trap animals for sport—a sea change is underway in the way society represents relations between men, women, and animals. In thousands of news and media reports, books, blogs, and films, women have been celebrated for taking up new roles as pig farmers, cattle ranchers, butchers, and hunters. Killing animals is no longer men's work, the stories and images tell us, but the very horizon of women's empowerment. As Lily McCaulou writes in *The Call of the Mild: Learning to Hunt My Own Dinner*, an account of her transition from urban journalist to big-game hunter, "hunting is the final frontier of feminism."[4]

Such a notion, that dominating and hurting animals could be construed as a path to women's liberation, would have startled feminists of earlier generations. "Scarcely a human being in the course of history has fallen to a woman's rifle," Virginia Woolf observed in *Three Guineas*, "the vast majority of birds and beasts have been killed by you, not by us."[5] From the vegetarian Amazonian women in Charlotte Perkins Gilman's utopian sci-fi novel *Herland*, published in 1915, to Frida Kahlo's famous self-portrait as a wounded deer pierced with arrows, feminists have long emphasized the parallels between male domination of women and male aggression and cruelty toward nonhuman animals. By contrast, for today's "femivores"—as *The New York Times* has dubbed the scores of women who have flocked to farming, hunting, and butchery as a way to achieve a sense of empowerment—nothing could be more repugnant than the musty feminism of their predecessors, with its specter of an angry activist clutching her dog-eared vegetarian *Moosewood Cookbook* as tightly as she clung to her millenarian fervor. These post-feminists don't want to unseat patriarchy, they want a seat at the table; they want to *lean in*, and they want their grass-fed steaks lean, too. If the feminist slogan of the 1970s was that a woman needed a man the way a fish needed a bicycle, the message of femivorism is that today's liberated woman needs only a butcher's knife, killing cone, or hunting rifle.

More than a cultural curiosity, the femivore phenomenon has become central to society's efforts to stabilize and legitimate the failing meat economy. By depicting violence against animals as a form of women's empowerment and maternal care, femivorism is providing society with a new set of rationales for maintaining its endless violence against other beings.

THE NEW FEMININE MYSTIQUE

Until recently, the literary expositors of husbandry and hunting were nearly all men: writers like hunter-rancher Wes Jackson and organic agriculture expert J.I. Rodale, among others. More and more, however, it is now women who are leading the charge. Over the last decade, dozens of women have written memoirs recounting their experiences participating in forms of violence against animals as a way of achieving a purpose-driven life. Women have written books about designing "humane" slaughterhouses (*Humane Livestock Handling* by Temple Grandin) or becoming taxidermists (*Still Life* by Melissa Milgrom), about becoming cattle ranchers (*My Ranch Too: A Wyoming Memoir* by Mary Budd Flitner), or marrying them (*Righteous Porkchop* by Nicolette Hahn Niman), becoming butchers (*Killing It: An Education* by Camas Davis), or marrying them (*Cleaving: A Story of Marriage, Meat, and Obsession* by Julie Powell). By far the most common books in the genre are memoirs by women recounting their experiences as novice animal farmers. With dozens of such books in print, sporting titles like *Hit by a Farm*; *Confessions of a Counterfeit Farm Girl*; *Barnhart: The Incurable Longing for a Barn of One's Own*; *The Dirty Life: A Memoir of Farming, Food, and Love*; *A Girl and Her Pig*; *Sheepish: Two Women, Fifty Sheep, and Enough Wool to Save the Planet*; and *One Woman Farm: My Life Shared with Sheep, Pigs, Chickens, Goats, and a Fine Fiddle*, the women's farming memoir has become one of the most popular genres in contemporary women's nonfiction, and many of the books have become national bestsellers, earning lavish praise in *The New York Times* and on *NPR*'s "All Things Considered" (among other venues).

The woman's farming memoir resembles nothing so much as the *bildungsroman*, or coming-of-age novel, popular in the 19th century, which depicted the moral and psychological development and maturation of a youthful male protagonist. In the classic bildungsroman, the protagonist feels restless and lost, and casts about for some life purpose adequate to his passions and ambitions. The hero may struggle with self-doubt, lost love, and other hardships. By the end, however, after suffering and overcoming setbacks, he has triumphed, forging a new, more authentic self in the process. What we might term the *femivore bildungsroman* traces a similar narrative arc, recounting its author's painful journey on the road to self-discovery and self-reliance, but with this signal difference—the narrative path to self-transformation involves cruelty to others. Only by dominating and killing nonhuman animals can the hero forge a new self in the smithy of her soul.

In *The Feminine Mystique* (1963), Betty Friedan famously addressed the tedium and alienation of the suburban American housewife. Women who had most benefited from the economic boom of the 1950s, for whom life was now supposed to be good, now felt "a strange stirring, a dissatisfaction, a yearning" for something more. In interviews, women from all walks of life (though mostly middle-class white women) told Friedan of a "problem that has no name." "Sometimes," Friedan wrote, "a woman would say 'I feel empty somehow . . . incomplete.' Or she would say, 'I feel as if I don't exist.'" One tells her, "I've tried everything women are supposed to do—hobbies, gardening, pickling, canning, being very social with my neighbors, joining committees, running PTA teas," but nothing works.[*,6]

The authors of today's femivore farming memoirs, nearly all of them white and either comfortably middle-class or affluent, sound a lot like women profiled by Friedan in *The Feminine Mystique*, describing similar feelings of dislocation and alienation. As the books begin, the women are reeling from romantic or professional blows, or both. One former food reporter for the *Chicago Tribune* takes up animal farming when she finds herself "without income, heartbroken, and terrified" after being dumped by her husband and fired from her job. *Killing It: An Education,*

---

[*] As critics have pointed out, Friedan tended to conflate the experiences of educated white, heterosexual, middle- or upper-class women with women "as such," ignoring differences of class, race, and sexual orientation. However, this makes Friedan's analysis all the more relevant for my discussion here, since most "femivore" authors are drawn from much the same demographic group.

Camas Davis's chronicle of her transformation from magazine editor to celebrity butcher, finds the author walking away from her own personal ground zero, having recently lost a 10-year relationship and been fired from her job at the foodie magazine *Saveur*.[7] "I broke my own heart. I wrecked my career," Davis writes. "Who was I? Where was I?" Like many a restless American writer before her, Davis flees the wreckage of her life in the U.S. for the relative safety of Europe. Ernest Hemingway went to Spain to drink and watch bullfights; Davis travels to southwestern France to be tutored the fine arts of butchery and *charcuterie*.

For most of the memoirists, however, the problem isn't losing a job— it's having one. Alienated from corporate life and feeling "burned out, apathetic, and bored" with their "sheltered" or "spoiled" urban lives, the women walk away from jobs as journalists, editors, novelists, food critics, and marketing directors. Other privileged white women in the memoirists' Louboutin shoes might cope with their spiritual desolation by undergoing psychoanalysis, coaching soccer, or organizing a saving mission to Africa. For these women, however, only the farming cure will do. Feminists once dreamed of changing the world; all these memoirists want, however, is a farm of their own. Or, rather, an *animal* farm of their own. Though many of the women grow vegetables and fruit too, it is not part of their vision to lord it over an apple orchard or petunia patch. Forty acres, yes, but the mule's the thing. Driving the women from their urban lives is what Jenna Woginrich, the author of two farming memoirs, calls "barnheart," a condition suffered by "those . . . who wish to God we were outside with our flocks, feed bags, or harnesses instead of sitting in front of the computer screen," women who "are overcome with the desire to be tagging cattle ears or feeding pigs."[8] As Woginrich observes in *One Woman Farm*, farming is a way to prove that "as a single woman I can manage an entire flock."[9] For professional white women who've grown tired of having to please their boss one minute, then rush home to begin the second shift the next, controlling animals is a way to escape feeling controlled themselves—a way to signal a break not only with the corporate world, but also with the conventional aspirations of their sex and their class. "I'm damn sure an ewe trying to deliver a lamb doesn't care about meeting a spreadsheet deadline," Woginrich writes, defiantly.[10] Tired of being tethered to the corporate machine, now *she'll* do the tethering.

Bereft of community and a sense of deeper purpose, the women leave behind lucrative jobs in thriving metropolises like New York, San Francisco, or Seattle to homestead in rural townships in Michigan, Virginia, or Wisconsin either alone or with a lover, spouse, or (more rarely) a family in tow. For Susan McCorkindale, a senior marketing director at *Family Circle*, not even $400 sea-salt pedicures and a $30,000 year-end bonus can relieve the tedium and stress of her privileged life, leading her and her husband to buy and move to a 500-acre beef farm in Virginia. Jessie Knadler, a senior editor with a women's magazine, exchanges her life in Manhattan, where she "splurged on Miu Mius, partied hard, and lived for Kundalini yoga," for down-home life on a farm in "the badlands of Montana."[11]

Once ensconced in their farmhouses, however, the troubles begin. The amateur farmers make blunders, struggle with self-doubt, and are confronted with a slew of new challenges, from early frosts to broken farm equipment. The true flint against which the women strike their souls, however, are the animals they raise for slaughter. In *Chickens in the Road*, Suzanne McMinn's "coming-of-age story of a woman in her forties"—the chronicle of her transformation "from publishing diva to reluctant pasture princess"—raising animals satisfies her "deep-seated need to test myself" ("[m]ilking a cow made me prove myself every single day," she writes).[12] Similarly, for Kristin Kimball, an Ivy Leaguer from an aristocratic East Coast family, dominating animals effects her metamorphosis from party girl who "stays out until four, wears heels, and carries a handbag" to cowgirl who can "shoot a gun, dispatch a chicken, dodge a charging bull, and ride out a runaway behind panicked horses."[13]

Scenes in which the author exerts mastery over a large animal feature prominently in many of the books, as signposts along the road to self-sufficiency. Seeing another woman controlling a horse for the first time, Woginrich admires how she "converses with Steele through the black leather lines, her voice, and her carriage whip." Soon, Woginrich has learned this "language" herself, "the way a child learns it, by holding up things and repeating what they are out loud: *Carriage whip. Blinders.*

Singletree. Lines."[14] When a horse she's riding named Merlin balks at carrying her up a hill, Woginrich digs him sharply with her heel, then gives him the taste of rawhide—a piquant reminder to Merlin of the true nature of their "conversation." Crucially, the mastery the women achieve is real, not merely notional—the mental and physical domination of another being. As Kimball writes in *The Dirty Life*, controlling a horse means "you're on top, a position of power."[15] Indeed, for the first time in their lives, the women feel in control. "I rise up on the big pasture from the back of a horse," Suzanne McMinn reflects in the closing pages of her memoir. "And in my hands, I hold the reins."[16] In mastering the animal other, she has mastered herself.

Though each of the memoirs ostensibly tells a unique story of self-discovery through domination, there is a striking sameness to the books that complicates the authors' claims to having achieved existential authenticity. The title of Ellen Stimson's bestselling *Mud Season: How One Woman's Dream of Moving to Vermont, Raising Children, Chickens and Sheep, and Running the Old Country Store Pretty Much Led to One Calamity After Another* is representative of the themes—and literary sensibilities—of memoirs across the genre. The women all poke fun at their "greenhorn" farming ways, marvel at their new Carhartt mud boots, and crack wise about goat and sheep penises. Several recount identical "comical" showdowns with "mean" roosters, whom they "courageously" vanquish at the chopping block. "Bats and Bears and Skunks. Oh My" reads one chapter title; "Calves' Heads and Black Snakes and Groundhogs, Oh My!" reads another in a different book by a different author. Even as the women depict themselves as roughing it, meanwhile, enacting pastoral rituals that "people have been doing for thousands of years,"[17] they surf the internet, play FarmVille on their iPhones, and curl up at night to a Netflix movie and a fine Chablis after a hard day wrangling sheep, milking cows, and cutting off the heads of the sensitive creatures they lovingly depict as their infants and children.

MOTHERING "BABIES"—THEN KILLING THEM

There have been any number of farming memoirs written by men, including the bestselling *Bucolic Plague* by Josh Kilmer-Purcell, in which a gay couple leave their jobs in Manhattan to set up an animal farm on an old estate in the country.[18] As in the women's memoirs, the gentlemen farmers portray themselves in a self-deprecating and comedic light, as smug city slickers who get their comeuppance wading in cow dung and pig entrails. Like their female counterparts, too, the men portray their rural experiments as a way to achieve a sense of authenticity and connection to nature. Yet there are far fewer farming memoirs by men and, unlike the memoirs by women, the male authors don't couch their farming adventures as cure-alls for low self-esteem, romantic failure, or professional dislocation. Nor do they depict animal husbandry as a revelatory exercise in parental care-giving.

The first book to popularize the new gentlewoman farmer narrative, and the first to weave maternal and natalist themes into the discourse of a "new" animal husbandry, was Barbara Kingsolver's influential bestseller, *Animal, Vegetable, Miracle*—a critique of corporate agribusiness wrapped in a personal account of the Kingsolver family's experiences running a small organic animal farm. Portions of *Animal, Vegetable, Miracle* were devoted specifically to attacking animal rights and ethical vegetarianism, with the author chiding vegetarians for finding nothing wrong with "cutting the heads off lettuces," but becoming upset when farmers cut the heads off "crops that blink their eyes."[19] "Who among us has never killed living creatures on purpose?" Kingsolver asks, rhetorically. But Kingsolver, in fact, professes not to like the word "killing" at all, preferring instead to speak of "harvesting." While "harvesting" animals "is a lot less fun than spending an autumn day picking apples off trees," Kingsolver writes, it is "a similar operation on principle and the same word."[20]

Notwithstanding her attack on vegetarians as sentimentalists, Kingsolver anthropomorphizes the animals on her own farm, analogizing them to her own children. "April 23, my babies due!" she writes in her calendar, to mark the day the chicks she has ordered are to arrive from the hatchery. "Our turkeys would be pampered as children," she writes, explaining that she wants to instruct her daughter in the responsibilities of mothering. "Some parents would worry about a daughter taking on maternal responsibility so early in life, but Lily was already experienced," having helped care for chickens at the family's previous home.[21]

Since its publication in 2007, *Animal, Vegetable, Miracle* has inspired scores of similar memoirs by women who have emulated Kingsolver by running their own small-scale animal farms. Maternalism has appeared in these books too—a theme signaled on the books' covers, most of which feature photos of their smiling authors in mud boots and clutching chickens, lambs, or baby pigs, infant-like, to their gingham-clad chests. "We would make babies," Catherine Friend writes in *Hit By a Farm*, after she and her partner buy a farm in Minnesota to raise sheep.[22] Another author puts a "basket of gear and supplies" by her back door, like "a hospital suitcase for a mother-in-waiting" or "a midwife . . . preparing for a midnight delivery."[23] For memoirist Ellen Stimson, the decision "to foster a little girl and a little boy"—a pair of lambs—fills the author with trepidation, because "it had been a long time since I had had a baby."[24] As the pregnant animals approach their due dates, the women anxiously take their temperatures and check their cervixes. When the babies are finally born, the women are over the moon. "Ohmygodohmygodohmygod," Friend enthuses on birthing day. "We'd made a baby boy."[25] Cradling the "sturdy little wool-baby" in her arms, Suzanne McMinn feels "starry-eyed."[26] Pastures in birthing season are described as "nurseries" and "out-of-control daycare" centers,[27] while herding lambs is said to resemble a "fire drill in a kindergarten."[28]

For femivore memoirists who are single and childless, rearing farmed animals becomes a way to achieve an elusive motherhood. "I had become a single parent raising a goat," Jenna Woginrich writes, recounting how she learned to let down a goat's milk by massaging her teats.[29] Another author, lacking children of her own, writes of her joy in having "a baby on my lap," while boasting that her "skills progress to the point I can feed five babies at once."[30] In controlling the bodies of other animals, the women are able to demonstrate superhuman maternal powers. Slipping out of bed in the wee hours of the morning after breast-feeding their own newborns, the women go out and milk cows and goats, yielding brimming vats of milk that would make La Leche League green—or white—with envy. Ordinarily, a nursing mother goat can produce only a few pints of milk each day; Woginrich however is soon producing "more than 45 gallons of fresh milk" per month. "Holy cow!" she writes.

"Strike that. Holy goat! *I'm doing it!*"[31] In a fantasy of limitless fertility, the women "produce" thousands of eggs and breed llamas, sheep, pheasants, peacocks, ponies, cows, geese, pigs, alpaca, rabbits, ducks, and goats.

The traditional human dependent is of course not the domesticated pig, chicken, or llama, but the human infant. However, that kind of dependent, the sort demanding unwavering parental attention and care, has long been symptom and sign of woman's subordinate cultural status in patriarchal society. As long as women remain solely responsible for bearing and raising children, they remain socially disadvantaged. Having a child, in a way, is not merely to *have* a dependent, it is to *be* dependent. Hence the importance placed by feminists in the 1960s and 1970s (and still today) on universal free childcare, as a way of freeing women to pursue careers without feeling the need to bear children at all. Today's femivores, however, have gravitated to a new kind of "dependent," one that allows them to engage in the pageantry of maternalism but without the risk of being tied down. These are babies who can be "loved" and "cared for," but also gotten rid of once their company grows tedious. The memoirists want only ersatz children, ones requiring only a simulation of maternal love and responsibility. Casual indifference to the fates of their "babies" is thus the norm in the memoirs. When the women aren't killing the animals outright, they're killing them through malign neglect.

Animals die left and right on the women's farms, with such frequency that the reader needs a scorecard to keep up. Sheep get crushed to death between bales of hay. Chickens fall between slats of pallets or get "mashed between the side of the feeder box and the wall of the chicken house,"[32] or have their necks broken when the women accidentally crush them with heavy objects. One rabbit gets her leg caught in the steel mesh floor and tries to gnaw it off, dislocating her vertebra and paralyzing her "from the waist down."[33] Snowstorms on the McCorkindale farm leave behind what the author jokingly calls "a very nice dusting of dead chickens," when the suffering birds freeze to death.[34] Cows give birth alongside electric fences, incinerating their newborn calves. "Bad things happen," Catherine Friend observes blandly after one ewe gives birth along an electric fence, killing two lambs.[35] When she and her partner accidentally get their herd of sheep pregnant out of season, they correct the error by selling them all for slaughter. As more than one memoirist remarks, "There's a saying in farming, 'if you're going to *have* livestock, you're going to have deadstock.'"[36]

Such perils are meant to distract the reader from the fact that it is the authors themselves who've placed their vulnerable charges at mortal risk. It is they too who will betray their "babies" in the end, ensuring that not one of them escapes a violent death. When Kingsolver's chicks first arrive from the hatchery, the author finds them "adorable," recounting how "they imprinted on me as Mama and rushed happily to greet me wherever I appeared." Kingsolver confesses to feeling like "Cruella de Ville" for having deceived the young turkeys into mistaking her for their mother, since she has only taken them under her own wing in order to eventually kill them. However, once the chicks mature into young adults and begin exerting their own agency and will, Kingsolver no longer wants them around. "Many of us were relieved that year at harvest time," she writes. Right up to the moment of slaughter, Kingsolver nonetheless is still comparing her relationship to the birds to a relationship between mother and child, in a tacit acknowledgment that, unlike picking apples off trees, the violence she is to inflict is an act of betrayal. Moments before delivering the coup de grace, Kingsolver registers the "downy softness and a vulnerable heartbeat" of the animal whose life she is about to extinguish. "I felt maternal," she observes, "while at the same time looking straight down the [kill] pipe toward the purpose of this enterprise."[37]

In *Macbeth*, after Lord and Lady Macbeth have determined to murder King Duncan and his men, guests under their roof, Lady Macbeth privately begs the "spirits" to "unsex" her by "damming up the access and passage to remorse." Only by tamping down any "compunctious visitings of nature," compassion, can she proceed with her "fell purpose." The memoirists similarly suppress natural stirrings of empathy in order to destroy their vulnerable young charges. The result is a succession of grotesque scenes in which maternal love ends in unfeeling betrayal. "I stroked his warm, warty head . . . I could feel his heart beating, slowly," writes Novella Carpenter in *Farm City: The Education of an Urban Farmer* of Harold, the loving turkey she has raised, seconds before cutting off his head.[38] Catherine Friend meanwhile describes how she "clung fiercely to this tender animal in my arms, wanting to protect her from whatever dangers lay ahead," except for the most lethal of all—herself. When an affectionate lamb becomes smitten with Friend, following her around and demanding to be nuzzled and patted on the head, she names him "Mr. Playful" and gushes to her partner, "I feel like kissing him right on his nose." Weeks later, Friend sits in her pickup outside a slaughterhouse, weeping, as "Mr. Playful" is killed. By suppertime, however, she's right as rain again, and sits down eagerly to dine on the lamb's body. Eating Mr. Playful's "savory and incredibly tender" flesh, she writes, is her way of "honoring the lamb *that died*"—a telling use of the passive voice which, like Kingsolver's preference for euphemism, is meant to conceal the author's moral culpability in an unnecessary act of violence.[39]

Thinking about killing the pigs she's raised, Carpenter wonders whether the animals are "really as intelligent as everyone" says they are, and hence whether she would "end up keeping the beasts as seven-hundred-pound pets" or instead melt them down into fat. "Of course it would be the latter," she writes, "I knew myself well enough by then. A pragmatic farmer, not a soft sentimentalist."[40] Though Carpenter and other femivores often accuse vegans of "sentimentality," however, it is they who engage in sentimental depictions of the animals they exploit and kill, treating them not as individuals worthy of dignity or respect, but as platforms for the authors' own narcissistic displays of affect. In a conversation with another farmer about killing chickens, Carpenter remarks, "It's solemn," and recounts how they "both touched our hearts."[41] These sorts of empty gestures, like Friend crying in her pickup, or the *de rigueur* ritual of "thanking" the animal corpse before a meal, recur throughout all of the memoirs.

But sentimentality, a form of disguised bad faith, is not to be confused with genuine *sentiment* or feeling. As James Baldwin observed in his critique of *Uncle Tom's Cabin* and similar efforts by liberal white race reformers:

> Sentimentality, the ostentatious parading of excessive and spurious
> emotion, is the mark of dishonesty, the inability to feel; the wet eyes
> of the sentimentalist betray his aversion to experience, his fear of

life, his arid heart; and it is always, therefore, the signal of secret and violent inhumanity, the mark of cruelty.[42]

Baldwin's observation helps explain how sentimentality in these accounts can bleed so readily into open sadism. A dark undertow of violence runs beneath the femivore narratives, as caring and killing get woven into a lethal maternalism, in which images of infant care segue effortlessly into Grand Guignol spectacle. In *Bones, Blood and Butter*, Gabrielle Hamilton's memoir about becoming a chef, the author thus confesses that each time she changes diapers on a "noncompliant child" she's reminded of trussing chickens and wrangling eels. After Hamilton sends her lambs, "with their little crooked sets of teeth and milky eyes," to the butcher, she skewers their lifeless bodies "onto ten-foot poles made of ash" and recounts how she "roasted four or five of the whole little guys." In a macabre parody of maternal watchfulness, the author writes, "The lambs were arranged over the coals head to toe and head to toe, the way you'd put a bunch of kids having a sleepover to bed." Hamilton is fascinated by the sound of the lambs' blood as it drips "down into the coals with a hypnotic and rhythmic bliss . . . Hiss. Hiss. Hiss."[43]

Many of the memoirists speak of "getting their hands dirty," a euphemism for enacting violence. "I had daily intimacy not just with *dirt* but with blood, manure, milk, pus . . . the grease of engines and the grease of animals, with innards," writes Kimball in *The Dirty Life*.[44] Another memoirist observes that "most of my story" was "written in sweat, tears, and even a little blood."[45] And there will be blood. Buckets and buckets of it. Blood pouring out of the torn tracheas of cows, blood gushing out of the throats of thrashing pigs, caught with giant buckets. Perhaps, confesses Catherine Friend, even "more blood than I was comfortable with."[46] With despotic fury, the women stab rabbits, shoot terrified raccoons, dismember deer, and roam the barnyard lopping off heads. Farms become abattoirs, cemeteries, killing fields. In *Chickens in the Road*, Suzanne McMinn traps a raccoon, then shoots him with a rifle as he cowers in the cage. "Wow," she writes, "I felt strange. I'd just killed an animal. I felt good and bad all at the same time."[47] But the truth is, she feels very, very good. Though the women wonder whether they'll be "tough enough" when the moment of truth comes, they prove eager and even impatient to kill.

When journalist-cum-hunter Lily McCaulou kills her first animal with a well-placed "head shot"—"a clean, perfect kill" of a pheasant in a canned hunt—she experiences "euphoria." Driving home, "I roll down the windows, crank up the radio, and sing at the top of my lungs," she recounts. Like a man boasting of having deflowered his first virgin, the author writes that "no other kill . . . evokes such pure elation as my first." McCaulou—who compares herself to a modern-day Diana the Huntress—soon graduates from killing birds and small mammals to exterminating much larger animals. Her moment of arrival comes the day she finds herself "kneeling before a bull elk, up to my shoulders in blood," "drenched in blood and laughing" at her "earlier squeamishness."[48] For other memoirists, too, shedding the blood of animals becomes a way to symbolically reenact earlier rituals of female maturation—a way to signify loss of a childlike innocence in the acceptance of the "adult knowledge"—as Lierre Keith puts it in her anti-vegetarian screed, *The Vegetarian Myth*—that "death is the substance of life."[49] In a kind of reverse transubstantiation, real blood gets transformed into something metaphysical—an aesthetic of the sublime and a newly "authentic" self. In Carpenter's *Farm City*, the author symbolically invokes the rite of menses when she renounces her former vegetarianism by throwing out her *Moosewood Cookbook* and replacing it with *The Encyclopedia of Country Living*, an instruction manual on DIY slaughter that becomes "marked with blood," Carpenter says, with her first kill.[50]

A leading force in locavore politics in the San Francisco Bay area, Carpenter is an especially eager killer of animals, someone who enjoys seeing them die. Of the first pigs she has raised, Carpenter writes, "I was going to have to kill one of Simon's babies . . . Yeah I gotta find someone to execute those fuckers." She hires a female butcher named Sheila to do the deed, telling her, "I really want to see the pigs die." Later, when she learns in a phone call that Sheila has gone ahead and killed the animals without her being there, Carpenter is so infuriated that she slams down the phone and screams, "Cunt!" Seeing the dead pigs' dismembered bodies for the first time, Carpenter impulsively reaches over to a pig's severed head and scoops its raw brains into her mouth, pronouncing them "delicious."[51] In another passage, Carpenter boasts of the "bloody revenge" she enacts on an opossum who'd made his way into the poultry enclosure one night. Recalling "the cuteness of my ducks, and the goose who would rest her head in my lap," Carpenter takes a shovel and brings it "down on the opossum's neck," thrusting repeatedly until his head rolls off. "Caught up in protecting my babies," she quips, "I had become a savage."[52] Yet her fierce determination to protect her "babies" is nowhere in evidence just a few weeks later, when she carries a trusting white duck into her house, places him in the bathtub, and decapitates him with a pruner. "He quacked and swam around for a few minutes . . . I merely squeezed the loppers shut. The duck went from being a happy camper to being a headless camper. I plucked and eviscerated him outside on a table."[53]

Such flippant passages, in which the author openly mocks her victims, give the lie to the memoirists' repeated claims to "love" and "respect" animals. Friend finds it amusing when a lamb strays against an electric fence and receives an 8,000-volt shock (a voltage so high that it burns a hole in a leather glove), causing him to shoot "straight up in the air" and to run crying to his mother as the other lambs "scatter in panic."[54] When lambs are born on Friend's farm, she and her partner "steal it from its mother" in order "to do things to it." "We sneak up to a pair of sleeping twins and each pick one up. The ewe no longer sees her babies on the ground and panics."[55] Similar heartbreaking scenes, of traumatized sheep and cows returning day after day to the ground where they last saw their babies, sniffing the ground and lowing in distress, can be found in many of the memoirs, their authors betraying not the slightest remorse or sympathy for their victims. The women even joke about the impending doom of their victims, finding humor in their very guilelessness and vulnerability. Woginrich, observing that the pig she has raised will soon "die in the same place where she has spent the last three months sleeping and eating," remarks, "It will surprise the hell out of her." And it does. On the fateful morning, as Woginrich reaches down and scratches the pig's ear, the pig turns and looks at her "curiously," wagging her "little curled tail" and making "gentle" noises. "I'm proud of this Pig," Woginrich writes. Soon, a trio of hired killers arrives in a truck, seizes the trusting animal, slashes her throat, and carves her body up into slabs. Woginrich sticks around to watch. It's her way of taking "responsibility," she writes. "I *need* to be there," she says, to bear witness to the "whole process, from holding a piglet in a dog crate, squealing in my arms, to the day its head lies on a snowbank."[56]

HUNGER GAMES

In 1974, a young chef at a feminist food collective called Moosewood published a new book of vegetarian recipes.[*][57] The *Moosewood Cookbook* soon became one of the most popular cookbooks of all time, and the name of its youthful author, Mollie Katzen, became synonymous with vegetarianism. In 2007, however, the author of the iconic *Moosewood* announced that she had started eating meat again. "For about 30 years I didn't eat meat at all, just a bite of fish every once in a while, and always some dairy," Katzen told an interviewer with *Food and Wine* magazine. "Lately, I've been eating a little meat. People say, 'Ha, ha, Mollie Katzen is eating steak.' But now that cleaner, naturally fed meat is available, it's a great option for anyone who's looking to complete his diet." Katzen now claimed to have been misunderstood all these years. She'd never said that she didn't "want people to eat meat;" she'd only "wanted to supply possibilities that were low on the food chain." The heroine of vegetarians everywhere now mocked them. "For people who are against eating meat because it's wrong or offensive to eat animals," Katzen said, "even the cleanest grass-fed beef won't be good enough."[58]

Katzen's about-face represented more than a change in diet—it was the repudiation of a movement and a moment when many Americans, particularly many women, had for the first time become open to a new way of relating to food and to animals. How had the nation gone from the feminist-vegetarian *Moosewood* to the spectacle of women hunting moose in the woods?

---

*   Moosewood was one of a number of feminist restaurant collectives at the time that sought an alternative to hierarchical (hence patriarchal) managerial practices.

Undoubtedly, many women have been drawn to animal husbandry for many of the same reasons that men have, including a longing for a more "authentic" relation to nature and the food economy, and as part of a more general cultural reaction against veganism and animal rights. However, to fully grasp the significance of the femivore phenomenon, we must attend to the specific historical and cultural plight of women in the early decades of the 21st century. As we have seen, the mass media have depicted the mania for women hunting, fishing, and animal husbandry as "feminist." However, whether that is indeed so depends on how we construe the history and meaning of feminism itself, and specifically whether we find ourselves satisfied with a conception of women's progress that emphasizes women's formal, rather than substantive, equality with men.

In the late 1960s and early 1970s, radical feminists had sought not only formal parity with men, such as equality in the workplace and in government, but also a broader transformation of patriarchal norms and institutions, including the overcoming of rape culture and an end to militarism, imperialism, and racism. As the feminist poet and essayist Adrienne Rich wrote in "Toward a Woman-Centered University" in the early 1970s, the question facing women wasn't merely whether they should be equal participants in society alongside men, but "whether this male-created, male-dominated structure is really capable of serving the humanism and freedom it professes." Rich and other radical feminists suggested that it was not, and that patriarchal society's "suicidal obsession with power and technology" was incompatible with general liberation and a just society.[59] True women's liberation thus implied not merely formal equality between men and women, but the creation of a new society, one based on principles of universal equality, freedom, and nonviolence. It was out of this same vision of a more just world that eco-feminist theorists like Marti Kheel, Josephine Donovan, Ynestra King, and Carol J. Adams would soon go on to highlight human oppression against other animals as one of the most destructive features of patriarchal society. The highwater mark of these efforts was Adams' breakthrough book, *The Sexual Politics of Meat*. Published in 1990—the 20th anniversary of Kate Millett's influential feminist classic, *Sexual Politics*—Adams' *The Sexual Politics of Meat* argued that the killing and consumption of animals had long been associated with masculinity, and that women and animals alike are objectified, fragmented, and subjected to violence under patriarchal relations.[60] By the time Adams' book appeared on the scene, however, the women's movement had been in decline for years, and feminist interest in vegetarianism, too, had waned. With the election of President Ronald Reagan in 1981, a period of broad political reaction had set in, transforming the political and cultural landscape and leading to a retrenchment of traditional gender norms. The conservative backlash against feminism—along with internecine squabbles within the women's movement itself, including conflicts over identity politics, movement priorities, and competing currents of feminist theory—had fragmented the women's movement and sapped it of its former grassroots momentum. Liberal feminism, oriented largely around winning formal parity with men, now came into ascendancy. As a consequence, more radical elements within the movement—those that had questioned the underlying structures and values of the patriarchal system, including speciesism—were eclipsed. Mainstream feminism thus moved further away from environmentalism, vegetarianism, and animal rights.

By 1990, many women had gained entry into previously closed professions and had won key legal victories for reproductive rights and against discrimination in the workplace. However, women's advances in the workplace hadn't altered their fundamental status, which remained one of social subordination to men. Women remained responsible for the bulk of domestic labor and child-rearing, they were still paid less than their male counterparts, and they remained as susceptible as before to male sexual assault and abuse. For white middle-class and upper-class women, the group that had gained the most from post-70s feminist reform, equality had come to seem both tantalizingly close and frustratingly out of reach. As Susan Faludi observed in *Backlash: The Undeclared War Against American Women*, in an echo of Betty Friedan's diagnosis of "the problem that has no name" decades earlier, "Behind this celebration of the American woman's victory, behind the news, cheerfully and endlessly repeated, that the struggle for women's rights is won, another message flashes. You may be free and equal now, it says to women, but you have never been more miserable."[61]

I want to suggest that it was this contradiction—between the promise of gender equality, on the one hand, and women's continuing status as the social inferiors to men on the other—that created the cultural opening for a regressive project in which middle-class white women, partly under the mantle of feminism, have channeled their frustration and rage over the unfinished business of sexual equality into animal husbandry and other forms of animal harm. The fact that the phenomenon has arisen during a period of patriarchal retrenchment and neoliberal austerity— i.e., amidst a rollback of women's rights and a cultural retreat into various private "localisms" that came at the expense of broader civic engagement—is no accident.

The publication of Michael Pollan's bestselling *The Omnivore's Dilemma* in 2006, followed the next year by Kingsolver's *Animal, Vegetable, Miracle*, helped to consolidate a new pastoral ideal in America, one that romanticized small-scale animal farming and the meat economy. During this same period, a group of women in San Francisco issued a manifesto for "locavorism," a new grassroots consumer movement oriented around buying locally farmed produce and animal products. Locavorism became popular among middle-class consumers interested in pushing back against corporate agribusiness and hoping to regain a sense of "connection" to the land. Men and women alike were drawn into locavorism. But the effects of that were unequal. The influx of women into animal pastoralism siphoned off women's activist energies into a communitarian and depoliticized movement that substituted rural domesticity for a more robust conception of feminist struggle. As Kristin Kimball writes in her book, before she began running an animal farm, "the word *home* could make me cry," because "I wanted one. With a man. A house. The smell of cut grass, sheets on a line, a child running through a sprinkler."[62] After forsaking professional lives in the city, she and other post-feminist pioneers set furiously to work canning, preserving, pickling, gardening, knitting, sewing, quilting, baking, and making homemade jerky, transforming themselves into "domestic superheroes" (as one memoirist describes herself), in a ferocious return to stereotypically "feminine" activities improbably re-cast as tactics of *empowerment*.

However, since few women today welcome the idea of a total retreat to the domestic sphere, some countervailing demonstration of women's power within the domestic sphere is plainly needed, in order to paper over the contradiction between the femivore memoirists' avowed quests for authenticity and independence, on the one hand, and their longings to fulfill traditional gender roles, on the other. Domination of animals provides it. In the femivore memoirs, violence against animals serves as a kind of psychic ballast, keeping the women from sinking entirely under what would otherwise be merely another form of conventional domesticity. By "mothering" animals, then killing them, the women have found a way to square the circle of the new femininity, which demands that women be both vulnerable *and* strong, domesticated *and* self-sufficient. By raising pigs and sheep—then bearing eager witness to their deaths—the women are able to exhibit traditional caring behavior, while at the same time demonstrating the toughness and ruthlessness we stereotypically associate with men. Having spent their whole lives in a world centered around men and their brutal deeds, women can now take a piece of the action for themselves. Hence the "swagger"—as Jessica Applestone, co-owner of Fleisher's Grass-Fed and Organic Meats, calls it—among women taking her butchering class for the first time. "There's a macho performal [*sic*] nature that some of these people crave," she writes. "And what better a performance than the blood and guts of butchery?"[63]

Femivorism has given concrete form to cultural fantasies of a militarized white femininity, allowing women to claim a "transgressive" status while nonetheless engaging in practices that keep them within the safe bounds of existing patriarchal values, norms, and institutions. Many of the memoirists, while ostensibly seeking to demonstrate their strength and autonomy, nonetheless seek out male approbation, rather than (in most cases) meaningful connections with other women. The ritual of learning to wield a gun, that most potent cultural symbol of masculine power, features prominently in many of the accounts. "I ran my hand over the smooth, dark wood of the stock and shivered,"

Kimball writes, caressing her first rifle. "Hand me a bow and arrow or a rifle and *it makes sense*," Woginrich confesses. Fielding a gun for the first time, Catherine Friend thinks, "Gosh, this is fun. Hand me more bullets." After considering different weapons, Friend finally settles upon an air pistol, which she will use to kill groundhogs and other "pests" on her farm. (A young woman staying with her vows, "we're going to shoot those SOBs.") "I yearned for more space, more breathing room," Friend writes.[64] And, indeed, how better to carve out a little *Lebensraum* in the wilderness than with a blazing firearm? Soon, the hills around the memoirists' farms are alive with the sounds of gunfire, as the farms and their surrounds get transformed into free-fire zones for killing deer, opossums, pigeons, squirrels, and any other living being hapless enough to wander across the women's defense perimeter in search of food or shelter or a mate. Memoirists who describe themselves as liberals and progressives suddenly reveal a patriotic fascination with all things military. "I've always fantasized about being one of those Navy SEALs, Special Forces, or Delta Force dudes, I think it would be a blast," McCorkindale writes.[65] "I begin to understand why hunting is often compared to war," McCaulou confesses. Like a soldier victorious in battle, she and the other women keep the body parts of their victims—feathers, tails, teeth—as fetishistic tokens. Suzanne McMinn nails the tail of the raccoon she has shot to the front porch—as a warning to other "pests," just as colonial officials used to impale the heads of defeated Native warriors on poles at the town gate.

One might well argue that women waging war on animals is merely the continuation of liberal feminist politics by other means. However, as I have suggested, only in the context of the historical decline of feminism could causing harm to other animals come to be mistaken for women's empowerment. If animal agriculture really is a way for affluent white women to work through the conflictual nature of 21st-century femininity, it has yet to serve as an effective vehicle for challenging the prerogatives of men. With its false pieties of "respect" for animals, its love of guns, knives, and blood, femivorism is indeed best seen as a reactionary movement—a maladaptive response to the contradictions of patriarchal society—allied with some of the most destructive features of patriarchal culture. Femivorism is displaced aggression. Today's real-life Dianas and Katnisses may not be able to shatter the corporate glass ceiling with their arrows or send conservative state legislators scattering for cover before they can shutter another abortion clinic, but they can make some deer or pig *pay*. At the end of the day, however, sticking pigs is not the same as sticking it to the Man. Even the memoirists' insatiable hunger for meat and blood as "enlivening" foods—a recurring theme in many of the accounts—suggests nothing so much as a sublimated desire to participate in society as the true equals of men.

Feminine "Credibility"

As one might have expected, the idea that animals can be raised and killed "humanely" and with "compassion"—a myth crucial to perpetuating the injustices of the meat economy—has been adopted not only by organic farmers and locavores, but also by the world's largest meatpackers and industrialized farming companies. Smithfield, owned by the WH Group in China, the world's largest killer of pigs, thus advertises itself as the "World's Leader in Animal Care," while Tyson Foods, the world's biggest killer of chickens, boasts that its "Animal Well-Being" program "promotes the health, safety and well-being of the animals," while its company personnel act as "stewards" of the animals they exploit.[66] Indeed, the humane hoax is not confined to health food stores and farmer's markets. The very plasticity of "humane" discourse, the fact that it can be successfully deployed across small- and large-scale contexts, organic farms and inorganic ones, shows just how critical it has become to the functioning of the meat system. Within this discourse, femivorism is an important strategic asset. If "sustainable" organic animal farming is merely the flipside of industrialized animal agriculture, then femivorism is the ideological ligature that now binds the two systems together.

Judith Capper, a self-proclaimed "livestock sustainability consultant" to the U.S. cattle industry, has explicitly invoked her femininity to legitimate large-scale farming in agriculture. In a blog entry entitled "Do Moms Have Instant Beef Credibility?" Capper promotes the beef industry by linking stories of women as mothers, domestic providers, and nurturers to the "caring" work of industrialized animal agriculture. Noting that women "who have children are trusted by female consumers more than the traditional scientific image of an older man in a white lab coat," Capper urges male ranchers to ask their "wife, girlfriend, daughter, mother, granddaughter, or niece to . . . let the female consumer know why . . . beef is a great choice for our families, and why we spend time caring for baby calves almost as if they are our own children." Only women, Capper explains, can make "that female–female connection that, like it or not, does promote an instant degree of trust." At a meeting of the International Livestock Conference, one prominent cattle lobbyist praised Capper for helping "to improve the image of beef sustainability," noting that "Jude Capper is credible because she is female" and suggesting that Capper would become "even more credible when she has children" of her own. Recounting this incident on her blog, Capper revealed to her readers that she was seven months pregnant. "I am gaining credibility by the day . . . pound by pound . . . literally," she wrote. And with her new "baby bump," she would have even "more opportunities for conversations about the importance of beef in pregnancy nutrition."[67]

CONCLUSION

Reading the femivore accounts, it is easy to forget that the majority of vegans, as well as many of the leading figures in contemporary animal advocacy, are women—courageous individuals like Karen Davis of United Poultry Concerns, pattrice jones, the director of VINE Sanctuary, and Jenny Brown, co-founder of the Woodstock Animal Sanctuary. Such women are modeling relations of genuine care and respect for nonhuman animals by rescuing them from slaughterhouses, managing sanctuaries, and educating the public about the true nature of the animal economy.[*,68] Notably, however, it isn't these women's experiences being profiled in *The New York Times* or *The New Yorker*, nor their memoirs being awarded six-figure contracts with Harper & Row or Penguin or other big publishing houses. Nor has the culture industry taken any interest in publicizing the experiences of the many caring men who have also devoted their lives to animal advocacy—men like Robert

---

* An estimated 60% of vegans in Britain and nearly 80% in the U.S. are women.

Grillo, director of Free from Harm, or longtime animal advocate Kim Stallwood. Only women who kill are deemed worthy of media attention.

The reason why should be obvious. By creating a false distinction between "good" and "bad" forms of animal exploitation and violence, the animal industry has convinced the public that there is nothing wrong with animal agriculture, per se, only with the way it is practiced. However, it isn't just the animal industry that has a stake in this. Capitalists and consumers, conservatives and liberals, small-scale farmers and corporate industrial farms alike all wish to re-"naturalize" animal husbandry as a permanent, benignant fixture of the human condition. The new hoax of "humane" meat is thus a convenience for all, a way to neutralize animal advocacy and to fend off the bad conscience of society. In this context, cultural stereotypes of women as "natural nurturers" are proving more and more indispensable. By blurring the line between caring for animals and killing them, femivorism is reshaping cultural narratives around animals, gender, and dominion. And in doing so, it is removing from our collective grasp one of the last resources we have for resisting the violence at the core of our civilization—compassion.

John Sanbonmatsu, Ph.D. is an associate professor of philosophy at Worcester Polytechnic Institute. He is the author of *The Postmodern Prince: Critical Theory, Left Strategy, and the Making of a New Political Subject* and the editor of the book, *Critical Theory and Animal Liberation.* A leading critic of cellular or cultivated meat, Dr. Sanbonmatsu created and now curates the CleanMeat-hoax.com website and is currently at work on a new book, *The Omnivore's Deception: What We Get Wrong about Meat, Animals, and the Nature of Moral Life.*

4

ONE BAD DAY

by Carol J. Adams, M.Div.

I am so tired of hearing people quote the "family farmer," saying: "Our cows have only one bad day."

Oh really? How do they know anyway?

Wasn't it a bad day when she was taken from her mother so that her mother's milk could go to humans, not her?

Wasn't it a bad day when she was forcibly made pregnant?

Wasn't it a bad day when her calf was taken away from her?

Wasn't it a bad day when a friend disappeared to go to her bad day?

Wasn't it a bad day when she was forcibly made pregnant through the violation of artificial insemination AGAIN because her milk was drying up? And then, AGAIN?

Wasn't it a bad day, each and every day that she was both pregnant and being milked by machine?

Wasn't it a bad day, each and every day that she was producing milk because she has been bred to produce more milk than is natural to her body, and so the weight of her udder caused strain to her back and hips?

Wasn't it a bad day, each and every day that her overgrown hooves stood on concrete and made her legs ache?

Wasn't it a bad day when she got an infection, and because the organic farm doesn't use antibiotics, a few days were spent discussing options before they decided that, though she was only two years old, she would have to go to slaughter?

What's a bad day anyway? A bad day means that you are going to have some time in the future to look back and say, "Now, that—*that* day—*that* was a bad day." A bad day isn't the day your life ended; it's the day your life dipped, or tumbled downward, but in its label, there is also contained the promise that other days will be good days. As one person points out,

> Calling it 'one bad day' is a horrendous insult in itself. This isn't the same as hitting your toe on the coffee table or spilling coffee on yourself in the car. This is the equivalent of being dragged out of your house and shot in the head with a 20-gauge shot gun. This isn't something that will be better with a good night's sleep or an aspirin.

Each animal is a unique being, with a unique personality, but she is reduced to being a part of a money-making venture, and her individuality is so fungible it can be extinguished when she is no longer producing money for the farmer. As long-time animal advocate Kim Stallwood has pointed out, why are the people who are oppressing the other animals allowed to be the spokespeople and interpreters of the animals' experiences? Haven't we seen this reversal before when the abusers claim themselves as benefactors? First, they murder the victims; then they murder the language.

Carol J. Adams is a feminist-vegan advocate, activist, and independent scholar and the author of numerous books including *The Sexual Politics of Meat: A Feminist-Vegetarian Critical Theory*. Adams is also the author of books on living as a vegan, including *Never Too Late to Go Vegan: The Over-50 Guide to Adopting and Thriving on a Vegan Diet* (with Patti Breitman); *Living Among Meat Eaters: The Vegetarian's Survival Guide*; and *How to Eat Like a Vegetarian Even if You Never Want to Be One*. She is the author of the training manual, *Pastoral Care for Domestic Violence: Case Studies for Clergy* and has a Master of Divinity from Yale University.

5

REINFORCING RATIONALIZATIONS
AND A ROOSTER

by Hope Bohanec

These days, it seems that almost everyone dislikes "factory farming"—the cruel confinement, the antibiotics and hormones, the small farmer pushed out by the big corporate conglomerates. Ending big, industrial, faceless farming is something that almost everyone can get behind, but where do we go from there? How do we feed almost eight billion people sustainably and humanely?

I live in what I would argue is one of the most beautiful places on earth. Sonoma County, California, is just about an hour north of San Francisco's Golden Gate Bridge and offers a rural refuge from the hustle of San Francisco and the East Bay. The winters are mild and short, bringing a shag of bright green carpet to the hills that sparkle with dew from the winter rains. March brings swaying fields of yellow mustard and tiny purple and orange wildflowers on the hiking trails. A steady stretch of dry warmth carries all the way to October, with mild temperatures and the emerald hills turning golden under the ceaseless sunshine.

California produces two-thirds of the fruits and vegetables[1] in the United States, and the state is a top producer of cow dairy.[2] Most of this agriculture is found in the Central Valley along Highway 5, with endless acres of flat mono-cropping and millions of cows crammed together in bleak and boring pens, awaiting milking, or branding, or an injection, or prodding, and finally, slaughter.

Sonoma County's mild weather has made it a haven for agriculture. Farmers flock to this area of California hoping for a few productive acres to grow food and raise farmed animals. The "locavore"* craze is alive and thriving in the North Bay (the counties north of San Francisco including Marin, Sonoma, and Napa) and farming here is taking on a different taste. Eschewing the bad reputation of industrial farming, animal products produced here are sporting labels like "organic," "sustainable," "free-range," and other classifications enticing customers to pay more money for the same items produced just a couple hours' drive to the east in the Central Valley.

But in the North Bay, farmers are promising something different. Producers are pledging that the products were created in a non-conventional fashion, in which the animals are treated better and the land, air, and water is healthier. Does this smaller-scale farming of animals mean big improvements for their experience of life and their premature death? Or could this be just a marketing ploy to ease the public's newfound concerns about the true horrors of animal farming?

A Humane Revolution?

The hard work of farmed animal advocates in the last three decades has been astonishing. With little money, resources, and very few activists compared to other social and environmental justice movements, we have managed to expose the dark truth concealed behind the barn doors. Most folks now know, on some level, that not all is well for animals raised for food. They know that something is not right "down on the farm," whether it's antibiotic use, overcrowding, food safety issues, or some other undefined feeling of unease. The truth is being revealed and people are concerned.

A recent study found that nearly two-thirds of grocery shoppers agree that humane treatment of animals raised for food should be regulated and should also be a concern for society, yet only about one-third of consumers feel that they are well informed about issues such as hormone/steroid/antibiotic-free, cage-free, free-range, pasture-raised,

---

* The preference for or emphasis on buying locally produced food for environmental, political, and ethical reasons.

and certified humane labels.[3] So, while there is a desire for better animal farming practices, there is a lack of knowledge of what that means, what the labels suggest, or what is really going on. Consumers rely on the manufacturers' and retailers' guidance and honesty, yet the stories they tell are designed to sell products, not to report the truth. The labels, websites, promotional materials, and representatives spin a new narrative of peaceful pastures and happy animals, but the reality all too often resembles the same universal and cruel practices of any conventional operation.

The organic label is a prime example. While organic certification can certainly reduce environmental impact and is one of the only labels we will talk about in this book that actually has some rigorous regulatory oversight and onsite farm inspection, many consumers believe this label signals a better life for the animals used to make the product. On the contrary, a report evaluating consumers' views of the organic label states:

> Although the common assumption that organic standards currently include animal welfare provisions is a misconception, organic foods such as grass-fed beef succeed precisely because of the consumer assumption that organic certification in meat, poultry and dairy case foods is inherently linked to animal welfare.[4]

The truth is that the organic label only minimally addresses the numerous animal welfare issues and inherent cruelties in animal agriculture. The most concerning issues, such as separation of babies from mothers, painful body mutilations, and slaughter at a young age, are not addressed at all. Not only are the organic standards weak on welfare, but because of the nature of the organic certification, organic products can be *even worse* for animals. An example is organic dairy products.

Unethical Organic Labeling

Even in organic dairy operations, the standard is filthy conditions, mechanical over-milking, painful cauterizing of cows' horns, trauma from the violation of artificial insemination, and the severe stress of having every newborn calf taken from her mother after giving birth, causing some cows to bellow with grief for weeks. Because of the physical strain and emotional anxiety, cows used for dairy production often suffer from mastitis, an infection of the udder which can cause swelling, open sores, pus, discharge, bleeding, and terrible pain from the milking machines. In conventional dairy farming, cows presenting symptoms of mastitis are often given antibiotics and other medications to clear up the infection. However, the organic regulations don't allow for antibiotics and other pharmaceuticals to be administered to the cows due to the preferences of consumers regarding their own health, so a cow suffering with infections or diseases is not given the medical attention she needs.

While investigating organic dairy production, I spoke to a Sonoma County farmed animal veterinarian who wished to remain anonymous. He confided in me that he saw cows in the most advanced stages of mastitis—with open sores on their udders flowing with pus, in severe pain at milking with stinging, tender teats—on organic dairies. He reported that there appeared to be an increase in the worst cases he has seen in decades of dairy vet care because so many farms were transitioning to the new organic standards that don't allow for the medications that the animals need. Owners and managers of organic dairy operations won't take a sick cow out of production because they would lose money. As a result, cows with painful and miserable illnesses are left to suffer untreated. How can this be considered humane? These are just some of the unforeseen consequences when practices change for supposed "improvements," yet the underlying fundamental problem of commodifying sentient beings' bodies is the practice that must end.

Humanewashing

To create a profitable product, most inherent cruelties in meat, dairy, and egg production are impossible to circumvent and still make a profit. This is the dirty little secret that the animal farming industry doesn't want the caring consumer to know. The truth is that to create enough animal food to feed a hungry planet, producers can't make a profit on cow dairy if the baby calves are not taken from their mothers. They can't make a profit on chicken's eggs if chicks are hatched with their mother hen in a nest. They can't make a profit on *any* animal product if they offer a comfortable retirement to the animals who are not producing at a high volume. Therefore, "humane treatment" will never be anything more than a marketing ploy on the product's website.

The reality is starkly different from what the ostensible messages on labels and assertions in the slogans would have us believe. Such fabricated stories the marketers tell that largely conflict and contradict reality are what have come to be called "humanewashing." Like the more widely used term "greenwashing" (where a product is advertised as being eco-friendly when it actually is not), "humanewashing" describes labels, signs, advertisements, and articles designed to paint a soothing picture of the farmed animal's experience to ease the buyers' concerns. The truth is all too often far from what is being illustrated. As the President of United Poultry Concerns, Karen Davis, notes, "This includes the humanewashing types of farmers and retailers who advertise sentiments designed to attract conscientious consumers eager to believe that they can have slaughter and humane treatment in the same package."[5]

"Mindful" Meats?

When you drive around my long-time home of Sonoma County, especially just on the outskirts of most of our cities, there are indications of animal agriculture everywhere. I often drive by dairy operations with signs posted that say, "Real California Milk" and "Certified Organic Dairy," appeasing the passers-by with the implication that "only good things are happening on *this* farm." Yet, if you look closer, you may see rows and rows of white plastic "calf hutches," like uniform cartons of milk, each containing a tiny baby calf who was taken from her mother at birth, chained to the hutch in all weather extremes—alone, frightened, and miserable. For each of these calves there is a grieving mother who will never know her baby, traumatized with each calf dragged away from her after birth.

Most people have no clue what is truly going on inside animal agriculture facilities, especially inside the slaughterhouse—that ominous place that ends all tomorrows for farmed animals. There is a slaughterhouse down the street from where I lived for many years in Petaluma, on a major road just outside of downtown. For decades it was called Rancho Veal. Of course, veal has been exposed as the poster child of cruelty and most people now agree that confining a baby cow so tightly that he can't even turn around, feeding him a malnourished diet so his muscles don't develop properly, and then slaughtering him when he is just weeks old, is cruel and shameful. But what people don't realize is that most animals who are slaughtered for meat are just weeks or months old, and have suffered similar egregious treatment, when they take their fateful journey to the abattoir. Most people also don't know that the veal industry is *deeply connected* to the dairy industry. Veal calves exist only because males are a by-product of continuously pregnant dairy cows.

The Rancho Veal slaughterhouse was acquired by a local beef producer called Marin Sun Farms and the building received a fresh coat of bright white paint complete with their looming logo, two stories high, on the front of the building. On the west wall, facing the oncoming traffic heading to downtown Petaluma, they added huge letters spelling out the name of a producer they are in partnership with, "Mindful Meats." When I first drove by this sizable new marketing endeavor, I had to pull over and take a moment for a figurative face-palm. Shaking my head, I pondered what I was seeing. It's truly appalling and offensive, and as a spiritual person, I see this as an egregious appropriation of the "mindfulness" concept.

THE IMPLICATIONS OF BEING MINDFUL

The term "mindful" has recently come into the ethos of Western culture from Eastern religions and philosophies such as Buddhist, Jain, and Hindu *dharma*s.* There is now a plethora of books, podcasts, workshops, and social media groups on "mindfulness" generally stemming from the teachings of Buddhism and Hinduism, which teach meditation and a capacity to increase one's awareness of one's self and one's actions. Inspired by dharma traditions, mindfulness teachers and guides tell us that to be "mindful" is to be aware of the present moment and to be sensitive that one's thoughts and actions have reactions, for ourselves

---

*   *Dharma* means "religion" or "tradition," although the term "religion" when applied to Eastern traditions can often be thought of differently than Euro-American religious traditions.

and others. "Mindfulness," inspired by the ancient traditions of the East, implies deep thoughtfulness, kindness, and gentleness that arise when striving to live by these principles, for ourselves and our relationships.

Furthering the teachings of mindfulness, other ideas associated with Eastern religions are *ahimsa* and *karma*. *Ahimsa* literally means "non-violence" and conceptually may be understood as "dynamic compassion." For many Eastern religions, *ahimsa* is the highest principle of ethical conduct and universal harmony, and above all, one should not take the life of any sentient being. It is believed that all life is sacred, and we have no right to take this precious gift.

Karma is also connected to being "mindful" in the dharmic sense, as our actions have repercussions for ourselves, others, and the planet. Whether you are a spiritual person or not, many believe in some form of the adage, "what you do comes back to you." Eating meat, dairy, and eggs not only has a negative impact on our health, but everything that goes into the production and transport of the final products to grocery stores and restaurants is devastating the environment. A recent study found that meat and dairy industries surpass fossil fuel production as the biggest polluters on the planet.[6]

Vegans can have a clear conscious that we are doing what we can to ease the suffering of animals and helping preserve the environment. In the ancient traditions of the East, there really is no act associated with more negative karma than needlessly killing another sentient being. Our actions have consequences, and killing sentient animals is considered *adharmic* in Eastern traditions—it's one of the worst actions someone can choose. Taking the life of another being will have devastating effects for a person's spiritual development and cause significant suffering to the perpetrator. But more importantly, these teachings show that animals have the same spiritual composition as us. In other words, our differences as species are merely material and not as definitive of our true nature, which is instead characterized as our spiritual equality. Therefore, all sentient beings have the same right and desire to live, and we should respect and protect them insofar as we are able. Being vegan is the *least* we can do.

Twisting a Term

What the owners and managers of this business imply by announcing "Mindful Meats" on the slaughterhouse wall is that there is something different happening inside this building now, that they are being "mindful" when they are slitting the throats of adolescent animals. It is flagrant humanewashing. To imply that those who are killing animals for financial gain are being "thoughtful" or somehow "kind" or "careful" in that institution of hopeless horror is a vicious, insidious falsehood. Unfortunately, this is emblematic of a novel narrative strategy of propaganda attempting to put a new spin on a wretched practice. A fresh coat of white paint cannot cover the deep stain of barbarism and merciless violence that cowers beneath this bogus declaration of "principled" bloodshed.

The internet has given us a glimpse inside the slaughterhouse, and if you have the stomach to search YouTube for "undercover slaughterhouse investigations," this dark world is exposed with animals desperately struggling to free themselves from the shackles that drag them to their death. Awaiting slaughter, their eyes are wide with terror as they hear and smell what is ahead for them. Workers kick, prod, punch, throw, and push animals, grabbing them and breaking tails and wings. The animals clamber on top of one another in panic trying to get away, but there is no escape. After witnessing this, I cannot imagine what a nightmare this would be to experience and pray that a day will come where no animal ever suffers at the slaughterhouse. To pretend that there is anything going on for animals in that grisly place of death other than fear, panic, anxiety, pain, and distress is nonsense. It is disrespectful to the concept of "mindfulness" and those who embrace this tenet as a guiding influence of spiritual awareness in their lives. Indeed, to ignore, endorse, benefit from, or participate in the anguish of the slaughterhouse is quite the opposite of "mindfulness." It is truly insulting and deeply troubling that this term would be appropriated by the animal agriculture industry.

Some argue that what we see in videos is not the norm, that it's only a few "bad apples." Yet every time an undercover investigator goes into one of these facilities, they emerge with hours of footage of abuse after only being there for days or weeks. It's not a few bad apples; the entire barrel is rotten—that's because it's animals who are being commodified, *not* apples. There is no humane way to take the life of an animal who does not want to die. The "norm" is a culture of violence that begins with baby animals being dragged from their mother's love and comfort to a life of incredible stress and misery. They endure beaks sheared off with a hot blade and other painful body mutilations without pain relief. Their lives are permeated with stress, boredom, and sorrow, all ending at the terrifying slaughterhouse.

NEW MARKETING, SAME SUFFERING

Meat marketers have always used words like "young" and "natural" and "farm-fresh" to sell flesh. But the savagery of their industry has been repeatedly exposed, so they are scrambling to find new words that ease apprehensions. Words like "mindful," "humane," and "happy" are simply new marketing strategies to appease concerned consumers, but as I reveal in my book, *The Ultimate Betrayal*, no matter the label, the standard is suffering, and cruelty is customary.

I long for the day when slaughterhouses are relics of a violent past; a day when we could not even imagine the sick ritual of killing animal after animal, day after day, second after second. I envision a day when we confront this industry with awareness, with real *mindfulness*, of what the true cost of their bottom line is, exposing the shadow of their euphemisms with the light of truth. I believe we will see a day when no human has to suffer the terrible trauma of working endless hours covered in innocent blood, a day when we see the awful irony of putting the word "humane" on a package of an animal's severed body parts. When we are *truly mindful*, we will come to realize the full consequences of consumer actions and see that all animals deserve to live free of human commodification and killing.

THE RESCUE OF KUKKUTA AND THE ROOSTER DILEMMA

One year, on the day before Easter, I got a call from a friend who was worried about an injured rooster in the Walgreens parking lot about five minutes from my house. A feral population of roosters and hens have made their home in the fields of tall grass and parking lots around Peet's Coffee and Walgreens in Cotati, California. It's the same area where I had recently rescued a mother hen and her six newborn chicks from a gas station and took them to a local farmed animal sanctuary. The chickens have become a novelty around there. Peet's puts out water for them and people come just to hang out with the colorful birds, feeding them bits of scone and taking their pictures. But the population is growing, and because of the popularity of "backyard" chicken keeping, more and more roosters are being dumped there.

I drove out to see what was going on and there was a police car parked outside the Walgreens. I asked the officer if she was there because of the rooster and she said yes, that Walgreens had called the Cotati police concerned about him. Another rooster had been bullying him for hours. We found the poor soul lying on the ground in the middle of a parking space with blood splattered around him on the pavement. The larger rooster was pacing triumphantly back and forth, hovering over him like a champion fighter taunting his opponent. I shooed away the tormenter and had a look at the poor guy. He was frozen in shock. His face, head, neck, and comb were covered in murky blood and his left eye was swollen shut with fresh blood dripping out of it.

I asked the officer what she was going to do, and she said that she didn't know. I sat next to the pitiful little guy and was able to put him in my lap and get a good look. He had a lot of blood on him, but the only injury I could find was to his eye. I couldn't find any wound on his body, neck, or comb. I told her there was a good chance he could recover, but she said they would probably "put him down," as no one would want to drive him all the way up to Animal Control on Easter weekend. I didn't want to ask what method of killing she would use, and he would likely be euthanized at Animal Control anyway, so I ended up with a rooster in my car. I knew that I was his only hope and that he would be my responsibility. I had just recently tried to help someone find a home for a rooster a few weeks before, so I knew that no sanctuary in the area would take a rooster, but there was no other choice. His life was now in my hands.

For seven days he didn't move. We put him on soft towels in an animal carrying crate and he just sat there, frozen in place. The poor soul was so traumatized. He was not interested in food or water. We tried to entice him with blueberries, pasta, apples, rice, bananas; nothing worked. His eye was so swollen it was the size of a marble, and the blood had dried stiff and black all over his head. I got some antibiotic cream and applied it to his eye twice a day. A few times, I took him out of the crate and set him in the sun for a while, trying to enliven him, but he would just sit, motionless and listless. Every morning I ran to the crate to check on him, so afraid that he might have died during the night. We named him Kukkuta—Sanskrit for "rooster."

THE TRAGEDY OF UNWANTED ROOSTERS

The only reason Kukkuta needed to be rescued was because people eat eggs. You don't see the connection? Allow me to elaborate. Because of the tireless work of animal advocacy organizations like United Poultry Concerns and others, there's a growing awareness that hens suffer terribly in the egg industry. In much of the North Bay area, people have bought into the "farm to table" ethos and want a more natural and "humane" experience with their animal-derived foods. This area consists of many wealthy and rural people who are buying chicks from feed stores and off Craigslist and are raising their own chickens for eggs. This may seem like a positive trend, but there is a hidden hindrance—for every hen born to provide eggs, so is a rooster who cannot.

Roosters are unwanted because, of course, they don't lay eggs. They also crow, so they aren't welcome, or even legal, in many neighborhoods. Most areas of Sonoma County will allow up to 12 hens, but no roosters. Because they are worthless to the egg industry, male chicks are killed just hours after emerging from their shells in the hatcheries. They are thrown away alive by the billions, dumped into huge trash bins to suffocate on the weight of their brothers and die slowly of dehydration or freeze to death. Many are ground up alive in maceration machines where sharp blades like huge blenders chop up their tiny bodies for fertilizer, pet food, and other products.

Determining the sex of a chick is not an exact science. As a result, baby males are shipped to feed stores and sold as hens. A backyard chicken hobbyist is surprised when one of her chicks starts crowing, so she "gets rid" of him. It's increasingly difficult to find homes for roosters. Overwhelmed animal shelters end up euthanizing most of them. Other roosters get dumped on the side of the road. This is what's happening in Cotati. People see chickens there, so they dump their unwanted rooster thinking he will be fine, but this is not necessarily so, as we saw with Kukkuta. Not only do they face the threat of predators and possible starvation, roosters are territorial, and as the numbers increase, the newcomers may have to face a bird defending his territory and might be injured, stressed, or even killed. This is what happened to our sweet rooster.

KUKKUTA'S ROAD TO RECOVERY

The swelling of Kukkuta's eye slowly subsided and on the seventh day of being a guest in my small cottage, he stood up and walked out of the crate and started drinking some water. I was thrilled! He dunked his head in the bowl of water again and again, washing the crusted blood off his face and comb. The next morning, I heard him crow for the first time and it was a joyful sound, a robust celebration of life! He recovered quickly after that and he was a perfect gentleman, never pecking when I reach for him or kicking when I pick him up. He was a gentle soul.

At first, he needed about a four-foot radius of "personal space," unsure of his rescuers' intent. But soon he would come right up to me, following me around everywhere. He talked to me with sweet clucks, bocks, and coos of affection and gratitude when I gave him food. He was so full of life, busy all day and loved to interact. I was mesmerized watching him.

A NEW LEVEL OF LOVE

Being vegan for 30 years, I have long respected chickens' lives, but I had never lived with a chicken. Kukkuta awakened something incredibly special in me. I love him so much, and while I had a strong vegan philosophy before, now more than ever I simply can't imagine anyone purposely killing a sentient individual like Kukkuta. I now see animal slaughter on a different level of unimaginable. Everything in me wanted to protect him and keep him alive. This is a love I wish everyone could experience, for you can never again think of harming an animal after knowing this kind of love and compassion. The whole experience enriched my life, strengthened my understanding of veganism, deepened my commitment to protecting chickens, and most of all, I will never forget my friend Kukkuta.

WHAT IS REALLY EXTREME?

I was having a conversation with someone recently who propounded the "too extreme" argument that anyone who has been vegan more than a few months has inevitably had to endure. "Veganism is too extreme," we are told. But I've come to believe that these statements are completely devoid of any logical value. They are placeholders existing in a vacuum of failing rhetorical validity. In other words, the "extreme" argument is completely meaningless, but somehow gives the illusion of rhetorical weight.

The argument rests on a faulty premise that being "extreme" is inherently bad. But I rather like the idea of being *extremely* intelligent, *extremely* compassionate, *extremely* thoughtful, *extremely* virtuous, or extreme in any of the manifestations that general goodness occurs. We might even say that extreme goodness is actually greatness. And greatness is something that we all aspire toward, or at the very least, admire.

It is as if we are somehow expected to valorize mediocrity, as if we shouldn't want to be extreme, even in matters that are considered virtuous, such as the values of compassion and sensitivity to social justice that veganism often implies. Instead, if we accept the "extreme equals bad" premise of this argument, we are led to believe that we should appraise what the medium level of achievement is of our current society, and then emulate that and not deviate from the average bandwagon of our mediocre contemporaries.

But social advancement necessitates a movement away from equilibrium and mediocrity into the realm of what might be currently considered "extreme." Any innovation or advancement in society, by the very definition of the term, is an innovation *away* from what is normative, and advancement *away* from social averages is, by its very nature, *extreme*.

The label "extreme" then becomes a pejorative label employed by conservative elements who perceive advancement as a losing proposition for their privileged position. And what greater instantiation of privilege is there than the killing of others simply for one's own pleasure, which is an accurate description of the carnist[*,7] lifestyle.

We might argue that what is truly extreme is slitting the throat of a sentient animal, causing her to choke to death on her blood, cutting her up, cooking her, and eating her. That might also be considered very extreme if we take the vantage point of compassion to be normative, instead of accepting violence as such. With this compassion as our center of orientation, eating animals is certainly *extremely* cruel, *extremely* disturbing, and *extremely* disgusting. How is choosing beans over blood too extreme? How is wanting to reduce harm to animals too extreme? How is choosing food that could help reverse climate change *and* heart disease too extreme? These types of acts are only extreme when we consider violence to be the norm and accept normative behavior blindly.

What is so "extreme" about veggie burgers, oat milkshakes, and tofu scramble? Absolutely nothing.

Extreme Labeling

This perception of veganism being "too extreme" is part of what feeds the popularity of animal products labeled "humane." The idea that there are kinder, gentler ways of breeding and killing animals on a smaller scale is highly appealing to a public seeking anesthetization against complicity with an industry that is increasingly being exposed for its cruel practices. People want to believe they don't have to take what are "extreme" measures that deviate from the norm of meat eating or make what is perceived as drastic changes. The industry is offering a "middle ground" where you can buy cage-free eggs and organic dairy and "happy" meat. What consumers don't realize is that labels lie, and *extreme* suffering is inherent in all animal agriculture.

---

*   Carnism is a concept used in discussions of humanity's relation to other animals, defined as a prevailing ideology in which people support the use and consumption of animal products, especially meat. Central to the ideology is the acceptance of meat-eating as "natural," "normal," "necessary." The term *carnism* was coined by social psychologist and author Melanie Joy.

EXTREME CRUELTY

Eggs sold at natural foods stores or at the farmer's market support cruel hatcheries where baby chicks suffer and die by the billions and chickens still face painful debeaking, miserable overcrowding, and a horrifying slaughter at a young age. No matter the label, mother dairy cows and calves are separated very soon after birth, causing both to grieve for the other. There is no retirement plan; all animals with "alternative" and "humane" labels on their flesh and fluid products will go to a sickening slaughter at a young age.

Yet the animal agriculture industry is crafting a pleasant story about "improved conditions" and "happy" animals living "better" lives. This way, consumers are made to feel that they don't have to go to "extremes" and can keep their burgers, milkshakes, and scrambled eggs—a perception that is of course in the interest of the animal agriculture industry's bottom line.

After three decades of research and activism, I can confidently say that exploiting animals for their meat, dairy, or eggs can never be both profitable *and* humane. It simply can't be done. I go into extensive detail about this in my book, *The Ultimate Betrayal.*

To assure that animals will be forever free of exploitation, we need to be extremely courageous and say, "No more!" Animals' flesh, eggs, and milk should not be considered food. As long as we consider meat, dairy, and eggs to be food, there will be *extreme* mistreatment, *extreme* exploitation, and *extreme* suffering.

THE STATEMENT "STOP FACTORY FARMING" IS NO LONGER NECESSARILY A VEGAN SENTIMENT

Much of the progress made in the last few decades exposing the cruelty in animal farming is the result of the strategic denouncement expressed by the powerful term, "factory farming." For decades, animal activists have inscribed the motto "End Factory Farming" into brochures and splattered "Stop Factory Farming" on protest signs with red letters dripping like blood. This incriminating term conjures images of endless rows of animals in barren cages, filthy windowless warehouses, and animals suffering and dying on manure-covered concrete floors—images that are increasingly familiar and made available to us via social media.

The ubiquity of these images and conditions associated with "factory farming" has spawned a pervasive condemnation. Everyone, it seems, can rally together and agree that we must stop "factory farming." But this rallying cry has created an unforeseen consequence, one that animal exploiters are taking full advantage of. Producers who sell the flesh and fluids of animals can simply state that *their* product is *not* factory farmed; it's organic, local, humane, cage-free (insert any number of misleading labels here). Likewise, when consumers hear these offensive two words, they are now thinking, "Oh, but my meat (or dairy or eggs) isn't *factory farmed*; I buy it at Whole Foods" (or "it's organic," or "it's free-range," etc.).

WATCH YOUR LANGUAGE

I so often hear advocates for farmed animals say, "99% of meat, dairy, and eggs are factory farmed." Again, now a consumer will think that their humanely labeled animal products are in the one percent that we have told them is acceptable because it is not factory farmed. Do animal advocates really believe that one percent of animal agriculture is somehow pampering the animals with comfortable, relaxed, happy lives where there is no separation of families, no painful body mutilations, and no terrifying slaughter? It is simply untrue. *All* commercial animal farming is factory farming. As long as animal bodies are commodified, there will be exploitation and suffering. As Robert Grillo states in his book *Farm to Fable*,

> The truth is that all commercial farming qualifies as factory farming based on the ancient production model of using animals as resource objects, with total control over their reproduction, the stealing and trafficking of their offspring, standard bodily manipulations (both physically and psychologically traumatizing), destruction of their families and social order, intensive biological manipulation and selective breeding, and of course the systematic domination, violence, and slaughter in their infancy or adolescence. All of the above are necessary in any kind of farming to render their flesh and secretions into products of consumption.[8]

DANGEROUS COMMON GROUND

The popular reprobation of "factory farming" has inadvertently created a demand for products labeled with euphemistic terms associated with "alternative," "small-scale" animal farming. This was not the initial intention of the term. Many advocacy groups originally used the term for the purpose of *ending all* exploitation and killing of farmed animals, as they do today.

But there has been a shift in the last few years, a shift toward small-scale, "humane" animal farming, and now everyone, it seems, can get behind ending factory farming—the animal rights activists, as well as the consumers and producers of meat, dairy, and eggs. This is unintended and dangerous common ground whereby the rhetoric of the animal rights movement has been appropriated by our opposition to promote the very products we seek to condemn. Now when we are denouncing animal products with the term factory farming, we are ironically repeating the marketing slogans of an increasing sector of animal industries.

Factory farming has come to imply that only the conditions the animals are kept in are of importance, and that taking an animal's life—the slaughter itself—is unproblematic. The marketing experts of the animal farming industry brandish this term to make people believe that as long as it isn't a "factory" or "industrial" setting, as long as it's not a mega-size farm, as long as the animal had some kind of minimally "natural" or "comfortable" life, then it is acceptable to slaughter the animal for the enjoyment of the conscientious consumer.

Many organizations want to "end factory farming," but still promote the killing of young animals for human consumption. These organizations support smaller farms with supposedly better conditions, but as I reveal in my book *The Ultimate Betrayal*, no label tells the whole story and "alternative" farming can be just as bad and is, in fact, in most cases, no different from so-called factory farming for the animal's experience or the impact on the environment.

ALL ANIMAL FARMING IS "FACTORY FARMING"

If a chick is hatched into this world in a sterile metal drawer without the comfort of her mother and a soft nest—that is factory farming. If a calf is ripped from his mother at birth and is kept separate from her and other cows, alone and frightened, chained and unloved—that is factory farming. If an animal has her beak burned off, her tail cut off, his genitals ripped out—that is factory farming. If an animal is hung upside down with his throat slit open and blood gushing out in a horrifying slaughter—that is factory farming. *All* animal farming is "factory" farming. And if all animal farming is factory farming, the term is meaningless except for those producers who seek to distinguish their products from the factory-farmed strawman. We must say *all* farming of animals is cruel, *all* animal agriculture is abusive, there can never be a humane way to breed, confine, and kill animals for their flesh, milk, and eggs.

The term "factory farming" no longer implies a vegan message. It no longer necessarily suggests a desire to stop the exploitation and killing of farmed animals. Those who work towards this important goal must abandon the term, or we risk inadvertently repeating what has become a marketing slogan of our opposition. Instead, we should be more specific and use the term *animal agriculture*. This encompasses *all* animal farming. We must be careful to speak in ways that express the truths that *all* farming of animals is exploitive, *all* farming of animals is abusive. Let's shift our language and the consciousness around this issue, and push beyond "humane" exploitation. It's time to retire the term factory farming.

What do we want? *To Stop Animal Farming*! When do we want it? *Now*!

Don't Waste Your Money

Because I have done extensive research in the area of humane labeling, I am often asked—which are the best brands to buy? What company has actual ethical eggs? What organic milk is the most humane? Years ago, when I first started to research these labels, I thought that I would be saying things like, "Free-range/cage-free/organic is better, but going vegan is best," and "So-and-so humane certification is better, but going vegan is best." No. That was not the result of my research. I found that no label, no product, no company, no rancher, no store, no farmers market—*no one* could guarantee that the animal had an improved life or death over a conventional product. It's just not the case. There were too many instances where the alternative label or farm was, for all practical purposes, the same as or even worse than conventional. There are cases where it was a bit better, but not necessarily from one particular certification or label. It varies from farm to farm, so I am unable to give any recommendations and in fact, I now tell people not to waste their money. There are numerous and blatant system-wide cruelties that the labels and certifications do not address. I feel consumers should not support these labels, as it is flagrantly false advertising and pure deception. Instead of switching labels or brands, it's better to reduce animal product use and eventually eliminate it.

Numerous lawsuits back this realization that the fiction communicated by the producers of alternative animal products and the reality of their products are starkly different. There are far too many to list, but I will highlight a challenge by the Animal Legal Defense Fund (ALDF) that is a typical characterization of these litigations. The complaint was filed in August of 2019 against Tillamook County Creamery Association, a producer of cow dairy products. The class action lawsuit was filed on behalf of a group of Oregon consumers who feel they have been deceived by Tillamook's marketing, violating Oregon's consumer protection laws. ALDF's website states:

> Tillamook's advertising campaigns are designed to mislead consumers that the company's products are sourced from humane, pasture-based, small-scale family farms, where animal care standards exceed those of other dairy companies. But this is far from reality.[9]

After a thorough investigation, the primary facility that provides most of the dairy has 70,000 cows in "inhumane, industrialized conditions." There are no cows out in the rolling grassy hills, as Tillamook's website and advertising declares. The reality for these tens of thousands of cows is continuous confinement indoors on a cement floor and excessive milking by robotic carousels. The cows are violated by artificial insemination, and soon after giving birth, their calves are taken away from them, causing psychological trauma to both mother and offspring.

The egregious undercover investigation videos and subsequent litigation accusing these companies of misleading consumers keep piling up.

AN EXTREMELY COMPASSIONATE WORLD

I believe that ultimately, society will evolve and come to the realization that we should not kill animals. This is the logical and compassionate evolution of the concern for humane treatment of animals.

Even as I speak out against "humane" labeling, I believe that it is an indicator of a positive progression. People want animals to be treated with dignity and respect, to be free of suffering and sadness. The rational progression of this compassionate treatment will lead to only one conclusion—we should never take an animal's life. Mitigating climate change and heart disease are benefits of eliminating animal products, but ultimately this is an issue of justice, kindness, love, and compassion. Living vegan is a revolution in compassion, and the world certainly needs a sizable dose of compassion right now. The environmental and health benefits are significant (and undeniably backed by science), but ultimately it's about asking ourselves—what kind of people do we want to be? Do we want to cause mass suffering and kill when it is not necessary? Veganism is not extreme in anything but compassion, and an extremely compassionate world is what we need more than anything right now.

Hope Bohanec has been active in animal protection and environmental activism for over 30 years and published the book, *The Ultimate Betrayal: Is There Happy Meat?* She is a nationally recognized leader and speaker in the animal protection movement, executive director of the non-profit Compassionate Living, host of the *Hope for the Animals Podcast*, and co-founder of the Humane Hoax Project and the Ahimsa Living Project. Over the last three decades, Bohanec has worked for national non-profits such as United Poultry Concerns and In Defense of Animals, organized numerous campaigns and events, and contributed chapters to two anthologies.

6

HOW COLONIZATION HELPED TO NORMALIZE THE HUMANE HOAX

by Christopher "Soul" Eubanks

M any first-time mothers become flowered with unconditional love when they look into the eyes of their newborns. Their hearts race as they feel an unexpected layer of emotion added to their existence that they didn't realize they were capable of developing. These thoughts and feelings rush through new mothers every day. Mother cows feel the same intense bond with their babies, but for cows used in dairy production, these precious moments are quickly ravaged by grief and turmoil as their newborn calves are torn from them—the males to be killed just a few months later, the females raised to be repeatedly impregnated to produce milk. The mother cow's cries and obvious psychological distress is the only language needed to know what she is experiencing. This crime against compassion is only one example of the cruelty of the humane hoax that's been ingrained into our civilization after millennia of abusing animals and was hyper-inflated after the native people of America were decimated by colonization.

Colonization is defined as "the action or process of settling among and establishing control over the Indigenous people of an area." Animal abuse and oppression existed long before colonization, but the mass scale of violence and exploitation towards Black, Brown, and Indigenous people that occurred during the colonization of the American continents, and numerous other Indigenous lands, has shaped much of our modern culture. For centuries, these systemic tools of oppression have made mass violence and large-scale slavery a significant part of world culture that is still poisoning numerous aspects of our social as well as physical world. Operating under these normalized systems of violence has spearheaded high crime rates, mass incarceration, and military-like weaponry into U.S. culture that has desensitized many of us to the violent psychology that permeates our world.

When Black, Brown, and Indigenous people were stripped of their culture and heritage, they were terrorized by their oppressors into accepting new cultural norms to the detriment of their own existence. This psychological warfare consisted of separating "fair" skin slaves from darker skin slaves, fueling colorism, feeding slaves undesirable animal remains such as pigs' feet, ears, and intestines, and forcing the mass consumption of cow secretions (dairy) into their diets. Over the course of generations, some of these oppressive processes have been passed down to future generations of people of color, which has allowed animal agriculture to prey even more on vulnerable people in these marginalized communities. This systemic oppression is a part of the fabric that takes place to uphold the humane hoax.

The normalization of sexual abuse, slavery, genocide, and mass oppression towards entire groups has allowed our society to accept the unjust systems that uphold them as routine and commonplace in our world. Not only have we become victims of this discrimination, we have also been conditioned to participate in the perpetuation of these abusive practices towards our fellow humans, as well as nonhuman animals.

Humans have never been the biggest or strongest of species, but we were able to use our unique cognitive capacity as an advantage to dominate other animals. During ancient times, various survival tactics were essential to humanity's wellbeing, but today many of those same tactics are shunned, outlawed, and shamed. We have used our unique intellect to blur the lines between survival and cruelty, allowing us to cause unnecessary harm to trillions of nonhuman animals every year. While early humans hunted and wore the fur and skin of animals for survival, we have used our ancestors' circumstances to justify our use of animals for food and clothing, animal testing, and a variety of unnecessary forms of abuse of nonhuman animals. This hoax has led to us exploiting animals across the globe for entertainment, fashion, and various unethical and unnecessary reasons.

The humane hoax is a lie that allows our society to believe that unnecessary killing can be done in an ethical manner. We have been predisposed to violence towards nonhuman animals so much that most of our culture assumes this violence is necessary for our survival. Many people not only don't question violence inflicted on nonhuman animals, but they also don't question if nonhuman animals deserve autonomy over their own bodies and the basic rights of "personhood." The perpetrators of this oppression have been covered not only by years of normalized violence, but also trillions of dollars of marketing, social programming, and conditioning.

Capitalism, which is a product of colonialism, has also fueled the humane hoax by using profit as a way to exacerbate the oppression of nonhuman animals. Nonhuman animals were exploited long before capitalism, but capitalism, under the umbrella of colonialism, has made it easily digestible to consume the lies of animal agriculture. This emotional warfare on the spirit of our collective consciousness helps our society to ignore the layers of nuance that exist when we attempt to extend our compassion beyond humanity. It also permeates how people from the dominant group often address human rights issues.

When people say "all lives matter" in response to Black Lives Matter, they are discounting the particular ways systemic oppression has targeted Black people, and also people of the global majority. Carelessly grouping everyone into the same crowd and ignoring nuance is a dangerous ideology and toxic framework that allows us to believe that deceptions like humane slaughter are possible. Overlooking these layers of nuance creates gateways towards the paths of thinking that allow us to accept the mass oppression of nonhuman animals and justify cruelty towards them. Not only has this impacted how those from the dominant socio-economic class view these issues, but it also impacts how marginalized groups unknowingly carry out oppressive thinking towards other oppressed groups.

Sometimes members of oppressed groups unintentionally resent other oppressed groups because they often feel they are in competition with them for society's compassion. Some people from marginalized groups feel that nonhuman animals get the understanding and sympathy for their oppression that we as marginalized people deserve. In the television show *Woke*, the main character Keef has a traumatic encounter with the police and spends most of the season suppressing his anxiety from the encounter while also feeling unacknowledged by his peers and society at large around his trauma. His emotions erupt later in the season in an episode that centers around a koala named Kubby who is killed after escaping from the local zoo. Keef lashes out at a crowd of people attending a candlelight vigil for Kubby because he interprets their compassion for Kubby as ignoring the police brutality and oppression he, and to a larger extent Black people, experience daily.

After his meltdown, Keef realizes his actions were a combination of him not addressing his trauma and sees how his anger was misdirected toward those grieving for Kubby. While some people who advocate for nonhuman animals lack empathy for human rights issues, these two aren't automatically mutually exclusive. Our compassion should be consistent for all oppressed beings experiencing mass exploitation, violence, and oppression, but the more we allow humane hoaxes to persist, the more oxygen they will create for other oppressions to breathe.

What allows discrimination and oppression to thrive is the idea that "others" are separate from us. When we are able to disassociate from others, be they human or nonhuman animals, this can lead to the justification of mistreatment towards them. We have an endless number of labels that have been immorally used to pit us against others and hide the truth. "Others" are just a different version of ourselves existing in different bodies who want to live, and to live free of suffering.

In order for us to combat the humane hoax, we are going to have to analyze how this hoax impacts not only nonhuman animals, but also our entire society. We will have to examine its poisonous roots and how it also permeates our activist communities. As the humane hoax has been passed down from generation to generation, the suffering it creates is also passed down, be it through normalized toxic behavior or the victims that suffer at the hands of this violence. As long as we allow poisonous ideologies like the humane hoax to exist, it will not only prevent the liberation of nonhuman animals, but it will also prevent humanity from achieving true collective liberation for all.

Christopher "Soul" Eubanks is a climate, human rights, and animal rights activist who was raised in Atlanta, Georgia and has dedicated himself to doing advocacy work that combats all forms of injustice. After learning about the horrors of animal exploitation, Eubanks became vegan, helped co-organize Atlanta's first ever animal rights march, and founded Apex Advocacy, advocating for collective liberation through animal rights. He plans to use education, public speaking, and creativity as tools to advocate for the climate, a vegan lifestyle, and the end to all forms of injustice.

PART 2:
GREENWASHING

7

GREENWASHING A BLOODY BUSINESS

The Planet Can't Survive "Sustainable" Animal Farming

by Lorelei Plotczyk, M.B.A.

During family walks in our rural Massachusetts neighborhood, we stroll past animals grazing, pecking, and lounging about on a small working family farm. Motorists wait in amusement as freshly dust-bathed chickens leisurely cross the road. Our toddler daughter giggles in delight and does her best goat impression as a cow glares at us briefly, then resumes munching on hay. Eggs are regularly hand-collected and, every so often, a trailer comes by and the cast of characters changes. The operation is made economically viable through a small network of subscribers. But can Old MacDonald–style operations like these sustainably produce plentiful animal products for the human population?

Quite simply, the answer is E-I-E-I-*NO*. Because it adds an extra step on the food chain through which humans feed ourselves, animal agriculture, no matter how it is done, has a massive ecological footprint. "Raising livestock* is such an antiquated way to derive nutrients from the Earth," Climax Foods founder Oliver Zahn—who is also an astrophysicist—tells

---

* Although degrading and deindividualizing, words like "livestock," "cattle," and "poultry" (and "production" instead of "farming") counter romanticized associations and are sometimes used throughout this chapter when referring to the commodification of animals domesticated for agricultural exploitation (but not to describe the animals themselves, unless someone is quoted doing so, as the human activity of livestock production/use is the agent of destruction).

Grist. "Instead of eating plants [directly], we funnel them through the extremely complicated machine that is an animal." As dictated by a natural principal—that most of us are taught in school—known as the 10% law, an average of only 10% of consumed energy is passed up each trophic level, so tremendous energy losses are incurred when farmed animals "convert" plants into meat, dairy, and eggs. University of Cambridge researcher Bojana Bajzelj also cites these "basic laws of biophysics" for animal agriculture's inefficiency, stating, "Agricultural practices are not necessarily at fault here—but our choice of food is."

Since only a small fraction of caloric energy reaches the top of a food chain, a large material base is needed to support heavy meat-eaters within *any* population size. While nature's relatively scarce obligate predators provide balance, devastating externalities result from billions of humans adopting animal-centric dietary norms, which unfortunately are globally considered aspirational and associated with wealth and status.* Yet the lower one eats on the food chain, the more resources are spared, including vast areas of land to help disrupt the climate and extinction crises—all while significantly decreasing biosecurity risks, including zoonotic diseases.†

Within the well-documented "climate–diet link," scientific consensus positions minimal animal consumption as key. Replications of quantitative science over the past few decades prove the farmed animal sector's significant contributions to widespread environmental degradation that plant-based diets significantly minimize. A systemic review by the Intergovernmental Panel on Climate Change (IPCC) attributes this disparity not to farming methods, but, once again, to "well-known energy losses along trophic chains." Among the most noteworthy of many supporting studies is a 2018 meta-analysis of global food systems, the largest of its kind, assessing farming's ecological impacts over several years.[1] The study's lead researcher, University of Oxford's

---

* The tendency for each nation's meat and dairy consumption to rise along with its affluence is so consistent that researchers have coined it as "Bennett's law."

† Multiple research studies cite increasing human demand for animal-based foods as a major driver of zoonotic disease emergence, specifying that livestock (including free-range) production serves as a primary bridge for viruses in wild animals to cross over to humans.

Joseph Poore, concludes, "A vegan diet is probably the single biggest way to reduce your impact on planet Earth" on several levels. Beyond just avoiding *industrial* farming, Poore specifies that "avoiding consumption of animal products delivers far better environmental benefits than trying to purchase sustainable meat and dairy."

THE OMNIVORE'S *REAL* DILEMMA

In their research, however, many experts note humanity's reluctance to acknowledge the planetary toll of animal-centric diets. Even when implicated, greenwashing—disinformation (often industry-generated) that presents an environmentally responsible public image giving consumers permission not to change—typically follows.

Animal farming, which currently occupies 45% of the global surface area,[2] poses an incontrovertible ecological dilemma: extensive free-range methods are less efficient yet considered more sustainable, while intensive methods are more efficient but considered less sustainable. Due to the Earth's fixed land constraints and the 10% law, dispersing domesticated animals more sparingly over land and using more "natural" slower-growth methods can only produce relatively small amounts of their flesh and bodily fluids for collective human consumption. Meeting demand, therefore, requires concentrating large numbers of these animals in industrial buildings and feedlots—but doing so also entails massive tracts of land for growing feed crops, amongst many other environmental tradeoffs.

No magical workaround exists for animal agriculture's core inefficiency, because humans' secondary consumption of plants as processed first through farmed animal bodies (which primary plant consumption bypasses) is so ineffectual. Pasturing free-range farmed animals on grasses takes up *more* land while producing the *least* amount of food; farmed animals occupy more than a quarter of all ice-free land on Earth,[3] yet minimally 90% of animal products are estimated to come from Concentrated Animal Feeding Operations (CAFOs).[4] Because traditional small, localized animal farms need vast areas of land (often exceeding availability),[5] the Earth's biophysical limits necessitate even further *intensifying* animal farming to continue the current global trajectory of increasingly animal-centric diets. Researchers have coined terms like "peak livestock," "peak meat," and "peak pasture" in an attempt to quantify a "safe operating space" for livestock production. Alas, a 2019 study from Ecological Economics notes "livestock" production's ongoing "transgression of several planetary boundaries," and concludes: "Efficiency measures alone are unlikely to mitigate the sector's environmental impacts to a sustainable level."[6]

The barnyards and pastures depicted on typical product packaging— exuding a halo effect over the farmed animal sector as a whole while providing consumers with a "psychological refuge"[7] to assuage their guilt over the more blatant cruelty and eco-impact of CAFOs—are biophysically incapable of accommodating the bulk of collective demand for animal-based foods. Phasing out CAFOs, as estimated by postdoctoral fellow Jan Dutkiewicz and his colleagues, would necessitate reducing U.S. meat production and consumption by over 90%.[8] Far more commonplace are relatively small meat reductions— often exaggerated or offset with more dairy and eggs—that experts call insufficient given wealthy nations' sky-high baseline livestock consumption levels.[9] Proposals for rich nations to prioritize plant-based foods typically face backlash, while others include subjecting farmed animals—already biologically altered for optimal exploitability through generations of selective breeding—to experimental measures that are narrowly focused and prohibitively expensive and ultimately include ecological trade-offs, obscuring the need for drastic dietary change.

LIVESTOCK'S LONG GREENWASHED SHADOW

No reform is too outlandish, it seems, apart from removing the unnecessary extra step in the chain of humanity's food production by replacing animal farming altogether. Why is that? Widely erased historical context helps explain the tendency for many otherwise savvy environmentalists to stop at advocating a return to the animal farming systems of yore.

Domesticating animals long ago dramatically severed them from their natural state, as did endlessly converting environments to farm them. Through animal agriculture, herding cultures imbalanced ecosystems and often turned fertile lands into desert.[10] A 2017 study in the journal *Nature* finds that land conversion for grazing livestock has been preventing the absorption of greenhouse gases long before industrial times,[11] while 2018 research describes increasingly intensive animal agriculture occurring 3,000 years ago.[12] Over time, humans have continued replacing native biodiverse habitats primarily with pastures, feed crops, and farmed animals. Viewing such landscapes as normal or even natural is due to a phenomenon called "shifting baseline syndrome," in which environmental knowledge is lost over time and works to distort each generation's perception of how even the most "sustainable" livestock production has heavily modified the natural world.

The social consequences of an activity that, by its very design, exponentially amplifies humans' environmental footprint appear to be no accident. Domesticating animals for food, per the late renowned historian Alfred Crosby, has enabled "the direct control and exploitation of many species for the sake of one,"[13] and, as author Jim Mason notes, allowed humans to "exert domination not only over animals and nature but over other people and their lands and cultures."[14] Animal food-related land expansion has long justified conquests and war, pointed out as far back as 380 BC in Plato's *Republic*, while a 2014 research article on "the rise of cattle culture" in the Bronze Age notes "the use of domesticated cattle as a material and symbolic source of power" for the elite class.[15] Regarding the ravages of "cattle colonialism," which was "central to the expansion of the Spanish, British, and American empires," Hayley G. Brazier invokes "a rich field of scholarship that has emphasized the significance of domesticated animals as tools of imperialism."[16,*] Among them is historian Virginia DeJohn Anderson's thorough account of how Europeans saw animal husbandry[†] as divinely ordained to "improve" and "civilize" the Americas' previously livestock-free colonized lands and people; colonists viewed their free-range herds' steady proliferation with "pride, not concern" despite driving ecological shifts incompatible

---

*   That emphasis, however, remains sorely missing from educational materials.

†   The term "animal husbandry" alone arguably positions animal farming as part of man's perceived dominion over animals and women alike.

with Indigenous peoples'* food practices.[17] The ability to eat animal-centric diets, previously reserved for Europe's wealthy, became part of America's immigration appeal. In 1813, essayist Percy Shelley lamented that "the most fertile districts of the habitable globe are now actually cultivated by men for farming animals, at a delay and waste of ailment absolutely incapable of calculation."[18]

Despite widespread modern-day disdain for the colonists' land greed, their most land-intensive activity is rarely articulated and, worse, remains dominant. Today, animal agriculture occupies 41% of land in the U.S.[19] and pasturing alone occupies 56% of (similarly colonized, previously livestock-free) Australia;[20] in both places, meaty barbeques are synonymous with patriotism and steakhouses with celebratory indulgence. And just as "the importation of European animals and the destruction of local fauna, flora, and local foodways were justified," per the text *Studies in Global Animal Law*, "by the goal of 'improving' agriculture and population health,"[21] cattle ranching remains exalted as indispensable and "regenerative" even where it was entirely colonist-imposed, with plant proteins often devalued as inferior. The cultural capital and lobbying power of "cowboys"—and the animal agriculture sector's revolving door to government roles—reap extensive subsidies, bailouts, and disaster relief along with exemptions from ecological reporting and regulations.

Complex factors, therefore, create the lens through which humanity's animal food reliance is historically romanticized and assumed as still obligatory. Animal agriculture greenwashing is informed not by science, argues researcher Vasile Stănescu, but belief in a "'natural' order of humanity's supposedly benevolent domain over other animals"[22]—which many authors connect to a domination-based worldview that is continuing to drive social and environmental injustice. Feminist author Carol J. Adams links humans' self-serving dominion over other animals to patriarchy;[23] academics and authors Aph and Syl Ko show how the

---

* Up to 90% of Indigenous people were decimated by livestock-derived European zoonotic diseases, which historically rose in prevalence with animal domestication and were unleashed globally on previously livestock-free cultures through colonization. The toll of livestock culture's global expansion was less visible and direct in this sense than its related land grabs and ecological alterations, but often even less survivable for colonized people.

Eurocentric concept of subhuman animality is racialized;[24] activist Christopher Sebastian McJetters demonstrates related connections to white nationalism;[25] and Mi'kmaw scholar Dr. Margaret Robinson examines how social and systemic barriers to Indigenous peoples' veganism ultimately reinforce Eurocentric values and practices.[26]

GREENWASHING LABELS

Deeply rooted speciesism and a tradition of animal domination and use contextualize, at least partly, an ongoing disconnect enabling the blatant greenwashing of animal agriculture. But do the specific labels and claims hold any weight? The most ubiquitous concepts are critiqued below.

Local Meat, Dairy, and Eggs: Fooled by "Food Miles"

The complex, resource-intensive total life cycle of animal products generally not only makes their "local" descriptors largely misleading, but "food miles" are far less ecologically significant than assumed.

The local food movement arose after widespread reporting that, per researcher Rich Pirog, produce typically travels 1,500 miles before reaching one's plate. "Food miles," however, as Pirog himself clarifies, are "not a very good measure of the food's environmental impact."[27] Eating local, in fact, "is one of the most misguided pieces of advice" to reduce one's footprint, explains the scientific platform Our World in Data. "Greenhouse Gas (GHG) emissions from transportation make up a very small amount of the emissions from food and *what* you eat is far more important than where your food traveled from."[28] A 2018 research study determined that reducing meat and dairy products matters far more than consuming local foods, because transportation only accounts for 11% of total food emissions, with 83% released during production (before the food reaches the market).[29] Food miles' impact pales, therefore, in comparison to the tremendous resource and energy losses incurred by producing animal foods anywhere.

Not only is the food miles metric of marginal ecological relevance, it also fails to consider many nonlocal aspects of "local" livestock production. Breeding facilities often send animals, such as newborn chicks, long distances. Animal farms then require various inputs that are transported far and wide, like plastic calf hutches, feeders, water tanks, irrigation equipment, syringes, vaccinations and antibiotics, minerals and supplements, genetic materials for selective breeding, and, most significantly, animal feed. In 2017, campaign group Mighty Earth exposed food companies, some of whom boasted that their meat was "local," importing soy-based livestock feed grown on cleared South American rainforests.[30] Alfalfa grown for "local" California dairy operations is sent to Saudi Arabian dairies, while the Midwest's soy crop is exported to feed pigs in China. Crop- and food-processing byproducts are also transported to livestock operations to supplement feed.

An additional local caveat exists: slaughter. As widely reported, many of Australia, Europe, and the U.K.'s farmed animals are sent to overseas slaughterhouses on live transport ships. Less discussed is how "local" farmed animals are often sent hundreds of miles away (and back in pieces) to the same slaughterhouses as CAFO-raised animals, since closer custom facilities are often highly restricted.[31] Just 50 U.S. slaughterhouses—industrial facilities generating their own excessive air and water pollution—kill and "process" 98% of cows and the vast majority of the nation's farmed animals (causing, among other horrors, "bottlenecks" during COVID-19–related closures), while just 0.2% of commercially available meat results from "on-farm slaughter."[32] Yet even this latter "best case scenario" is greenwashed. "Mobile Slaughterhouse Units," reports James McWilliams, author of *Just Food*, "are polluting our backyards with plasma-flecked wastewater, blood, and offal— dangerous byproducts that they're ill-equipped to handle properly," and so these very rare U.S. Department of Agriculture (USDA)–approved trailers are "authorized to leave behind a literal bloody mess" that will likely end up in waterways.[33]

The "local meat" charade deepens. The flesh of foreign-raised animals, if slaughtered or even just partially butchered domestically, can "receive a 'Product of U.S.A.' stamp," per a Bloomberg report. "Instantly, cows that spent most of their lives thousands of miles away suddenly become American bovines."[34] Slaughterhouse "byproducts" are also shipped to various product manufacturing plants, greenwashed as "upcycling." Finally, because of cultural taboos and consumer preferences, various animal parts are exported for foreign consumption, explaining, as agricultural economist Darrell Peel tells NPR, "why millions of pounds of beef" are "flowing back and forth in both direction[s] across the U.S.–Mexico border."[35]

Even if an animal product's total life cycle is somehow truly local, the "food miles" takeaway should be that far more resources are lost from converting food through animals—that extra step on the food chain— than from simply transporting it. Despite extensive storage systems for seasonal and terrain-specific feed and forage crops, livestock die-offs and mass "cullings"[*] routinely occur during weather events or disease outbreaks, predation, and other traumas, making animal farming far from a failproof year-round local food source. Despite presumptions that vegan food is inherently not local or accessible, many areas' native crops that are nutritious, hardy, and adaptable have simply been deprioritized. In fact, despite the "locavore" movement's heavy focus on animal foods, research shows its proper practice often *requires* eating more plant foods, since locally limited land availability often conflicts with animal agriculture's land-intensive nature.[36]

Organic Meat, Dairy, and Eggs: Hard On the Wallet and the Planet

Much like going locavore, choosing organic animal products is consistently found to have ecologically negligible benefits compared to eating low on the food chain by going vegan. Foregoing animal agriculture production methods that increase efficiency and decrease costs requires devoting more resources and expenses to match dominant "conventional" systems' yields. Without these efficiency shortcuts, organically raised farmed animals typically take longer to raise while requiring more acreage, food, and water—all to produce smaller and costlier amounts of milk, eggs, or meat. Therefore, farming animals organically is often even *worse* for the environment.

Certification restrictions alone dictate organic livestock production's amplified material cost. The USDA states that organic regulations "require that animals are raised in living conditions accommodating

---

[*]   Culling is a euphemism used to describe killing and disposing of animals, often en masse, as opposed to slaughtering them as scheduled for commercial use.

their natural behaviors (like the ability to graze on pasture)" and are "not administered antibiotics or hormones."[37] Logically, such conditions require either accessing more space to spread out the existing animals or allowing fewer animals in the existing space, and to further reduce yields by foregoing growth hormones. The restrictions also stipulate the animals be "fed 100% organic feed and forage"—but given that organic crop farming produces up to 34% lower yields than conventional,[38] feeding farmed animals organically would guzzle even *more* land.

Rather than fretting over organic labels (and food miles), specifies Tara Garnett of the Food Climate Research Network, the real question about any food's eco-impact should be, "Did it come from an animal or did it not come from an animal?" Indeed, Foodwatch data from 2009 shows that omnivores can reduce their impact just 8% by going organic— or a whopping 87% by instead going vegan (further increasing to 94% by going organic vegan).[39] A more recent 2020 study confirms once again that organic meat production incurs similar or worse climate damage than conventional; per *The Guardian*, its takeaway is that, regardless of whether grown organically, "all plants have far lower emissions than animal products."[40]

Grass-Fed Meat: A Lot of Hot Air

Few things illustrate our disconnect more clearly than the belief that giving over yet *more* land to what is already the Earth's most land-intensive human activity—and for disproportionately small returns—can somehow make it more sustainable. Yet this greenwashing theme continues.

Allowing farmed animals to graze or forage on grass pastures is widely considered an ecofriendly alternative to grain-based systems, yet grazing provides the *least* food using the *most* acreage. Therefore, as an international team of scientists demonstrates through GlobalCalculator.org, only a small portion of humankind can regularly be fed meat from pastured animals. Such methods could never scale up to significantly feed the global population now, let alone in the future. As renowned journalist George Monbiot observes in *The Guardian* that "switching from indoor production to free-range meat and eggs," although widely perceived as more humane (regardless of reality, as examined elsewhere in this book), is actually "crueler to the rest of the living world" because it swallows up even more land.[41] A 2014 research article joins many other studies in debunking the rampant greenwashing of grazing, which occupies more than three billion global hectares "with a majority suffering degradation in ecological condition. Losses in plant productivity, biodiversity of plant and animal communities, and carbon storage are occurring as a result of livestock grazing."[42]

While beef is frequently consumed in wealthy nations, it is often reserved for special occasions globally due to the singularly high land and resource cost of farming ruminants (animals with multiple stomachs for digesting grasses). Research from 2018 confirms that exclusively grass-fed beef production systems cannot sustainably scale up without dramatically reduced beef consumption levels.[43] Consider the differing mechanisms of grain and grass "finishing" cattle as follows:

Grain finishing: Per environmental researcher Matthew Hayek (who led the above research), cattle bred for beef being grazed in pastures outnumber those being fattened in feedlots at any given moment by five to one. This is because, under dominant production systems, cattle are grazed (or are seasonally fed hay and forage supplements) for several months before being sent to feedlots for grain "finishing" pre-slaughter. This final step dramatically *speeds up* their growth.

Grass finishing: Authentic "grass-fed beef," on the other hand, entails slower cattle growth simply because producers bypass grain finishing and instead continue grazing cattle on grasses long after their feedlot brethren have been slaughtered. Skipping grain finishing dramatically *slows down* their growth.

Grasses lack protein density and have the lowest "feed conversion ratio" (FCR) of all, meaning very little of it is converted into meat and dairy. Compared to grain, digesting grass also causes cows to produce more methane, a potent greenhouse gas. Per Hayek's study, given current beef consumption levels, a U.S. shift to entirely grass-fed systems would require farming many additional cows—whose longer lives and all-grass diets would generate more methane—and, impossibly, 270%

more land to yield the same quantities as grain-finished beef; otherwise, national beef consumption would need to decrease by nearly 73%. Yet cattle ranching is already the overwhelmingly dominant U.S. (and global) land use *even with most producers utilizing the efficiency shortcut of grain finishing.* We cannot continue current levels of meat-eating, Garnett has stated, let alone shift to grass-fed ruminants that require "huge tracts of additional land," since globally, "the consequences would be devastating."

Grass-Fed Dairy: "Grass-milk" Will Never Be Green

Although a rash of 2020 headlines used faulty industry research to claim so-called grass-milk is "greener" than soy milk,[44] grass-fed dairy is wildly inefficient. *On Pasture*, an "online magazine for graziers," explains that "zero grain dairy farming is very challenging, so there are still a relatively small number of farms doing it successfully." Among the dairy farmers interviewed who tried shifting to grass-fed systems, it states, "Many of them had either reduced herd size or added additional acreage of both pasture and harvested forages." All experienced "lower milk production levels." The main tips summarized include: "Your cows will need to eat a lot more forage to replace the grain they aren't getting," so "make sure you have enough land for the increase in forage consumption." Many farmers reported that using more land and resources to produce so little milk, even when sold at a premium, was ultimately not financially sustainable.[45]

Even the leading grass-fed dairy brand in the U.S., Maple Hill Farms, startlingly concedes (amidst many unsupported sustainability claims) on their website that, unless slaughtered, each post-fertile cow "becomes bad for the environment as a result of her carbon footprint: it uses environmental resources, produces greenhouse gases, and does not serve an ecological purpose."

"Pasture-Raised" Birds and Pigs: Feeding on Consumer Misconceptions

On any viable commercial operation, pasturing and foraging represent a secondary low-growth input for monogastric (one-stomached) animals like pigs and so-called poultry birds, who primarily convert processed and fortified animal feed (typically made from plant protein like corn, soy, or wheat) into meat or eggs. Despite connotations, therefore, labeling pork, turkey, chicken, or eggs "pasture-raised" conveys little about the animals' actual diet.

As one livestock specialist explains in a university resource on farming pigs, "Pasture should be considered a nutritional supplement and playground for monogastric animals, not the main source of their nutrition." Unless their primary source of sustenance is feed, the specialist bluntly states, "pastured pork production will not be sustainable at any level or from any standpoint."[46] Another university resource similarly concedes that although "many pastured poultry enthusiasts like the fact the birds are able to graze" alongside cows and sheep, "they get almost no nutrition from the grass itself." Although a portion of chickens' nutrients can be obtained from insects and seeds in the pastures, it varies greatly according to conditions and seasons. "Therefore, it is important for producers of poultry in pasture systems to provide a year-round supply of a prepared feed." The resource repeatedly emphasizes that feed must be made available for pastured poultry "at all times."[47] Farmed animals are not wild animals and mostly rely on humans for their nutritional needs.

When it comes to pasture-raising chickens, apparently, even greenwashing is being greenwashed. An article on the site Pastured Poultry Talk describes how "traditional poultry integrators" are engaging in a form of greenwashing that they are calling "pasture washing," by characterizing birds as "pasture-raised" despite raising them in stationary barns on overgrazed dirt lots. A telltale way to know whether a farm is really pasture-raising chickens at all (regardless of the practice's true ecological impact) is by their prohibitively small scale and output. "Scale in pastured poultry may be 1,000 birds or it may be a couple hundred thousand in a year," the resource admits, and the economic approach "features direct-to-consumer relationships."[48] These products—so costly and scarce that they are not even available at the typical grocery store, let alone cafeterias, stadiums, and hospitals—are *still* not "sustainable" compared to consuming plants directly.

Heritage Breeds: A Tradition of Violence

Touted as ecofriendly, farming pre-industrially developed "heritage breeds" of domesticated animals* cannot scale beyond niche markets, as exemplified by the following discussion on a homesteader's blog. "Even with a LOT more time," the author laments about attempting to raise such chickens, "they were still much smaller than the modern meat breeds" when slaughtered.† A fellow homesteader adds that "many bags of extra food" are needed for heritage breeds "scarfing down plenty of high priced organic chicken chow," adding that even more bedding material is required for the additional feces generated.[49] The website Hello Homestead similarly advises its audience that raising heritage breeds requires more inputs because "slower growing" animals must remain alive longer (to reach a viable slaughter weight). Regardless, as Robert Grillo discusses in his book *Farm to Fable*, groups like the Livestock Conservancy glorify farming "traditional livestock breeds that were raised by our forefathers" in "a bygone era," who "once roamed the pastures of America's pastoral landscape" and today could face "extinction." In reality, writes Grillo, colonial-era livestock cultures "wreaked havoc on ecosystems" and "the process continues today, particularly on so-called pasture-based or free-range farms, which require more land use and more confrontations with indigenous species."[50]

GREENWASHING CLAIMS BEYOND LABELS

Climate Disruption

Like powering buildings and vehicles with fuels made of fossilized matter, obtaining caloric energy from animal-digested plants is a secondary, indirect, and inefficient way to obtain the sun's energy. Not

---

*   Although pre-industrially developed, there were faster-growing, higher-yielding farmed animals who were already being selectively bred by the 18th century to have disproportionately massive bodies atop spindly legs (as depicted in paintings of the time), a historic aspect of livestock "heritage" rarely mentioned.

†   Disturbingly, the author admits that along with ultimately preferring a "Frankenchicken" breed's much higher "carcass weight" yielding more meat, they consider their slaughter a "mercy killing, because the birds get so big their bodies fail under the strain."

only does producing one calorie of animal protein versus plant protein require more than ten times the fossil fuel inputs,[51] but the animals emit additional powerful greenhouse gases through their own digestion and waste, as does the fertilizer used to grow their feed. Meanwhile, maintaining large tracts of previously converted land for livestock production (again, humanity's largest land use) suppresses the possibility of significant global reforestation, or otherwise rewilding, to absorb huge amounts of carbon, while continued land conversion for ever-expanding livestock production releases yet *more* carbon previously stored in the trees and plants.[52]

Some studies on animal agriculture's climate impact neglect a full lifecycle analysis by excluding factors like feed production and land use, while industry spokespeople mischaracterize the sector's emissions as "natural processes," "less harmful" than other sources, or merely "cow farts." However, farming animals hinders a healthy carbon cycle through complex inputs, outputs, and opportunity costs that compound the climate catastrophe in various ways. Beyond climate change, farming animals is driving land use changes, habitat and biodiversity loss, freshwater overuse and pollution, and ocean depletion, the impacts of which make it increasingly foolish to divert resources to livestock production and harder to manage livestock-driven burdens such as zoonotic disease outbreaks and pandemics, antibiotic resistance, and food-borne illness. Once again, the solution is not in reforming animal agriculture, but in our food choices. "Researchers have shown that even when accounting for future improvements in agriculture," the World Resources Institute explains, "shifting the diets of higher-income consumers toward plant-based foods remains essential for meeting climate targets."[53]

Greenwashed High Tech Workaround Proposals

Some of the most widely hyped yet implausible tech fix proposals that would ostensibly reduce animal food production's climate-warming emissions are as follows:

- **Seaweed feed additives**: Adding seaweed to cattle feed cuts the levels of methane they belch out during "grain finishing." A 2019 study, however, cautions this "may not be a realistic strategy" for several reasons. Harvesting, freeze drying, and grinding wild seaweed to feed the world's 1.5 billion farmed cows "would deplete the oceans and cause an ecological problem in trying to solve another," as would cultivating the seaweed in aquaculture operations instead. Seaweed effectiveness may be impacted by storage and cattle microbe adaptation, plus cows dislike the taste of seaweed, so tend to eat less feed that contains it; when they do eat feed containing seaweed, they belch out bromoform, an ozone-depleting gas.[54] "We need to reduce emissions from livestock," says Leeds University professor and Chatham House research director Tim Benton of such solutions. "That needs to come from dietary change"—of humans, not cows.[55]

- **Methane-capturing face masks**: Two sons of an Argentine cattle rancher are launching a mask for farmed cattle that Bloomberg says contains "a set of fans powered by solar-charged batteries sucks up the burps and traps them in a chamber with a methane-absorbing filter," plus a built-in accelerometer and GPS sensor to ensure productivity. Cattle producers, already working under "very tight margins," can subscribe to Zelp cattle mask service for $45 per bovine annually or more for tracking data. "Zelp will join a growing roster of solutions to the cow burp problem," notes Bloomberg, which "have seen little success so far." One of Zelp's founding brothers admits that the environmental impacts of cattle production "will not be solved without radical solutions. Some consumers will choose to go vegan, and some will choose to eat less beef." However, Zelp will surely go down in history as radically ridiculous.

- **Anaerobic digesters**: Livestock production generates far more manure than the Earth can safely absorb or handle; in the U.S. that is 3 to 20 times more than humans produce.[56] Waste "lagoons," found in both large- and small-scale farming, emit greenhouse gases and pollute waterways, but spraying them onto farmland (a common "solution" to the problem) jeopardizes nearby communities' health. Anaerobic or methane digesters on livestock farms aim to reduce "carbon hoofprints" by converting manure into electricity. The Center for Food and Safety, among many others, calls them B.S. (pun intended).[57] Biogas digesters, yet another income stream for livestock producers that only partially address an entirely self-generated problem and require large public investment, are water-intensive, and leave unprocessed toxic sludge behind.

While these and other greenwashing proposals to reduce the emissions from animal agriculture elicit excitement amongst "livestock sustainability consultants" and journalists covering "green" topics (the latest headline at the time of this writing being "MooLoo: Scientists potty-train cows to help cut greenhouse gas emissions"), none can resolve the dangerous climate cost of everyone eating high on the food chain.

Greenwashing Claim:
"Livestock Production Absorbs Carbon and Regenerates the Soil"
Whether the methods are applicable, widely adopted, scientifically validated, or truly effective, "regenerative grazing" proponents attempt to reframe livestock production altogether as a climate *solution*. As Hayek explains, however, "efforts to reduce the cattle's footprints by getting them to trample some of their carbon back into the ground"—mostly into the top layer of the soil only, making it a temporary solution either way—"rely on shaky science and do not seem to work on a large scale." The multiple studies debunking so-called regenerative grazing's benefits include research published in the International Journal of Biodiversity, which states, "Leading range scientists have refuted the system and indicated that its adoption by land management agencies is based on these anecdotes and unproven principles rather than scientific evidence."[58] And a two-year, peer-reviewed study released in 2017 citing 300 sources thoroughly rejects these methods and makes it clear: "grazing livestock—even in a best-case scenario—are net contributors to the climate problem, as is all livestock [production]."[59] Grazing animals, regardless of methods, swallows up massive acreage that could be liberated from agriculture altogether and largely rewilded for maximum carbon sequestration and biodiversity conservation. For an in-depth debunking of the extraordinary claims surrounding "regenerative"

ranching, see Nicholas Carter's chapter, "Grazing vs. The Planet: The Failed Attempt to Greenwash Animal Farming," in this book.

Earth's Land Crisis

"Our land use and agricultural practices," declares Yale research, "rival climate change as a global environmental threat."[60] While livestock production overwhelmingly dominates human land use, plant foods supply most global calories by far. A 2018 study describes meat as a "land-intensive" food and plant foods as "land-sparing"—so much so that a plant-based shift, per Poore's research, would free up an area of land equivalent to the U.S., European Union, China, and Australia combined.[61] Instead, sadly, cattle ranching (the largest deforestation driver in every Amazon country) continues overtaking the planet's remaining Indigenous territories and reserves.

Greenwashing Concept: "Deforestation-Free Beef"

The term "deforestation-free beef" seems to defy beef production's astonishingly land-intensive nature. In reality, the Bureau of Investigative Journalism, among others, has established that major U.S. companies, including Walmart, Costco, and Kroger, have been selling beef directly linked to Amazon deforestation;[62] verifying otherwise is difficult given rampant cow laundering (when a farm with environmental violations sells animals to a "clean" farm to circumvent monitoring systems)[63] and the unlabeled use of imported soy-based feed. Regardless of where or how recently it was converted, once richly forested land is widely used for beef production. Half the U.S. was covered in forests before about 70% of it was cleared, mostly for post-colonial agriculture[64]— again, dominated in terms of land use by livestock, and especially beef, production. In the U.K., all sheep and cattle grassland pastures sit on previously forested land, including once temperate rainforest that would otherwise revert back and soak up 12 years' carbon emissions while still retaining the ability to feed its population.[65] Brazil, therefore, is simply doing what other nations have for centuries. Producing the planet's most land-intensive food, beef, for regular global consumption requires overtaking vast land areas that are far more ecologically valuable in their native state—all for relatively little food. Sadly, "beef" alone uses more than half of the world's agricultural land, but accounts for less than 2% of calories and 5% of protein consumed worldwide.[66] Such a land-hungry undertaking as beef production, clearly, can *never* rationally be "deforestation-free" at scale.

Greenwashing Rallying Cries: "Cow or Plow" & "Soil Not Soy"

Unlike clearing forests, using grasslands for cattle ranching purportedly "saves" them from being plowed over for crops like corn and soy. Buzzworthy terms like "cow not plow" and "soil not soy," however, create false dichotomies. Not only are ranching and conservation inherently in conflict, but the primary use of corn and soy is animal feed. During conversion to ranching, formerly biodiverse grassland vegetation, including prairies once of incalculable value for Indigenous peoples to gather various seeds,[67] is homogenized into farmed monocultures of grasses (often imported long ago for that purpose and continually farmed at the expense of native grasses) to feed vast herds of domesticated ruminants. Protecting more grasslands from agriculture, *especially* livestock grazing, would mitigate climate change, as 2010 research shows that agricultural soils contain 25% to 75% less organic carbon than undisturbed ecosystems.[68] Given plant-based diet's land-sparing ability, research shows that 42% of U.S. crop land could be freed up by simply replacing beef with beans alone.[69]

Greenwashing Claim: "Livestock Utilize Marginal Lands"

"But livestock use lands that can't be used for anything else!" Positioning animal agriculture as land's sole "use" and value that is otherwise "empty" or "wasted" is a persistent colonial-era trope. The term "marginal lands" is merely a flexibly defined economic descriptor for land with little apparent agricultural value purely from a human consumer perspective, and it says nothing of its value to the rest of the living world. In many cases, land became considered marginal in the first place *because* of livestock grazing. Further, agricultural grazing on marginal lands is even *less* productive than on fertile pastures (already a slow-growth method itself); in southwestern deserts where the grass and shrubs are sparse and low-quality, domestic animals must cover many miles to get enough calories to be commercially viable, wreaking environmental havoc in the process. Using such lands to produce paltry yields of animal products comes at tremendous conservations costs. The marginal lands argument largely hinges on the following false premises:

- **"We must produce food on marginal lands":** This claim is certainly not applicable to wealthy nations, where plant-based diets can negate the need to use so much land for food production.* Elsewhere, in lower income countries, livestock use is an overemphasized solution for less arable lands that is often counterproductive (as discussed further on).

- **"Marginal lands have no other/better uses":** According to the earlier-mentioned study written by an international team of experts and published by Food Climate Research Network: "While 'grass-fed' animals may not be dependent on arable-based feeds, the supposition that they are using spare land that could not be used for something else is mistaken." Other uses given include nature conservation, forests, bioenergy, and plant food cultivation.[70] The most significant use would be reforesting and rewilding vast areas for crucial carbon sequestration.

- **"Crops won't grow on marginal lands":** Examples of hardy, human-edible plants that grow in difficult conditions include leafy greens, fruit, roots, buckwheat, rye, barley, quinoa, amaranth, and several leguminous plants.[71] This includes places with seemingly non-fertile sand; after all, the arid West's top irrigation use is growing alfalfa for dairy farms. "Although seldom discussed in relation to world food production," states a 1979 scientific journal article, "tree crops on rough and marginal lands have a potentially valuable role to play in supplementing traditional cereal and grain crop agriculture."[72] Regardless of which foods can be farmed where, University of

---

* The ecological cost of transporting foods (already widely done in our globalized world, including with livestock production's feed and other inputs) to areas lacking access to enough arable land, if needed, is much lower than using marginal lands for livestock production.

California research from 2016 find that vegan diets require far less land overall for food production—and whether or not they can "use" all available land is largely negated by the fact that they *do not need to*, which comes with massive ecological benefits. The study specifies that "dietary change towards plant-based diets has significant potential to reduce the agricultural land requirements of U.S. consumers and increase the carrying capacity of U.S. agricultural resources."[73]

Earth's Water Crisis

Household measures can only save so much water, since agriculture accounts for 92% of humanity's water footprint.[74] Per 2011 research, "The water footprint of any animal product is larger than the water footprint of crop products with equivalent nutritional value." Once again, not farming practices, but "the unfavorable feed conversion efficiency for animal products" is pinpointed.[75] Over one half of the U.S. and nearly one third of global freshwater consumption for *any* use is *just for livestock production*,[76] also the top nitrogen and phosphorus polluter of global waterways.[77] Comprising only 2.5% of water on Earth, freshwater's sustainable use is incompatible with globally increasing livestock-centric diets draining aquifers that take thousands of years to recharge.[78] Abundant scientific research finds that livestock production is dangerously straining global water resources, which some experts call "the next oil" that will drive global conflict.

Greenwashing Claim: "Grass-Fed Cows Use Rainwater"

Beef and dairy production's astonishing water use is greenwashed by the notion that grass-fed cows solely use "green water" (rainwater) falling on pastures before returning to the water cycle, versus irrigated "blue water" from already gravely overdrawn aquifers and rivers to grow feed. In truth, most agricultural pastures are irrigated at least seasonally, and again, feeding ruminants grasses is land-intensive yet low-yielding, which is why most are finished on (irrigated) grain (with seaweed added to reduce methane, remember?). Regardless, rainwater reliance for grazing animals is precarious amidst increasingly frequent and severe droughts, and 70% of U.S. beef cattle are already raised in drought-stressed states.[79] Globally, reports increasingly describe helicopter water deliveries going to pastured animals, with other grazed herds starving to death or being killed en masse. Animal grazing also drives deforestation, *further* exacerbating droughts. Continually breeding hungry, thirsty megafauna to graze on vast areas of ostensibly rainwater-fed pastures is a liability when famine, floods, and droughts are increasing in frequency due to climate disruption.

Food Waste and Hunger

While millions of humans globally are malnourished and deprived of basic staple crops, wealthy nations consume around twice the protein they need—mostly in the form of resource-intensive animal protein.[81] According to 2018 scientific research, feeding 2050's projected global population will require "replacing most meat and dairy with plant-based alternatives."[82] Otherwise, researchers anticipate "growing inequities as growing land use for meat consumption by rich countries causes rising food costs for staples" relied upon globally.[83] Even among pastoralist communities (in which meat is generally eaten sparingly to begin with) like Kenya's Samburu tribe, per international reporting, many are embracing "a greater dependence on plant growing" while recognizing livestock production as "an increasingly unsustainable livelihood option." Regarding food waste, research finds animal agriculture's "opportunity food loss" is larger than conventional food loss that reaches landfills,[84] as over a billion tons of harvested crops can produce only about a quarter million tons of animal products.[85] At the consumer level, discarded foods of animal origin have the greatest material cost.[86]

Overall, staple crops like cereals, legumes, tubers, and roots account for about 90% of the world's caloric intake, while animal products provide comparably little.[87] While livestock-centric diets undeniably help create the artificial scarcity and inflated staple crop prices that serve elite interests, world hunger is also dictated by resource allocation, and shifting agriculture away from livestock reliance must happen methodically versus overnight. To avoid further strain on global food resources, however, those with food choice, access, and autonomy can move the needle by helping normalize plant-based diets.

Greenwashing Claim: "Livestock 'Upcycle' Human-Inedible Food"

Animal agriculture's unconscionable strain on global food resources is greenwashed by the narrative that farmed animals primarily "upcycle" human-inedible biomass and leftovers into meat, dairy, and eggs. While research from 2017 finds that farmed animals' diets are collectively only 13% grain,[88] this statistic was expressed by dry weight. The *weightier* density of their diet is comprised of far less *nutritionally* dense materials than grain—like grasses, fodder crops, crop residues, and various by-products—simply because inordinate amounts are required for any meaningful impact. Highlighting feed-source percentages without context "obscures the sheer magnitude of stuff [farmed] animals eat," explains Hayek, because although "only" 13% of animal feed is grain, that comprises one third of the grain on Earth! Along with a third of the world's grain, livestock production *also* inhales mountains of these other relatively low-impact materials, which a breakdown of their actual caloric/protein value would help illustrate.

Grasses and fodder crops fed primarily to massive ruminants, of course, are not genuinely "leftovers" at all, since they are farmed over vast land areas for that purpose. Lumping in oil seed cakes—the protein-rich "meal" portion of certain seeds and beans, including soy—as upcycled materials is similarly misleading, since soybeans are grown primarily to extract the meal for livestock production (especially pigs and birds, who cannot digest grass), resulting in cheap oil byproduct.* Regarding crop residues and other byproducts, per researchers, livestock producers' "high usage of low-impact by-products is typically offset by low digestibility and growth,"[89] necessitating that massive amounts of arable land are still reserved for growing feed. Either way, better uses for genuine crop byproducts exist and continue being developed.

Framing the issue in terms of "food/feed competition" also distracts from the devastating wildlife conflicts and other eco-impacts of animal

---

* Soybeans actually have a low oil content, containing the least oil of all major oilseeds and about four times more meal than oil, so food processors are only swimming in cheap soy oil because so much soy is grown to feed livestock.

farming. Despite the half-truth that "livestock turn food we can't eat into protein," as one greenwashing website proclaims,[90] plants that humans *can* eat already provide more than enough protein using a fraction of the land. Either way, a 2015 study determines that feeding livestock exclusively "ecological leftovers" would necessitate drastic reductions in meat consumption yet "still results in environmental impacts that cause several planetary boundaries to be transgressed."[91] Rather than mass-breeding animals as humanity's giant garbage disposal to inhale low-impact materials *in addition to* endless acres of corn, soy, and grain, 2019 research finds that feeding the world requires the inverse: "replacing most meat and dairy with plant-based alternatives, and greater acceptance of human-edible crops currently fed to animals."[92]

Greenwashing Term: "Nose to Tail" Dining

The "ethical omnivore" movement champions eating "nose to tail" (every edible part of a carcass, including offal) along with baby and older animals (often discarded "byproducts" of livestock production) to reduce waste. Again, these are more of those "less-bad" solutions that, while making a massively wasteful process slightly less so in one regard, certainly cannot make it sustainable. Plant-based diets bypass animal production's extra step on the food chain altogether—along with this entirely avoidable yet supposedly "ethical" obligation to eat the otherwise discarded heads, brains, organs, babies, mothers, and fathers of deliberately bred sentient individuals.

Biodiversity Loss

Computer modeling estimates that the Earth is currently losing multiple species each day,[93] a "biological annihilation" that scientists are calling the "sixth mass extinction." Unsurprisingly, given its unrivaled land use, multiple researcher studies cite animal agriculture as the single largest driver of habitat loss and species extinction worldwide. Among them is 2015 research stating that "reducing meat consumption" is the key to biodiversity conservation,[94] a 2017 World Wildlife Fund (WWF) summary report finding that excessive animal product consumption is responsible for most biodiversity loss,[95] and, most recently, two 2021 studies' collective findings, as summarized by media outlet *Vox*, show that global meat production is on track to "wipe out thousands of species in the next few decades."[96] Our global terrestrial mammal biomass (combined weight) is now dramatically dominated by humanity's continually bred farmed animals crowding out what little wildlife remains.[97]

Greenwashing Animal Ag as "Conservation"

In the U.K., whose heavily modified landscape was long ago deforested into patchworks of sheep and cattle pastures and eradicated of predators, groups like the government agency Natural England championed so-called "conservation grazing" and claim, "Livestock grazing is essential for the management of many of England's most important wildlife habitats." Meanwhile, the "range conservation" field of employment is characterized as crucial for U.S. land management but truly serves ranching interests; per Texas Tech University, range conservationists "focus on maintaining the health of range ecosystems so they can continue to be used for domestic or wildlife animal production." Such paradoxical narratives not only conflate nature's authentic biodiversity with variations in human-domesticated breeds, but mistake exploitation for conservation.

In reality, animal agriculture of all forms swallows up habitats, homogenizes biodiversity, and decimates wild animals. Per National Geographic, the USDA's Wildlife Services agency "specializes in killing wild animals that [are perceived to] threaten livestock—especially predators such as coyotes, wolves, and cougars."[98] Yet carnivores naturally exist in relatively small densities and are ecologically necessary and appropriate, as are the native herbivores deemed mere "forage competition" for livestock production. Using USDA data, wildlife biologist Erik Molvar explains, "one cow-calf pair eats a similar amount of forage as two elk or eight mule deer, and therefore would be estimated to displace that number" of those animals.[99]

The wildlife conflict created by continually mass-breeding and widely distributing hungry human-dependent animals is *only exacerbated* by "sustainably" farming them over vast land areas. California's Point

Reyes National Seashore is among those areas forcing out native Tule elk to accommodate organic dairy operations.[100] The Tule elk are dying of starvation and dehydration as fences deny them access to their native grasslands and water sources. To protect ranching interests, bison and wild horses are routinely rounded up and/or slaughtered from the midwestern U.S. to the southwest.[101] Even wildlife reserves and refuges largely serve to keep nature's animals away from livestock operations to prevent forage competition, predation threats, and disease spreading. Grazing animals is even greenwashed as "wildfire prevention" in (historically livestock-free) current wildfire hotbeds like California and Australia, yet it mostly just suppresses nature's fire defenses[102] while maintaining and further spreading invasive fire-fuel grasses,[103] at a tremendous cost to the native biodiversity.

Greenwashing Claim: "Livestock Function Like Wildlife"
While methane-emitting ruminants have long roamed the planet as an autonomous part of nature's functional food chain, ecologically extractive farmed animals are human-dependent, mass-bred, and "produced" by humans using converted forest and other formerly biodiverse ecosystems that otherwise would be absorbing methane and other greenhouse gases. Among the experts debunking the narrative that livestock production has functionally replaced the ecological role of native herbivores is ecologist George Wuerthner, who points out crucial differences regarding population density, distribution, concentration, preferences, mobility, diversity, symbiosis, and more.[104] Other livestock proponents claim that grazing farmed animals is now necessary to carry out the ecosystem services that wild grazers once did in order to return lands to their pre-livestock state of health using . . . livestock? Far from nature's symbiosis, again, animal grazing is the very activity primarily displacing nature in the first place. Greenpeace Alaska co-founder and environmental activist Will Anderson clarifies: "We can accomplish magnitudes of recovery more if conservation biologists introduce native species in tandem with the end of animal agriculture. As it dies, ecosystems will thrive."[105]

Greenwashed High Tech Workaround Proposal: Invisible Fences

The countless acres of fences separating farmed animals from natural ecosystems interfere with wild animals' seasonal migration, separate vulnerable family members, and unnaturally increase their predation risk. One proposed solution, reported in *On Pasture*, is a virtual system said to "improve agriculture, animal welfare and the environment all at once" using a GPS collar to shock animals who surpass pasture boundaries—but "will the cost for the collars and the monthly service fee for the web portal service combined with anticipated profits from access to more forage offset the material and labor costs of your current fencing?" Granting livestock producers access to yet more land is, of course, far from an environmental benefit. Either way, this high-tech proposal of fitting billions of farmed animals with shock collars seems implausible and yet another form of cruelty for them to endure.

GREENWASHING DAIRY, EGGS, CHICKEN, HONEY, AND FISH

Greenwashing Dairy (Beyond "Grass-milk")

The basic mechanisms and inefficiencies vary little among dairy operations, regardless of size or type: they exploit the lactation functions of large mammals with massive caloric and water needs for comparably little product. Additionally, attempts to repackage veal, a cruel dairy farming byproduct, as "sustainable" or "conscientious" consumption will inevitably fail. Ironically, *Edible Magazine* proclaims that buying veal throws a "lifeline" to artisanal dairy farms in crisis over "the ascent of alt-milks (like oat and almond),"[106] which have much smaller land, water, and emissions footprints while bypassing the unwanted calf predicament altogether.

"Micro-dairy" models, such as the U.K.'s much-heralded "calf at foot" dairy, only exacerbate grass-fed dairying's baseline inefficiencies. By granting calves some access to their lactating mothers (which most dairies prevent beyond the first few hours or days of birth), even *less* milk is diverted for human consumption. But dairying, by design, cruelly entails frequent breeding *and* slaughter (explaining why, as industry publication *Drover's* admits, "beef is a byproduct of the dairy industry"[107]); otherwise, given its high herd "turnover," populations would logically explode beyond environmental limits. Calf-at-foot systems could not possibly scale beyond niche markets to feed a meaningful portion of our current (let alone growing) population.

Despite relentless spin from those deeply invested in the notion of "sustainable dairy," Jay Wilde of Bradley Nook Farm in the U.K. provides a reality check. In a video documenting his transition away from dairy farming, Wilde points to a massive stockpile of hay bundles, frequently replenished just for his small remaining herd of seventeen—a fraction of what larger working dairies require. "And that just shows the environmental impact of keeping livestock; because ours are not producing anything, they eat ten of these a week just to live." If the animals were being used for milk, he adds, they would have "enormous energy demands," including protein "grown on what used to be grassland or forest or which is now intensive cropland" for feeding cows. Wilde, now working with an organization called Refarm'd to help animal farmers transition to oat milk production, points out that a plant-based shift is not about putting farmers out of business, but changing with the times and embracing better opportunities.[108]

Greenwashing "Poultry" Products

While homesteaders experiment with heritage breeds and higher income consumers custom order "pasture-raised" birds for their holiday feasts, CAFOs churn out the vast majority of "poultry" and all animal products. Chickens' meat and eggs, regardless of their source, are frequently presented as "more sustainable" than beef, which is like saying that gas-guzzling vehicles are sustainable if private jets are the only other option. As articulated in *The Ecologist*:

> White meat tends to be far worse than alternatives such as beans and other legumes, in terms of greenhouse gas emissions but also food security, deforestation, and other forms of pollution. . . . That white meat is less bad in greenhouse gas terms than the worst food does not serve to render it sustainable, especially given the scale of the problems we face.[109]

The largest tonnage of animal feed worldwide—the production of which WWF research cites as the leading driver of species extinction—goes to poultry production, since humans consume approximately 65 billion chickens annually. Even soybean cultivation's massive ecological footprint is primarily owed to poultry farming's heavy reliance on soy-based feed, including celebrated "pastured" chicken producers and "sustainable" turkey farms with Thanksgiving waiting lists. According to the World Resources Institute, every nine calories of crops fed to chickens produces only one calorie of food for humans.[110] Other research finds that double the protein can be produced from growing plant protein instead of raising poultry for meat, or 40% more than eggs.[111] "Eliminating eggs and replacing them with plants that offer the same nutrients would make it possible to feed one million additional people," Phys. org summarizes, while eliminating chicken meat "could feed 12 million more people."[112] Unlike soy-fed animal foods like chicken (generating staggering amounts of bones mummifying in landfills, an environmental disaster in itself) and eggs,[113] animal-free soy (and other plant) foods—often nearly indistinguishable from the former—are a land-efficient and climate-smart protein.

Greenwashing Honey and Beekeeping

The widespread misconception that beekeeping is eco-friendly conflates native pollinators with insects that humans domesticated as "livestock" long ago, imposed globally along with animals like cattle during colonization, and continually mass-bred. "Beekeeping is often promoted as a way to conserve pollinators," explains pollinator researcher Olivia Norfolk. However, "it's the equivalent of farming chickens to save wild birds."[114] Similarly, scientist Juan P. Gonzalez-Varo describes beekeeping as an extractive activity like cattle grazing. And just as cattle ranching displaces ecologically appropriate native herbivores, beekeeping displaces more efficient native pollinators.[115] Per Gonzalez-Varo, beekeeping's agricultural problems are falsely lumped in with wild pollinators' biodiversity issues (much like "livestock conservancy" and "conservation grazing"). A 2018 study, however, shows that beekeeping harms native pollinators through disease spreading and pollen (food) competition,[116] mirroring similar conflicts between wild and domesticated herbivores. Furthermore, feral honeybees unleashed on the planet through beekeeping are *the primary threat* to native pollinator populations.[117]

Replacing so many of the world's wild herbivores and pollinators with domesticated animals like cattle and honeybees is driving ecological homogenization and, with it, the unprecedented need for commercial crop pollination services (ironically, a common justification for continued beekeeping). Instead of maintaining the negative feedback loop that humans create by exploiting honeybees and other animals as "livestock," shifting to plant-based farming, especially veganic systems,* would encourage more crop diversity and spare massive areas of land to restore wild pollinators' and other native species' rightful place.

Greenwashing Fishing

Seafood production's ecological devastation is also being widely greenwashed away. Like forests, oceans are climate-healing carbon sinks—but fishing dramatically interferes with the marine food web's delicate balance and decreases levels of emissions-absorbing phytoplankton.[118] Privately-run organizations reap financial rewards by certifying "sustainable" fish species, ever-changing as each inevitably becomes overfished, while endangered and non-target species are decimated as "bycatch" in indiscriminate nets and thrown back into the ocean dead and dying.[119] Torn and used fishing nets and other gear are widely discarded and left to litter the oceans as fish and other marine life get caught, trapped, and die in the "ghost gear."[120] While often presented as ecofriendly for bypassing the more well-known problems with trawling, fish farming is a trade-off that seriously threatens freshwater and ocean health, marine life, and human biosecurity.[121] Like farming land animals, aquaculture relies on animals (including apex predators like tuna) inefficiently "converting" feed, which is often made from soy and even wild caught fish. Researchers estimate that only "19% of

---

* Veganic farming is organic farming without animal inputs such as blood meal, bone meal, fish meal, manure, etc.

protein and 10% of calories in feed for aquatic species are ultimately made available in the human food supply."[122] Additionally, both wild and farmed fish are now fed to farmed land animals (whose runoff in turn pollutes the oceans and other bodies of water), further diminishing marine life populations.

While less unsustainable fishing methods exist, they cannot sustainably enable the frequent, affordable, and entirely discretionary collective human consumption of marine animals. Renowned marine biologist Dr. Sylvia Earle states, "I personally have stopped eating ocean wildlife because I think they're more important alive than dead. And I think now is the time to make a serious issue of this." What of remote tribes and wild animals who genuinely need to eat fish for survival? "That is all the more reason," Fish Feel founder Mary Finelli points out, "for those of us who don't need to eat fish to not eat them." For too long, "saving the oceans" has referred mostly to preserving humans' ability to wantonly exploit the oceans' amazing and varied animals, but truly saving their home requires taking them off our plates.

From Greenwashing to Green

The rampant greenwashing and humanewashing of animal exploitation systems cannot erase the horrific moral wrong of defaulting to them when viable alternatives exist. Far from a "humane" or "sustainable" (let alone scalable) model, Old MacDonald-style farms' most effectual function is simply to present animals as ambassadors sanitizing and normalizing their own exploitation—overwhelmingly carried out in CAFOs—and its ecological toll. Commodifying other sentient beings by the billions to reinforce a false sense of human dominance, let alone for an acquired taste or texture, is not remotely worth jeopardizing the natural world on which we *all* depend. Luckily, humans eating high on the food chain and otherwise exploiting other animals is no more part of some non-negotiable "natural order" than is burning fossil fuels for our energy. Whether the animals are farmed locally or organically, given seaweed-supplemented feed or wearing gas-capturing masks, grazed "regeneratively" or on lands deemed otherwise "useless,"—or whatever dubious proposal hits the headlines next—nothing can meaningfully change animal agriculture's innately resource-intensive mechanisms and deeply problematic framework. Hopefully, my daughter's generation will be the one savvy enough to finally embrace the *truly* green and humane possibilities of a shift to vegan living.

Lorelei Plotczyk holds a B.A. in Visual and Media Arts, as well as an M.B.A. with an Environmental Management specialization. Through the years she has written and produced content for the television and marketing industries, along with various animal justice–focused platforms and her own science-based environmental campaign Truth or Drought. After a decade-plus stint in Southern California, she now resides back in her native Massachusetts with her husband and daughter (both fellow vegans!).

8

GRAZING VS. THE PLANET

The Failed Attempt to Greenwash Animal Farming

by Nicholas Carter, M.A.

The idea that the land needs farmed animal grazing to thrive is not just pseudoscience, it appeals to the "culture over scientific evidence" ethos, falsely asserting that when you eat animals, you are somehow helping the environment, when that is the complete opposite of reality. This is all part of a new movement called "regenerative agriculture" that's premise is to incorporate farming animals within otherwise sustainable plant farming. The grazing methods go by many names—rotational grazing, holistic grazing management, short-duration grazing—but they all tout something better for land, climate, and biodiversity: regeneration. To regenerate is to regrow or fix something and restore it to a better state than it was before. This is ironic as, in most cases, land is terribly degraded *because of* animal farming, and while there is a spectrum to the degradation, the collective environmental impacts of grazing animals pale in comparison to benefits of farming plants or rewilding.

Many consumers want to eat better, both ethically and environmentally, and are turning to trendy solutions like so-called regenerative farms to source their food. Local farms with grass-fed animals being bred and raised for food are growing in popularity. Consumers envision happy animals on a farm with a vast, biodiverse pasture habitat. The problematic reality is that we are now aware, after a slew of studies, that farming grass-fed animals has an even larger ecological footprint than confinement systems.[1] Furthermore, where food is sourced from and the transportation of it (how "local" the food is) is approximately 10% of its environmental footprint—and only 1% for beef. A 2008 study entitled "Food-Miles and the Relative Climate Impacts of Food Choices in the United States" found that "Greenhouse gas emissions (GHG) associated with food are dominated by the production phase, contributing 83% of the average U.S. household's 8%," and that, "transportation as a whole represents only 11% of life-cycle GHG emissions, and final delivery from producer to retail contributes only 4%."[2] The overwhelming scientific evidence points to the need to shift our food system to emphasize a plant-rich diet, but the largely baseless claims of carbon-neutral beef and other local free-range meats, dairy, and eggs are a dangerous distraction that must be addressed.

Regenerative agriculture needs to shift away from greenwashed farmed animal grazing and only include plant-based agriculture that truly regenerates biodiversity, increases carbon sequestration, uses low levels of land allowing rewilding, regenerates our health, and lowers the risk of zoonoses. Conservation agriculture, a type of sustainable and diverse plant farming that doesn't involve any animal inputs, is one of the best models of how we need to farm for the planet.[3]

GRAZED AND CONFUSED

The causes of our climate catastrophe have largely been focused on fossil fuels. There is no doubt that the carbon dioxide emitted from burning fossil fuels for energy has played a major role. However, even if we successfully shift away from fossil fuels and live in a utopia of electric cars, renewable energy, and clean energy grids, the farmed animal sector's continued business as usual alone will account for at least 49% of the allowed emissions under the Paris Agreement for maintaining only a 1.5°C increase in temperature goal by 2030.[4] This shows the urgency of addressing both fossil fuels *and* animal agriculture to avoid enhancing the climate crisis. This is largely because Big Livestock is a major polluter just like Big Oil and the top five meat and dairy companies combined emit more greenhouse gases than ExxonMobil, Shell, or BP. This is despite a lack of reporting and accountability as "most of the top 35 global meat and dairy giants either do not report or underreport their emissions."[5] Naturally, one may think this is just an issue of industrial mass confinement of animals. In fact, it is instead an issue of farming animals as a whole, no matter the size or scale of the operation.

Let's explore the impacts of climate change when animals are moved from confinement to pastureland. First, it's important to understand that only ruminants like cows can shift to an exclusive grass diet; monogastric animals like pigs and chickens require a large part of their diet to be supplied by various crops, such as grains, soybeans, and alfalfa.

Does shifting cows from feedlots to pastureland help sequester carbon in soils? Key to this discussion is an extensive two-year report by TABLE, a food and climate research group,[6] who conducted a meta-analysis of 300 sources, all related to soil health, regenerative and other forms of grazing, methane, and farming as a whole, which included almost a dozen authors and universities like Oxford and Cambridge. In terms of the big picture and scaling up of grazing, they concluded:

> It would be physically impossible for the animal protein production produced today—about 27 g/person/day—to be supplied by grazing systems, at least without an unthinkably damaging programme of forest clearance, which would vastly increase the livestock sector's already large contribution to global GHG emissions.[7]

This report attempts to answer the question: "Do 'grass-fed' systems hold potential to help address our climate problems, or is their overall contribution damaging?" The question is limiting as it doesn't factor in wider environmental issues, such as biodiversity, water footprints, health, food safety, and zoonoses, but the central question is key for those proponents of regenerative grazing claiming it as a "cure for climate change."

Ultimately, along with many other researchers not directly funded by animal agriculture, they concluded that only under very specific conditions can grazing help sequester carbon, and even then it is small, time-limited, easily reversible, and substantially outweighed by the

GHG emissions these grazing animals generate. The maximum global potential (of carbon sequestered in these soils), in the most optimistic conditions and using the most generous of assumptions, would offset only "20%–60% of emissions from grazing cows, 4%–11% of total livestock emissions, and 0.6%–1.6% of total annual greenhouse gas emissions."[8] Let's put that into perspective. Right now, grazing livestock take up about 37% of all ice-free land.[9] All that land, in the best, most generous scientific estimates, will not even sequester 2% of total annual greenhouse gas emissions. On the other hand, protecting forests from being cleared for grazing, and allowing native grasslands to rewild, draws down significantly more carbon, some of which can stay in the soil or biomass for the long term.

Missing from much of the discussion about shifting to grass-fed cattle is methane, despite the fact that 50–75% of increased methane emission from 2003 to 2010 was due entirely to livestock.[10] Methane is an important consideration when discussing animals in confinement when compared to shifting cows to pasture. In the United States, transitioning animals to pastureland would increase their relative methane emissions by 43%, as grass-fed cows release more methane than grain-fed. Methane is also undervalued in how it's compared with CO_2 over 100 years, yet it is 84 times as potent in the first decade after it's emitted.[11] Methane goes into the atmosphere with a much stronger potency and dissipates fairly quickly compared to carbon dioxide. Most estimates of U.S. agriculture use the 100-year time frame for Global Warming Potential (GWP), instead of a more accurate 20-year timeframe. The IPCC recognizes the validity of shorter time horizons—there is no firm requirement or advantage to using the 100-year time horizon. The Intergovernmental Panel on Climate Change (IPCC) has stated: "There is no scientific argument for selecting 100 years compared with other choices (20 or 10). The choice of time horizon is a value judgement because it depends on the relative weight assigned to effects at different times."[12] Some climate scientists will claim putting a 20-year timeline on methane means you only want to address climate change for 20 years. That argument is made solely to try to avoid addressing agriculture when, in fact, if methane is addressed quickly, we will see results quickly (within a decade or two)—likely within a timeline needed to avoid critical feedback loops that could melt the permafrost and significantly ramp up climate disruption. Of course, we need to address CO_2 quickly as well, but what's emitted will still be in the atmosphere causing issues for 100 more years before we see effects. There is a significant benefit to focusing on reducing methane, and at least 37% is coming from animal agriculture.[13]

Shifting to a plant-based diet can free up significant land, not only reducing the amount of grazing land, but also freeing up vast square acres that are used to grow feed for farmed animals. Growing feed crops for farmed animals is an extremely inefficient process. Plant-based farming is already scalable to feed everyone, but the vast majority of crops are inefficiently fed to animals. For every 100 calories of grain fed to farmed animals, we only get 40 calories of milk, or 22 calories of eggs, or 12 calories of chicken, or 10 calories of pork, or 3 calories of beef. This is an extravagantly inefficient and wasteful way to feed the world.[14]

FARMED ANIMAL PLANET

When we think of what the Earth's land is used for, many think of big cities, industrialization, and perhaps some areas of wild nature. The reality is we live on a planet dominated by farmland, primarily for raising animals for consumption. This is despite the vast majority of farmed animals being in miserable, indoor, confined spaces, out of sight.

Ten thousand years ago, the biomass of land vertebrates was broken down as 1% humans and 99% wild animals. Today it's 1% wild animals, 67% livestock, and 32% humans.[15] It was the agricultural revolution that shaped how our planet looks today—a deforested, colonized, urbanized, human and farmed animal dominated mess. Forests cover around one third of the Earth's land mass and are the most biologically diverse ecosystems on land, home to over 80% of animal, plant, and insect species. Yet they have been largely cut down to feed our addiction to meat, dairy, and eggs, and even more is destroyed every day to graze more animals under a disguise of sustainable shifts to humane meat.

Many vital ecosystems are threatened by animal agriculture, and this industry is in fact the leading cause in the reduction of biodiversity, which is mostly from deforestation. Brazil's Cerrado area, the most biologically diverse savannah in the world, is deforested from the production of half of the country's soy crops that are grown to feed farmed animals. The diversity of wild species in the area is threatened by the rapid increase in animal feed production and the 40 million cows per year that this region produces.

Looking at the United States only, if the country were to completely shift to grazing cows on pasture, the U.S. beef production would require 63% to 270% *more land.*[16] Keep in mind, the animal farming industry already uses almost 50% of all continental land in the U.S. A shift to grass-fed beef, especially at current consumption levels, is biophysically impossible without mass deforestation.

Meanwhile, replacing beef with beans in the U.S. could free up 42% of U.S. cropland and significantly reduce GHG emissions, accomplishing 75% of the 2020 carbon reduction target.[17] Choice A: Replace beef with beans in the U.S. and free up to rewild at least 42% of U.S. land. Choice B: Graze all cows in the U.S. and use 63–270% more land, as well as increase methane emissions by 43%.[18]

Animal agriculture uses 35–45% of all ice-free land. What is the sequestration potential of this land better purposed as rewilded land, either as forest or vegetation? The ecologist William Ripple, who has studied this in detail, concludes: "In terms of short-term climate change mitigation during the next few decades, if all the land used for ruminant livestock production were instead converted to grow natural vegetation, increased CO_2 sequestration of 30–470% of the greenhouse gas emissions associated with food production could be expected."[19] In fact, 42% of pastureland globally used to be forest or woody savannas.[20] The carbon sequestration value and biodiversity benefits from land simply being rewilded and left for nature to restore is considerable and could possibly absorb enough CO_2 to turn the tide of the current climate disaster. Shifting to a global plant-based diet by 2050 could sequester 332–547 gigatons of CO_2 from the rewilded land—that's equivalent to 9–16 years of global CO_2 emissions.[21]

It's often said that three-quarters of agricultural land is marginal land, meaning it can't grow crops due to lack of rain and degraded or rocky soil. However, much of that land was made marginal due to poor grazing practices in the first place. A much better use of this supposedly subpar land is to rewild it with vegetation that sequesters carbon. There's no credible evidence that cows improve this land more so than allowing it to rewild. One will also find that forests do quite well on their own without human intervention, not requiring fertilizers or manure.

It is true that not every acre of land currently used for grazing animals, which ranges from 26 to 45% of the ice-free land surface, can be used for plant farming. An assessment of this vast amount of land used for grazing farmed animals shows it uses 1.5 times more than all forested land, 2.8 times more than cropland, and 17 times more than urban settlements.[22] However, the percentage of this land that is actually suitable for crops is beside the point as only a small fraction of it is actually needed to feed the world with plants. Animal agriculture currently requires 83% of global agricultural land in order to return a mere 18% of human calories.[23] In the U.S. alone, 70% of grains, 70% of soy, and 60% of corn production is fed directly to farmed animals. There is ample fertile acreage available to feed everyone a plant-based diet in the U.S. The land that is "unsuitable" can be rewilded to help absorb carbon. In fact, growing food exclusively for direct human consumption could increase available food calories by as much as 70%, which could feed an additional four billion people.[24]

Case Study: Greenwashing Beef to Appear Climate Neutral

One of the animal farms put on a pedestal in the U.S. is White Oak Pastures (WOP) in Bluffton, Georgia. They commissioned a study by consultancy Quantis to show their claimed level of regenerative grazing perfection in 2019. Quantis released a report[25] showing how WOP cows have a 111% lower carbon footprint than conventionally farmed cows and how they stored more carbon than emitted in their lifetime. Quantis also released a report a few years ago "proving"[26] bottled water is environmentally friendly. Clearly, Quantis has no concern about accepting funding and finding the results that the paying customer wants, which in the case of the bottled water, was the hugely unethical and environmentally destructive company Nestlé. Quantis went beyond "proving" the environmental friendliness of bottled water to urging it be promoted in National Parks.[27] That should be enough to completely disregard any results from Quantis, but let's entertain it here.

Quantis concluded, "The WOP beef is potentially on-par or better than other non-beef protein sources with regard to its carbon footprint," but then clarified, "Within our margin of error, there is a potential that the WOP beef production is climate positive." This means using the right methods, as one would expect given the body of evidence on this matter, climate-positive cows emit more emissions than they help sequester into the ground. But WOP's website simply states, "White Oak Pastures is storing more carbon in its soil than its pasture-raised cows emit during their lifetime. . . . Shop Now: Carbon Negative Beef." This is blatant greenwashing. But let's look deeper. The Quantis report for WOP uses a 100-year timeframe for accounting for methane with no discussion of why it doesn't use a 20-year timeframe, which the IPCC has used. Keeping the time horizon at their 100 years versus 20 years decreases the potency of methane by about 2.5 times, which makes it easy to show that their impacts on climate change are not as bad. The report also does not account for the carbon absorption potential of their land if it was transitioned to forests or rewilded. It only compares to conventional forms of grazing. Overall, for a true and very basic environmental assessment, an acre of land is only as good as its alternative uses. This is a key strategy used by regenerative grazing proponents. They appear to have positive outcomes because their tactic is to compare it with vastly worse forms of grazing animals instead of rewilding the land—the far better option every time.

The Quantis report on White Oak Pastures has since been peer reviewed.[28] The results showed this style of farming at White Oak Pastures actually uses 2.5 times *more land* and is not carbon neutral at all. This is despite their attempts to build carbon in the soil by bringing in feed not grown on their farm and cycling it through animals, cherry picking estimates on the land to favor results that could show grazing methods were the reasons for land sequestration, when there were many other land management actions—inputting compost, using cover crops, growing lentils for nitrogen fixing in the soil—that were the real reason for land improvements. This goes to show, even in the most generous situations, with funded bias and creative accounting, so-called sustainable meat is just a hoax and a distraction designed to help people feel better about their bad habits.

To understand what White Oak Pastures is trying to be, it's important to understand where the ideas come from. They are in fact considered the preeminent example for the work of Allan Savory. Savory became famous for his TED Talk, "How to Fight Desertification and Reverse Climate Change."[29] According to the Savory Institute, Holistic Grazing Management (HGM) is a process of decision-making and planning that gives people the insights and management tools needed to understand nature, resulting in better, more informed decisions that balance key social, environmental, and financial considerations. They claim peer-reviewed science *cannot determine* if their methods in fact work. Experimental validation, they say of course, offers the best process for evaluating whether holistic management works. This alone should throw up red flags. Savory reveals himself with this quip he offered to a journalist for *Range* magazine, which profiled him in 1999, "You'll find the scientific method never discovers anything." His claims that his grazing methods reverse climate change have been thoroughly debunked, repeatedly:

1. Savory's claim of sequestration rate of 2.5 tons of carbon, per hectare, per year, is substantially higher than all other peer-reviewed estimates for pastureland.

2. The amount of grassland to which this is applied—5 billion hectares, according to Savory—is considerably greater than most estimates of the area of global defined grasslands that can even loosely be described as grazing lands. The Intergovernmental Panel on Climate Change, in a report on land use,[30] considers global grasslands to be 3.5 billion hectares.

3. It is extremely unlikely that this constant high sequestration rate could be maintained for 40 years since the rate of accrual diminishes over time as soils approach carbon equilibrium.

4. Last, Savory does not consider the significant increases in methane and nitrous oxide that would result from higher herd numbers to maintain supply.[31]

Any possible gains in soil health or carbon sequestration on pastureland are likely to be modest, are not exclusive to rotational practices, and will be time limited—and the problems of the other greenhouse gases, methane, and nitrous oxide, as well as using far more land for far fewer animals, do not go away. Contrary to what Savory and others say, it's not just about *how* we farm. The issue first lies more in *what*, or rather *who*, we farm. Only focusing on how, as someone who does environmental assessment, is like saying how we drive (perhaps slower to use less gas) is better than not driving at all or riding a bicycle.

So, what's the solution? We can restore three billion hectares of land by shifting to plant-based eating. What does that number represent? That's equivalent to all of Africa, or all of the Americas! Forty-two percent of grazing land used to be forests, and if we can return the original forests on that land, the carbon storage would increase by 265 gigatons from its present value.[32]

Transformation: Incentivizing the Switch to Plant Production and Conservation
I mentioned earlier about the Cerrado, a tropical savanna in Brazil with huge ecological importance. The region's soil, deep roots, and trees store around 13.7 billion tons of CO_2—that's more than China's annual emissions.[33] This region is under constant threat as a world leader of soy feed crops for farmed animals mostly in China and Europe. While halting this deforestation is complicated, since landholders there can deforest up to 80% of their land for agriculture, there are still some obvious solutions. Rewarding carbon storage and providing biodiversity credits for landowners is key. But lobby groups' and livestock industry's subsidies incentivize growing feed crops and make it more profitable than keeping a rainforest intact. Global cooperation is needed to incentivize landowners to conserve their forests, rewild, or transition to growing food for humans directly.

Another possibility is switching from raising chickens to growing hemp. That's exactly what Mike Weaver is doing after some help from the group Transfarmation.[34] Weaver is part of Mercy for Animals' new Transformation Project, which helps farm owners transition from animal husbandry to growing sustainable crops for plant-based products. He's now using his old chicken barns to grow industrial hemp, which removes more CO_2 per acre than many other crops. This will also earn him a greater income and employ four times as many people as chicken farming did. One ton of harvested hemp fiber sequesters 1.62 tons of CO_2, and every part of the plant is used. The seeds become healthy food and the stalks are useful for eco-building materials. Hemp naturally regenerates the soil it grows in and is one of the most sustainable crops. Hemp can also be grown almost anywhere, requires relatively low inputs of fertilizer, herbicides, or pesticides, and needs little water, land, and maintenance.

There's also the Rancher's Advocacy Program (RAP)[35] that has helped countless ranchers and animal farmers switch to more sustainable plant farming. Former chicken and cow farmers Jennifer and Rodney Barrett are becoming mushroom farmers. While the reasons behind these changes are varied, including the economics, ethics, and environment, there is no doubt that this is a trend that will continue as the climate and biodiversity crisis worsens. It's time for government groups across the world to collaborate and support farmers and landowners to be part of the solution, creating subsidies and incentives to encourage these critical transitions.

With every acre of land used to grass-feed a cow, as well as the acre next to her that is likely used to grow corn, sorghum, or soybeans to supplement her feed, we could grow ancient grains, beans, green leafy vegetables, fruit, nuts, and provide thousands more pounds of food per acre, without having to take her life. The 2021 United Nations Food Systems Summit and groups like Eat-Lancet are working on the awareness and urgency for governmental support and global cooperation to encourage plant-rich diets. The goal is to create a Paris Agreement for food, and to set achievable and practical goals for a global food system shift towards more plant-based and sustainable diets.

Veganic Agriculture: The Truly Regenerative Farming

While it is well documented that natural ecosystems will almost always store more carbon than agricultural land, a quiet but growing trend of stock-free—otherwise known as veganic farming—can protect and restore land and offer a prosperous economic future for farmers and regions alike.

Veganic farming (or vegan organic farming) is broadly defined as the organic cultivation and production of food crops focusing on a minimal amount of harm or exploitation to any animal. This method avoids the common inputs of pesticides, livestock manure, the use of blood meal, bone meal, fish meal, feather meal, and slaughterhouse by-products that are regularly utilized for fertilizer even in organic crop systems.

Instead of implementing monocultures, veganic farming employs polyculture techniques using a variety of plants in the same area to coexist and work with one another. The vast majority of veganic farming uses no-till practices to avoid disturbing what carbon may be stored in the soil, as well as companion planting to maintain garden insect balance to avoid the need for pesticides.

Sustainability and soil regeneration is at the heart of veganic farming. It can include some or all of these methods of soil fertility maintenance including green manure, vegetable compost, crop rotation, and mulching. It also may include hay mulch, wood ash, or composted organic matter like grass clippings, seaweed, comfrey liquid, or nettles. Of note, stock-free farms use identical practices as veganic farms, although usually used when it's mainly an economic versus ethical motivation.

Veganic farming is not new; farming specifically without domesticated animal inputs dates back centuries. The biggest issue with veganic farming is the lack of awareness and communication around this highly sustainable form of food production. New certifications for farms like the accredited Biocyclical Vegan Standard[36] are helping to raise awareness of the benefits of this form of cultivation. In addition, this program participates in research projects on humus accumulation and sustainable soil fertility increase through the use of biocyclic humus soil on a purely plant-based basis.

Johannes Eisenbach, who is a farmer and expert in soil building with the Biocyclical Vegan Standard in Europe, is working with farmers to help build high quality humus soil through compost methods, free of any animal inputs. This group is working with farmers, grocers, and food brands to use this new Biocyclic Vegan label as a gold standard to highlight the most sustainable plant farming methods.

There are some barriers to being able to scale up from this style of farming to meet the world's food demands of today. Most importantly, we would need a network of local compost facilities that produces and collects plant-based raw materials. But the benefits would be huge. We would no longer rely on nitrous oxide emitting manure or synthetic fertilizers, or at least not to the massive level currently used. A great place to start would be our major food waste problem, which has been identified as one of the top five issues that must be addressed to reverse global warming.[37] We could repurpose food waste for industrial compost systems and feed two birds with one hand.

At this stage of the environmental crisis, we're past the point of having the luxury of small incremental changes. Rewilding and sustainable plant-based production systems are clear solutions that address many root problems. There are cultural and social barriers to change, but there's no sense in preserving traditions that result in countless ethical atrocities and an uninhabitable planet. We need a movement that values coexistence with nature and respect for land and the wildlife on it. To spark a movement to rewild the world, and address both the climate and biodiversity crises, we must shift away from animal agriculture and transition to global plant-based food system.

Nicholas Carter has a Master's in Environmental Practice and is a freelance writer, researcher, consultant, and co-founder of PlantBasedData.org. He focuses on the scientific links between agriculture and planetary health. His Master's thesis analyzes the various estimates of greenhouse gas emissions attributed to animal agriculture. Carter's writing and research have been featured in *The New Republic*, *Plant Based News*, *Sentient Media*, *Forbes*, *Maclean's*, and *Planet Friendly News*. Transitioning to plant-based farming systems has also been a focus where he's written about sustainable farming practices with A Well-Fed World and others.

9

NEW AND IMPROVED?

Deconstructing the Narrative of So-Called Better Meat

by Robert Grillo

When I discovered food activist Diana Rodgers and her film project, *Sacred Cow*,[1] I quickly realized I had stumbled upon yet another iteration of the all-too-familiar "better meat" story that is resonating with a growing consumer base interested in sustainability and animal welfare. While *Sacred Cow* may represent one of the latest variations on the theme, the ideas expressed here borrow heavily from the 2008 documentary, *Food, Inc.*, featuring key protagonists Joel Salatin and Michael Pollan. Rodger's film affirms that the "better meat" movement is alive and well, which makes it all the more important to understand and evaluate the story lines and branding of this increasingly popular cultural phenomenon and identify the fictions that drive it.

Like Ms. Rodgers, I too have a history of work in food marketing, which included major food brands like McDonald's and Kraft Foods. This experience gave me a behind-the-scenes perspective on how marketers sell not only products, but ideas. This "better meat" story has become all too predictable to me. My book, *Farm to Fable: The Fictions of Our Animal Consuming Culture*, is, in part, an exposé of how corporate food brands impact our culture and food choices.

Beyond our shared experience in marketing, she and I also share concerns with most "better meat" advocates about food justice, the plight of farm workers, food sustainability, and the corporate consolidation of our food system. In this sense, we both conscientiously object to our current highly centralized and industrialized food system. However, while her advocacy precludes the possibility of animals as anything other than commodities, mine includes a genuine empathy and respect for the sentience of all animals, farmed and wild, which rejects the idea of animals as a resource for humans to use in any way. Such empathy is fundamentally lacking in any ideology that regards animals as commodities—as simply "meat."

Any "humane" rhetoric will always obscure a lack of understanding that animals' consciousness and sentience is sufficient to deserve lives free of victimization and violation for profit. Without empathy, the "better meat" argument fails to adequately address their professed concerns for humans, nonhumans, and the planet. We need only to look at the intentional fires ravaging the Amazon to see that the industry that profits from the exploiting and killing of animals is also destroying Indigenous people and their land, wildlife, and whole ecosystems to make way for cattle grazing and the growing of soy and corn to feed farmed animals, thus contributing to the growing climate emergency.

Necessity as Moral Neutralizer

As much as its proponents seek to differentiate "better meat" from "factory farming," the foundation of the argument for "better meat" is strikingly similar to its corporate farming counterpart. Both arguments are rooted in the mistaken premise that animal agriculture is a foregone conclusion and proceed from there. As Rogers has claimed in an interview, "In order to have a truly sustainable food system, we absolutely need to have well-managed animals in the mix." But is this adamant claim of necessity true? Even if we assume for the sake of argument that it is true, it does not justify the exploiting, killing, and eating of animals merely because they are needed for, say, grazing and manure. We could just let them live and graze. And yet that is exactly the ethical leap that "better meat" asserts, claiming that our only obligation to these animals is to treat them with a modicum of "respect" during the short time we allow them to stay alive and, the oft-repeated, to "honor the life" that was taken by not wasting any of their body parts.

As I stress in my book *Farm to Fable*, making the case for necessity is of central importance to the defense of animal agriculture in all its manifestations, whether large corporate entities or small farms. If true, *necessity* might be the one credible defense for an industry that exploits and kills farmed animals for profit. It is, however, not true, as evidenced by the millions of people who are thriving on a vegan diet. Farmed animals are not the only victims in this paradigm of "necessity." The more land given over to grazing, the greater the number of wild creatures who are displaced, forced from their habitats, or brutally trapped, gunned down, and bludgeoned to death. In fact, the powerful ranching and farming industries successfully lobby our government to brutally exterminate tens of millions of wild animals every year. None are safe, be they wild horses and donkeys who are "competing" for grazing land and water, or predators such as wolves and foxes who are a threat to livestock. This taxpayer expense is in addition to the billions of dollars of tax-funded subsidies and bailouts that farmers and ranchers also receive.

FARMED ANIMALS AS PROXIES AND SAVIORS?

Some argue that "well managed animals in the mix" are not only a necessity for a sustainable food system, but essential to the very survival of the planet. Alan Savory, for example, who has inspired many farmers in the "better meat" movement, predicts dire consequences for humanity and the planet if we don't quickly adopt "holistic management and grazing" methods. The paradox implied in this approach has raised much skepticism of Savory's big assertion.

A recent report by *Vox* describes an attempt at a "holistic grazing strategy," where artificially bred bison, raised and slaughtered for profit, are used as grazing "proxies" for their indigenous counterparts who once roamed ancient grasslands before being hunted to extinction or forced from their habitat in the name of ranching. While this effort may include some genuine interest in ecosystem restoration, it does not acknowledge the role of the animals as an integral part of the system; these bison are not allowed to live out the whole of their natural lifespan or to die of natural causes, as they will be killed in a fraction of their lifespan for buffalo burgers.

Here we see animal exploitation inserting itself into the conflicting goals of restoring ecosystems to what they were prior to their destruction caused, in large part, by previous eras of animal domestication, hunting, and trapping. Ironically, such *conservation* serves our interest in continuing to consume animals.

But if farmed animals are *not* necessary, then the asserted ethical basis for "better meat" loses its footing. What remains are appeals to culture, nature, and tradition—appeals that historically have been used time and time again to justify all forms of oppression, of humans as well as of animals.

Today we see innovations in agriculture that are proving how unnecessary and obsolete the farming of animals is becoming,[2] including greenhouse agriculture[3] (successfully established in cold and hot climates not previously suitable for growing crops), no-till cultivation, green manure (plant compost in place of animal manure and other animal by-products), the replacement of harmful pesticides and other methods that reduce the impact on the land, animals, and ecosystems.

Beyond "Necessity"

"Better meat" advocates often call for truth, facts, transparency, and authenticity, which appeals to people who want to know more about "where our food comes from." Their consideration of the farmed animals, however, never actually moves beyond that of resource or commodity, which has allowed for the exploitation of animals by humans for millennia. Instead of arriving at some new-found respect and recognition of the animals they affectionately fondle in promotional photos and videos, they ultimately betray their own empathy, as well as the very bodies of those animals. The act of reducing the living animal to a slab of meat is the ultimate symbol of the exploiter's dominance and objectification of the victim. A victim of sexual assault might describe being treated like a "piece of meat," and "red meat" is often used to describe, metaphorically, someone vulnerable to attack.

Yet the "better meat" worldview willfully denies the intersectional nature of oppression as it crosses the human–nonhuman species divide, and affirms its speciesist and rigid categorizations of "pet," "food," "game," etc. "Better meat" euphemisms, with such expressions as "well managed," "humanely raised," "responsibly raised," "harvested," and "processed" simply reinforce the idea of farmed animals as mere commodities and do not allow for a shift to the acknowledgement of animals from that of objects to sentient beings.

Faulty Foundation: The Fictions

The unavoidable flaw in their logic is the double standard. If the conditions that proponents of "better meat" are advocating for farmed animals were applied to the species we call companion animals, it would be considered torture and abuse, and in some states and counties, be criminally punishable.

This leads us to unpack a host of other fictions, beyond the fiction of "necessity," that are commonly featured in "better meat" branding.

Fiction 1: There's a big difference between factory farmed meat and better-raised meat.

There are at least three issues to look at in this statement. The first is the nature of the two things being compared. The second is how such a comparison reflects a shallow view of the complexity of nonhuman animal consciousness and suffering. And the third deals with the buzzword itself, *factory farming.*

As mentioned earlier, "better meat" advocates typically compare their model against the worst-case scenario, industrial farming, knowing full well that anything looks better in such a comparison. A more honest, apples-to-apples comparison would be between two systems that share common sustainability goals, such as rebuilding soil, carbon sequestration, and reducing overall environmental impact—for example, comparing the "better meat" solution and the veganic farming of plant foods discussed earlier.

Aside from the comparison itself, is the difference really that significant? Yes, "better meat" animals typically spend a short time on pasture (which, arguably, is not necessarily "better," as it can leave defenseless domesticated animals unprotected from wild predators and extreme weather), yet the fundamental circumstances of their lives remain largely the same. The focus on "treatment" alone conveniently ignores the many other forms of suffering that result from being used as a commodity, regardless of the level of treatment even in the "best-case scenario." Other key areas of suffering to consider are:

The suffering of breeding. All domesticated farmed animals have been subject to intensive breeding and biological manipulation to "optimize" their muscle tissue growth and milk, egg, or wool production. This has taken a heavy toll on their bodies, resulting in frail bones, painful abnormalities, susceptibility to disease, and premature death. Weak, sickly, or injured animals are considered a liability and, therefore, not only given no medical care but are instead taken out of production and either sent to slaughter or simply left to dehydrate, starve, and die.

The suffering of commodification. Until very recently, we have failed to recognize that *use* is indeed a form of abuse. Being used as a resource against their will for someone else's gain causes great physical and psychological suffering to animals who clearly demonstrate their desire to live freely, and who resist being dominated and denied the ability to express their essential interests and preferences. Any type of farming requires that animals be stripped of their freedom, denied their agency, and subjugated to the will of their owners.

The suffering of dependence. We often hear farmers claim that *animals don't mind, are not aware, or don't care what happens to them.* But the whole point of the process of domestication has been to mold animal bodies and minds into this state of subservience, dependence, defenselessness, and vulnerability. The farmed animal today is the result of thousands of years of systematic capture, confinement, domination, and intensive breeding for traits that make them docile and less resistant to being used and treated as a piece of property. As a result, like human children, they are completely reliant on us for food, water, and protection. We cannot underestimate the psychological effects this has on them.

Peaceful Prairie Sanctuary describes it best in its brochure by pointing out that we dictate:

where they will live;

if they will ever know their mothers;

if, and how long, they will nurse their babies;

when, and if, they will be permitted to see or be with their families and friends;

when, where, or if they will be allowed to socialize with members of their own species;

when, how, and if, they are going to reproduce;

what, when, and how much they will eat;

how much space they will have, if any;

if, and how far, they will be allowed to roam;

what mutilations they will be subjected to;

what, if any, veterinary care they will receive;

and when, where, and how they are going to die,

Finally, what does the phrase "factory farming" actually mean, if anything? If we look beyond the buzzword, we find that a factory model of animal production is as old as civilization itself. For example, most people would agree that an operation that can artificially incubate and hatch thousands of chicken eggs into chicks per day most certainly qualifies as a factory farm, yet we can travel over three thousand years back in time to ancient Egypt to find these practices, where some of the first high-production artificial incubators were developed. Use of the term factory farming—which refers to the mass concentration of animals in an assembly-line environment (and all the horrors that go along with it)—falsely suggests that some viable alternative exists. The truth is that all commercial farming qualifies as factory farming based on an ancient production model of using animals as resources, with total control over their reproduction, the stealing and trafficking of their offspring, standard bodily mutilations that are both physically and psychologically traumatizing, destruction of their families and social order, intensive biological manipulation and selective breeding, and of course the systematic slaughter in their infancy or adolescence.

All the above are necessary in any kind of farming to render their flesh and secretions into products of consumption.

Fiction 2: It's completely unrealistic that everyone will give up meat, so vegans should instead join the fight for better meat.

Putting aside the caricature of "realistic vegans" advocating for "better meat," I question this appeal to practicality, i.e., that it is more realistic for their niche market flesh to become the staple that feeds the masses, rather than inexpensive yet highly nutritious vegan options like lentils, grains, and beans. Their claim that as demand increases, prices will drop, is also erroneous. According to Dave Simon, author of *Meatonomics*, "grass-fed and pasture-raised are both dependent on using costly and shrinking real estate, rather than technology, so I would expect prices to go up with increased demand." What is *truly* unrealistic is the notion that the grass-fed system could be described as sustainable on a scale required to drive prices down to a level that could be even remotely affordable to the vast majority of consumers.

Equally baffling is the suggestion that "better meat" is a more nutritionally sensible choice than nutrient-dense plant foods for those of limited means, especially in cases where one cannot afford both. The world's Indigenous populations have consumed a diet of mostly grains, legumes, and vegetables because that has historically been their only affordable option. The idea that vegans should favor better meat advocacy over more affordable and nutritious plant foods shows just how out-of-touch this idea is from the class and economic realities of Main Street America.

Finally, the belief that not everyone is going to adopt a certain practice means we should abandon it for something more "realistic" is misguided, especially when the proposed "better meat" solution isn't remotely realistic. Furthermore, the fact that the vegan population in the U.S. has risen dramatically over the last few years surely has more to do with promoting veganism, rather than meat. Misrepresenting veganism with the outdated labels of "utopian" and "remote" reinforces the belief that it is more complicated than a simple act of reaching for one product over another on the store shelf. Veganism is as accessible in practice as it is in principle—a rejection of animal exploitation—for the same reasons that we reject human exploitation, which has no more to do with purity or perfection than does the same rejection of any oppression.

Fiction 3: I believe that it's wrong to impose moral choices on others.

It is impossible to impose or force someone to accept an idea, moral or otherwise, simply by advocating for it. "Better meat" proponents advocate for one position, while vegans simply take the position that the world would be a better place with less violence and suffering, that it is *better* to not abuse our power over others, *better* to choose to spare an animal the fate of being born for the sole purpose of being subjected as a youth to a violent death—because we can. And vegans argue that this represents a *better* choice—a choice consistent with our already existing beliefs in harm reduction—than the choice of so-called "better meat."

Another inconsistency in the "better meat" view is in its advice of not *imposing* moral choices, as they often advise people to stop eating so much industrially produced chicken. As a chicken rescuer, I fully understand the gravity of the immense suffering of birds, but it seems arbitrary of them to single out vegans as "pushing or imposing their views" as they readily dole out advice on what to eat as well.

It's also worth noting that activists for other causes are never dismissed as "pushing their views" when they are simply working toward their goals and demands for human rights issues or a livable planet. Encouraging eating vegan foods to avoid animal exploitation and environmental degradation from animal agriculture is not urging personal choices, but inspiring ethical imperatives.

Fiction 4: There are a lot of ethical dilemmas in the plant food industry too.

Some plant crops are particularly destructive to rainforests, Indigenous communities and other native species, as well as exploitive of slave and child labor. In discussions of veganism and animal rights, some people justifiably point to coffee, bananas, palm oil, and chocolate as being among the most unethical crops. The problem with this critique is that it often singles out vegans,[4] as if only vegans—and all vegans—are responsible for the existence of these products.

First, it's important to point out that none of these crops are essential for human nutrition or for which there are no satisfying substitutes. Nonetheless, it is fair to challenge vegans—and everyone else for that matter—to consider the harms caused to marginalized communities, workers, and wildlife in crop farming. It is also important to point out the efforts of veganic agriculture[5] to minimize all of these harms through greenhouse agriculture,[6] no-till cultivation, green manure (in place of animal manure and other animal by-products), the replacement of harmful pesticides, and other methods that reduce the impact on the land, animals, and ecosystems. I will note here that vegans, being aware of unjust food issues, are often vocal proponents of these reforms. The bottom line is that an ethical vegan seeks to reduce harm wherever possible and practical, but never claims to rise to the impossible standard of perfection. Those who dismiss veganism in such a manner are invoking the perfection fallacy.

Second, it is a false equivalence to conclude that the impact of vegans—even vegans who occasionally consume cashews, bananas, coffee and chocolate—is the same as the impact of those who regularly consume a combination of animal products and these ethically problematic plant crops. Consider the following statistics to fully appreciate the impacts of eating animals:

70% of food related greenhouse gases (GHGs) come from animal products.[7] Animal agriculture produces more GHGs than all global transportation combined.[8] Swapping beef with beans could have helped the U.S. meet more than 50% of its emissions goals by the year 2020.[9] "Beef contributes 34 times more climate pollution than legumes like beans and lentils, pound for pound."[10]

We feed about half the world's edible grain crop to farmed animals.[11] It takes thirteen pounds of grain to yield just one pound of beef.[12] Soy and lentils produce, pound for pound, as much protein as beef, and sometimes more.[13] Raising animals is the number one cause of global deforestation.[14] Humans consume only about 6% of global soy, while farmed animals are fed 70%.[15] "Livestock systems occupy 45% of the global surface area," according to International Livestock Research Institute.[16] One acre of land yields 12 to 20 times more plant food than animal food.[17] If U.S. farmers took all the land currently devoted to raising animals and used it to grow plants instead, they could sustain more than twice as many people as they do now.[18] Farmed animals use about one third of the planet's freshwater resources.[19]

Animal agriculture is the greatest driver of habitat loss globally and the leading cause of species extinction and ocean dead zones.[20] Meat, dairy, and egg operations overproduce and then dump millions of pounds of animal products every year as our government bails them out with 63% of all farm subsidies.[21]

This is not to diminish the suffering of children in the chocolate industry or the impact of coffee plantations on the rainforest, but we can have the greatest positive impact by going vegan. And once vegan, our sensitivity to issues around food increase and there is a whole host of other concerns to consider and confront, such as these problematic plant crops. The act of going vegan opens us up to unraveling the layers of deception and misinformation that blind us to the harms we are causing this planet, and veganism often leads us on a journey that does not just end with replacing animal products. As vegan pioneer Donald Watson articulated many decades ago, the journey is about exploring what is "possible and the practical" in reducing harm in the world.

Fiction 5: Plants are sentient too. Plants are capable of complex communication.

Both Michael Pollan and Joel Salatin have helped popularize the theory that vegans and vegetarians are hypocritical in ignoring the *feelings* of plants. They do this by half-hearted attempts at blurring the distinctions between plants and animals, and therefore confusing the important ethical considerations we make for sentient beings. While sentience may exist on a spectrum, the fact that we may not all agree on exactly where to draw the line does not in any way prevent us from acting on what we already know with absolute certainty. For example, we know that all the animal species we exploit for food are highly sentient, possess advanced cognitive abilities, and have the self-awareness of being an individual with specific roles within a complex social group.

To his credit, Pollan's observations on plant behavior are interesting in their own right,[22] yet the conclusions he draws from them often conflate plant responses to environmental factors with sentience. One example is his article in *The New York Times*, about which Pollan himself tweeted, "Cool piece on how pea plants communicate with one another, possibly raising some tough issues for vegetarians. . . ." One of Pollan's critics, Adam Merberg, who shares a faculty position at UC Berkeley with Pollan, points out in his blog that Pollan's argument for consistency would make sense only if he didn't eat plants—an argument, he writes, "that has nothing to do with whether the person making the argument cares about plants or animals, and everything to do with proving that an argument fails to meet its own standards of consistency."[23]

Aside from the Pollanesque plant defense arguments, there is a commonsense reason why we don't hesitate to walk our dogs in the park on the grass (without giving the grass a second thought), yet if someone were to intentionally step on our dog's paw on that walk, we would find this morally objectionable. Similarly, the animals we exploit for food clearly and regularly demonstrate that they are highly sentient, emotionally complex individuals who are aware of and value their individual lives. Sentient beings have self-awareness and, on the most fundamental level, an interest in avoiding pain, suffering, and death.

Plants, not animals, are the foundation of our diet and our survival. Raising animals for food requires vastly greater amounts of plant and crop production to feed those animals than crops produced for direct human consumption, so *more* plants are "killed" for a diet including animal foods. For this reason alone, the principle of harm reduction that "plant advocates" are using would compel us to eat a plant-based diet. While none of us can live completely cruelty-free, the notion that everything we eat, whether of plant or animal origin, has the same moral weight is ethically dishonest.

Fiction 6: Eating animals is a personal choice.

The important keyword here is "personal." When we personalize something, we typically seek to shield it from public scrutiny. The subject of eating animals was never characterized as personal until vegans at the table made food choices a matter of public discourse and consequence. Personalization is the meat-eater's reaction to being *outed* publicly and an attempt to divorce ethics from food choices, thereby denying the fact that someone suffered as a result of such choices. For all their insistence that their choice to eat animals must be respected and unfettered, the choice to eat other animals ironically annihilates choice and free will for others—those other animals—who were also designed by nature to be free agents like ourselves. The unavoidable truth is that eating animals is the choice to dominate, violate, and kill them against their will. It is also a choice to betray our empathy.

Fiction 7: The farming of plants is not inherently better, nor does it cause less harm than animal production.

This statement is false for four important reasons.

1. Staple crops are necessary for human health and survival. We can live without consuming animal products, but we will become malnourished without the nutrients we get from plants.

2. Intention is a critical factor by which we evaluate the morality of an action or behavior. If killing certain animals in the process of raising necessary staple crops is morally objectionable, then our accountability for their deaths certainly cannot be rectified by breeding even more animals into existence for the sole purpose of exploiting, slaughtering, and profiting from their carcasses.

3. It is factually wrong. Common sense alone tells us that growing plant crops to feed millions of animals raised for human consumption has a greater impact than raising crops for direct human consumption. Even if, instead, we allow animals to graze on grasses, this method wastes even more land, water, and other resources and therefore can only serve a wealthy niche market.[24]

4. We have evidence of the "harm footprint" of various foods. An Animals Visual study shows the number of wild and domestic animals killed directly by slaughter, as well as through crop harvesting, in order to produce one million food calories from eight different categories of food.[25] One million calories of beef kills 29 animals, while the equivalent calories of vegetable and grain crops kill between 2.5 and 1.7 animals.[26]

Fiction 8: Everything eats and is eaten.

When someone says, "Everything eats and is eaten," they seem to be implying a conclusion that goes something like, "Therefore, eating animals is justified because it's natural." But there are many common, natural behaviors we see in both domestic animals and wildlife that we would find immoral and offensive to engage in ourselves based on modern societal standards. We would never attempt to justify them by citing how other species regularly engage in them. The fact that males of various species often sexually force themselves on females who clearly seek to escape such assaults is one example. We don't point to this biologically *natural* behavior in other species as a moral defense for rape in our own species. And yet, when it is convenient for our argument, some use this exact logic when they suggest that eating animals is okay because "everything eats and is eaten," or "animals eat other animals, so why shouldn't we?"

"Everything eats and is eaten" is also an inaccurate statement. Yes "everyone eats," but not everyone eats other sentient beings. In fact, only about 10% of all animals are actually carnivorous[27] and many of these are scavengers, which feed on decomposing corpses. Most animals are omnivores and herbivores. Then there are parasites and other non-sentient life forms that feed on decaying animal and plant matter. Does the fact that parasites eat decaying animals mean we should eat roadkill?

The worst suggestion in "Everyone eats and is eaten" is that we are somehow biologically predetermined to eat animals and therefore abandon any moral consideration for our actions. It suggests we should ignore two important factors that determine the morality of any action: necessity and intention. Yet only true carnivores kill and eat animals out of a necessity to survive, while we consume animals unnecessarily. We have the power to choose to inflict suffering and death or spare both. When we knowingly choose to inflict suffering on someone for the pleasure we derive from it, this is not just unnecessary, it is a betrayal of our belief in harm reduction and our basic morality of compassion.

Some of these very same "excusitarians" identify as "animal lovers." They would witness an individual animal being harmed in a public space and condemn the act and may even intervene to stop the abuser. Yet when we pay others to systematically harm animals on a mass scale, confined to windowless slaughterhouses, it suddenly becomes grounds for celebrating and fetishizing the taste of their body parts.

"Everything eats and is eaten" conflates human omnivores with the likes of obligate carnivores or even obligate omnivores who kill and eat other wild, free-roaming animals out of necessity, while we go about artificially breeding, raising, and killing herbivorous animals trapped in confinement who we have intentionally bred to be submissive and defenseless against us. In short, we've created a rigged game stacked against the victims in which we claim a hollow victory.

Fiction 9: We should use the whole animal and buy directly from a farmer.
It will also help consumers honor the life that was killed for their nourishment.
The idea that we can redeem ourselves from inflicting suffering and death on an animal by "honoring his life" has its roots in ancient herding and hunting cultures. Author and law professor Sherry Colb describes this as a ritual intended to absolve the guilt one feels for having caused another sentient being harm. "Indigenous people—like us—created ways of coping with their own violence against animals through rituals of denial. Some Indigenous hunters have given thanks to animals for gifts the animals never consented to bestow," writes Colb.[28]

The popular trope of using the whole animal is based on cherry-picking the animals we just so happen to find edible or exploitable according to the dictates of our culture. We do not concern ourselves with the bodies of almost all other animals that are defined as inedible, let alone consider it a "waste" not to use their bodies. But even if wasting were a genuine concern, we would never claim that using all the body parts honors other animals to whom we ascribe greater value. We don't honor the lives of our companion animals by eating them. And we are actually offended by human atrocities in which the perpetrators used many of the body parts of their victims: extracting gold fillings, making soap from fat tissue, and using brains and other organs in experiments. So how can it be that doing the same to other species delights us with honor? This ancient anthropomorphic myth that animals consented to sacrificing their well-being and life to the higher purpose of serving us is as pervasive today as ever.

Fiction 10: People should visit a well-managed farm or volunteer on a farm to better understand the role animals play in our food system.

People should *then* go visit a sanctuary so they can better understand the *important difference* between how the same animals regarded as resources on farms are valued as individuals in sanctuaries. One can learn a lot about animals from those who have devoted many years to cleaning up the mess that farmers and homesteaders leave behind, including all the unwanted and discarded offspring such as male dairy calves and other unmarketable beings who sanctuaries rescue and provide with forever homes. It can be transformative to get to know these animals as the individuals they truly are when they are given an opportunity to express themselves. This only happens when they are not under the pressure of producing something for us.

It is also transformative to visit a slaughterhouse or attend a vigil to get "up close and personal" with animals as they are trucked into slaughterhouses in the dead of the night, from all kinds of farms, who have endured hours upon hours of a grueling journey to their deaths. We see the complete despair of weeks-old chickens gasping for air and the terror of months-old piglets and cows who are forced to crouch in their own feces and denied water, food, and protection from the inclement weather.

CONCLUSION

In so many respects, the case for "better meat" is ironically neither *better* nor emboldened by any new or innovative assertions. It is more of a new-age rebranding of ancient myths with a persistent appeal to *necessity* at its core. The world, however, is becoming increasingly aware that animal products are not only unnecessary for our health and survival, but that our surviving a climate crisis and environmental collapse will necessarily rely on abandoning animal agriculture. Nevertheless, the "better meat" movement continues to push its own brand of "ethical" animal exploitation in the name of environmental stewardship. Beyond its softer, gentler facade lies the same patriarchal oppression of animals, nature, workers, and marginalized communities.

Under increasing pressure, "better meat" struggles against veganism. To retain its caring consumers by promising brands that will satisfy their conscience as much as their appetite, it at once seeks to address concerns and objections popularized by veganism while striving to divert the public discourse away from veganism. But in the end, the prospect of a better world through better meat is a fantasy. Like Dorothy pulling the curtain back to reveal the Wizard of Oz, we discover not an awesome supernatural power capable of fulfilling our fantasies, but rather a cowardly bully who shrivels at being caught in the act.

Robert Grillo is the founder and director of Free from Harm. As an activist, author, and speaker, Grillo draws insights from popular culture, sociology, psychology, ethics, and social justice to bridge the gap between humans and other animals. As a marketing communications professional for over 20 years, Grillo worked on large food industry accounts where he acquired a behind-the-scenes perspective on food branding and marketing. His book, *Farm to Fable: The Fictions of Our Animal-Consuming Culture*, exposes the many ways we have all been conditioned into a culture where mass animal consumption is the norm. Other published works include contributions to *Caged: Top Activists Share Their Wisdom on Effective Animal Advocacy* and *Circles of Compassion: Connecting Issues of Justice*.

10

A FOX GUARDING THE HENHOUSE

Can Animal Agriculture Reform Itself?

by Matthew Chalmers

Twin crises are engendered by animal agriculture: a moral crisis of cruelty and an environmental crisis that endangers the entire planet.

Let's examine these crises. The Humane League U.K. ran a campaign in 2018 called One in a Billion.[1] It follows the life of Frank, a chicken raised for meat. He is one of the billions of chickens slaughtered in the U.K. each year, or nine billion in the U.S. He begins his life as a single yellow fluff ball in a vast dark shed. As he begins to develop, pain permeates his frame. His genes have been engineered in such a way that his body grows at an alarming rate. His breast muscles bulge and his body grows to be unnaturally heavy. Struggling to walk, he is unable to explore the crowded barn where thousands of others like him totter about restlessly. He may be stricken with lameness, green muscle disease, wooden breast syndrome, or sudden death syndrome.[2] All of these are about as unpleasant as they sound for these energetic and curious creatures, whose complex hierarchies and wide range of natural behaviors remain distorted, frustrated, and unfulfilled amidst the chaos of animal farming. Each bird is an individual, with a distinct personality; each one is mutilated by painful procedures like debeaking,[3] each one ends up electrocuted, gassed, their throats slit when they are just a few weeks old. Across the world, six and a half thousand of these sentient beings are killed *every second*.

It is the same story with pigs, whose tails, testicles, and teeth are yanked out without anesthetic; with cows who scream when they are burned with a branding iron or when their calves are taken away; and with fish whose sensitivity to pressure makes for an agonizing death, crushed and suffocated on boat decks. The intensity and scope of the suffering is simply unimaginable.

Most people love and cherish animals; it is up to us to choose consistency in our behavior, to notice that when lambs run and frolic, they look just like puppies. There is nothing that distinguishes the moral worth of one such creature from another, apart from arbitrary roles society has assigned them, one destined for friendship, the other destined for dinner.

The moral crisis is not limited to the rest of the animal kingdom. Humans involved in animal agriculture are rarely, if ever, the better for it. Slaughterhouse work is one of the physically harshest and most emotionally destructive jobs on the planet.[4]

Most slaughterhouse workers have no other employment options; many have served time in the judicial system or are undocumented migrant laborers who cannot find other employment. Doing this job involves the supervision, killing, and butchering of thousands of living animals who moan, fight, cry out, and even try to befriend their killers. It is toxic for the human mind. Take this example from a BBC feature on a former slaughterhouse worker.[5] Of all the vicious acts and hushed up cruelties she witnessed at her stint in the abattoir, the image that stuck with her most vividly, forever tattooed on her mind, is that of a pile of bloody cow skulls, stripped bare of their flesh but with their still-intact eyes staring helplessly at her under long wet lashes. Another first-hand account comes from Josh Agland, an Australian slaughterhouse worker–turned–vegan activist, who testified that he witnessed a collapsed cow left on the kill floor overnight before being killed the next morning. She was pregnant; her baby was cut out of her body. He says the hide-pulling machine still gives him nightmares.[6]

The data supports these anecdotes. A 2009 study found that abattoir employment coincides with spiking rates of violent and sexual crime.[7] Drug and alcohol abuse also skyrocket, and mental illness tends to abound.[8] The animal industry ravages the psyches of those unlucky enough to serve as its employees. As ever, the most vulnerable and defenseless, innocent animals and marginalized people, are soaked in suffering while corporate bigwigs are weighed down by ever-expanding wallets.

As animal agriculture perpetrates this ethical nightmare, karma has come seeping into the world like blood on parchment. A second crisis is fueled not only by agriculture but by the emergence of an economic system that prioritizes the relentless consumption by individuals over the needs of the whole. The situation is so dire that the term "ecocide" is now used to describe it: the planet is heating, species are dying out at an alarming rate, forests are being levelled, and water is being made toxic by agricultural effluence.

In New Zealand, two thirds of all rivers are not swimmable due to pollution from the dairy industry alone. This once pristine landscape, visually immortalized by the epic *Lord of the Rings* movies, is now toxic to most life forms. Dogs have died after swimming in and drinking from rivers that are infested with bacteria like salmonella. In the U.S. state of Wisconsin, children are dying of blue baby syndrome, caused by water sources badly contaminated by nitrates from cattle feces. In England, there is no longer a single river of a good *chemical* standard, and a mere 14% remain of a good *ecological* standard.[9] A large source of this pollution is the waste runoff from animal farming.

Animal agriculture is also one of the leading causes of deforestation. Cattle ranching is behind 80% of deforestation in the Amazon and accounts for 83% of global farmland, but yields only 18% of our calories.[10] Shrimp farming is destroying habitats such as mangrove swamps—vital carbon sinks—in Southeast Asia.[11] Rising sea levels, extreme weather events like droughts and hurricanes, natural disasters that cause wars, which in turn generate mass migration and refugee crises, and other catastrophic developments—these are the shocks and punches that will rain down upon civilization if we do not address climate change.

The effect of animal agriculture on the globe and on all sentient beings is nothing short of catastrophic. This must be acknowledged before we investigate solutions. Animal agriculture is an ethical emergency, and our response to it must be stringent and immediate. Although regulatory laws continue to be passed, they largely lack the requisite urgency or scope. The agricultural industry, often referred to as "Big Ag," has a hoard of money and influence and possesses massive political power across the globe. Some legislators and regulators have prodded Big Ag and pleaded for change, and it has nodded tepidly in response. Meanwhile, little changes. The industrial leaders offer their own phony solutions, whilst maintaining, more or less, the status quo. Yet if the crisis is as severe as all the science indicates, why aren't the laws changing? Why can't the industry be reformed?

Self-Interest

Upton Sinclair, author of the infamous 1906 meatpacking exposé *The Jungle*, quipped that "it is difficult to get a man to understand something when his salary depends upon his not understanding it."[12] This remark is an ironclad argument against self-regulation. If an industry is characterized by destructive externalities or morally dubious features, it makes little sense to expect said industry to adequately regulate its behavior of its own volition. An external corrective must be administered.

As it stands, modern agriculture underpins a moral and ecological crisis, and reform has been glacial in pace, meagre in scale, and has mostly come from the farmers themselves in the form of pacifying labels and soothing stories of "humane" and "sustainable" reforms.

Power does not simply give away its own influence unprompted, it needs to be pushed. This is abundantly true of the agricultural industry today, which is given a free pass to pursue its own self-generated reforms on its own leisurely timetable. This is insufficient. The industry's attempts to certify "humane" welfare standards, either self-certifying or in league with pro-farming government bodies, as well as initiatives to move toward the questionable panacea of regenerative agriculture, are falling far short of what science and philosophy demand. This is not to disparage the expertise of farmers whose knowledge could be instrumental to transforming modern agriculture. Yet the farmers' perspective, naturally concerned with preserving the profit margins of their businesses, will inevitably be tainted by self-interest. Their expertise is also limited to improving production and price per pound, not animal welfare and wellbeing or addressing the complexities of climate disruption. Their testimony alone cannot be relied upon.

Global animal agriculture has an estimated worth of two trillion dollars. JBS, the world's largest meat company, makes around fifty billion dollars in revenue each year. The industry is ginormous, and its owners and proprietors are wealthy, well-connected, and powerful. The global trend toward larger and more concentrated industrial agriculture has continued to grow. In the U.S., 66% of food products come from the 4% of farms that make over $1 million in annual sales.[13] This system has expanded to the benefit of an increasingly small number of companies and individuals with ever bigger stakes dominating the industry. It has lined their pockets with gold. Of course, these people will seek to conceal their practices. Those who have made their living creating and defending animal agriculture as it now exists will not engage in a good faith effort to reform or revolutionize it, let alone abolish it. From their perspective, why fix something that isn't broken? Consumers are still buying meat, dairy, and eggs; investors' dividends are still being paid. They are not the ones slipping on the blood and grease on abattoir floors, or drinking poison water, or having their habitats torched. It is not their problem, and as long as it remains profitable to carry on with the status quo, the meat industry will not change, contrary to whatever soothing assurances they may make to the contrary.

The market mechanism has led to *some* hopeful developments in changing the composition of the food industry. A growing demand for plant-based products has led a handful of major meat firms to rebrand themselves "protein companies" as they wade into the plant-based industry.[14] Consumers are presented with a widening variety of choices when it comes to food options. However, there remain valid reasons to be suspicious of these meat companies. Their moral crimes are inexcusable, and ongoing caution is essential to ensure that the perpetrators cannot obscure their violence with greenwashing and plant-based schemes.

The problem with the profit motive is that it is inherently amoral; whatever sells is preferable. Although there is genuine demand for ethical and environmentally friendly products, it is possible, with clever labelling and advertising, to parade select items as meeting this demand criteria when in fact they do nothing of the sort. The number of vegans and vegetarians is increasing, but not rapidly enough to render the animal industry irrelevant any time soon.[15] Whilst the growth of these consumer habits may prove to be exponential, the damage that animal farming might wreak in the meantime, particularly for the billions who will continue to be goaded onto kill floors, remains unacceptable.

REGENERATIVE AGRICULTURE

Regenerative agriculture refers to methods which seek to improve both commercial and environmental outcomes. The policies that sport this description are diverse and tend to revolve around maintaining soil quality, which proponents say is crucial to crop yields and sequestering carbon from the atmosphere. Some of the practices that fall under the umbrella of regenerative agriculture, particularly around regenerative plant farming, are promising and constitute valuable reforms to our agricultural methods. Yet, by the same token, these techniques are in some cases nowhere near as effective as advertised at combatting climate change. Indeed, one major question is this: who determines what regenerative agriculture is? There is no centralized or certified body that determines if a farm is suitably regenerative. That is to say, anyone can call their farm a regenerative farm, and nobody is checking to see if their claims are bogus. This was explosively exposed in an article, first published in *The Ecologist*, in which one writer got an entirely fictional farm to be certified as regenerative.[16] If this can happen, it follows that opportunistic farmers, catching wind of growing environmental consciousness, can profit from the regenerative label without changing anything of significance about their business. This is exactly what has happened with unregulated labels like "humane" and "free-range." In a windowless building with thousands of hens, an open door to a small concrete area or tiny muddy yard can constitute "free-range," as the birds have "access to the outside."

A pertinent example comes from packaged food giant General Mills. In the spring of 2019, it announced a plan that set out to put one million acres of land in the U.S. under regenerative agriculture policies by the year 2030.[17] However, as revolutionary as this program may sound, much of it proved to be simply hot air. It was a public relations stunt rustled up by suits with little substance behind it.

Adopting regenerative measures will be purely optional for farmers in the General Mills program. Ben Lilliston, of the Institute for Agriculture and Trade Policy, pointed out that this means farmers could set their own targets, self-report their results, and hold no accountability for the outcomes of their efforts, or lack thereof. This self-directed scheme is therefore altogether spineless, and General Mills' show of ecological altruism is exposed as a facade. It is not good enough for the industry to devise schemes wrapped in green ribbons, we should not leave pollution to be regulated by the polluters themselves.

There is some evidence in favor of regenerative agriculture, particularly regenerative crop farming. Healthy soil microbes, which flourish in untilled land, help sequester carbon. However, this is unlikely to be a fix to global heating; studies have found varying results, but healthy soils only compensate for 10–30% of greenhouse gas emissions from a given farm.[18] As long as toxic pesticides and generous helpings of harmful fertilizer remain in use, soil health can only do so much. Indeed, no-till farming* is a fundamentally insecure way to combat climate change, for if the land swaps hands, or the farmer changes their mind, the soil need only be tilled once afterwards for the carbon capture to be reversed. In terms of durability or efficiency, "regenerative agriculture" is simply not in the same league as *rewilding*, where regrowing genuine, vital ecosystems can create a sturdy reservoir of carbon and actually counteract the planet's heating.[19]

Additionally, the meat industry has been keen to capitalize on the regenerative name. Regenerative animal agriculture is almost a contradiction in terms. People like Allan Savory, the founder of so-called regenerative cattle ranching, has been widely exposed as a fraud.[20] Grass-fed beef is often not simply from animals raised on grass; these cattle often need supplementary grain feed to maintain the profitability of their flesh. Indeed, due to their low energy diet, grass-fed cows tend to grow more slowly and thus produce more methane over the course

---

*   No-till farming minimizes soil disturbance from tilling, which helps keep carbon in the soil.

of their lives, polluting the atmosphere in the process. An Oxford University report that looked into grass-fed livestock had this to say: "This report concludes that grass-fed livestock are not a climate solution. Grazing livestock are net contributors to the climate problem, as are all livestock. Rising animal production and consumption, whatever the farming system and animal type, is causing damaging greenhouse gas release and contributing to changes in land use."[21]

Making plant farming more commensurate with the environment, using less pesticides, improving soil health, and bolstering local ecosystems represent regenerative farming at its best. There are few people who would sneer at this approach, even if it falls short of being the comprehensive solution to climate change that some of its advocates claim. However, regenerative *animal* agriculture, with only spotty or specious science supporting it, is a thoroughly flawed suggestion. As the foundations of the regenerative ranching argument are so shaky, its champions sometimes retreat from their environmental claims and grasp for a different argument altogether. They settle on the fact that grass-fed is high welfare, that cows grazing in fields are beautiful and natural, like bison on the prairie—that the cows love living in this way.

This may be so. Yet they surely do not love being painfully branded or castrated; they do not consent to having their children and friends taken from them; nor do they cherish the bolt gun that shoots between their eyes or the knife that slashes their throat. Killing animals who desire life is not good for their welfare. A genuine concern for the wellbeing of animals leads down one track only—that of veganism.

THE HONEST FARMER

There is an enduring cultural image of the honest farmer, the trusty laborer who, with loving hands, pulls life out of the earth. His animals are cared for, doted on by hand and reared from bottles like human infants. When the time comes, and the slaughterhouse truck comes creaking down the track to ferry his animals away, he accepts their fate with grim resolve and a quiet tremble of his lip. Even the founders of the U.S. waxed lyrical about the noble art of agriculture. Thomas Jefferson wrote in a 1787 letter to George Washington that he hoped the nation would not become distracted from "[a]griculture which is our wisest pursuit, because it will in the end contribute most to real wealth, good morals and happiness. The wealth acquired by speculation and plunder is fugacious in its nature and fills society with the spirit of gambling. The moderate and sure income of husbandry begets permanent improvement, quiet life, and orderly conduct both public and private."[22] Revering farmers is a pastime as old as the nation.

This is not meant to disparage farmers, whose work we all rely on to survive, and whose jobs are harder than most. Yet it is clear that modern agriculture has not contributed to "good morals and happiness," and in fact falls far short of these ideals. Animal agriculture manufactures violence and destruction, resulting in animal cruelty and poisoned ecosystems. An industry that creates and financially benefits from these outcomes cannot be trusted to remedy them of their own free will.

There is a commonly held belief that if you buy from independent or organic sources, perhaps frequenting a farmers market and befriending your producers, then you have done your due diligence. Direct communion with farmers, who are assumed to hold direct communion with the earth, provides a cheap way to quash persistent feelings of guilt about where one's food comes from. Yet all animal products come from a system in which animals are merely commodities, who possess value only as an egg layer, a milk producer, or a corpse. All animal products come from ranches that produce emissions and generate animal waste that must be treated and stored, but so often is not.

The issue is not that farmers should not be trusted because they are inherently dishonest people. It is because they are simply regular people that they cannot be trusted. Farmers are not motivated by altruism or rural chivalry. Their businesses are not dictated by the logic of "good morals and happiness." They are motivated by the bills they must pay and the profit they must make to survive. It is naïve to believe otherwise. Farmers may be experts in their domain; succeeding in agriculture of all different stripes requires technical knowledge by the bucketload. However, they are not climate scientists, or ethicists, or experts in animal cognition or animal welfare. Indeed, even if farmers were authorities on animal welfare and carbon emissions, their behavior likely would not change.

They need to know about animal welfare insofar as it helps them produce a profitable product. They need to know about their local climate insofar as it affects the planting seasons and soil health. They are proficient in managing a business but have no incentives to act in the best interests of the wider society or the animals who constitute their property.

The reality is that prioritizing animal welfare and avoiding the climate catastrophe necessitates the abolition of animal farming and all animal agriculture to transition to plant food farming. It would be unreasonable to expect even the most honest and decent farmer to take such steps. Some are, but large-scale change must come from external pressure.

"Humane" and "Green" Meat

We have already explored the fact that those who seek to make meat "green" often have been led by spurious science or self-interested desires to rebrand a system which science routinely exposes as unsustainable and cruel. These rebranding initiatives also serve to muddy the waters when it comes to animal welfare.

Take the example of Natural Prairie Dairy, an organic dairy farm in Channing, Texas, which was the subject of a 2019 investigation.[23] The U.S. Department of Agriculture (USDA) regulations for raising organic farmed animals contain a number of welfare provisions, which vary by species. Animals are expected to have adequate access to water, to outdoor areas and natural light, to be protected from severe weather, to be free from crowding, and to live in housing that reduces "the potential for livestock injury." Although the larger part of organic regulations is dedicated to topics like the use of pesticides and antibiotics or the sources of animal feed, it is clear that animal welfare is considered a part of the organic brand and is sold to consumers in this way.

Natural Prairie Dairy leaned into this high welfare image, selling itself as a little bucolic patch of Eden. Its website proclaimed that "[a] sustainable farm ecosystem means giving our cows the very best care." The reality proved to be far different: squalid stalls choked with manure; cows with bloated udders rife with infection; animals collapsing and shuddering in pain and exhaustion. "Downer cows," those too sick or weak to stand, were kicked and battered with shovels. Their necks bent and twisted into their bodies and tied with ropes, the animals were carried away in excavators like so much garbage. Some of the most disturbing footage was of force-feeding procedures. As many of the cows were lame or sick with infections of the udder (mastitis[24]), they were force-fed by untrained staff. The images are truly frightening: cows crammed into a huge metal vice, ropes yanking their nose rings and sharp metal tubes slithering up their throats, their eyes wide with incredulity and fear, shrieking in terror. This is not what people imagine they are paying for when their good intentions bring them to the organic meat or dairy section of the grocery store.

Egg production presents another harrowing example. Eggs labelled organic must come from chickens who have some access to the outdoors. Consumers imagine pods of plucky chickens darting amongst foliage and undergrowth, roosting in toasty straw-filled cabins, and greeting each sunrise with heartfelt choruses. The sad reality is commonly a suffocating rabble of animals, squawking with discomfort, agitation, and pain; sick chickens with feathers so badly pecked away that the animals look poisoned or cancerous. This is too often the story of free-range and organic egg production. Indeed, to obtain the status of organic certification, U.S. egg producers are required to moderate their antibiotic use while maintaining cramped disease-ridden environments, which lead to chickens suffering unnecessarily from debilitating diseases and infections without proper medical attention. Even the greenest animal products will inevitably be tainted with cruelty, and high welfare standards will always be undermined if their implementation destabilizes profits.

There are numerous institutions whose self-professed *raison d'être* is to protect animals from the cruelties of farming. That, of course, includes only the cruelties up to the point of slaughter—that ultimate act of unnecessary evil is taken as a given. On principle, many such welfare groups do deserve credit. Those that pursue better welfare outcomes whilst also promoting animal liberation, for example, seek to remedy what suffering they can within our current paradigm, while also working to build a new one. However, some welfare organizations can act as fronts for the animal industry and provide the means of easing consumers' consciences whilst maintaining animals in a state of agony.

In the U.K., the Assured Food Standards, a private organization that sprang out of the agricultural industry in 2000, applies its "Red Tractor" label to a host of products and suppliers, and high animal welfare is central to this certification. "Buy Red Tractor and you're buying happy lives for animals," goes the rhetoric.[25] Yet since 2018, despite inspections rarely being conducted unannounced, a whole catalogue of atrocities has been documented at their facilities. These include the killing of piglets by smashing them against walls, the use of hammers to kill pigs, and leaving chickens to rot in conditions of extreme suffering. This may be superficially surprising. However, is the Red Tractor label there to protect animals, or is it there to sell meat? The Assured Food Standards functions little more than as a mouthpiece of the food industry. Farms bearing this label, even when having been exposed torturing intelligent and sensitive pigs, supply major supermarkets like Sainsbury's, Morrison's, and Tesco despite the fact that the chair of the Assured Food Standards, Baroness Lucy Neville-Rolfe, was an executive director on the board of the supermarket Tesco from 2006 to 2013. Why would Red Tractor inspectors raise a red flag when they see desperate and dying creatures, when raising a red flag means undermining the basis of their livelihoods?

When it comes to animal cruelty, self-regulation is not an option. Anticruelty laws must be enforced by a third party and informed by scientific standards. What science says is good for animals aggravates commercial interests. The Better Chicken Commitment, devised by animal welfare experts and researchers,[26] outlines a number of measures that should be considered the bare minimum in the striving toward high welfare. These measures include no live-dumping or shackling, no cages, enrichments added to the chickens' environment such as litters* and natural light. A "humane" standard like this should be a benchmark, as it is at least developed by experts in animal wellbeing. Although some companies have signed onto this program, the change it represents globally is fractional. Indeed, even if all companies adopted

---

*   Litter is a straw or other plant matter used as bedding for animals

such measures, abuse would still abound. Without adequate surveillance there could be no guarantee that the standard was fully enforced, or that excess cruelties weren't inflicted on the animals by workers. Genuine change must be universally implemented by a third party. The only suitable candidate for such a task is the state.

REGULATION, LEGISLATION, LIBERATION

The state must regulate both the environmental impact and the extreme cruelty perpetrated by modern agriculture. There are several components to this process.

First, those regulations that do exist must be implemented and further funding must be provided to this end. There has been some change in the regulatory environment around agriculture in recent decades. Legislative acts in the U.S., such as the Animal Welfare Act, the Clean Water Act, and the Federal Insecticide, Fungicide, and Rodenticide Acts, mean that there are some regulatory instruments at work in that country. However, these legal instruments are as dull as molars. For example, the Clean Water Act is meant to regulate the discharge of pollution from point sources into natural bodies of water. A point source is a discrete man-made conveyance like a water pipe or ditch, which directs effluence straight into, say, a river. Such practices are not outlawed outright—a permit from the National Pollutant Discharge Elimination System is required to discharge from a point source. Yet the regulation has nothing to say about nonpoint source discharge, which is a leading cause of water pollution today.[27] This is mostly runoff from fields that are covered with fertilizer, which then contaminates water sources with high levels of sulfates, nitrates, and harmful bacteria. In Wisconsin, for example, dairy farm runoff has so poisoned the groundwater that drinking water in some areas has double the recommended nitrate content.[28] This has devastating consequences for human health. Excess nitrate consumption has been linked with cancer, thyroid disease, and damage to reproductive issues.[29]

Therefore, although legislation and regulation do exist, they are spotty and outdated, ignoring serious aspects of the harm animal agriculture perpetuates. More inspectors must be recruited, their training made more rigorous, and their goals redefined. This may seem a pipedream at present. Organizations like the USDA or DEFRA in the U.K. exist to facilitate the efficient running of agriculture, rather than to create obstacles for it. This is part of the reason why so much environmental devastation and animal abuse continues to burn like an unwatched fire, away from the distracted eyes of society. However, state inspectors must prioritize, as a matter of moral obligation, the wellbeing of billions of animals and the continued environmental impact of animal farming.

The question of how we get there must have a political answer. Agriculture is increasingly appearing on the political menu. U.S. politicians like senators Elizabeth Warren and Cory Booker have led the way in this regard, pointing out some of the injustices of modern farming. Yet what they point to is the tip of the iceberg; like drool splashing on a cave floor, we have yet to look up and reckon with the monster.

The obvious tactic would be to emphasize agriculture's environmental recklessness, and to harness the public's burgeoning ecological awareness to pressure the state into further regulating farming and exposing regenerative animal agriculture for its failings. This is an essential step. Although we have previously established that regenerative plant farming is not without merits, it is limited and needs regulation and implementation by heavily funded, ethically motivated agriculture policies at the state and federal levels.

Government officials must strongly endorse plant-based diets. Subsidies must be shifted from animal agriculture to plant farming, and a savvy government must leap at the opportunity to invest millions in innovative meat alternatives, which can sustain a truly ethical and green diet of the future. People must exert pressure on the cumbersome mechanisms of the state and the representatives who operate them. The climate emergency will not wait for us; energized activism is required to pressure our democracies into funding and legislating a new paradigm into being, or risk our destruction.

Funding and the enforcement of existing regulations will be only a start, however. Animal rights advocates, therefore, must be more strident than ever in making the case against eating meat in a changing zeitgeist and economy where alternatives are becoming more available. Animal products must become a political issue, and cruelty a topic of genuine debate. Advocating for better welfare and superior environmental policies can help get this topic on the table. Our ecological crisis has empowered many people and fostered an appetite for change. Compassion for animals is fundamental to this change—recognizing how similar they are to us rather than how different, recognizing that humanity, in our arrogance, has willfully placed ourselves at the center of consciousness on Earth. If we can learn to respect animals, to appreciate individuals of other species, to place ourselves not in the center, but included in the whole of life on Earth, then we accept the deepest values of equality and generosity. We become more capable of extending our consideration to other humans, to nonhuman animals, and to the planet, with its vast and fragile constellations of life.

Nature and all of its brilliant sentience has long enraptured humanity. Even today it attracts our attention to nature documentaries or keeps us waddling in eager crowds to zoos, marine parks, and wildlife reserves. People say that they like animals—many say they love animals. However, our goal must be to say that a lifestyle which pays for animals to die for our pleasure is directly contrary to our benevolent instincts. There is a rope that ties the appetizing cutlet, blasted by the sterile lights of a supermarket, all the way back to a living, breathing, sensitive creature whose life was cut horribly short. The consumer's cash, clinking about in the supermarket register, is the same money that guides the hand that sticks a knife into an animal's jugular, snatches away a calf from a panicked mother, or burns a chicken's beak down to a stump.

It is scientists and experts who must determine the best course of action for farmers to take, rather than allowing farmers to rely on self-diagnoses and prescriptions. External and neutral arbiters must be appointed as regulators, and funds must be moved to provide incentive for agricultural policies that are truly designed to address climate change and general wellbeing. Yet this is only a first step. As the myopic profiteering of animal agriculture will continue competing with the wellbeing of humans, other creatures, and the planet, we must cease breeding and farming animals altogether.

Matthew Chalmers is a U.K.-based writer and activist who has reported on the way animals are treated in agriculture, society, and culture. His articles span topics from animal industry euphemisms to the movies *Babe* and *Seaspiracy*, to the uniqueness of humans and the role of nature in the COVID-19 pandemic. He holds a B.A. in History at Durham University and an M.Phil. in Egyptology at the University of Cambridge. Chalmers work has appeared in *Current Affairs*, *Sentient Media*, *The Ecologist*, *History Today*, *Vegan Life*, and *Bright Lights Film Journal*.

11

THE ETHICAL VEGETARIAN MYTH

by Sailesh Rao and Lisa Barca, Ph.D.

"When you change the way you look at things, the things you look at change."—**Wayne Dyer**

Human supremacism propagates the Ethical Vegetarian Myth, defined as the myth that the human consumption of milk and eggs is a mutually beneficial ecological relationship with other species. This chapter seeks to debunk the common view that a lacto-vegetarian or ovo-vegetarian lifestyle is not only ethical, but has negligible additional ecological impact compared to a vegan lifestyle.

This view stems, in part, from a local sensitivity analysis (LSA), which is misleading when extrapolated out on a global scale. In contrast, our global sensitivity analysis (GSA) shows that an ethical* lacto-vegetarian or ovo-vegetarian lifestyle would actually *amplify* the ecological impact of animal agriculture by an order of magnitude and therefore be highly unsustainable. Human consumption of eggs and nonhuman milk is unethical due to the reproductive exploitation, confinement, and slaughter of the cows and chickens bred in both large and small dairy and egg-farming operations.

While vegetarians are moving in the right direction by making a conscious effort to make their diets more ethical, vegetarianism unfortunately does not benefit either the environment or the lives of

---

* "Ethical" is included in the name to specifically address the "humane" version of lacto-vegetarianism (using, for example, ahimsa milk).

nonhuman animals exploited for food. The Ethical Vegetarian Myth cajoles vegetarians into a false sense of moral assuagement, persuading them that abstaining only from meat will lessen the myriad harmful effects of animal agriculture on both the ecosystems and the sentient beings whose milk and eggs are stolen and commodified. The Ethical Vegetarian Myth tells consumers that, compared to meat, dairy and eggs are benign and humane products, but this fails to take into account that the dairy and egg industries are inextricably connected to the meat industry. Those under the influence of this myth believe that because the animal must be alive at the time of the extraction of her bodily fluids, the process is ethical and sustainable. We intend to debunk this myth by bringing to light the violence and devastation behind these products, and by demonstrating that veganism is, therefore, the only viable and ethical way forward.

THE HUMAN SUPREMACY MYTH

In *The Myth of Human Supremacy*, Derrick Jensen debunks the near universal, unquestioned belief in *scala naturae* or the "Ladder of Nature," with humans at the top and all other animals and species below.[1] He points out other species' unique and essential gifts that aid the functioning of ecosystems in which they belong. He shows that when humans assert superiority over the rest of the natural world, we orient ourselves against nature by taking an unjust and fundamentally unsustainable position. Indeed, the species nomenclature we give ourselves, *Homo sapiens*, Latin for the "wise hominid," should clue us in to the egocentric narcissism and human supremacism that pervades our culture.

Human supremacism is the cultural bedrock on which all other forms of supremacism flourish. If we do not assert superiority over other species, we cannot possibly assert superiority over other members of our own species. Conversely, when we assert superiority over other species, we normalize their oppression, along with the oppression of humans engaged in their oppression, thereby watering the roots of colonialism, racism, ableism, patriarchy, and other forms of social discrimination.[2]

Human supremacism distorts science. It makes us accept the protein myth, which claims that we can only get our protein from meat even as we observe the largest land herbivores on the planet, elephants, getting their protein exclusively from plants. It makes us believe the calcium myth—that we can only absorb calcium from milk—without questioning the bovine absorption of calcium from leafy greens. It also propagates the Ethical Vegetarian Myth, the myth that the human consumption of milk and eggs is a mutually beneficial ecological relationship with a few other species in the animal kingdom.

AN ECOLOGICAL CRISIS

The French philosopher François-René de Chateaubriand once said, *"Forests precede civilizations and deserts follow them."* What he omitted is that the conversion of forests to grazing lands is the most likely intermediate step in this desertification process. It is becoming increasingly clear that unless we reorganize ourselves into a civilization that does the opposite— turns deserts back into forests—we will soon be facing extinction.

Of the 130 million square kilometers of the ice-free land area of the planet today, only 9% is original forests, while 37% is grazing lands for our ruminant farmed animals, 19% is deserts and mountains, 22% is managed forests for timber, and 12% is cropland.[3]

Half the cropland output is going to feed farmed animals, while just one-quarter goes to feed humans directly. That one-quarter of the cropland output, which is entirely plant-based, constitutes a whopping 85% of the food that we consume by weight, while animal agriculture provides just 12%, and seafood the remaining 3%. Farmed animals are consuming almost five times as much food as all humans while providing just 12% of human food, and yet the Ethical Vegetarian Myth persists.

The scientific method relies heavily on an "unbiased observer" interpreting data. Since such an observer is truly a mythical creature, biases occur in science. To minimize such biases, science relies on a peer-review process to sift out bad science. However, since the vast majority of scientists consume meat and dairy, the peer-review process itself can become a carnist echo-chamber, thereby distorting science. In our Animal Agriculture Position Paper,[4] we have shown that such distortions have already occurred in United Nation's reports on climate science.

Therefore, it is worth examining whether such distortions have occurred in the science on the ecological footprint of diets.

Using data from the U.S. Department of Agriculture (USDA) and the Life-Cycle Analysis (LCA) of the greenhouse gas emissions of food substances from various sources, the often-cited Shrink That Footprint website reported that the lacto-vegetarian diet causes just 13% more greenhouse gas emissions than the vegan diet, 1.7 tons of carbon dioxide equivalents (CO2e) per person vs. 1.5 tons for the vegan diet.[5] While this analysis can perhaps be dismissed as non-peer reviewed and therefore not credible, in 2016, Peters et al. claimed to have shown, using a biophysical simulation model, that the carrying capacity of the continental U.S. was highest for the lacto-vegetarian diet—even more than that for a vegan diet.[6] According to their calculations, 807 million people can be supported within the continental U.S. on a lacto-vegetarian diet, 787 million people can be supported on an ovo-vegetarian diet, whereas just 735 million people can be supported on a vegan diet. This scientific paper made it seem like raising cows strictly for dairy and chickens strictly for eggs is highly desirable from a sustainability perspective.

If true, this would be excellent news for egg and dairy producers and consumers since these products have been historically associated with a seemingly benevolent human relationship with animals instead of keeping them in intensive farming facilities and slaughtering them. Therefore, it is worth scrutinizing this claim from the perspective of ethical lacto-ovo-vegetarianism, where the cows and chickens are treated as members of the extended human family and only their excess mammary and menstrual secretions are extracted for human consumption. Indeed, the Peters et al. claim that the carrying capacity of the continental U.S. is maximum for a lacto-vegetarian diet implies that everyone in the U.S. would be consuming just dairy products and no one would actually be eating the cows in that optimum carrying capacity scenario.

In 2018, Poore and Nemecek claimed to have shown that the water footprint of cow's milk (600 liters/liter) is only slightly worse than the water footprint of almond milk (400 liters/liter).[7] If almond milk is truly almost as water-intensive as cow's milk to produce, it reinforces the Peters et al. claim that lacto-vegetarianism is the optimum dietary and lifestyle choice for humans. Therefore, in this paper, we will scrutinize this Poore–Nemecek claim as well.

LOCAL VS. GLOBAL SENSITIVITY ANALYSIS

In the proverbial story of the six blind men describing an elephant, each man conducts a local examination of the elephant and determines that it is a tree (a blind man touching a leg of the elephant), a snake (trunk), a wall (body), a spear (tusk), a rope (tail), and a fan (ear). This shows that a Local Sensitivity Analysis (LSA) can be misleading when extrapolated out on a global scale. For instance, the LSA of flat terrain might lead one to globally extrapolate that the earth is flat.

In a LSA of lacto-vegetarianism, we examine the impact of a single individual switching to lacto-vegetarianism while everyone else continues with the status-quo consumption of meat, dairy, and eggs. Since this individual switch would have a negligible impact on the total number of animals raised and slaughtered, as will be demonstrated below, the LSA becomes an exercise in apportioning the ecological impact of raising a cow between the dairy, beef, and leather "outputs." If we choose to assign the vast majority of the ecological impact to beef and leather while minimizing that apportioned for dairy, such creative accounting would make lacto-vegetarianism seem truly benign from an ecological perspective. However, like blind men describing an elephant, we would be fooling ourselves.

In contrast, a GSA considers the impact of a global change and examines it in its totality. In order to assess the impact of lacto-vegetarianism, it examines what would happen if the whole world adopted lacto-vegetarianism and compares it with what would happen if the whole world adopted veganism.

GLOBAL MATTERS

For such a global perspective, Bar On et al.have estimated that the biomass of farmed mammals today is nearly triple the biomass of all the wild mammals that lived 10,000 years ago, while the biomass of wild mammals has diminished by over 80% in the same period.[8] The present-day biomass of farmed mammals is dominated by grazing animals such as cows, goats, and buffalos. Consider that humans have cut down almost half the trees on the planet[9] since the dawn of civilization mainly to create grazing land for farmed animals, displacing an estimated 464 Gigatons of Carbon (GtC) from vegetation and soils and emitting them into the atmosphere.

When trees are cut down to create grazing land, the carbon stored on that land decreases by an order of magnitude. Rao et al. showed that if current grazing land is restored to native forest biomes that existed on that land in the 1800s, that would increase the carbon stored on that land more than ten-fold, from 27 GtC to 292 GtC.[10] Therefore, the diminished carbon storage on grazing land compared to the forests that they replaced is a fundamental greenhouse gas emissions penalty of animal agriculture, which is ignored in an LSA, but properly accounted for in a GSA.

As of 2018, humans were extracting 840 million tons of milk every year from 808 million milk producing animals, including cows, buffaloes, goats, and sheep.[11] The total number of cows, buffaloes, goats, and sheep was 3.7 billion, which means that 22% of these animals were producing milk. In a lacto-vegetarian world, for each milk-producing animal, there would be a male counterpart, as there are equal numbers of each sex born to each of these species. For cows, milk production occurs over roughly one quarter of their natural lifespan before they are sent to slaughter to be ground up into hamburgers today. In such an ethical lacto-vegetarian world, these animals considered "non-producers" would live out their natural lives, quadrupling the number of animals. Each milk-producing animal lactates because she recently gave birth to a calf. If the baby is allowed to drink half the milk, and the other half is used for human consumption (as is often cited as an "ethical" situation for milk production), that would further double the number of animals needed to produce the same amount of milk. Therefore, in an "ethical" lacto-vegetarian world, the number of animals needed to produce the same amount of milk is 12.8 billion, *roughly four times the total number* of cows, buffaloes, goats, and sheep in the world today. Since we are already using 37% of the ice-free land area of the planet just to graze farmed animals, it would be impossible to find the necessary grazing land for quadrupling this animal population, not to mention the significant increase in greenhouse gas emissions.

Next, please note that the current world production of milk—840 million tons per year—works out to a daily average of 286 ml of milk per person, which is little over one cup (250 ml) per person per day. The USDA recommends a daily average of three cups of milk equivalent per person per day, for which we would need to increase the global population of cows, buffaloes, goats, and sheep to 33.6 billion, effectively increasing the current cow, buffalo, goat, and sheep population *by a factor of nine.*

In a vegan world, we can safely assume that current agriculture land is more than sufficient to produce all the food that humans need (as so much currently goes to animal grazing and growing feed), which means that 37% of the ice-free land area of the planet can be restored to forests, wetlands, prairies, and other carbon-absorbing wild areas. According to the HYDE database of the fossil record,[12] 41% of that grazing land was forests in 1800, while it is unknown how much of the remaining grazing lands were deforested before 1800. If native forests were restored on 41% of grazing lands today, that alone could sequester 265 GtC—more than the 240 GtC that were added to the atmosphere through human activities between 1750 and 2015.[13] Therefore, a vegan world would literally reverse climate change while also restoring the biodiversity of the planet.

A GLOBAL VEGAN ETHIC

Next, let's consider the case of ethical ovo-vegetarianism. At present, 7.6 billion birds, who are bred and killed for their eggs, each produce about 210 eggs per year for human consumption.[14] This level of egg production is astounding considering that the jungle ancestor of the modern-day chicken laid about 12–15 eggs per year. Such extreme acceleration of the egg-laying cycle of birds has grisly consequences for the health of the birds as most of them are "spent" (considered "used up" and sent to slaughter) after about 18 months, roughly one-sixth to one-eighth of their natural lifespan.

In an "ethical" ovo-vegetarian world, let's assume that the chickens are allowed to live out their natural lives at what would be normal egg production rates. That would require the number of birds to increase by a factor of 84 to 140 to produce the same number of eggs. Then, we would also need to let the male birds, who are currently killed when they are just hours or days old, live out their natural lifespans, which would further double the number of birds. Finally, harvesting just half the eggs—letting the other half be used for hatching baby chicks—would further double the number of birds by a factor of two. In total, the number of birds in an "ethical" ovo-vegetarian world would be 120 to 200 times the total number of chickens on Earth today, or about *2.5 trillion to 4.3 trillion*. It is impossible for such "ethical" ovo-vegetarianism to be sustainable, much less optimal, on planet Earth. Further, eating just one egg per day is as bad as smoking five cigarettes per day in terms of life expectancy, making it unclear why we would contemplate transforming into this lifestyle in the first place.[15]

The ethical ramifications of dairy and egg consumption are profound, even in a fictional (and economically and environmentally impossible) situation in which male chicks and male calves were not slaughtered as unproductive waste products of the egg and dairy industries, and even if their mothers were not also killed at a fraction of their natural lifespans. The ethical dimensions of these products also include the exploitation of the female reproductive system, no matter the label or size of the farm, causing immense harm to female nonhuman animals in terms of their biology and their natural inclination to care for their young—a bodily and emotional drive that is just as strong in these bovine and avian mothers as it is in human mothers, but which is commonly ignored by those concerned with bodily self-sovereignty as a basic right. As American law professor Dr. Sherry Colb asserts:

> One aspect of dairy and egg production, beyond the killing and the suffering that both require, independently disturbs me as a woman. It is the use of female animals as reproductive slave. . . . Because of their uniquely female capacities, capacities that they share with human women, we exploit laying hens and dairy cows every moment of their lives and then slaughter them or throw them away when their reproductive productivity diminishes.[16]

Cows and hens used for their milk and eggs—in both large industrial farms and small "family," "organic," or "local" farming—have been bred to maximize their rates of lactation and ovulation without concern for the physical and psychological impacts this has on the animals themselves. Because of the unnatural quantities in which their bodies produce milk and eggs due to human manipulation of their genetics, cows and hens commonly suffer from osteoporosis due to the calcium leached from their bodies in milk and egg production and other ailments of the bones. In the case of cows, mastitis, a painful inflammation of a cow's udder—and for hens uterine prolapses and other painful and often fatal reproductive maladies—is common, among other agonizing illnesses and harms.

Anyone who favors rights for human women and identifies as feminist should be concerned about these abuses of the female body, and about the fact that these female animals are forced into reproductive activity against their will through a process that has aptly been described as rape. For instance, dairy farmers use an apparatus to restrain cows while forcibly inseminating them and casually refer to this restraining device as a "rape rack." Journalist Katrina Fox asks, "how could I call for my own reproductive autonomy while actively supporting the assault on female nonhuman animals' reproductive systems through the consumption of dairy? . . . It's contrary to feminism to defend one type of female body while using and abusing another."[17] Along similar lines, according to law scholar Carmen M. Cusack, "Cows are the victims of rape, but feminists ignore them. Mainstream feminism condemns rape but ignores the connection between the sexual abuse of women and cows because feminist theory and law legitimize human superiority and speciesism."[18] We concur with these positions and maintain that dairy and eggs are a feminist issue, and that there is no ethical consumption of these products in the contemporary industrialized world.

COMPARING WATER FOOTPRINTS OF TREES AND ANIMALS

The earth currently has approximately half the trees of 10,000 years ago, while the biomass of mammals has increased by a factor of four, mostly in the form of farmed animals. Therefore, to restore the ecological balance on Earth, we need to be planting more trees and reducing the biomass of farmed animals. Yet, scientific comparisons on the water footprint of dairy milk vs. almond milk have been used to discourage the switch to almond milk from dairy milk on the pretext that its water footprint (400 liters/liter) is almost the same as that of dairy milk (600 liters/liter).[19] It is interesting to note that missing from the discourse is the incredibly low water footprint of oat milk, hemp milk, and many other plant-based milks, but let's focus on the almond comparison.

Trees are integral to the desirable conversion of salt water into fresh water, while animal agriculture is responsible for the undesirable conversion of fresh water into salt water in the water cycle. Trees absorb underground water through their roots and transpire it through their leaves. Along with the water vapor, trees also emit microorganisms that become the nucleus for raindrop formation. Such condensation creates a low-pressure zone over the trees, which sucks water vapor from over the ocean to shower rain over the trees, thereby creating a "Biotic Moisture Pump" to convert salt water into fresh water. Conversely, when forests are cut down to form grazing lands for animal agriculture, there will be more microorganisms above the ocean than above land and the Biotic Moisture Pump reverses, converting fresh water into salt water,[20] thereby desertifying the land.

Therefore, the water footprint of tree nut products should rightly be viewed as a "negative" footprint in that the greater it is, the more efficient the tree in creating fresh water in the water cycle. Of course, this assumes that the trees are part of a larger ecosystem that is thriving, instead of being part of monoculture plantations that have to be maintained using pesticides and other poisonous means.

It is estimated that humans have reduced the number of trees on Earth by 2–3 trillion over the past 10,000 years. Replanting these trees while restoring native ecosystems would increase the total number of trees on a thriving planet Earth to 5–6 trillion.

At present, the world produces 840 million tons of dairy milk. In order to produce the same amount of almond milk using almonds, that is, one cup of almonds per liter of almond milk, we would require 8.4 billion mature almond trees, about 0.2% of the total number of trees on a thriving planet Earth. In order to meet the USDA recommended three cups of milk per person per day, we would need to increase that to about 0.5% of the total number of trees on the planet. Contrast that with the ecological devastation that needs to occur in order to produce adequate amounts of dairy milk in an "ethical" lacto-vegetarian world as stated above.

THE FUTURE IS VEGAN

On the pristine earth that existed 10,000 years ago, the dry weight of vegetation was about 1,000 billion tons (1,000 Gigatons, Gt) and the dry weight of wild mammals was about 0.2 Gt.[21] Today, wild mammal populations have been decimated while the human population itself has a dry weight of 0.2 Gt, and we need to eat about 1.6 Gt of food each year. We are now facing the question: how much of that food should come from animals if we have to simultaneously restore the balance in global ecosystems and ensure that future generations have a thriving planet to live in?

Far from reducing our demands on the planet, "ethical" lacto-ovo vegetarianism actually increases our demands by an order of magnitude over what we do today. In contrast, the rejection of human supremacism and the adoption of veganism, while organizing human society around the task of turning deserts into forests, would lead to a thriving human civilization on a thriving planet Earth. Therefore, the logical analysis, as well as the crisis situation in all our global ecosystems, calls for a complete moratorium on animal foods so that ecosystems can be restored and the planet can heal. There is an abundance of diverse plant foods available on the planet to sustain our human population as we go about the task of extricating ourselves from this crisis situation.

Once we acknowledge that humans have caused climate change on the planet, we must automatically shoulder the responsibility to fix it. Therefore, it is time for humans to wean ourselves from our mother cow, buffalo, goat, and sheep and grow into our mature ecosystems' role as the climate regulating "thermostat species" of the planet. While vegetarians are moving in the right direction by making a conscious effort to make their diets more ethical, we have shown that vegetarianism unfortunately does not benefit either the environment or the lives of nonhuman animals exploited for food. We have also shown that the Ethical Vegetarian Myth lulls vegetarians into a false sense of improvement and contentment, while ignoring the violence and devastation behind egg and dairy products. We conclude that veganism is, therefore, the only truly sustainable and ethical way forward.

Dr. Sailesh Rao is the founder and executive director of Climate Healers, a non-profit dedicated towards healing the Earth's climate. A systems specialist with a Ph.D. in Electrical Engineering from Stanford University, Dr. Rao worked on the internet communications infrastructure for 20 years after graduation. In 2006, he switched careers and became deeply immersed in solving the environmental crises affecting humanity. Dr. Rao is the author of two books, *Carbon Dharma: The Occupation of Butterflies* and *Carbon Yoga: The Vegan Metamorphosis*, and an executive producer of several documentaries, including *Cowspiracy: The Sustainability Secret, What the Health*, and *A Prayer for Compassion*.

Lisa Barca is a lecturer in the Honors College at Arizona State University, where she teaches humanities and writing courses and seminars on the ethics of humans' relationships with other animals. Her current research centers on critical animal studies, media ethics, rhetoric and ideology, and the intersections of feminism and animal rights. She holds a Ph.D. in Romance Languages and Literatures and has published in the past on topics ranging from modernist poetry to media representations of gender-based violence. Dr. Barca is a contributor to the volume *Meatsplaining: The Meat Industry and the Rhetoric of Denial*, forthcoming with Sydney University Press, and her writing appears in the academic journals *Comparative Literature* and *Critical Discourse Studies*, literary anthologies for undergraduates, including *The Manifesto in Literature* and *The Literature of War*, and popular publications such as *Ms.* magazine.

PART 3:
LANGUAGE AND LABELS

"There are numerous horrible and heartless agricultural practices that are universal and essential to making a profit. Alternative operations cannot circumvent such practices, and the consumer is left uninformed, unaware, and assuaged by the reassuring label."
—**Hope Bohanec**, *The Ultimate Betrayal: Is There Happy Meat?*

12

CORRUPTING THE LANGUAGE OF ANIMAL WELFARE

by Devatha P. Nair, Ph.D.

Language has historically provided humans with the requisite context and distance essential to consume animal products and disengage from the miserable, short lives animals lead en route to slaughter. By using words and contexts that imply that nonhuman animals are both different and inferior, language has made it acceptable for humans to tolerate the inhumane treatment of nonhuman animals for food and other products. The language used to describe the lives of farmed animals has convinced unsuspecting consumers that killing animals is necessary to maintain human life and even contributes to "sustainable" farming practices. It is also the crafty use of language in the stories we tell ourselves that allows us to fawn over an animal at the zoo and still be able to consume another animal a few moments later for lunch without raising too many existential qualms.

As consumers, we have reluctantly become aware of the atrocities inherent in farming animals, largely due to the proliferation of graphic images that capture the inherent cruelty of raising animals for slaughter and consumption. In response to heightened consumer concerns, the past decade has witnessed the strategic commandeering of animal welfare terms by the proponents of animal agriculture who are keen to maintain the status quo. Spurred on by consumer awareness and the lack of regulatory oversight on food labeling, terms such as "all-natural" are bandied by those who profit from animal agriculture to both calm consumer concerns and charge a premium on animal-derived products. But the terms hardly mean what they imply. For example, I was surprised to learn that the term "all-natural"[1] beef does not mean that a cow was raised on lush, green-pastured meadows and grazed on natural grass over the course of her life. I was even more shocked to find out that the label does not restrict the use of antibiotics and growth hormones in her feed during her lifetime. Instead, the term only applies to how her carcass was processed after slaughter and indicates that her flesh was subject to minimal processing.[2] The label has no implications whatsoever for animal welfare and does not imply that humane or ethical practices were followed while she was being raised or slaughtered.

Redefining terms to imply that the humane treatment of animals is possible within the framework of animal agriculture—known as humanewashing—has been instrumental in providing the discourse necessary for the continued exploitation and abuse of animals. By adopting vocabulary and language used by animal advocates and subtly reframing the context of phrases and expressions via labels, marketing, websites, and other promotion, animal agriculture aims to quell consumer concerns regarding the miserable lives that sentient beings lead in the production of animal foods. This chapter briefly examines the role that language has played over the years in enabling the exploitation of nonhuman animals and, more recently, the deliberate doublespeak and obfuscation of language commonly used to describe the treatment of animals.

Most consumers care about the environment, farm and slaughterhouse workers, sustainable practices in agriculture, and the humane and ethical treatment of animals. Many people are willing to pay premium prices for animal-derived products and stay loyal to companies that assure us that our ethical and environmental concerns are being addressed in the way the business is conducted. Companies, in turn, make known their awareness of customer concerns by using product labels that describe how the product was procured, processed, and packaged for sale. This practice, successfully utilized by proponents of animal agriculture in combating consumer complaints over the past decade, has two inherent flaws. First, manufacturers often exploit the grey areas created by the lack of firm legal definitions and use misleading language, such as "humane" or "all-natural" or "free-range," on their product labels. Second, and more importantly, labels that tout animal welfare claims perpetuate the myth that it is possible to "humanely" run any enterprise whose very foundational tenet is the systematic exploitation of our fellow sentient beings.

Human compassion is governed by a set of contradictory emotions and cognitive dissonance. Its inherent complexity allows us to express outrage and dismay at the three billion animals killed by the wildfires of 2020,[3] while calmly accepting as inevitable that over three billion land and aquatic animals are slaughtered every day for human consumption.[4] To be able to accomplish this emotional feat with minimal discomfort, we rely on language to provide the requisite discourses necessary to build our stories. We reconcile the contradiction by accepting the death of animals in wildfires as a tragedy, a one-off that is unlikely to happen very often and therefore deserving of our concern and condemnation. On the other hand, the organized industrial-scale slaughter of animals within animal agriculture is discussed as an inevitable but necessary evil required to maintain life as we know it on this planet. But as animal activists continue to counter these discourses with details and graphic imagery that expose the misery of farmed animals, and as environmental activists draw attention to the widespread destruction caused by intensive animal farming operations, consumer concerns surrounding animal welfare and the environment have sharply increased. Therefore, the vocabulary of animal agriculture, and the discourses it enables to ensure that consumers continue to demand animal products in high numbers, has to be actively chosen and constantly updated. Carefully constructed discourses by animal agriculture proponents tell us the stories we want to hear; even more importantly, they enable us to make peace with the contradictions that permit us to call ourselves animal lovers as we cuddle a companion animal and simultaneously ignore the organized exploitation and slaughter of other sentient beings.

Animals have been deliberately confined to language that markedly seeks to box them into stereotypes that designate them as "different" and "less than"—both necessary conditions that allow us to justify exploiting them.[5] Take the example of the number of pig-related metaphors in the English language with negative connotations. Porcine metaphors are usually used to describe sexist, disgusting, and lazy behavior, falling in with other anthropomorphisms that describe negative behavioral traits attributed to nonhuman animals that we actively exploit.[6] While humans and pigs are different species, we are both highly sensitive and emotional beings, and our capacity to suffer, both physically and psychologically, is the same. We now know that nonhuman animals are sentient beings, capable of experiencing pain as well as a wide range of emotions including fear, joy, grief, and happiness.

The vocabulary of a language can also be deconstructed to reflect the inherent prejudices of its people. As compelling historical records, vocabulary can be used to study evolving relationships between different tribes of humans, and also to document the relationship between humans and the environment.[7] Over the past decade, Arran Stibbe has studied ways in which language has been used (and abused) to structure and direct our interactions with animals.[8] He points out that we rely on destructive discourses to justify the way we relate to nonhuman animals. Destructive discourses are continually reinforced by organizations with profit-driven motives and provide us with the narratives we need to justify the exploitative and cruel relationship we currently have with our fellow sentient beings. The vocabulary within destructive discourses further empowers us with euphemistic terms necessary to distance ourselves from the realities of animal abuse, exploitation, and slaughter. For example, while referring to the selective breeding, fattening, and slaughter of a pig for her meat, we are provided with terms in the industry such as "sow durability" or "pork production," and in the retail sector, "fresh" or "humanely raised," thereby allowing us to distance ourselves from the mass cruelty and slaughter of these individuals that are required to enable us to eat the flesh of a fellow sentient being.[9]

While destructive discourses strive to make it acceptable and, indeed, inevitable that sentient beings have to be exploited for human survival, not to mention profits, counter-discourses are used by animal activists to draw attention to the exploitative ideologies of the meat lobby and the realities of animal agriculture. Stibbe points out the need for yet another discourse, an alternative one that firmly acknowledges the importance of animals at the center stage of our ecosystems and the pivotal role that nonhuman animals play in enabling human lives on Earth. In the absence of a narrative that examines the individuality of animals and acknowledges their existence beyond our need to confine and slaughter them, we are condemned to treat them as property and utilize them as commodities, to our own detriment.[10]

DOUBLESPEAK

For several decades, intensive animal agriculture and independent family farms have provided meat and dairy products to consumers in the U.S.[11] And while animal welfare concerns in animal agriculture have recently gained attention, it has fallen on the proponents of animal agriculture to conjure up the vocabulary and the language to ensure that the status quo can be maintained. Maintaining the status quo in animal agriculture will provide both the psychological refuge by which consumers can continue to eat meat and use animal products, and a means by which animal agriculture can prioritize profits over animal welfare. Doublespeak is often the method of choice employed by animal agriculture to maintain business as usual.

Doublespeak and the vocabulary of doublespeak consist of a word or phrase to intentionally introduce ambiguity within a sentence or a concept, thereby obscuring the meaning of simple words and ideas. Thus, by introducing ambiguity, doublespeak also provides alternative narratives to the intended meanings of words and ideas. In short, doublespeak muddies verbal waters. When confronted with the graphic reality of the lives of farmed animals bred for exploitation and slaughter, consumers demand an explanation. Animal agriculture responds by providing a counter-reality enabled via labels and marketing and built using the vocabulary of animal welfare activists.

The doublespeak on animal product labels and marketing provides a false sense of security to the consumer, who feels they are doing their part for animal protection. A report published by the Animal Welfare Institute showed that the U. S. Department of Agriculture (USDA) typically requires no evidence to back up claims made on the label that relates to the treatment of animals in farms.[12] When the USDA does issue labels pertaining to the treatment of farmed animals, it is generally done based on the documentation provided by the agricultural organization seeking its approval. With jurisdiction limited to slaughterhouses and meat processing plants, federal inspectors assigned with the task of verifying claims on the labels have limited access to information and have no credible way of learning firsthand the plight of animals on farms or the manner in which they are confined and maintained throughout their short lifespan. Labels provided by third-party verification organizations, such as Certified Animal Welfare Approved by AGW,[13] often claim to uphold better animal welfare standards as they require audits that ensure that certain standards are maintained during production, transport, and slaughter practices, but the difference from standard practice is woefully minimal. The strategy works to ensure profits are maintained and the "Certified Animal Welfare Approved by AGW" label has been shown to have the "single highest impact on consumer purchasing of any food label."

However, consider the fact that without the execution of a young sentient being that has been bred for the specific purpose of slaughter at a fraction of his or her natural lifespan, there cannot be animal flesh on one's plate. Without the exploitation of sentient beings that involves confinement, selective breeding, forced insemination to maximize productivity, monotony, severe boredom, and chaotic, terror-filled moments before slaughter—be it on an industrial farm or in an independent family-owned, pasture-raised organic facility—there can be no animal products available for human consumption. Let's examine doublespeak in the context of the all-encompassing term that is currently used with abandon, both by animal welfare activists and proponents of animal agriculture—the term "humane" animal slaughter.

Just as There Is No "Happy Meat," There Can Be No "Humane Meat"

The Oxford English Dictionary defines the term humane as "having or showing compassion or benevolence." There is no compassionate way to kill an animal who wants to live. No sentient being goes willingly to slaughter. No matter how ethically and kindly the animal is treated throughout her short life, a sentient being will never walk willingly to her premature death.

On the contrary, treating an animal raised for slaughter with compassion, gaining his trust, and then killing him when he reaches the target weight within four to six months of his life is the ultimate act of betrayal in our relationship with another fellow sentient being.[14] By setting the basic construct that animal exploitation and slaughter are an inevitable and necessary evil for human beings to survive—a practice that must go on as an evolutionary imperative and because there is no viable alternative—proponents of animal agriculture do not leave room for any counter-discourses, yet millions of people are thriving around the world without consuming animal products.

Instead, what is presented as a viable alternative by animal agriculture is an offer to treat an animal "humanely" and "compassionately" during his short lifespan and improve his quality of life before slaughter. This has led to the introduction of a cacophony of labels that are aimed at presenting animal exploitation and slaughter in a more palatable light for consumers. They include "cage-free eggs," "free-range chickens," "ethically sourced," "pasture-raised," "antibiotic-free," "Certified Humane," and "Animal Welfare Approved," to name a few. While certifications are an attempt to calm well-meaning consumer concerns over the treatment of animals, they are often used as a smokescreen to obscure a multitude of evils. For example, what a consumer who diligently buys "cage-free eggs" may not stop to consider is that there is much more cruelty inflicted on chickens who are selectively bred to produce eggs than the size of their confinement, such as chickens being brutally debeaked (a process where a portion of the beak of the chicken is burned off), or the monotony of life in a barren building, or the lack of sunlight, or the terror experienced as she is led to slaughter once her egg production has waned.

The inappropriate use of the term "humane" by the animal agriculture lobby is an example of doublespeak and has given rise to what animal advocates are calling "humanewashing." Humanewashing is defined as the practice of making misleading claims about the treatment of animals or the conditions in which they are born, raised, or killed.

Beyond Labels and Laws

There has been a deliberate absence of any meaningful laws to protect farmed animals. Animals raised for food are explicitly left out of the Animal Welfare Act. The two outdated federal laws that govern animals used in agriculture—The Humane Methods of Slaughter Act (1958) and the Twenty-Eight Hour Law (1994)—exempt all poultry species, which contributes to 98% of land animals bred for human consumption.[15] The so-called ag-gag laws, which restrict audio and video recording within animal agricultural operations without the owner's consent, are put in place to prevent consumers from finding out about the miserable plight of animals in these facilities. They are certainly not in place to protect the animals.[16] Ag-gag laws over the last decade are a significant setback to the already woefully deficient animal welfare laws and are a major blow to the tireless efforts of animal protection activists.

Countless animal activists have risked their lives repeatedly to inform the public of the conditions of our fellow sentient beings on intensive animal agriculture operations, organic family farms, and slaughterhouses. As consumers, we should now be well aware of the terror-filled lives of extreme cruelty that our fellow sentient beings experience, be it during confinement, en route to slaughter, or in their final terrifying moments on a conveyor belt before being slaughtered. Therefore, labels and laws notwithstanding, ignorance surrounding the cruel and horrifying lives that animals lead on farms has become less of an option for consumers. As the practices within animal agriculture are now open to consumer scrutiny, the proponents of this industry realize that discourses that worked in the past to sidestep this basic construct— that animal agriculture is based on the exploitation and execution of a sentient being, often conducted in the most horrific ways—have to be continually updated. In addition to strongly objecting to any discourse that acknowledges animals as sentient beings, proponents of animal agriculture continue to push language that designates nonhuman animals as "not on par" with humans and therefore, clearly, the suffering and terror they undergo cannot be compared to human suffering. When used skillfully and authoritatively, language can be relied on to maintain a power structure that does not question convenient assumptions.[17] Kinder, more ethical lifestyles that examine the construct that other living beings besides humans have a place on our planet, and acknowledge that nonhuman animals have a right not to be exploited solely for our benefit, are simply not discussed within destructive discourses. With the foundational construct asserting that animal exploitation and slaughter is non-negotiable, the rest of the discourse, such as the so-called "humane" treatment of sentient beings, is touted as granting concessions to nonhuman animals out of human largesse. It is worth considering that the basic construct—that humans need to exploit and consume animals for their survival—has been repeatedly debunked. The growing number of healthy, thriving vegans across the globe is a clear and present argument against this destructive narrative.

By either deliberately or inadvertently muddying the waters with doublespeak, the proponents of animal agriculture attempt to counter any criticism regarding the treatment of animals bred for food. This strategy ensures that the crux of the animal agriculture business continues to remain untouched. And business is thriving—it is estimated that currently a staggering 60% of mammals on Earth are animals raised for food,[18] with poultry alone representing 70% of all live birds on the planet, surpassing the total number of wild bird populations.[19] The numbers are expected to grow exponentially in the coming decade, and any incidental compassion shown to the animals to quell consumer concerns is projected to come at an increased cost to the consumer, thereby further protecting the bottom-line of the industry. A recent research survey sampled U.S. consumers on their concerns regarding the welfare of farmed animals and their readiness to pay for products with welfare certifications.[20] The respondents of the survey indicated that they were willing to pay 30–50% more for eggs and poultry that were raised under labels that indicated "trustworthy welfare certification." Over 50% of the consumers surveyed also indicated that they were willing to pay up to five dollars extra per entrée in restaurants that served welfare-certified animal products. Labels and claims have become intimately tied with profits, with well-meaning customers willing to pay a premium for "humane" animal-derived products, especially if the labels imply higher welfare standards than those of conventional farming operations.

Language, labels, and humanewashing aside, consumers of animal products are complicit in sustaining an industry that has its very foundation built on the exploitation of our fellow sentient beings. Currently, 72 billion land animals and over 1.2 trillion aquatic animals are killed for the products demanded by humans every year[21]—and there is no dearth of labels positioned to serve as a panacea for consumers who continue to want to believe that there is a humane way to exploit and slaughter an animal. This fallacy forms the crux of the humane hoax and profit-driven animal agriculture has been successful in propagating this discourse. Animal agriculture does not have to be an inevitable, non-negotiable part of living on Earth—we have the power to put an end to the unnecessary suffering of our fellow beings by consuming plant foods that don't involve confining, exploiting, and slaughtering nonhuman animals. There is simply no label, no marketing campaign, no comforting image, nor reassuring advertising that can rationalize, assuage, or justify the inherent cruelty of animal agriculture.

Devatha P. Nair has a keen interest in the subtle power of language and the role it plays in constructing stories that in turn define our realities. She writes for *Sentient Media* and is a part of their editorial team. She is also a materials scientist whose research is focused on developing polymer-based platforms for biomedical applications. She is vegan and lives in Denver, Colorado.

13

KINDRED SPIRITS OR COMMODIFIED OBJECTS?

Disconnection and Perception in the Humane Hoax

By Dr. Joanne Kong

ORIGINS

The origins of the humane hoax are clearly tied to altered perceptions rooted in the development of the herding culture. Prior to the establishment of tribal and agrarian societies, humans lived as opportunistic eaters, gathering, hunting, and scavenging for food. In a nomadic existence, humans existed with other animals in a complex web of life, highly observant of nonhuman animals' unique abilities and behaviors, and fascinated by the powers they seemed to hold.

As human cultures developed, a shift in this relationship began to take place. Along with a rise in population, people began to abandon nomadic lifestyles, seeking and settling in places where food, shelter, and land for growing crops were available. Agriculture slowly took hold, as did the concept of ownership, not only of land, but of animals as well, beginning with cows, sheep, and goats. This marked a critical change in our perceptions of animals; we began seeing them not as kindred spirits, but as commodities, objects, and tools for our use. The ultimate rise of urbanization and consumerism, which shaped the foundations of our modern culture, served only to reinforce this view of animals as units of production within industries whose sole goals were efficiency and profit. As described by Jim Mason in *An Unnatural Order,*

> Buried beneath the demands and devices of dominionist culture, the need for animals—as exercisers of human empathy and nurturance, as kindred beings in the unity of creation, as feeders and informers of the psyche—is hard to see. Their importance in these ways is not (to use computer-ese again) easily called up on our screens. Our software today is dominionist and utilitarian, and it calls up only the value of animals as resources or tools.[1]

This change in the perception of humans towards nonhuman animals thus created a hierarchy, the sense that all beings are *not* equal in status. Rather, human animals assumed a position of superiority. Accepted was the notion of nonhuman animals as "others," less deserving of compassion and respect. As Michael Mountain writes,

> I am not an animal." Over thousands of years, we humans have sought to separate ourselves from the rest of nature, to see ourselves as superior and "exceptional." We don't even like to be reminded of the fact that we *are* animals. *They* are animals, *we* are humans. . . . As long as we're in denial about our own animal nature, almost any effort to treat our fellow animals with the respect we grant each other is doomed to fail.[2]

This accepted position of power and dominion over other animals, together with the human need to feel that their actions are justified, has led to the contradictory nature of the "humane hoax." Regardless of the circumstances and conditions in which animals are raised, nothing should distract us from this central truth: these innocent beings are victims of exploitation. Their lives culminate in a violent death at our hands—how can this ever be considered humane? This lies at the core of what all manifestations of the humane hoax are—distractions from, and distortions of, the most atrocious acts of cruelty and violence ever exacted upon other species.

EMOTIONAL VALUE

The humane hoax has deep ties to the ways in which consumers make their purchasing decisions. A large part of these choices connects to the so-called "emotional value" of the product—in other words, how it makes the consumer *feel*. We are, after all, emotional beings, and naturally feel drawn to make a purchase if we perceive we are doing good in the process. Thus, where animals and animal products are concerned, buyers are deceptively led into the trap of making choices that are anything but humane. Think of the proliferation of product labels we see in grocery stores, such as "free-range," "cage-free," "free-roaming," "grass-fed," "pasture-raised," "high welfare," "Certified Humane," and "Animal Welfare Approved." Sadly, such terms continue to deceive consumers into believing they are making ethical food choices, when in actuality there is not only an astounding lack of oversight, regulation, and consistency in such claims, but a built-in ambiguity that misleads consumers. For example, 63% of Americans believe that "free-range" chickens live outdoors in natural settings,[3] when in fact the birds are generally crammed together in horrifying indoor warehouse facilities, suffering from fear, debilitating injuries, and industry-standard mutilations. Additionally, food packaging and promotion reinforces a false reality, showing pictures of animals in pleasant, sunlit fields, happy and healthy. All these marketing ploys, aimed at appealing to buyers' "feel-good" perceptions, do nothing to erase the fact that these animals are brutally killed at a fraction of their natural lifespans.

FALSE EQUIVALENCES

Another aspect of the humane hoax that has conditioned consumer behavior is the creation of false notions that certain animal agricultural practices are, by their very nature, "humane." One of the most common is the idea that small or local farms are ethical. But regardless of whether an animal spends her short life in an industrialized facility or on a small rural farm, the result is the same: the animal has been denied her freedom along with the ability to engage in natural behaviors. The scale of the operation is irrelevant; to the industry, all farmed animals are nothing more than objects, and cruel common procedures are universal to making a product profitable. Through their commodification, any recognition of their individuality and will to live has been violated. Furthermore, on small farms it is tragic that connections of trust are sometimes forged between the animal and his "owner," only to be horrifically betrayed when it comes time for the animal to be slaughtered.

Along the same lines, the animal agriculture industry touts the convenience of two supposedly more humane slaughtering practices: 1) Mobile slaughter units, where a trailer comes directly to the rural farmer with "everything you need," and 2) DYI (Do-It-Yourself) slaughter, a type of false empowerment that there is some kind of intrinsic worth in killing the animal yourself. The latter is the same slaughter process that is found at large abattoirs, just done "on the farm" with animals gasping for their last breath—bleeding out in the grass. DIY slaughter has a history of horrific botched killings when the inexperienced hobbyist causes more suffering than was ever intended. It is deeply unsettling to see how far these practices move consumer perceptions away from the act of killing that is taking place; instead, it's called "harvesting" the animal, or "putting the animal down." Decentralizing animal slaughter away from large, industrialized facilities does nothing to erase the fact that innocent beings suffered the ultimate loss of their lives.

DISTANCED AND DISCONNECTED

In dispelling the myth of the humane hoax, the challenges of creating a new paradigm of compassionate awareness are undeniable. The deeply ingrained acceptance of animal exploitation, whether through the food, research, clothing, recreation, or entertainment industries, is so broad and habitual that I often describe it as an invisible thread running through the fabric of our lives, existing without question. Sadly, ethical discussions are not at the forefront of broad public awareness; the humane hoax persists with the underlying acceptance and expectation that animals will be killed, with massive indifference.

As a culture, we have allowed ourselves to live in a state of deep disconnection from our kindred animals, numbed from seeing them as worthy individuals with the same behaviors we all share and value as sentient beings. Labelling and marketing descriptions only exacerbate this divide and distort our perceptions, diminishing our ability to embrace our shared animal nature. Cows are "beef," pigs are "pork," birds are "poultry," and animal flesh is "meat." We hear the terms "lab rats," "circus animals," and "farm animals," with the intrinsic implications that animals serve a utilitarian purpose for humans. Furthermore, consumer messaging ingrains the idea that only "real leather" and "real fur" will do. Many of us remember the slogan, "Beef—Real Food for Real People." The animals are nothing more than units of profit in a food system driven by corporate interests and unbridled industrial growth.

Likewise, workers in the harrowing conditions of slaughterhouses and meatpacking facilities are victims as well. They suffer extraordinarily high rates of physical injury, psychological and emotional trauma, social withdrawal and PTSD, leading to increased incidences of domestic violence, as well as drug and alcohol abuse. Timothy Pachirat, who worked undercover for five months in a Midwest slaughterhouse, writes the following:

> Exploring industrialized killing from this vantage point draws attention to the distance we create through walls, screens, catwalks, fences, security checkpoints, and geographic zones of isolation and confinement. It reveals the distance we create by constructing and reinforcing racial, gender, citizenship, and education hierarchies that coerce others into performing dangerous, demeaning, and violent tasks from which we directly benefit. It makes visible the distance we create with language—in the ways we avoid precise descriptions of repugnant things, inventing instead less dangerous names and phrases for them.[4]

How telling that at the beginning of the global pandemic, the plight of workers was addressed only insofar as their illnesses from COVID-19 brought disruptions to operations and "meat supply chains." Clearly, the false narrative continues—that consuming animals is necessary to a functioning society. Our culture as a whole has become desensitized, accepting and normalizing the violence that takes place on a massive scale against billions of innocent animals, every second of every day. How stunningly hypocritical is Smithfield's tagline, "Good food. Responsibly."

To speak of my own personal experiences, my upbringing reflects a particular aspect in which the consumption of animals has become culturally celebrated—namely, that of culinary excellence. My father and especially my aunt had reputations as superb cooks, the latter with a notable reputation in which she was praised as the "Julia Child of Cantonese cuisine." I have many memories of Chinese dishes intricately and meticulously prepared and admired—shark's fin soup, chicken feet, beef tongue, chrysanthemum fish balls, red-cooked pork, pig's feet, and more. In this cuisine and many others, there is also the idea that lesser-consumed animal species (lamb, duck, squab, baby goat, and octopus, for example) are delicacies, special treats to be savored with the senses. It is indeed disturbing to realize the perceptual disconnect taking place here: the brutal killing of a kindred being has come to be disguised as culinary art. I look back with shame at the fact that my younger self did not possess the awareness to realize *whose* body parts I was consuming, yet I hope it provides me with the necessary perspectives to help others on their vegan journey, and to do it in a way that is positive and not judgmental.

Ultimately, ending the humane hoax will only be possible when we make the choice to abandon the practices of food production that are rooted in suffering and the violation of every animal's desire to live. While we are making progress, the task is a difficult one. What is called for is a true revolution of the heart, rising above material self-interests to a new, deeper spiritual awareness. This is not some vague notion—in truth, it is a movement of our collective consciousness toward seeing ourselves in all others. It's a new perception in which boundaries and divisions no longer separate us, and a higher level of caring for ourselves, animals, and the planet is grounded in the knowledge that we are all connected.

Dr. Joanne Kong has been praised as one of the most compelling advocates for plant-sourced nutrition today. Her highly-praised TEDx talk, "The Power of Plant-Based Eating," is placed on numerous websites internationally. Author of *If You've Ever Loved an Animal, Go Vegan*, she is profiled in *Legends of Change* about vegan women changing the world, and she is an editor of the book, *Vegan Voices: Essays by Inspiring Changemakers*. She also appears in the 2021 documentary *Eating Our Way to Extinction*, narrated by Kate Winslet. Her vegan advocacy has been recognized around the world, with international talks in Italy, Spain, Germany, Norway, Canada, and India. Dr. Kong is a critically acclaimed and award-winning classical pianist on the faculty at the University of Richmond, and she combines her musical artistry and public speaking to advocate for animals, veganism, and the environment.

14

"HUMANE EGGS" AND "HAPPY WINGS"

A Look Behind the Labels

by Karen Davis, Ph.D.

Many people are buying "free-range," "cage-free," and "organic" products as perceived alternatives to conventional poultry and eggs. "Free-range" and "cage-free" convey positive images of chickens living outdoors in sunshine, fresh air, and open space. Historically, the term "range" meant that, in addition to living outside and getting exercise, the birds could sustain themselves on the land they occupied, but this is no longer the case. Birds raised for meat in the United States may be sold as "free-range" if they have U.S. Department of Agriculture-certified access to the outdoors, a requirement that isn't monitored.[1]

Consumers understandably confuse "free-range" and "cage-free" labels. Eggs sold in the U.S. may be labeled "free-range" even when thousands of hens are confined in a shed with little or no access to the outdoors. The exit may be very small, affecting only those closest to it, and the "range" may be merely a mudyard. But whereas "free-range" implies some sort of outdoor access for the hens, "cage-free" means that, while the hens are not squeezed into wire cages, they are packed together in densely crowded, unhealthy buildings from which they never emerge until they are deemed "spent" by their owners.[2]

Adding to the confusion is the word "organic." Legally, organic animal farming refers to the ingredients that are fed to chickens and other farmed animals. Created in 1990 by the United States Congress under the Organic Foods Production Act, the National Organic Program is administered by the USDA.[3] Since 2002, the USDA has been charged with certifying that products labeled "organic" come from animals who were fed no antibiotics, growth hormones, or animal byproducts. Synthetic pesticides and fertilizers, bioengineering, and ionizing radiation are also prohibited.

The Organic Program further stipulates that poultry products labeled organic must be sourced from birds who had access to the outdoors, although an exception is made whenever avian influenza outbreaks threaten the poultry and egg industries.[4] The USDA does not verify organic products. It appoints organic certifiers to authorize the Certified Organic or USDA organic labels. This arrangement contributes to the lowering of standards, including misleading and often fraudulent claims in which "conventional" and "alternative" farming practices converge.

"THE HAPPY HENS"

In 1992, a group of caring people and I visited two small-scale egg farms in Lancaster County, Pennsylvania: The Happy Hen and Sauder's Eggs. Twenty years later, we visited a farm in Nelson County, Virginia, called Black Eagle.

"The Happy Hen Organic Fertile Brown Eggs" were advertised as satisfying "the demands of today's health-conscious consumers." The hens—"docile" yet "hardy"—were described as "free running in a natural setting." They were characterized as "humanely housed in healthy, open-sided housing, for daily sunning—something Happy Hens really enjoy."[5]

The Happy Hen was an enterprise of Pleasant View Farms, a family poultry business run by Joe Moyer, who drove us to a remote Amish farmstead where the three Happy Hen houses were located. Through the netting at the front end of a long shed, we saw a sea of chicken faces looking out. Inside, the birds were wall to wall. They were severely debeaked, and their feathers were straggly, drab, and worn off. When we commented on their feathers, Moyer said, "We have a saying: The rougher they look, the better they lay."

Each 9,000 square–foot shed held 6,800 hens, with one rooster per 100 hens. Each bird had a maximum of 1.5 square feet to "run free" in. The three Happy Hen sheds were identical. As we approached each one, the faces of the chickens close to the netting looked out at a leafy countryside on a June day they would never enjoy.

Though chickens can live from five to twenty years, the Happy Hens were deemed "old"—"spent"—at fourteen months. "Old" and "spent" are economic terms meaning that the number of eggs the hens are laying no longer justifies feeding and maintaining them, even though each hen could potentially continue laying eggs for years, having been bred for this purpose.

At the point of being "spent," the Happy Hens were reclassified as "Moyer's Uncaged Hens" and trucked in crates to live poultry markets in Pennsylvania, New Jersey, and New York City, where they fetched a dollar per bird compared to 25 cents or less at a spent fowl plant. A spent fowl plant is a specialized slaughter facility for "spent" flocks of birds that are used to produce fertilized eggs for breeding or for human consumption. Following slaughter, they are trucked to rendering plants for processing into soups, pies, sausages, pet food, farmed animal feed, and so on.

Moyer's Happy Hens had nubs and stubs and jags instead of beaks. A couple of hens pecked as best they could at our shoes. When I knelt down, they immediately showed interest and curiosity. They did not act as if they would be "docile" if they had a real life. And if they're so "docile," I wondered, why are they debeaked?

HOME ON THE RANGE

Sauder's Eggs is a large battery-caged hen operation with plants in Pennsylvania, Ohio and Maryland. Sauder's also produces cage-free eggs for consumers willing to pay more. According to the website, Sauder's employs 120 family farmers who raise 6.2 million hens with an output of 1.5 billion eggs a year.[6] At the time of our visit to one of the Sauders' Amish contract farms, their eggs from uncaged "free-roaming hens" were priced at $2.89 a dozen compared to $1.03 a dozen from hens raised in the company's conventional battery-cage facilities.[7]

The farm we visited had 4,200 hens in a shed that was said to provide each hen and the 40 roosters enclosed with them two square feet of living space per bird. All were debeaked. We asked why the birds had so little individual floor space, and were told, "A hen won't lay as many eggs if she gets exercise. Also, active hens need more feed, making the eggs cost more to produce. Caged hens get lower-power feed, so their eggs cost less." It should be noted that feeding farmed animals is the biggest cost of raising them, averaging 70 to 75% of the total.

The backs of many of Sauder's hens were featherless. When we asked why, we were told, "They're ready to go out"—that is, to be slaughtered. The hens were destroyed after just a year of producing one egg every two or three days. Metal nest boxes lined the walls and a slatted platform ran the length of the shed for perching. The farmer said that in his view, the hens would be better off outside where "they are not likely to peck each other" and because "chickens love earth worms which they know are good for them." Yet these thousands of birds would never see the outdoors.

BLACK EAGLE FARM

An article in the *Nelson County Times* in April 2008 announced that by June there would be 24,000 chickens on a 1,000-acre farm called Black Eagle Farm, making it "the largest organic, free-range, egg producer in the state" of Virginia.[8] Ralph Glatt, the farm president, estimated that the hens would lay 20,000 eggs a day and that the number of hens would likely double by the end of the year to fill the close to football-size facility. They would have places to roost inside, exposure to natural light and air, and access to the outside with an average of five feet of space per bird within a fenced yard. Farm manager John Dobbs said that while other farms in Virginia already produced organic and free-range eggs, Black Eagle would be the first to produce and market such eggs on a large scale.

In 2010, we published a report in our quarterly magazine *Poultry Press*, "Black Eagle Farm: Story of an Organic Egg Scam."[9] In it, we described the appalling cruelty revealed at the farm in documents obtained by an attorney in the course of investigating a complaint about malnourished dogs at Black Eagle. Located 100 miles from Richmond,

Virginia, and 130 miles from Washington, D.C., Black Eagle portrayed itself as a "traditional family farm with a long history of treating our animals and the environment with respect" and a "sustainable producer of USDA organic, animal-friendly natural livestock products."

Documents obtained by the attorney revealed an absentee owner, unpaid bills, and malnourished dogs, pigs, and sheep. A veterinarian with the Virginia Department of Agriculture and Consumer Services discovered a building with 25,000 hens described in her report as "thin to emaciated," with many dead and dying birds on the floor. Farm personnel told her the hens had been unfed for seven days in November, five days in December, and for two straight weeks earlier in the year.

Through December of 2009, veterinarians with the Virginia Department of Agriculture and Consumer Services emailed each other back and forth, eventually authorizing an emergency ration for the surviving hens to hold them until after Christmas Day. They told each other that no private veterinarian was available to attend to the hens and that industry veterinarians like themselves do not bother with smaller farms like Black Eagle. Discussion centered on "depop"—depopulating the hens on December 27th and trucking them to a North Carolina rendering company. New hens would be brought to the farm in 2010.

In phone calls with me, former Black Eagle Farm manager John Dobbs described the depopulation of the flock he witnessed in December of 2009. Instead of going to a spent fowl slaughter plant, the hens were painfully gassed with carbon dioxide (CO_2) on the premises—a terrifying and common egg industry method of killing "spent" hens.[10]

"We gotta play baseball with these chickens?"—Black Eagle Farm owner Dr. Ralph Glatt during the "depopulation" of the surviving hens in late December 2009.

"Burning the hell out of them with CO2."—John Dobbs to Karen Davis, April 22, 2011.

"I think it freezes their lungs."—Ralph Glatt to Karen Davis, June 20, 2011.

CARBON DIOXIDE GASSING PROCEDURE
DESCRIBED BY JOHN DOBBS:

Shut the lights off. Grab the hens by their legs off the perches and floor, take them out of the house and stuff them in metal boxes 2 ft. wide x 5 ft. long x 3 ft. deep. Put 200–500 hens in each box. Four or five metal boxes in all.

Stick a rubber hose attached to a CO_2 tank inside the box and shoot cold CO_2 into the box through the nozzle until the hens flop around. The birds on top burn and suffocate to death from the freezing CO_2.

The birds on the bottom of the boxes won't die. When the boxes were opened they ran around and employees whacked them with boards. One employee put a bird on the ground and another struck her with a board like he was hitting a baseball. Ralph Glatt said, "We gotta play baseball with these chickens?"

After this, if any hens were still alive, "you just pull their heads off. You're not supposed to truck them if they're still alive."

John Dobbs worked for Black Eagle for three and a half years. He grew up on a hog farm where he shot cows and "knocked" piglets, but he said that the killing of these hens was the worst cruelty he ever saw. He said the metal box–CO_2 procedure for depopulating "spent" hens was developed by the caged layer industry. He said, "I'm a big advocate of banning the boxes. Better to gas the whole house at once."

OUR VISIT TO BLACK EAGLE FARM, JUNE 20, 2011

In June of 2011, two staff members and I visited Black Eagle Farm with egg-industry businessman Bob Pike. His business, GCB Foods in North Carolina, markets eggs to retailers from farms said to have met inspection standards. In 2010, Humane Farm Animal Care (HFAC) decertified Black Eagle as a "humane" operation based on the abuses revealed in the records obtained by the attorney in 2009.[11]

Our tour of Black Eagle included Bob Pike, Ralph Glatt, a Nelson County Animal Control officer, and a farm employee. Of the four units housed in a single building (two "cage-free," two "organic"), two were said to be empty at the time of our visit. Each unit was designed to hold 12,500 hens, making 50,000 hens in all. We viewed a unit holding 12,500 "organic" brown hens through glass. They covered every inch of space on the floor and on the platforms above the floor. Each hen supposedly got a 1.4 square foot of space for herself under the "organic" and "humane" standards set for aviary units like these, we were told.

Next, we visited the "cage-free" brown hens in a unit holding 9,000 hens, including what Bob Pike called "salvage" hens diverted from other egg farms in the process of depopulating their own flocks. Moving "salvage" flocks from one farm to another is a common egg industry practice, he said. Since the cage-free unit we visited was 3,500 hens short of its 12,500-hen capacity, the hens we walked among had some space to move about on the floor and on the platforms, which included sloping strips of plastic for laying their eggs behind little flapping curtains the length of the building. These plastic strips were what they called "nests." On the floor was a thin layer of musty wood chips, and overhead fans were running, although John Dobbs told me that "when you visit these places, they'll be sure to turn the fans on right before your visit."

A passageway was called the winter garden. Separated by glass from the green vegetation visible outside, the floor of this area was covered with hens. John Dobbs had told me, "They like the winter garden because they gravitate naturally toward sunlight." We petted and talked to these hens, crouched down and gently picked up a few, holding them and trying to impart to their spirits that we cared about them and were sorry, *so sorry*. They were a little shy but mostly friendly and interested, but we had to go. We asked if we could please take some hens back to United Poultry Concerns to live in our sanctuary, but the answer was no. We would have to leave them behind, except in our memories. How were these innocent and defenseless creatures, so young and full of unexpressed life, "depopulated"? Were they gassed in the metal boxes, burned and frozen and kicked around like footballs? By whatever means, their death would be brutal. Bob Pike told us their time was almost up.

In December of 2011, I spoke with Bob Pike. He said Black Eagle Farm "is all organic now." The farm "grows its own pullets (young chickens) to 16 weeks, then transfers them to the laying facility." Each of the four units had its own "isolated pasture area" for the hens to go outside sometimes. A company in California was Black Eagle's new organic certifier. When the hens are depopulated, he said, they go to various slaughter facilities in Pennsylvania, Georgia and Virginia. Some are "salvage flocks." Salvage flocks are trucked to other egg farms, depending on who wants them and pays the best price.

Humane Animal Care

Lest it be thought that the conditions I've described are rare or are no longer practiced by the majority of alternative egg producers, I must point out that, while some businesses may treat their hens better, investigations of alternative poultry and egg farms typically reveal practices and attitudes that do not meet consumer expectations—expectations that are cultivated not only by the companies and retailers they do business with, such as Whole Foods and Pete and Gerry's Organics, but also by animal welfare organizations that support "humane animal care" through certification programs that gloss over the facts.

In part, the deception arises from the popular notion that free-range, cage-free, and organic farming is essentially a collection of small, local enterprises, distinct from industrialized operations like, say, Tyson Foods and Perdue Farms in the meat industry, or Cal-Maine and Rose Acres in the egg industry. But as a 2019 report on the organic food industry in *The Washington Post* explains, contrary to the pristine image of organic egg production, "many conventional egg producers have organic subsidiaries that operate on a vast scale, 100,000 laying hens housed in a huge building, their federally mandated access to outdoor space winkingly fulfilled by screened porches." This hoodwink relates in part to the fact that "many of the original organic food companies are now owned and subsidized by huge conventional companies. Kellogg's owns Kashi, General Mills owns Annie's, Perdue owns Niman Ranch, etc."[12]

These companies, like all businesses seeking organic accreditation, pay the organic certifiers for their service. As a result, unscrupulous relationships between the certifiers and the certified can flourish financially to benefit both parties, enabling practices that are completely at odds with organic to hide behind fraudulent labels and the inflated prices they command.

An example is Nellie's Free Range Eggs. Owned by the New Hampshire–based company, Pete and Gerry's Organics, Nellie's Eggs, which can cost up to eight dollars a dozen, are labeled "Certified Humane." In 2019, People for the Ethical Treatment of Animals (PETA) filed a lawsuit alleging that Nellie's Eggs falsely depicts hens ranging on open pastures and being cuddled by children, when in fact Nellie's hens are crammed inside long confinement sheds holding 20,000 hens per shed with little more than a square foot of living space for each hen.[13]

As in all commercial egg production, the newborn brothers of Nellie's hens are destroyed at the hatchery as soon as they break out of their shells in the mechanical incubators. Newborn roosters in egg industry sectors across the globe are ground up alive, suffocated, or electrocuted to death. Unlike birds bred for meat, for which purpose both hens and roosters are raised and slaughtered, male birds in the egg industry—other than those born specifically for use in the breeder flocks or the fertilized egg market—are destroyed because they don't lay eggs.

Pete and Gerry's Organics disputes the PETA lawsuit's claims, asserting through the company's chief executive: "Our humane practices stand in sharp contrast with the overwhelming majority of egg producers in the U.S., and we can confidently say that our family farms have a flawless history of upholding our high animal welfare standards."

All agribusiness companies claim "high animal welfare standards." Moreover, it is only by comparison with the worst conditions and practices of industrialized animal farming that any commercial trafficker in animals can claim to be "humane." It isn't just industry. Mainstream journalists have been known to contribute to the misperception of alternative animal farming as a positive or "not so bad" experience for the animals involved.

For example, Tom Philpott, writing in *Mother Jones* in 2015, discusses an investigative video produced by an animal rights organization of a Petaluma Farms operation in California that supplies "organic" and "cage-free" eggs to Whole Foods Market and Organic Valley. In "What Does 'Cage-Free' Even Mean?" Philpott does not question the truth of the videos. Yet he writes that "compared to the vast Iowa facilities that triggered a half-billion-egg salmonella recall in 2010 . . . (they) actually look pretty good."[14]

Just a few paragraphs earlier, Philpott had described the houses that he says comparatively speaking look pretty good: "lots of birds wallowing tightly together, often amidst what looks like significant buildup of their own waste . . . birds with blisters, missing feathers, one clearly caked with shit—along with birds that appear to be in decent shape." So what is a reader to make of this nonsense, and why does Philpott choose the word "wallowing," which, though technically correct, suggests that the birds are more disgusting for being trapped in the muck than their abusers are for making them live in it?

Animal welfare organizations also contribute to public misperception by contrasting smaller operations favorably with "factory farming" and leading consumers to believe they are helping chickens and turkeys, not by being vegan, but by purchasing the birds and eggs whose owners the welfare organizations endorse. But as political activist Harriet Schleifer observed, "The public comes to feel that the use of animals for food is in some way acceptable, since even the animal welfare people say so. This cannot help but make it much more difficult to eliminate the practice in the future."[15]

Not every animal welfare organization seeks to eliminate the use of animals for food, however. In 2012, the American Society for the Prevention of Cruelty to Animals (ASPCA) announced a $151,000 grant to Frank Reese, owner of the Good Shepherd Poultry Ranch in Lindsborg, Kansas. Flush with this grant, the Good Shepherd Poultry Ranch, which at the time was producing 72,000 hatching chicken eggs and 30,000 hatching turkey eggs per season for the poultry meat business, would now "be able to increase this amount to 600,000 chicken eggs and 100,000 turkey eggs per season," according to ASPCA spokesman Bret Hopman, who called Good Shepherd "the market leader in the sale of chicken and turkey products that come from birds raised entirely outside of the factory farming industry."[16]

This non-factory farming claim is a lie. A commercial poultry operation is a form of factory farming, including the fact that the birds do not incubate and hatch under the body and care of a mother hen, but in industrial hatcheries like Murray McMurray in Iowa. McMurray alone ships 100,000 or more chicks to buyers each week through the U.S. Postal Service as airmail. As many chicks die in the mail, hatcheries often stuff two or three baby roosters into a box of female chicks as "packers," since, as previously noted, they are otherwise destroyed.[17]

It is unethical for an animal welfare organization to support the view that billions of consumers can eat megatons of products from animals raised "humanely" on non-factory farms. Human beings will never set aside vast acres of land to accommodate billions of animals living "free-range," even if it were economically feasible, which it could never be, and if we had the arable land to spare, which we do not. Yet this ludicrous prospect is put before a public willing to believe the impossible, "since even the animal welfare people say so."

Killing "It" Is Personal

Seeking to distinguish themselves from factory farmers, the "ethical" meat people employ a rhetoric of "respect," even "reverence," for the animals they kill. An example is a woman named Camas Davis, founder of a "meat collective" that is part of an "ethical meat movement." In July of 2018, Davis appeared on the National Public Radio show *Fresh Air*, hosted by Terry Gross.[18] In the jargon of this movement, she told how farmers and butchers "revere" and "respect" the animals they kill and cut up, and how calling an animal "it" comports with "respect" for the animal, which turns out to mean nothing more than "using every part of" the corpse.

In a flat voice she described fitting pigs with electricity wired into "head phones" clamped onto the pig, supposedly to stun the animal. She conceded that this "humane" procedure doesn't always work, judged by the pig's reaction. Asked which animal she first killed with her own hands, she said a chicken. She said chickens have a "reptilian brain" that causes them to "calm down" before you scramble their brains by sticking a knife through the roof of their mouth.

Since the "ethical meat movement" invokes the pre-factory farming era as its model, it's important to strip this model of humane trappings, which a dip into the history of traditional farming makes easy. For example, a book called *Marketing Poultry Products*, published in 1937, describes the traditional farming practice of "braining" a bird prior to cutting the bird's throat:

> In braining, the beak is pried open and a cut is made through the roof of the mouth through a carotid artery or jugular vein to the base of the brain with a knife, which can also be inserted through the bird's lower eyelid to the brain. The knife is then twisted in the brain to paralyze the bird to facilitate immobilization and feather release: "It is necessary that the brain be pierced with a knife so that the muscles of the feather follicles are paralyzed, allowing the feathers to come out more easily."[19]

The method of inducing muscular paralysis in poultry with a knife the old-fashioned way was replaced in the twentieth century by dragging the birds facedown through electrified water troughs in the industrialized slaughter plants that replaced traditional slaughter. Camas Davis equates the muscular paralysis of fully conscious birds with "calmness." In fact, the birds are in excruciating pain, but being paralyzed, they cannot express their agony, whether caused by a knife in the brain or by volts of electricity pulsing through their bodies and faces. A former Tyson chicken slaughter plant worker, Virgil Butler, described the chickens he killed for years in Arkansas before quitting the business: "They have been 'stunned,' so their muscles don't work, but their eyes do, and you can tell by them looking at you that they're scared to death."[20]

Meanwhile, the big corporations are eager to cash in on the alternative farming trend. Steve Striffler, in *Chicken*, describes how Tyson Foods "jumped on the organic bandwagon with its Nature's Farm Organic Chicken," proclaiming that the chickens slaughtered under this brand name are raised on an "all-natural . . . vegetable diet of organically grown grains . . . , plus a blend of the natural vitamins and minerals they need (just like you) to grow up strong and healthy." Unlike Tyson's billions of "regular" chickens, these organic chickens are said to have "room to spread their wings" before they are slaughtered and placed on an "environmentally friendly recyclable" tray.[21]

What Tyson's move into the alternative chicken meat production sector shows, Striffler explains, is how easy it is "to produce 'healthy' organic and free-range chicken in a way that differs very little from industrial chicken" and "why companies such as Tyson have moved so quickly into organic chicken. It requires very little change in the way that industry leaders do business."[22]

Like Tyson, Perdue Farms has a "free-range, organic" chicken product. Television commercials in 2019 showed CEO Jim Perdue and his sons outdoors with a few bright-white chickens with bulging breasts at their feet. Yet even as this commercial was airing, the USDA was assisting producers who prefer keeping their birds indoors, citing everything from the weather on a particular day to the risk of the chickens or turkeys coming into contact with wild birds carrying an avian influenza virus.

In *The Way We Eat: Why Our Food Choices Matter*, published in 2006, co-authors Jim Mason and Peter Singer describe a visit to Pete and Gerry's Organic Eggs in New Hampshire, where they found 100,000 debeaked hens confined in six long sheds. The manager explained that the sheds were "sealed" and that the hens had little interest in going outside anyway, in what the authors describe in the book as "a bare patch of dirt."[23]

Similarly, an investigator with East Bay Animal Advocates discovered conditions at Diestel Turkey Ranch, a "free-range" farm in Northern California and a supplier to Whole Foods Market, which in 2005 announced an initiative called "Farm Animal Compassionate Standards." Investigated in 2004 and 2005, Diestel Turkey Ranch turned out to be a standard turkey operation complete with debeaked young turkeys crowded miserably together inside filthy sheds and not a turkey outside to be seen.[24]

THE AVIAN INFLUENZA EXCUSE

Poultry and egg producers tell the public that the avian influenza viruses that ravage domestic flocks are the result of birds running wild in the fresh air and open skies. The way to control the viruses, they insist, is to lock up every domestic bird, exterminate all birds in the affected region, and start over. For the industries, these disease outbreaks and mass exterminations are no big deal, just part of the cost of doing business. Armed with government reimbursements and insurance policies, producers can exterminate billions of birds at a time and restock their facilities without losing a cent.[25]

In 2019, the *Los Angeles Times* reported that Southern California was "plagued by an outbreak of a highly contagious viral disease that can affect all species of birds but is most deadly to chickens. . . . To stop the spread of the virus, more than 1.2 million birds, mainly chickens, have been euthanized [*sic*] in heavily affected areas, some of which weren't showing symptoms or hadn't been infected yet."[26] The death squads—"poorly trained temporary workers hired without sufficient background checks and put into the field without sufficient training" by the California Department of Food and Agriculture—entered people's property and killed their birds using "gassing, gunshot, and blunt force trauma." These methods are not "euthanasia"—which means a merciful death.[27]

In all such outbreaks, and increasingly as a matter of year-round policy, government authorities encourage or require corporate and residential owners alike to lock their birds permanently indoors, away from waterfowl and wild birds—away from the natural world altogether.

These government directives undermine the performance of free-range and organic husbandry. The National Organic Program is under attack from within, aided by the state and federal departments of agriculture. An article published in 2019 states:

> The NOP standards require outdoor access for livestock, grass for ruminants and dirt for scratching for poultry. Shortly after the creation of the NOP, a chicken farm, where the chickens never walk outside but only access the outdoors by spending time on a porch, applied for certification. Today, most eggs with the organic label come from similar farms.[28]

IT'S NOT A BIRD. IT'S A BUSINESS.

The degradation of animals is an inherent part of raising them for food. Their food is chosen; their social, familial, and physical environment is controlled; their reproductive organs and activities are manipulated; and how long they live is determined by humans. They can be abused and killed at will based on economic "necessity." An example in poultry and egg production is the routine culling—killing—of birds who are not gaining weight fast enough or laying enough eggs. Whatever compassion a person may initially feel for birds slated for commercialization, once they become a business, the business mentality takes over.

So while it may be that a hen in a cage-free facility suffers less than a hen in a wire cage, "cage-free" is not cruelty-free for birds who yearn to be outdoors digging in the soil, sunbathing, dustbathing, perching in trees, running around, and socializing. Having maintained a sanctuary for rescued chickens for many years, I've watched their natural behavior and innate cheerfulness revive under the influence of sunshine, fresh air, and the earth under their feet. A well-managed organic or free-range system can be an improvement on the standard industrialized model of production, but it does not solve the problem of the unnatural isolation of the birds from other sexes and age groups of their species. It does not solve the problem of taking life merely for the sake of profit or because one likes the taste of chicken soup. It does not solve the problem of disguising the violence with language designed to deceive the public.

Not long ago, I watched a video produced by an egg farm featuring a large number of brown hens in a field. They were young and vibrant, running in the grass. Close-ups revealed their bright eyes and eager faces—faces I have come to know well in my work. The narrator explained that these hens would soon be "spent." I pictured them being grabbed upside down and shoved into kill-carts, transport crates, or metal boxes as their hearts beat rapidly in fear. The next stop could be a live poultry market, a battery-cage facility, or a spent fowl plant hundreds of miles away. Most likely they would be deprived of food two or three days before being carried off or gassed on site, in order to reduce the amount of fecal matter and because farmers do not feed animals who are no longer earning their keep.[29]

Conclusion

"When her body goes limp with comfort, I stretch her neck."

Having held many roosters and hens in my lap and watched them close their eyes trustingly in the comfort of my care, I felt keenly the betrayal of a woman named Gina Warren, who went from being an environmentally motivated vegetarian (so she said) to being a killer with a proud sense of power in herself when she goes to work on a small farm in California. In "The Chicken Project," she writes, without irony, of the farm's "free-ranging" chickens:

> When Cody opened the door of the henhouse, the first thing that hit me was the smell. The ammonia stench clogged my throat and nose, and while my eyes didn't literally water, I wished they would've because of how badly they burned. I cannot imagine what a factory farm might smell like, with chickens piled one on top of the other, surrounded by feces, and suffering blindness and ammonia burns from the poorly ventilated air. Which is nothing like Cody's farm, but good God it reeked.[30]

There is no sense of compassion in this person's sordid account for the hens who are forced to live in the micro-factory farm shed with its tiny outdoor run. The shed reeks with filth and toxic gasses only because "Cody" never cleans it. Warren describes massaging the hen she is preparing to kill and "watching her warm eyes close" trustingly in her lap. She watches the hen, not lovingly, but conscious that she is going to close those eyes forever and that she is using the hen's trust as a lure to kill her. This may seem like a far cry from industrialized chicken farming, but it illustrates the moral psychology of animal farming, and it evokes the essence of why "humane" animal farming is a false hope and an unsustainable illusion.

Karen Davis, Ph.D. is the president and founder of United Poultry Concerns, a non-profit organization that promotes the compassionate and respectful treatment of domestic fowl, including a sanctuary for chickens in Virginia. Inducted into the National Animal Rights Hall of Fame for Outstanding Contributions to Animal Liberation, she is the author of *Prisoned Chickens, Poisoned Eggs: An Inside Look at the Modern Poultry Industry*; *More Than a Meal: The Turkey in History, Myth, Ritual, and Reality*; *The Holocaust and the Henmaid's Tale: A Case for Comparing Atrocitie*s; and other works, including her children's book *A Home for Henny* and a vegan cookbook *Instead of Chicken, Instead of Turkey: A Poultryless "Poultry" Potpourri*. Her latest book is *For the Birds: From Exploitation to Liberation*, published by Lantern Publishing & Media.

15

HUMANE MYTHS AND MEDIA

The Reproduction of Speciesism in Mainstream U.S. News

by Lisa A. Barca, Ph.D.

Most reflective people come to see the violence inflicted on nonhuman animals in the food system as an atrocity. Once they learn about the severity of the violence, the staggering numbers of victims, and the clear sentience and desperate, futile attempts at resistance that these beings demonstrate, this conclusion is practically inevitable. A major part of advocating for an end to this atrocity is getting people to stop reflexively looking away, instead allowing themselves to see, in many cases for the first time, the subjectivity of nonhuman beings and the injustice of humans' oppression of them. Those committed to full justice for animals view all use as oppression—there is no such thing as "benign" use, an "interspecies bargain" in which nonhumans consent to our utilizing their bodily products or taking their lives in exchange for feeding or housing them, or any other human-imagined scenario in which it is justifiable to exploit them.[1] Especially in the contemporary world, we have no need to use them for food or any of the other contexts in which we impose unfathomable abuse upon beings who have a right to life, liberty, and to not being the property of others.

The movement for nonhuman animal rights has made some headway in fostering awareness about the injustices inherent in our use of other animals, an endeavor aided by the growing number of videos, books, and first-person accounts by those who have chosen to stop looking away and to share what they have learned. In this complicated and challenging process, however, new rhetorical and marketing gimmicks, created by industry and heavily promoted in the media, have emerged to encourage people who potentially care to keep looking away, or to come just to the precipice of looking without fully seeing. One such deceptive discourse that has proven highly effective in propping up the most harmful industries on Earth, those that exploit nonhumans for food, is that of "humane" treatment of commodified nonhuman animals. Designations such as "humane," "cage-free," "free-range," "grass-fed," and an array of others have become not only persuasive sales pitches when affixed to particular products, but have translated into powerful ideological tools in their own right apart from their appearance on any individual commodity. For people who empathize with nonhuman animals and do not want to think of themselves as causing them to suffer, the idea of humane products can assuage their conscience and deflect the cognitive dissonance of caring about these beings while eating them. Yet an investigation of standard practices in "humane" agriculture, which will be discussed in this chapter, reveals that immense suffering is indeed involved. Scientific information on human nutrition confirms that this suffering is unnecessary; mainstream health organizations such as the Academy of Nutrition and Dietetics, for instance, have deemed vegan diets healthful for all life stages,[2] so there is no reason to continue consuming the products of sentient beings' bodies, no matter how "humanely" these individuals have supposedly been controlled and killed.

The dominant ideology that enables humans' needless violence against other animals is speciesism, or the pervasive cultural belief system that views nonhuman animals as less morally important than humans and sees their value as lying in their potential to serve human interests.[3] One of the most powerful avenues through which speciesism is instilled and reinforced is mass media, including the journalist sources through which many people inform themselves about events and issues. Virtually all U.S. news outlets are for-profit enterprises clamoring for popularity and revenue.* Because of these structural factors, combined with journalists and editors themselves having been enculturated within dominant societal traditions, media tend to reinforce the status quo, which almost always includes being deeply speciesist. Speciesism is ubiquitous in media not only because of its generally pro-establishment orientation, but also because of its embeddedness with animal-products industries—for instance, through reliance on advertising revenues.[5]

It is therefore unsurprising that along with the rise of "humane" marketing come media stories celebrating this allegedly kindhearted commodification. These news items routinely feature interviews with those who profit financially from nonhuman animal agriculture, whose views of the beings under their control reach audiences of millions with little challenge or checking of factuality. Such articles allow exploiters to portray themselves as animals' benefactors, exemplifying what critical animal studies scholar Vasile Stănescu has identified as *biopolitics*, or legitimating harm through a rhetoric of care that claims to help the very victims that are harmed.[6] Such fictions of "care" in journalistic media propagate pro–animal use messaging on a mass scale, propping up both standard agribusiness and the "humane," "alternative" market, since the markets are mutually reinforcing through their common promotion of animal consumption.

The articles selected for analysis in this chapter appeared in major U.S. news sources and report in some central way on supposedly humane treatment of nonhuman animals commodified for food. Out of dozens of such articles that I reviewed, I have selected three representative examples to analyze. While varying in focus and tone and ranging from standard industrial exploitation to "locavore" farming and do-it-yourself slaughter, they all reinforce the objectification of nonhuman animals as end-products, omitting representation of them as individuals with subjective experiences. Because the articles selected for analysis (like the majority examined overall) contain references to women's involvement

---

*   Although National Public Radio (NPR), included in this chapter's analysis, is nonprofit and receives some public funds, 29% of its revenue comes from corporate sponsors or "underwriters," which have included Cargill, Koch Industries, and the mega-billionaire Walmart-owning family; so they are far from free of corporate influence.[4]

in "humane" agriculture, I focus where relevant on the gender politics of the news accounts, with the more central goal of showing how this is one of many devices contributing to the trivialization of nonhuman animals' experiences and lives.

THE ABSENT REFERENT: INVISIBILITY AND OBJECTIFICATION

While discussions of "humane" farming in media might seem to promise a pathway toward making nonhuman perspectives visible and challenging speciesism, quite the opposite is true. A partial explanation of this invisibility in plain sight can be achieved using feminist author and activist Carol Adams' concept of the *absent referent*, which refers to animals' identities being erased through the culturally reinforced denial that prevents most people from connecting the nonhuman animal–derived products they consume with the living beings who were killed for those products. "Behind every meal of meat is an absence: the death of the animal whose place the meat takes. The 'absent referent' is that which separates the meat eater from the animal and the animal from the end product," Adams explains.[7] (Although she develops the absent referent particularly in the context of "meat," it is also applicable to chickens' eggs and cows' milk, because the hens and cows whose bodies produce those substances are made invisible as individuals.) Adams has argued that although humane and do-it-yourself exploitation models claim to make slaughter and the living animals themselves more visible than in conventional agriculture, the violence against animals and their objectification as consumable parts are still completely operative in these models. The result is that nonhuman identities, emotions, and value as individuals are just as invisible in "humane" as in conventional exploitation.[8]

In media, this manifests as animals being shown or mentioned as tools in stories on human interests, so that truthful depictions of their subjectivity, individuality, and suffering—the combination of which is often required for people to begin taking nonhuman interests seriously—are excluded. In fact, the distortions and fabrications required to keep nonhuman animals' objectification intact while making them visible in "humane" narratives may be more harmful than their invisibility; the journalistic accounts analyzed below, for instance, allow widespread circulation of speciesist ideas without respectful or truthful perspectives to balance them.

In short, nonhuman animals are "visible yet unperceived," as activist and author Karen Davis has put in reference to animals in journalism.[9] The experiences and interests of nonhumans are absent, while their bodies are displayed.

SELLING "ETHICAL MEAT" ON NATIONAL PUBLIC RADIO

Camas Davis is a celebrity of the "ethical meat" industry. She runs the Portland Meat Collective, where customers can buy high-priced nonhuman animal remains and join in ritualized violence through offerings like lamb and rabbit slaughtering classes costing hundreds of dollars per session. National Public Radio's interview with Davis on the program Fresh Air with Terry Gross was timed to promote the release of Davis's book, *Killing It*, so a few words about the book are in order before examining the interview. Appearing next to the copyright and at the beginning of each chapter is the silhouette of a pig with lines dividing the anatomical sources of various "cuts" of meat. This familiar graphic, just like the ones seen in millions of conventional places where pigs' remains are sold, is the first clue to the objectifying view that Davis's book constructs of nonhuman animals—an outlook no different than that of standard agribusiness. Another sign of this objectifying viewpoint is the book's title—*Killing It*. Referring to nonhuman animals with the impersonal pronoun "it" is a characteristic marker of speciesist objectification; advocates for nonhuman animals are conscious of language's role in shaping ideology and the consequent importance of using personal pronouns for all sentient individuals.[10] That Davis not only includes this reifying "it" in her title, but uses it in a play on words that is presumably humorous (evoking the colloquial expression "killing it," i.e., doing a great job), adds insult to injury, making a joke of what can arguably be characterized as murder.

Like the title of Davis's book, that of NPR's transcription of the interview is revealing: "Food Writer Becomes A Butcher to Learn the Value of Meat" (original capitalization). Again, one sees an instrumentalized view of nonhuman animals: she became a butcher not to learn about her relationship with animals, as those in the "ethical food movement" sometimes claim. Her stated goal is not to learn the value of the sentient beings whom she butchers for profit (since such a notion would be obviously incongruous even for the casual observer). It is to learn "the value of *meat*," the dead commodity. This is a value of utilization—what humans can gain from exploiting others—not "value" in the sense of the inherent worth of an individual such as a pig, who has a personality, interests, emotions, advanced cognition, preferences, and feels love and fear. All of that is obliterated by valuing her or him ("it") as "meat."

It is useful here to elaborate on Carol Adams's application of the *absent referent* to "locavore," "do-it-yourself" slaughter since Davis is one of this fad's leading representatives. Regarding the ruse of visibility underlying this trend, Adams argues:

> The locavore movement and other friendly slaughter assertions are not making the entirety of the (dead) animal visible. . . . [I]t is not available to us to know exactly how she lived her life, nor how she experienced her death. What we have is the pretense and premise that sufficient information is available for us to conclude that eating her dead body is okay. It is all within a very anthropocentric setting about what is made visible. . . . [Locavores] still hold an instrumentalized notion of the animal.[11]

Adams further illuminates this pretense of visibility by breaking the absent referent into a three-part structure, xyz: "x" for the literal death of the animal; "y" for the hiding of the death, as occurs with conventional products procured from the supermarket, etc.; and "z" for objectification, or "the lifting of the animal's death to a higher meaning through metaphor and consumption," which enables viewing the parts of what was once a conscious being as nothing but meat.[12] Adams further explains: "With the locavore movement, we see x and z still functioning (the objectifying, the eating of a dead object), but y . . . has been made demonstrably present" (the death isn't hidden). However, she continues: "These 'Nouveau flesh eaters' are still eating meat from a dead body whose life had been emptied of meaning by the freedom to kill that being."[13] I have presented Adams's framework before analyzing NPR's interview with Camas Davis because it helps make the otherwise bewildering detachment from violence that this interview demonstrates a little more decipherable (if no less disconcerting).

The "Complicated Puzzle" of "Ethical Meat Eating"

Terry Gross introduces the interview with anti-vegan framing: "A lot of people have become vegetarians or vegans for ethical reasons. . . . But my guest Camas Davis believes there are ethical ways of raising livestock, slaughtering the animals and eating their meat."[14] This implies that it is equally valid or even more preferable to "ethically" slaughter "livestock" than it is to be vegan, a claim which requires demonstration rather than mere assertion. The closest explanation that Davis offers consists of vague pseudo-intellectualism, rather than facts or sound reasoning:

> In my own education, I've found the more I went into those processes—be it slaughter or whole-animal butchery or turning a pig head into pate de tete—the more I thought—more deeply I thought about why I eat meat, how much of it I eat, where it comes from, and the more I was able to assess how comfortable I felt with certain parts of those production methods and which kinds of production methods felt right and which felt wrong—and so it's my theory—or it's a theory that I've developed over time through my own education—that the further in we go, the better choices we make and the more agency we have in changing that system that brings food to our table.[15]

"[T]urning a pig head into pate de tete" is an emblematic expression of the "z" component of the absent referent (objectification as parts). Meanwhile, Davis's deep thought about why she eats meat is never elaborated—in fact, no substantive attempt to justify eating other animals is provided in the interview. So, this "theory" that Davis developed through her "education" (which entailed watching others, mainly men, bully nonhuman animals, then doing so herself) seems no more than an impressionistic amalgam of self-serving delusion and supposedly anti-establishment ideas about "agency" to "change the system." The complete robbing of agency from nonhuman animals in this system, meanwhile, is unacknowledged. In reality, locavorism promotes not revolutionary change, but conservative, retrograde notions of an idyllic relationship with animals that never existed.[16]

In the absence of real ethical engagement, Davis obfuscates matters further through the distracting device of moral relativism:

Gross: So, what do you define now as ethical meat-eating?

Davis: Well, it's a complicated picture, and I think it can be very personal for people. I don't think we all sit on the exact same part of what I think of as the spectrum of meat-eating, and so it really depends on where you come from.[17]

It is not surprising that Davis's comments are so evasive; she is asked to define an oxymoron, "ethical meat-eating," which automatically engenders confusion in any attempted response. The characterization of choosing to oppress animals as "a complicated picture" deflects attention onto a nonexistent moral quandary, as does the appeal to such violence being "very personal for *people*," which erases nonhuman victims and draws on the cliché of meat-eating as a personal choice, as if this absolves moral accountability. Contributing to this spurious line of thinking is the invention of a "spectrum of meat-eating" and the idea that harming others "depends on where you come from." Would it be considered appropriate to say this regarding practices that willfully harmed humans? (One can only imagine how NPR audiences might react to that.)

Providing a laundry list of things she is "interested in" vis-à-vis her profitable enterprise of slashing defenseless animals' throats, Davis continues:

But, on a basic level, I'm interested in a couple of things—how land is used to raise the animals that we eat for meat. I'm interested in whether those animals are allowed to be the animals that they are, they're allowed to eat what they are meant to eat, they're allowed to move around the way their bodies were built to move around, that they're treated humanely. And that—in and of itself, that phrase, is debated quite a bit.[18]

Insinuating that "ethical meat" involves judicious land use is problematic, since it is beyond viable to debate that nonhuman animal agriculture is environmentally unsustainable, especially the "free-range" type promoted here. As author and activist Hope Bohanec has insightfully phrased it, we would need about "five planet Earths" to free-range all the animals currently raised for food, meaning that this style of agriculture is impossible to scale up and "can never be more than a niche market for a few elite buyers."[19] As for Davis's other listed "interests," although they appear to involve ethical deliberation, it is only spuriously. No individuals who are being "farmed" are "allowed to be the animals that they are," given the control of their reproduction, the engineering of every aspect of their lives to enhance their controllers' profitmaking, and, of course, their being killed as soon as it is more profitable to do that than to keep them alive, and before their muscles age, since people like eating the supple muscles of baby and adolescent nonhumans. The idea that this is consistent with being "treated humanely" defies both morality and reason.

Admitting that "this phrase [humane] is debated quite a bit," Davis leaves it at that and moves on to more convoluted contemplation of "ethical meat":

> I'm interested in what happens—inputs go in—what happens to the inputs when they come out of those animals—so pollution practices. And, you know, is the food safe for us? Do the animals have a good life? Do they have a good death? And then, on our end, when we're eating that meat, is it safe? Is it nutritious? Is it delicious? So, all of those things play into this complicated puzzle that is ethical meat.[20]

The discourse of "inputs" going in and coming out draws on an instrumentalizing concept of nonhuman beings as mechanistic "converters" of energy and resources. This speciesist characterization is followed by entirely anthropocentric issues like food safety, nutrition, and even deliciousness. How could the way dead animals taste be a component of "*ethical* meat"? It seems ethics have exited the conversation, except for the dubious notion of a "good life" under human control, and the truly bizarre idea of a "good death." These notions are quintessentially biopolitical: for instance, the violent killing of young, healthy individuals who don't want to die is presented as a "good" for those individuals.

Before providing an example from Davis's book of what she considers a good death, I want to point out how her smoke-and-mirrors rhetoric, in which she frames her ramblings as "this complicated puzzle that is ethical meat," attempts to mask the fact that the form of exploitation she promotes is just as objectifying as its more conventional agricultural counterpart. Based on Davis's definition of ethical meat discussed so far, it is clear that the absent referent (the erasure of the animal as a subjective being) is operative. Doing the killing oneself and making murder more visible (changing "y" in Adams's formula presented earlier) does not change the fact of the animal's death (x) or the reduction of that once-living being to a commodity (z).

To illustrate this, in the first pages of her book *Killing It*, Davis begins to make what she considers a "good death" visible by describing the corpse of a pig whom she has just watched others slaughter:

> She was big. I didn't even know pigs could get that big. And although I could see for myself the astounding girth of her, I had no way of wrapping my head around the sheer physical reality of such a weight, until the mechanical hand that had lifted up the dead old sow out of the concrete bath of scalding water accidentally dropped her, from five feet high, onto the hard, cold, concrete floor. It wasn't a thud, exactly. It was more of a ripple. A reverberating ripple of fat and skin and bone. Her heart was still in there, too, though no longer beating. . . . Without flinching, several men in dark-blue coveralls scrambled over to her body and attempted to push her back into the mechanical hand. As if this were actually possible. . . . 'She's three hundred kilos. Too big,' Marc Chapolard, who, along with his three brothers, had agreed to mentor me in the French ways of knife and bone, told Kate, my American translator and host, who told me.[21]

The emotional vacuity with which Davis describes the aftermath of violence causes one to wonder what kind of mindset makes such insensitive and objectifying remarks possible, as if she were observing a process as innocuous as an amusement park ride or museum exhibit.

To momentarily break from contemplating the horror, one might wonder why Davis had to go to France for her "education" in barbarity when there is plenty of it going on in the U.S. and she doesn't speak French. Perhaps a dash of the exotic—in this case, the romanticism of a rural Mediterranean setting in which domineering Frenchmen educate Davis in brutality—helps to sell books about "local" agriculture.

Below is more revelation of what Davis means by "humane" death (I am quoting at length to convey the narrative's disturbing nonchalance and the brutality of the "ethical" slaughter described):

> Just minutes before this pig carcass had accidentally fallen to the floor, a tall, thin, older gentleman, also in coveralls, had escorted the live sow through a wooden chute. As I watched her slowly make her way . . . Marc explained that she was done having babies and was going to be turned into sausage. Another man then secured what looked like a set of headphones on the sow's head. 'Are they going to play her music?' I asked. . . . Then, with the meaty part of his palm, the man pressed a big red button on the wall, which sent a quick electrical current coursing through the headphones and into the skin and the subcutaneous fat and the bone and then the brain of the seven-hundred-pound mama, who dropped to the floor and began convulsing. . . . 'That makes her senseless to pain,' Marc told Kate, who told me. This was the most humane way to kill a pig, he said. . . . 'She won't be dead until they bleed her.' When I looked back, another man had hoisted the pig up by way of a chain wrapped around her back leg. He stuck a long knife into the space between the sow's throat and where I imagined her heart to be.[22]

The objectifying lens through which this scene is described demonstrates the operation of the absent referent, even when killing is made visible. By Davis's trainer's admission, this is "the most humane way to kill a pig"; yet to one who views pigs truthfully as sentient individuals, it is a travesty to call these acts "humane." She is not only violently killed— she is "convulsing" on the floor, which only the wildest stretches of imagination could construe as "humane." But she is also oppressed in other ways. Bred to be abnormally oversized, she is oppressed by her biology. Used to "make babies" then brutally discarded once no longer birthing enough new victims, she is exploited for her maternal capacity. And she is exploited yet again by having her death callously chronicled in a self-promoting book. But what to make of Davis's at least using the personal pronoun "she" throughout this passage, as opposed to the "it" of her book's title? Does that individualize this gravely unfortunate "mama" at all? Perhaps. Yet an insidious, self-centered agenda seems to underlie even this.

FEMIVORISM AND REVERSE VICTIMOLOGY

In an ultimate expression of reverse victimology (making the perpetrator of violence a victim),[23] Davis compares the degradation and annihilation of this sow-turned-sausage with her own hard luck at being fired from an elite magazine writer job. This narcissistic comparison is facilitated by grammatically gendering the violated pig as female:

> This sow, I thought, had spent her entire adult life doing her job well. Her job was to make babies. Lots of them. Babies that could be turned into food for our tables. And then, one day, someone had deemed her no longer useful. And just like that, her job had ended. Hence the headphones and the electric shock and the blood. At least she could still be used for sausage. I'd spent my entire adult life doing my job well, too—although it didn't have anything to do with making babies for the dinner table. And then, one day, just a few short months ago, someone had deemed me no longer useful and my job had also ended. . . . Given the way things had gone in my life recently, I felt like I was the one who had just been dropped from a five-foot height onto a hard, cold concrete floor.[24]

To call being forced to "make babies . . . turned into food" for the "tables" of another species a "job," which denotes assent and remuneration, is not only morally bankrupt but also supremely illogic. In a total short-circuiting of empathy, Davis "identifies" with the pig not to actually grapple with the violence she has witnessed, but to bask in egoistic self-pity. This conveys an astounding ability to make everything self-referential, even when immense feats of logic-defying mental gyration are required. And this is another way in which truly identifying with the nonhuman animal killed for food is prevented from happening.

One way to contextualize Davis's warped comparison between herself being laid off from a job and a pig having her life violently ended is through the politics of the "femivore" trend in animal agriculture. Femivorism, as critical animal studies scholar John Sanbonmatsu chronicles in this volume, involves a surge of women leaving white-collar careers in order to "find themselves" through killing animals. Sanbonmatsu argues: "White middle-class women have been stymied in their quest for true social equality. Some women have consequently turned to the domination and killing of animals as a way to achieve a false sense of empowerment *as women.*"[25] This is exemplified in Davis's seeming delight in the sow's torment, as if she is vicariously avenging her own perceived rough treatment in the capitalist marketplace. On a simpler level, it is familiar bully psychology: forces more powerful than I am have wronged me, so I find sadistic solace in tormenting someone with less power.

The attempt to legitimate domination when it is made visible in "humane slaughter" narratives can lead to such roundabout and euphemistic language that it is sometimes hard to believe that the speaker is in earnest. This is seen in Davis's response to the question of whether a sentient being suffers while her still-beating heart pumps the blood out of her body after she's been electrocuted in the head and hung upside down:

Gross: So, with this pig that you were witnessing, headphones were put on the pig. Would you describe what the headphones are for?

Davis: The headphones are for electrocution. And I know that sounds terrible, but, essentially, the idea behind humanely slaughtering an animal is that you render them—quickly render them senseless to pain [. . .].

Gross: But the pig doesn't feel anything when the blood is being drained?

257

Davis: That's the goal, and that's the belief. If it's done wrong—
if the pig is not stunned correctly—and stunned is the term we
usually use in the industry to describe that part of the process—
then the animal will feel it. And you'll know pretty immediately.
So, the whole goal is to keep it, you know, pain-free. And I mean,
it's—there's a lot of debate about what happens in that moment and
whether or not it's—whether or not we can know or not. But based
on what science exists, that's sort of the conclusion that the industry
has come to.[26]

The hollowness of Davis's assertions are betrayed by linguistic hedging
("you know," "I mean," "sort of," etc.) and euphemisms ("headphones"
for electrocution implements, "stunning" instead of electrocution as the
"term we usually use in the industry"). There is also a pattern of admission
followed by denial: electrocution "sounds terrible" (because it is), *but* it's
just part of "slaughtering an animal." We can't really know what these
beings experience as their lives are slashed out of them, *but* we've "sort of"
decided in "the industry" not to worry about that. And this is indeed an
industry—not a "movement" to overturn oppressive conditions, but rather
a fresh ploy for profiting from them. The similarities to conventional
agribusiness are many, seen for instance in Davis's revelation that the
French men she learned slaughter and butchery from confine pigs in
barns despite owning ample land, which they use to grow food for the
imprisoned pigs.[27] Joking about their impersonal disposition toward the
beings under their control, Davis muses, "I think they respected the
animals, but they didn't name them Wilbur."[28] This mocks those who
care for animals enough to name them, protect them, and see them as
individuals.

MISREPRESENTING ANIMALS

There are many additional troubling statements in this NPR interview,
including some of the most tired stereotypes about "vegetarians" (who
wear tie-died shirts and don't think about eating animals as deeply as
Davis does) and animal activists (apparently prone to shouting Hitler
comparisons in public), as well as further false and objectifying claims
about nonhuman beings. Here is one indication of Davis's careless

misrepresentation of nonhuman animals' biological and cognitive characteristics:

Gross: So, what's the first animal that you slaughtered yourself?

Davis: It was a chicken.

Gross: And what did you consider to be a humane approach to slaughtering a chicken?

Davis: With any—really with any slaughter of any species, it's always the same. . . . And in the case of a chicken, hanging them upside down or setting them on their backs sort of turns their brains off. They kind of just stop moving. And they have sort of these reptilian brains that respond to that in a way that—they just sort of calm down and don't want to move anywhere. And so that's usually the first step in getting them comfortable. Yeah.[29]

The peculiar claim that forcing chickens upside-down sedates them is contradicted by widely available film footage of commercial chicken killing operations where birds are shackled upside-down and scream, struggle, and fight for their lives in that position. Indeed, it is a convenient fiction that hanging chickens upside down or forcing them on their backs "turns their brains off," as if they were machines, and that if they stop moving under such conditions, it is because they "*sort of* calm down" (that hedging again) or are "comfortable." A less convenient truth would be that they may become frightened, disoriented, and made so aware of their helplessness in the situation that some become immobilized or simply realize that it is futile to resist. An even more plausible interpretation is that if a particular human has been feeding a nonhuman animal, the nonhuman develops a feeling of trust and even affection toward her or his caretaker, making slaughter an act of "ultimate betrayal" as Bohanec has put it.[30] Despite more credible explanations for a chicken's possible lack of resistance in DIY killing, Terry Gross allowed Davis's far-fetched claims go unchallenged, disseminating to a wide, elite NPR audience the falsehood that chickens have such unsophisticated cognitive worlds that their consciousness can be turned on and off like an automated device. But that is precisely the point—to those who think that exploiting animals when we have no need to eat them is "humane," beings like chickens are mere widgets in a production system. To say they have "sort of these reptilian brains" (as if reptiles were also automata, another falsehood) counters the abundant information about chicken intelligence, emotions, and cognitive complexity that has been published in recent years, even in the mainstream press, so it is inexcusable for a high-level journalist like Gross not to challenge information that contradicts easily available scientific evidence.[31]

Through its unqualified counterfactual assertions, this NPR interview illustrates how the "ethical" meat business keeps the absent referent intact—in fact, entrenches it deeper with each denial of nonhuman subjectivity. As Carol Adams argues:

> For most eaters of dead animals, the structure of the absent referent means that the killing is off stage. But the structure of the absent referent does not require that the killing be off stage or unreferenced. It . . . renders the idea of individual animals as immaterial to anyone's selfish desires for consumption. . . . Killing an animal onscreen or by a local butcher in your own kitchen participates in the structure of the absent referent because it makes the animal as an individual disappear.[32]

This is what is seen in Davis's narratives about the nonhumans who she claims to treat ethically—they appear as violated in detail but are denied individuality and worth, reinforcing the speciesist framework through which most people have been enculturated to view animals commonly exploited for food. Despite grandiose claims to the contrary, nothing revolutionary or ethical is to be found here.

THE HUMANE MYTH AND INDUSTRIAL DAIRY PROPAGANDA IN *THE NEW YORK TIMES*

A different application of humane rhetoric appears in *The New York Times* full-page article "Changing the Face of the Dairy Industry," with farmer Tara Meyers as its protagonist. This paid public-relations piece for the

Land O'Lakes brand adopts the guise of a news article (with only a fine-print disclaimer about its paid public-relations status to distinguish it from any other article in the paper).[33] Journalism is rife with covert, paid public-relations material, so the PR-news-article hybrid form of this *Times* piece simply makes explicit what is a widespread feature of the "news."[34] It also demonstrates how big brands engaging in conventional agribusiness can capitalize on now-popularized "humane" rhetoric and femivorism without even presenting the facade of pastoral serenity put forth by locavore or do-it-yourself exploitation. The featured female farmer claims, "Everything revolves around the comfort and well-being of our cows"—a phrase reprinted in large font as a highlighted quote. Yet everything else in the piece belies that assertion, with its written and visual elements telling a story of standard, large-scale, mechanized production. And irrespective of this, as will be discussed below, dairy production is always inherently incompatible with cow well-being.

The article's headline reveals its PR intent—"Changing the Face of the Dairy Industry." It is not so much that the face itself is changing. Rather, the wording suggests that someone is actively "changing the face." In an almost certainly unintentional illumination of what is actually going on, the choice of phrasing can be read as indicating that the "change" at issue is the public-relations tactic of manipulating perceptions of the industry's "face," which, whether female or male, is a face of domination and oppression of female animals for their reproductive and mothering capacities, as cows only produce milk when pregnant and after giving birth. This change means nothing for the nonhuman victims, but by facilitating exultant narratives of care and visibility, it probably does sell more cows' milk and the fat isolated from it, otherwise known as butter.

The article/PR/advertisement begins with a nod to the pseudo-feminism that's its main ruse throughout, also drawing on nostalgic, patriotic tropes of self-sufficiency and industry:

FARM WIFE. It's a label with which Tara Meyer is far too familiar, when, simply, 'farmer' would do. She runs Meyer Dairy, just south of Sauk Centre, Minn., alongside her husband, Nick, the two waking at 4 most mornings for the first milking. The cows are milked again at noon and at 8 p.m.[35]

Mere props in the story, cows are superficially visible as commodities, invoked only in the context of their exploitation and the resources taken from them. The cows' experience of being "milked" three times a day by machines, instead of being with their calves—who have been abducted from them as occurs in all dairy production, large or small—is not referenced. The narrative later enumerates "numerous improvements to the dairy operation Nick took over from his parents," which include "milk-pumping motors that run only when necessary,"[36] presumably to save energy and lower the cost of mechanically taking milk from immobilized cows. Never mind that holding a cow captive to forcibly impregnate her repeatedly, rob her of her baby and the milk meant for him or her, and send her to the slaughterhouse at a fraction of her natural lifespan when her beleaguered body can no longer produce a profitable amount of milk is itself not necessary, but is rather a choice made by people intent on keeping this outdated industry alive.

MOTHERLY TECHNOLOGIES OF CARE

Wholly ignoring (as virtually all dairy advertising does) the natural relationship between bovine mothers and babies that humans destroy to steal cows' milk, the story presents Meyer as a nurturer of the calves she has caused to be orphaned. In a characteristic display of biopolitics, or concealing violence in a rhetoric of care for the victims of that violence, it is reported by Meyer:

> I'm responsible for the young stock, the baby calves . . . I take care of vaccinations for the entire 550-head herd, tracking their movements and health events with a computer program. And I handle the financials: billing, accounts payable, payroll, taxes, everything that goes into operating a successful business.[37]

Why are the "young stock, the baby calves" not cared for by their mothers? Perhaps the tragic scene of mother–baby separation inherent to all dairy, which is heartbreaking and traumatizing for both mother and calf, might dampen the audience's appetite for the commodities thus obtained. Instead, the focus is on Meyer's diligence in "taking care" of vaccinations; why the entire "550-head herd" would need them is another matter of reticence. But the photos in the piece, showing dozens of distressed-looking cows with ear tags standing shoulder-to-shoulder in crowded, muddy pens, reveal the unhealthy and stressful conditions in which these bereft mothers live. The large-font caption to one of the photos, in which Meyer walks smiling among her "herd," reads: "Sustaining the Farming Life for the Next Generation." Photo and caption thus invoke a double myth of sustainability and caring pastoralism—both of which are utterly inconsistent with animal dairy. There is also an ironic appeal to human family continuity that ignores how the pictured bovines are deprived of *their* families.

The technologized surveillance enacted by this motherly warden ("tracking their movements and health events with a computer program") is made to seem normal and even a benefit to cows, a kindly service performed by their captors. Contributing to this construction of normalcy are objectifying terms, such as "stock" (units of production), "head" (referring to a unique individual as an undistinguished part of a "count"), and "herd" (an undifferentiated mass difficult to care about when thus described). The audience is positioned to see the cows as things rather than beings, and to feel admiration for a woman who can handle business management, as if this were extraordinary in itself.

There are a few ways to interpret references to medical oversight and techno-monitoring as "care." One is through the insights of environmental ethicist Sune Borfelt and his co-authors, who identify such rhetoric as "welfare from a producer perspective," which does not construct the bucolic fantasies characteristic of consumers' typical notions of "welfare" (however also misguided). Instead, the "producer perspective" focuses only on issues that affect profits such as "protection from harsh or hot climate, access to sufficient food and water and clinical health, ensuring that the animal grows and complies with production goals."[38] Discussing the same phenomenon in different terms, John Sorenson refers to an "obfuscatory framework of industry discourse, which construes welfare as meaning only that other animals will be kept in salable condition until they are killed for maximum profit."[39] Similarly, commenting on Swedish dairy advertising, Jana Canavan notes: "Overemphasizing nonhuman animal welfare routines is . . . a successful marketing strategy that the industry uses for its benefit. The mention of cows' 'personal records' is actually the total system of tracking every aspect of the cow's life that is relevant to increasing milk yields. Such descriptions . . . give consumers distorted ideas about daily production routines and reassurances about the good intentions of farmers and 'dairy' firms."[40]

This focus on a mechanized "producer" concept of welfare is evident in the many photos in *The New York Times* Land O'Lakes article. Cows are not shown grazing on pasture as is characteristic of much marketing with a "humane" veneer. There is a photo of green pasture with no cows on it, then several photos of anxious or lethargic adult cows in crowded outdoor confinement. Perhaps the saddest photo is of Tara Meyer next to a tiny calf, just born and already with large, numbered tags—the ultimate emblem of commodification—pierced through her ears. The tags look tragically oversized on this tiny bovine baby already marked as an object. The caption reads, "Meyer examines a newborn calf birthed just hours earlier." Calf and woman stand in a sterile stall with a drinking bucket, almost surely containing the milk substitute given to infants like this one deprived of her mother's milk, pilfered instead for human consumption. As Meyer encircles the baby's neck with her arm, the calf's head is turned away, and one senses that the calf is not enjoying being "examined" for economically advantageous characteristics rather than fulfilling the powerful emotional and biological urge to suckle her mother's milk.

Given the story told by these photos and the article's other references to the unhappy conditions for cows, it is especially ironic to read: "Everything revolves around the comfort and well-being of our cows."[41] It is clear that everything instead revolves around human financial interests and the public-relations ploy of attaching hollow "women's empowerment" clichés to an industry whose very foundation is built on exploiting bovine females. Focusing on women participating in this violent industry as if this were cause for celebration deflects attention from cows as sentient individuals and onto a spurious, anthropocentric narrative. These human-centered deflections align with advice given in industry literature. For instance, referring to a 2016 article in *National Hog Farmer*, professor of rhetoric Mary Trachsel discusses how farmers are encouraged to counter activists' revelations of violence by focusing away from the animals: "The narrative endorsed by this article attempts to shift attention from the exploitation of pigs to the purported virtues of their oppressors. . . . Farmers are also encouraged to foreground their families, with pictures and stories of farm children and baby pigs occupying an especially favored place in the narrative."[42] In such narratives, nonhumans are made visible in such an objectifying manner that this visibility does not foster consideration of them as beings with feelings and interests.

The New York Times PR article is rife with other inconsistencies; for instance, an apparent swipe at global corporate power is offered: "WAIT. WHAT? Land O'Lakes, the brand synonymous with butter, is owned by farmers and not some massive multinational conglomerate?" referencing the co-op structure of the business.[43] Yet the photo caption directly above this attempt to make a mega-business sound like a "mom-and-pop" operation reads: "Meyer Dairy produces 2,670 gallons of milk daily," a massive amount of mammary secretion for one facility. Does this incongruity suggest that the authors are counting on an urban audience who knows virtually nothing (and wants to know even less) about the processes of taking cows' milk? Perhaps. What also seems at play, however, is a critique not so much of capitalism or large-scale profit-taking, but of the *multinational* aspect of "massive multinational conglomerate," enabling an appeal to the "local" and "American" foundations of the promoted company and tapping into the rhetoric of popular locavore models of exploiting animals.[44]

"She-I-O"

The rhetoric of this piece suggests that the deceptions of "humane" agriculture are transferrable to practically any type of enterprise, even when obviously conflicting evidence appears in the very same promotional materials. Public relations firms like the one hired to write this extended advertisement posing as a news article in the nation's paper of record have access to copious market and consumer research, and it is fair to assume that the versions of care and "well-being" presented were consistent with indicators of what would be persuasive for a substantial segment of the paper's audience. Land O'Lakes was so confident in this branding approach that it released a slick music video, mentioned in the article, called "She-I-O," in which female dairy farmers perform chores to an updated country-swing version of Old McDonald's farm.[45] As the *Times* piece reports, it "debuted in advance of National Women's Equality Day on Aug. 26 and went viral."[46] Among its choreographed emotional appeals is a young girl bottle-feeding an orphaned newborn calf, as if it were necessary for humans to care for calves when their mothers, invisible, are mourning for them. This anthropocentric deflection performs the biopolitical reframing of kidnapping as care, ensures cows' erasure as subjective beings, and enables the branding of dairy as "feminist."

This pseudo-feminist branding is ironic given that one of the main ways that cows are rendered invisible in dairy propaganda is through suppressing the inescapable fact of their femaleness and motherhood. As feminist academic Cory Wrenn has observed, industry rhetoric

> . . . encourages consumers to only superficially conceptualize 'dairy cows' as female. Subsequently, the audience will not be invited to acknowledge that they are actually mothers. Motherhood reminds the audience that these animals do not exist solely for the pleasure of the consumer. It is a reminder of their connectedness in complex social relationships, their responsibilities for others, their love for others, and others' love for them.[47]

In other words, femaleness and motherhood interfere with the functioning of the absent referent by truthfully placing cows in the context of their intra-species relationships apart from the roles that humans artificially assign to them. Wrenn continues:

> . . . the invisibility of childbirth, nursing, and parenting is a consistent theme. . . . Depicting these cows as mothers would disrupt the fantasy presented to the human consumer; the presence of calves forces the viewer to acknowledge the intended purpose of cows' breast milk. Instead, *farmers* are more frequently pictured nurturing calves when calves are visible at all. In this way, farmers are presented as caring stewards, while the bovine mothers are dematernalized. . . .[48]

The New York Times article enacts this dematernalization and the visual dissociation of cows from their calves with biopolitical justifications for the cruelty of dairy provided through photo-ops for farmers like Tara Meyer, seen as a hero for bottle-feeding the very calves she has abducted from their mothers.

The invisibility of bovine kin relationships, femaleness, and motherhood featured in the *Times* facilitate the absent referent in a somewhat different way than occurs in Camas Davis's "ethical meat" rhetoric. There, one saw violence made graphically visible, while speciesist objectification was equally rampant to justify such violence. In the Land O'Lakes ad, violence is only alluded to obliquely via representations of exploitative technologies and orphaned and confined cows, conveniently leveraged in a rhetoric of care. In both articles, despite their otherwise substantial differences, nonhuman animal identities are similarly obscured and falsified.

DESIGNER BEINGS AND TASTING SOMEONE ELSE'S "GOOD LIFE" IN THE NEW YORK POST

If *The New York Times* public relations article "Changing the Face of the Dairy Industry" exhibits a "producer"-based version of welfare involving farmers' technological surveillance, an article published around the same time in the *New York Post* focuses instead on consumers' idyllic fantasies about the beings they consume. Like the material examined so far, this article provides publicity for the specific animal-exploitation businesses referenced, allowed to portray themselves in the best possible light. The article's title— "Would You Pay $200 for a Designer Thanksgiving Turkey?"—positions the reader as someone who consumes turkeys' remains (which ignores vegan readers) and is affluent enough to consider the headline's proposal. "Designer" characterizes turkeys— communities of intelligent, social beings—as products "designed" for high-end consumption like fashion apparel. In accordance with this, the opening sentences set a glib and consumerist tone:

> After last year's debacle, Vicky Konstantinidis wasn't about to leave the centerpiece of her Thanksgiving dinner to chance. In 2017, the

Long Island resident had been a little late to place her turkey order to Feisty Acres, a North Fork farm known for its organic, heritage-breed gobblers. . . . 'It's the only turkey I'd eat,' Konstantinidis tells The Post. While she did ultimately wind up getting her two birds—at 6 to 12 pounds, Feisty's turkeys run smaller than the average supermarket kind—the stress was real, Konstantinidis says.[49]

The "stress" experienced by Konstandtinidis, a middle-aged white woman pictured elegantly dressed and strolling among turkeys whom she is eyeing as future centerpieces, surely must have exceeded that of the birds themselves. That the birds might experience any stress is altogether overlooked, as though the designations "organic" and "heritage breed" remove any need to consider their suffering. Yet these designations are gravely misleading, "Organic standards do not provide protection against routine mutilations, severe confinement, rough handling, long transport, or brutal slaughter of animals," Humane Facts reports.[50] Hope Bohanec notes that overall, "there is little difference between organic and conventional farming with respect to animals' experience in the process of production."[51] Activist and author Robert Grillo has in turn critiqued the "effort by the sustainable/humane food movement to popularize such euphemisms as *heritage breed*" so as to claim that beings thus labeled are "more natural, traditional, and better suited to their environment." In reality, he concludes, "heritage" is "just another euphemism strategically branded for an affluent and highly lucrative niche market."[52]

This upscale market thrives not only on the misleading sense of transparency that is typical of humane farming rhetoric, but also on the allure of high social status supposedly conferred by and reflected in consumption. The *Post* informs readers:

Regular old Butterball turkeys just won't cut it for home cooks of elevated tastes, who prefer their gobblers organic, pasture-raised and in-demand. Heritage-breed turkeys are particularly popular: As heritage-turkey farmer Amanda Andrews puts it, some of the historic species resemble 'what, like, the Roosevelts would've had on their table'. . . . Fans of such prestigious birds can wind up spending hundreds on their Thanksgiving meat—but they're willing to pay the price to avoid the genetically modified, large-breasted and too-young birds from the supermarket.[53]

The favorable contrast with conventional agribusiness is deceptive. It is true that "birds from the supermarket" have been genetically manipulated to have "breasts" so oversized—to accommodate the human preference for tasting the muscles and fat of birds' front torsos—that they can barely move and cannot reproduce naturally, thus necessitating that human workers manually masturbate male turkeys to obtain semen forcibly inserted into females.[54] Yet the genetics of "heritage breeds" have also been manipulated, along with their movements, mating, and relationships.[55] The shallow appeal to history and authority ("some of the historic species resemble 'what, like, the Roosevelts would've had on their table'") is as shaky as the other devices used here to glorify the mass-killing of sentient beings for a human celebration that could easily be carried out without victims of violence. It is implied that continuity, status, and respectability are conferred by imagined association with a past authority figure and based on the "breed" of nonhuman animal corpse socially showcased. The emphasis on status continues with the notion of "fans of such prestigious birds," displacing the idea of *prestige* from the human "gobbler" of the birds' bodies onto the bird-victim her or himself (much in the way "gobbling" itself is displaced onto the birds). This constitutes a version of what Grillo has called a "fictional device in which we turn animal victims into false heroes," and, I would add, project our domination-based values (prestige, victory, power, consumption) onto the vanquished nonhumans used as tools for reflecting an egoistic self-image based on possessing these qualities ourselves.

"You Can Taste That the Bird Lived a Good Life"

In case thoughts arise about the birds' actually abysmal status as commodified beings, readers are assured that "you can taste that the bird lived a good life."[56] Tasting someone else's "good life" is a supreme expression of the biopolitical narrative that exploitation benefits victims, and the focus on "taste" reveals the self-interest underlying the disingenuous fantasy. As Swedish political scientist Jana Canavan has put it, "Judging beings' happiness, as difficult and problematic as that may be, by measuring the quantity and quality of the products that they produce is nonsensical. That we are made to believe in such statements is a sign of our alienation to those who produce the products we buy."[57] Indeed, most readers are probably so alienated from animals such as turkeys, whom they have been conditioned to view as means to human ends and abstract symbols of human "traditions," that they are likely convinced by a few facile statements by people with no expertise in turkeys as living beings and a bias toward the profits or trivial taste sensations they will glean from their deaths.[58]

In one striking expression of cognitive dissonance, customers of upscale turkey farms effuse about visiting turkeys before slaughter. One buyer is said to value "seeing her meat in its natural habitat,"[59] which displays distorted thinking semantically by confusing subject and object: "meat" is dead flesh which no longer has any habitat, i.e., living area.[60] This bespeaks the reification ("thing-ification"), even in life, of these animals, which underlies the disingenuous claims about bonding or caring.[61] And it is self-evidently untrue that turkeys whose locations, movements, and lifeways are controlled by humans are living in a "natural habitat." Of another customer, we are told:

> Over the past two years, she's visited Feisty Acres no fewer than five times to bond with the birds she's buying. 'I saw them in the wild, running around,' says Konstantinidis, who lives an hour from the farm. 'They all ran toward me. They were just so beautiful.'[62]

How can appreciation of these birds' beauty—the one glimmer of truth in this otherwise delusional piece of journalism—be reconciled with the practice of killing and consuming them? Perhaps beliefs such as that they are "in the wild" rather than on a farm facilitate this dissonance by conjuring a supposed circle-of-life scenario in which their premature demise is a sad but necessary part of a "natural" process. This seems an instance of what Borkfelt et al. call the "willed blindness" of consumers who, through a desire to believe the implausible in order to maintain both consumption habits and positive self-evaluation, participate in constructing the hoax of "humane" agriculture.[63] Maybe vising the farm so often—five times in two years—serves as a ritual to absolve guilt over betraying these beings so trusting and sociable as to run toward the very person whose dollars ensure their violent demise. There is also the biopolitical consolation that, compared to their industrially farmed cousins, these turkeys "live several weeks longer, allowing them to develop more flavor."[64]

The *New York Post* exemplifies how the facade of animal visibility in stories of "humane" farming does not equate to respectful or truthful representation. Although living turkeys are shown in word and image, the violence of their deaths is omitted—nowhere in the article is slaughter described or even mentioned. This keeps the absent referent functioning in ways fundamentally similar to how it operates with the products of conventional animal agriculture. An instrumentalized and distorted version of nonhuman-animal identities prevails, rendering them invisible as individuals with subjective experiences.

CONCLUSION

The media stories analyzed in this chapter erase nonhuman animals' identities despite appearing to make these beings visible, which illuminates key underlying structure of "humane" narratives generally. This making of animals into absent referents showed up across different exploitation and narrative styles, from do-it-yourself slaughter to standard agriculture to consumer-driven pastoral illusions. The public reputations of the news sources examined are also diverse—NPR is often considered unbiased and "progressive," and *The New York Times* is widely regarded as the nation's "paper of record" and the apogee of quality journalism. The *New York Post* is a quasi-tabloid with a reputation as conservative and kitschy. Despite these differences, they were remarkably similar in their representations of nonhuman animals, all equally ignoring their interests and subjectivity.[65] The *New York Post* was the only of the three publications to contain any evocation, however minimal, of nonhuman animals' having personalities or likable characteristics, with NPR and the *Times* neglecting this entirely. Across all narratives, the perspectives of nonhuman animals themselves were absent. This entrenches speciesist modes of seeing rather than challenging this bias, as might initially be hoped given the focus on "humane" treatment, which appears to acknowledge sentience and moral worth.

Whether it is in stories on agriculture or in other contexts, representing the interests of nonhuman animals is imperative if the press is to adhere to its social responsibility to reflect relevant viewpoints of all those affected by the issues on which it reports. Carrie P. Freeman and Debra Merskin call for such inclusion, citing the United States' Society of Professional Journalists' code of ethics, which mandates that journalists "give voice to the voiceless."[66] Lending scientific credence to this call for media responsibility is vast scientific affirmation of nonhuman animals' sentience, including highly public affirmations such as the Cambridge Declaration of Consciousness—a statement by hundreds of world-class scientists asserting nonhuman animals' advanced cognition, emotional complexity, and capacity to suffer on par with humans.[67] This confirms what other researchers and many general observers have long known: that nonhuman animals, including the mammals, avians, and fishes commonly used for human food, have sensitive and sophisticated inner worlds. To deny that their experiences matter is inconsistent with both moral and scientific reasoning, and such denial can only be maintained through the irrational ideology of speciesism, propped up by the commercial entities that profit from its perpetuation.

Giving the embeddedness of dominant media with speciesist ideologies, it may be unrealistic to expect improved coverage until public opinion turns more pervasively against the exploitation of other animals and a greater number of conscientious advocates for nonhuman animals occupy positions in journalism. In the meantime, a few recommendations for journalists and editors include:

- Taking more seriously the perspectives of nonhuman animals by personalizing them and portraying their emotions and experiences, rather than dismissing their moral importance in a discussion centered on human interests.
- Balancing the opinions of exploiters with commentary from those who advocate for nonhuman rights and have no vested interest in their exploitation.

- Acknowledging that people's food decisions have serious impacts on nonhuman and human beings other than the consumer, thus avoiding the inaccurate framing of food as purely a personal choice or financial issue.
- Taking vegan readers into account by acknowledging their perspectives, explicitly or tacitly, rather than assuming news audiences are entirely non-vegan.

As veganism grows and the public becomes increasingly aware of the inherent cruelties of *all* animal agriculture, these changes are likely to emerge, however gradually. Until then, educating consumers about the speciesist bias in media is a step in the right direction.

Lisa A. Barca, Ph.D. is a lecturer in the Honors College at Arizona State University, where she teaches humanities and writing courses and seminars on the ethics of humans' relationships with other animals. Her current research centers on critical animal studies, media ethics, rhetoric and ideology, and the intersections of feminism and animal rights. She holds a Ph.D. in Romance Languages and Literatures and has published in the past on topics ranging from modernist poetry to media representations of gender-based violence. Dr. Barca is a contributor to the volume *Meatsplaining: The Meat Industry and the Rhetoric of Denial*, forthcoming with Sydney University Press, and her writing appears in the academic journals *Comparative Literature* and *Critical Discourse Studies*, literary anthologies for undergraduates, including *The Manifesto in Literature* and *The Literature of War*, and popular publications such as *Ms.* magazine.

16

MODERN FOODIE CULTURE

A Celebration of Violence

by Robert C. Jones, Ph.D.

"A true gastronome is as insensible to suffering as a conqueror."—**Abraham Hayward**[1]

The 2011 Sydney Writers' Festival featured late British food critic A.A. Gill and late American celebrity chef Anthony Bourdain in conversation with restaurateur Tony Bilson. A significant part of that discussion involves the trio ridiculing advocates of animal rights.[2] Decrying animal rights as a "false morality," Bilson—completely unaware of the unoriginality of his hoary critique—castigates animal rights advocates for what he sees as a misanthropic concern favoring animals at a time when countless human beings suffer. (Apparently, he cannot imagine a person being *both* an animal and human rights advocate). Bilson's comment prompts the following exchange:

> Gill: Well, I don't know if it's a false morality, I just don't agree with it. I also don't really care if animals suffer. If I'm perfectly honest, I don't give a shit!

> Bourdain: (laughs) I'd rather not see it.

> Gill: Once you've heard one pig scream, the second one's easier.

Bourdain: And he's right . . . you learn something about yourself when you kill a pig!

Putting aside the invective, their arrogance, condescension, ignorance, and revealing macho swagger, I want to instead concentrate on their *attitude*, a certain despicable indifference to the suffering and death of animals slaughtered for food. Not only their indifference, but the giddy, mocking, sadistic pleasure they seem to take in the suffering of nonhuman food animals. It is that attitude—an attitude not necessarily emblematic of foodie culture, but not entirely foreign to it either—that I'd like to discuss in this chapter. At the heart of such attitudes lurks the human prejudice, a human supremacy, a "speciesism," expressed in beliefs and behaviors (as well as societal practices and institutions) that hold that nonhuman animals are ours to use, to do with as we see fit.

In researching for this chapter, I found myself struggling to formulate a clear and precise definition of the term foodie, while simultaneously grappling to identify those most morally debased characteristics of foodie culture. However, as philosopher Ludwig Wittgenstein taught us, trying to identify the necessary and sufficient conditions for the proper application of a given term is a fool's errand; the best we can hope for is a "family resemblance."[3] To that end, here is a kind of rough-and-ready definition: A foodie is a kind of gourmand, a gastronome, an enthusiast who, for aesthetic reasons, purports to have an ardent or refined interest in food, who seeks new food experiences as a kind of hobby rather than simply eating for convenience or from hunger, and who is "willing to spend a considerable portion of his or her expendable income and time exploring, studying, and sampling food, with special interest in the pleasures of the tastes." Further, there is a certain kind of foodie—the person who gives "priority to their personal quest for interesting and delicious tastes over moral and health concerns"—who is the focus of this chapter.[4]

I further tried to get clear on those aspects of foodie culture—specifically those related to animals as food—that I find most morally objectionable. To that end, I devised the following rough taxonomic family resemblance. I have formulated four, non-exhaustive, loose distinctions I refer to as *moral-belief states* in relation to the treatment of animals used as food—including their flesh, bodily secretions, and zygote-containing roe—that describe the moral stance a person takes vis-à-vis the consumption of animal products. I employ (as philosophers are wont to do) a term of art in describing these four states, specifically, the term *akrasia*, from the Greek meaning "a weakness of the will; to act in a way contrary to one's sincerely held moral values." The four moral-belief states I wish to discuss in relation to foodie culture are as follows:

FOUR MORAL BELIEF STATES

1. Non-Akratic Ignorance

Individuals in this moral-belief state are ignorant of the moral issues surrounding the suffering and death of animals for food, and so experience no weakness of the will when trying to avoid consuming animal products since they don't try. Not because they are bad people, but because they are ignorant of the conditions under which nonhuman animals are raised as food. Some readers may find it unimaginable that there exist adult humans who remain ignorant of the plight of nonhuman animals used for food. However, a 2017 study found that despite decades of undercover investigations—including graphic video evidence, ubiquitous on the internet—58% of U.S. adults think that "farmed animals are treated well." The authors of the study interpret these results as suggesting that people either have insufficient awareness of the plight of food industry animals, or they just refuse to accept the evidence.[5]

The notion of consumer ignorance is even more complicated than might appear at first blush. A 2016 Dutch study examining consumer indifference toward meat eating focused on two types of people: (a) consumers who do not care and, therefore, ignore the issue, and (b) consumers who may care but strategically *choose* to ignore the issue.[6] The latter group (b)—the so-called "strategically ignorant consumers"— suffer from a kind of confirmation bias in which they *strategically ignore* information concerning the ethics of consuming animal products. Though fascinating, persons afflicted with non-akratic ignorance are not my focus here.

2. Akratic Non-Ignorance

Sadly, akratic non-ignorance is a rather common moral-belief state. Though individuals in this moral-belief state feel that the production and consumption of (at least some) animal products are morally problematic, they nevertheless suffer *akrasia*—weakness of will—when trying to resist, and therefore continue to consume animal products. These are folks the Dutch study refers to as "struggling consumers," those meat eaters with negative feelings toward meat consumption, yet with low scores on willingness to ignore and positive scores on perceived responsibility.[7] As with the first moral-belief state, those in this group are interesting, yet not my focus here.

3. Non-Akratic Non-Ignorance

Individuals in this moral-belief state believe that the production and consumption of animal products is *not* morally problematic, thus they suffer no weakness of the will when it comes to avoiding animal products since they see no moral reason to do so. This person is cognizant of and accepts the suffering of animals as a consequence (perhaps an unfortunate consequence) of food production and consumption. They believe the production and consumption of animal products is not morally problematic, usually for at least one of four reasons (known as the "4Ns")—namely, that the consumption of animal products is (a) normal; (b) natural; (c) necessary; or (d) nice.[8] This, too, is a common moral-belief state. Persons in this state recognize that animals suffer and die in food production. While they do not think that suffering and death are necessarily good things, they do accept the suffering as a necessary part of food production and perhaps even part of the "cycle of life." They also tend to have an attitude of speciesism, believing the superiority of humans and our right to use nonhuman animals as we see fit. People in this moral-belief state are often opposed to "factory farms" and industrialized food production methods. They may even express this opposition by purchasing only "locally produced," "artisanal," "humane" animal products. This category includes people like Michael Pollan and many others who self-identify as foodies.

4. Sadistic Non-Akratic Non-Ignorance

Like the third moral-belief state, the fourth moral-belief state involves non-akratic non-ignorance, but with a twist I call sadistic non-akratic non-ignorance. Like persons in the non-akratic non-ignorance moral-belief state, those in the sadistic non-akratic non-ignorance state believe that the production and consumption of animal products is not morally problematic. However, the crucial moral difference between the two is that persons in this moral-belief state reject that the suffering of animals is unfortunate. This rejection can manifest itself in myriad ways, including (a) indifference to the suffering and killing of "food animals"; (b) the mocking of the animals and their suffering and killing; and (c) in some cases, a celebration of the suffering and killing of animals. In these cases, knowledge of the animals' suffering actually adds to the exotic, hedonistic, debauched dining pleasure. For sadistic foodies, not only do taste preference and palate satisfaction trump all competing considerations, including issues of animal suffering or even animal welfare, but the addition of animal suffering in food preparation *increases* the foodie capital of the dish, the dining experience, and even themselves. Unlike other kinds of foodies, sadistic foodies relish the fact that animals had to suffer and die for their gustatory pleasure.

Particularly for sadistic foodies, the pursuit of new food experiences is best interpreted as an artifact of affluence, and in many ways is ultimately about power, prestige, and privilege—power over the animal, the food producers, the servers, etc.; prestige with other foodies and aspiring foodies; and the privilege to afford to seek out novel and exotic food and drink. Sadistic foodies can appear absolved from all moral culpability since moral culpability is hidden behind the fact that these practices are culturally, socially, and legally sanctioned, encouraged, and even aspired to. In light of this discussion, it should be clear that folks like A.A. Gill and Anthony Bourdain are paradigm cases of sadistic foodies. For these reasons, sadistic foodie culture is particularly morally debased, especially regarding the plight of animals used as food.

MUSINGS ON MURDER

Examples of sadistic foodies are ubiquitous. Describing her experience cooking lobster, Julie Powell, author of the best-selling *Julie & Julia: 365 Days, 524 Recipes, 1 Tiny Apartment Kitchen*, writes:

> Over a period of two weeks . . . I went on a murderous rampage. I committed gruesome, atrocious acts. . . . If news of the carnage was not widely remarked upon in the local press, it was only because my victims were not Catholic schoolgirls or Filipino nurses, but crustaceans. This distinction means that I am not a murderer in the legal sense. But I have blood on my hands, even if it is the clear blood of lobsters. People say lobsters make a terrible racket in the pot, trying-reasonably enough to claw their way out of the water. I wouldn't know. I spent the next twenty minutes watching a golf game on the TV with the volume turned up. . . . When I ventured back into the kitchen, the lobsters were very red, and not making any racket at all. . . . Poor little beasties.[9]

Commenting on these passages, B. R. Myers notes in *The Atlantic*:

> This is a prime example of foodies' hostility to the very language of moral values. In mocking and debasing it, they exert, with Madison Avenue's help, a baleful influence on American English as a whole. If words like "sinful" and "decadent" are now just a cutesy way of saying "delicious but fattening," so that any serious use of them marks the speaker as a crank, and if it is more acceptable to talk of the "evils of gluten" than of the "evils of gluttony," much of the blame must be laid at their doorstep.[10]

The indifference to animal suffering is only exacerbated by the mockery and sarcasm, a staple of sadistic foodie culture. The faux light-hearted sneering, the scornful, condescending laughter at the wanton suffering and death of these sentient beings for no reason other than the gustatory satisfaction of the sadistic foodie's will to power, reflects a kind of schadenfreude on steroids that is shameful. Feminist and author Carol J. Adams maintains that expressions of laughter at animal suffering indicate just how successful the animal rights movement has become. What was once acceptable—the suffering and death of food animals—is no longer so. But rather than assimilating the lessons of the animal rights movement, we instead laugh at and mock animal death, making the unacceptable once again acceptable.[11]

Further examples of sadistic foodie culture abound. In *Blood, Bones & Butter*, Gabrielle Hamilton's reverent tone belies her ghoulish glee as she recounts her sadistic carnage:

> It's quite something to go bare-handed up through an animal's ass and dislodge its warm guts. Startling, the first time, how fragilely they are attached. I have since put countless suckling pigs—pink, with blue, querying eyes—the same weight and size of a pet beagle—into slow ovens to roast overnight so that their skin crisps and their still-forming bones melt into the meat, making it succulent and sticky. I have butchered two-hundred-twenty-pound sides of beef down to their primal cuts, carved the tongues out of the heads of goats, fastened whole baby lambs with crooked sets of teeth onto green ash spits and set them by the foursome over hot coals, and boned out the loins and legs of whole rabbits that—even skinned—still look exactly like bunnies. But at the time of the chicken killing, I was still young and unaccustomed. I retrieved the bird off the frozen ground and tied its feet and hung it from a low tree branch so it could bleed out. . . . Once the bird bled out, I submerged it in boiling water to loosen its feathers. . . . Its viscera came out with an easy tug; a small palmful of livery, bloody jewels that I tossed out into the dark yard.[12]

I imagine that such graphic descriptions of what amount to the total and utter disregard for the suffering and death of a sentient being—not to mention the objectification and fragmentation of the body of the slaughtered chicken—are intended to elicit feelings of respect, awe, and admiration. When in fact, more appropriate moral sentiments would include horror, incredulity, and nausea.

In a 2015 article from *The Guardian*, we learn that:

> Noma's Japanese restaurant serves up a rare treat. . . . The world's best restaurant has opened a pop-up in Tokyo and its still-twitching, slightly gruesome menu, has critics salivating. . . . [T]he celebrated chef behind Noma, Rene Redzepi, has upped the sushi

and seasoning stakes with a creation featuring live jumbo prawns, topped with tiny black ants. At Noma Tokyo, perched on the 37th floor of the Mandarin Oriental hotel with views of Mount Fuji in the distance, the presence of half a dozen ants clinging to the wobbling flesh of each prawn is more than just a visual gimmick. With their natural reserves of formic acid, the ants give the botan ebi—or botan prawn—a sour kick. . . . In her review for *Bloomberg*, Tejal Rao recalled being confronted by a "pristine shrimp . . . so recently dead that its brain has yet to telegraph this information to the rest of its body. For now . . . it's all twitching muscle and whirring antennae." After regaining her composure, Rao described the sensation of biting into the prawn as "shockingly good."[13]

In the bestselling *Anything That Moves: Renegade Chefs, Fearless Eaters, and the Making of a New American Food Culture*, journalist and foodie Dana Goodyear chronicles (sadistic) foodie culture, writing:

"It's not Bacchanalian, it's Caligulan!" the woman to my left exclaimed one night at Totoraku, an invitation-only, all-beef restaurant in Los Angeles, as course after course of raw beef came to the table. She was a member of a dining group that calls itself the Hedonists. On my right, another Hedonist, a Totoraku regular who had invited me along, was photographing each dish with a macrolens and macroflash. I felt obliged to gulp down as much raw beef throat as I could and made sure that I was seen doing it.[14]

As research for this chapter, I conducted an interview with Elsa Newman, an experienced server from the exclusive Plumed Horse restaurant, a fancy French foodie favorite in Silicon Valley. In the course of our discussion, Newman provided keen insight into the precise phenomenon that I am getting at here, "Foodieism is really a way for foodies to talk about money. It's a disguise, a lead in for braggadocio. They don't talk so much about the food as much as they talk about their travels and material possessions."

On the issue of foodie sadism, Newman offered the following:

We offer two different kinds of caviar here. One is produced by rubbing the fish mother's belly rather than cutting it open. That kind costs $200 an ounce versus $90 an ounce for the run-of-the-mill caviar. When told that the difference in price is due to the fact that the belly rubbing caviar is more humane in that it doesn't hurt the mother, customers become turned off, and order the eggs from the slaughtered fish. But when you tell them that the $200-an-ounce caviar has slight and unique accents of cucumber, customers fork over the $200 an ounce without hesitation.[15]

Sadistic foodie culture is about more than food. It's about intent; it's an expression of cultural capital, economic power, power over the supply chain that must come together to make "exceptional, special dishes." As B.R. Myers notes in his brilliant 2011 tour de force takedown of (the oxymoronic) foodie ethics, "The Moral Crusade Against Foodies," "It has always been crucial to the gourmet's pleasure that he eat in ways the mainstream cannot afford. [W]hen foodies talk of flying to Paris to buy cheese, to Vietnam to sample pho . . . they're not joking about that."[16]

Of course, a foodie might respond to these aspects of foodie culture by pointing out that sadistic foodies are a small, elite, nonrepresentative segment of foodie culture. Most foodies are of the non-akratic non-ignorance type (moral belief state 3) who, though not indifferent to the suffering and killing of food animals, nevertheless do not see the production and consumption of animal products as morally problematic. Even Bourdain, in the discussion referenced above, tells us that he "want[s] [food] animals to live pretty happy, stress-free lives" (of course, because "they taste less delicious if they're mistreated").[17] That said, I can only wonder, how many non-sadistic foodies are in reality aspiring sadistic foodies? For those that are, it would seem that the main difference between non-sadistic foodies and sadistic foodies is wealth and access. And that's morally troubling.

THE HIDDEN HUMANE HOAX BEHIND FOODIEISM

Even foodies of the Michael Pollan sort—emblematic of a popular kind of foodieism—are themselves accompanied by their own troubling moral consequences. An increased awareness of the destructive nature of animal agriculture and fishing—including environmental degradation, individual and public health threats, and the atrocious conditions under which animals are raised—has led to a shift in attitudes toward meat production and animal products in general. This acknowledgment, coupled with a sentimental nostalgia for a time when a majority of Europeans and Americans were farmers and craftspersons, has fed a booming alternative food movement. Known as locavorism, foodieism, compassionate carnivorism, the sustainable meat movement, the humane meat movement, the happy meat movement, the nose-to-tail food movement, and the conscientious omnivore movement, this movement markets itself as free-range, grass-fed, organic, natural, and cage-free. For those who desire to consume animal products but are ethically troubled by industrialized animal agriculture, so-called "happy" meat, eggs, and dairy purport to offer an ethical alternative both to veganism and to the cruelty of the industrial farm, ensuring happier lives (and "humane deaths") for animals destined to become food. Measured against the vast majority of consumers whose lack of connectedness to their food enables the near-total erasure of suffering from their plates in the form of neatly shrink-wrapped, bloodless cuts of meat, so-called "compassionate carnivore" foodies perhaps deserve praise. Yet despite this supposed concern for the animals' lives and deaths, the details of their short and torturous lives and the brutality of their slaughter are kept secret, far from the public eye. In truth, an overwhelming majority of animals raised on "local" farms are sent to the same slaughterhouses, butchered alongside their kin raised in larger industrial settings. Animals raised in "humane" conditions are routinely overcrowded and suffer branding, dehorning, tail-docking, debeaking, castration, tooth-filing, ear-notching, and nose ring piercing, all without anesthesia.[18]

In "How Happy is Your Meat?: Confronting (Dis)connectedness in the 'Alternative' Meat Industry," geographer Kathryn Gillespie analyzes the tension between the desire for Do-It-Yourself (DIY) butchers to forge a connection to their food by involving themselves in every step of its production (including slaughter), and the Herculean efforts they make to disconnect themselves from the actual animal they will butcher in order to avoid a sentimental or emotional attachment to the hapless victim. For many "compassionate carnivores," the killing and eating of animals is justified by their interest in forming a consumer–food connection, where personally taking on the death of the animal acts as a means to more ethical eating, a way of honoring the subjects of slaughter while eating them. Yet, as Gillespie points out, even Michael Pollan advises DIY butchers to quickly disconnect from what it means to slaughter an animal. Gillespie incisively characterizes this most profound disconnect in the following way:

> All of the justifications for DIY slaughter as a way to connect to food, to become an artisan, to embody rusticity, and to make slaughter more humane are enlisted to conceal what the process really does. DIY slaughter connects participants to the violence against the animal, and not to the animal him/herself. This "connection" is a wholly false connection. DIY slaughter denies the actual connection we have with animals. Animals are still, in DIY slaughter, conceptualized not as individual animals but as products ready to become meat.[19]

A further problem with both "humane" and industrial agriculture is that they place animals in the category of the edible, ontologizing sentient beings as food. The transformation of an animal to a food object involves a kind of erasure in which a complex, sensitive being is made absent, stripped of all subjectivity, individual personality, interests, and desires (including the desire not to be harmed or killed). This ultimate and ghastly expression of speciesism *literally* transmutes a living being into an object to be severed and consumed.[20]

THE PERSONAL CHOICE RATIONALIZATION

Intimately connected to foodie culture is one popular justification for eating animal flesh and secretions—namely, the claim that eating meat is a personal choice. A common response to the suggestion that non-sadistic foodies ought to go vegan goes something like this: The matter of eating animals is a matter of personal choice, and matters of personal choice are not moral issues, so the matter of eating animals is not a moral issue. But rather than respecting such choices, vegans try and force their views on others, disrespecting people and their personal choices.

True, one's diet is a kind of personal choice. In fact, with rare exception (e.g., coercion), every action that we perform is in a sense a personal choice. However, a crucial conceptual and ethical distinction exists between two different senses of the term. One type of personal choice—*benign personal choice*—involves matters of taste that have little to no effect on others (e.g., whether I prefer to wear blue or brown socks today). A second type of personal choice—*pernicious personal choice*—involves actions (like consumer behavior) that may appear from our own perspectives to be benign, but which actually have grave moral implications, effects that sometimes may be invisible to us. Some choices we make are immoral. Some choices have victims. The choice to consume animal products may appear to be benign, but in fact, is a choice that involves a sentient victim. Thus, despite appearances, the choice to eat animals is not a case of benign personal choice, but rather a case of pernicious personal choice. Seeing animal food choices as instances of pernicious personal choice is a necessary step in assimilating nonhuman animals into our moral community.[21] The billions of animals kept in bondage and slaughtered each year would surely welcome the opportunity to exercise their personal choice, and if granted the choice, would prefer to live out their lives without human-inflicted exploitation and violence. Animals are forced onto the killing floor against their will. Any notion of choice has been taken away from them. Unless we are hedonistic solipsistic narcissists, the personal choice defense holds no sway. The inclusion of a victim removes any possibility of moral justification.

Further, animal agribusiness is the leading single cause of water pollution, air pollution, and climate disruption[22] such that, collectively, the consumption of animal products does impose and externalize the costs and consequences of such "personal choices" on others.[23] As if that weren't enough, animal exploitation and consumption remains the driving force behind viral outbreaks such as H1N1 (avian flu), H5N1 (swine flu), and the SAR-CoV-2 COVID-19 pandemic.[24] Clearly, to argue that eating animal products is merely a personal choice is to ignore and overlook important ethical consequences of such choices.

Of course, there is nothing inherent in foodieism that excludes plant-based fare, nor even ethical veganism. There are numerous vegan foodies who can attest to that. Once we remove animal suffering and exploitation from the foodie palate, the sadistic aspects of foodieism—at least as they affect nonhuman animals—dissolve. This benevolent foodieism may not suffer the troubling moral consequences that sadistic foodieism faces, but it must still contend with the exclusivity and elitism inherent in foodieism, a topic I will leave for another day. For now, it's sufficient to identify, as I have attempted to do here, those aspects of human psychology and behavior that drive us to divorce the gastronomic from the ethical, to willfully ignore that food choices *are* moral choices.

Robert C. Jones earned his Ph.D. in Philosophy from Stanford University. He is currently an associate professor of philosophy at California State University, Dominguez Hills. His research focuses on critical animal studies and animal liberation theory and activism through a variety of projects spanning traditional and novel areas of ethics, social justice, and food ethics. Dr. Jones co-authored *Chimpanzee Rights*, has published numerous articles and book chapters on animal ethics, and has given talks on animal liberation, speciesism, and human supremacy.

PART 4:
SPIRITUAL DIMENSIONS

17

HONOR KILLING

Spiritual Bypass and False Faith in Do-It-Yourself Slaughter

By Cogen Bohanec, Ph.D.

If the animal is small, I hold it while it passes. I hold it so that I never take for granted the life that leaves. I hold it so that perhaps it can feel my love and take some comfort from my gratitude. If the animal is large, I lay my hand upon them. Even as I cut the throat, I lay my hand upon them and I pray for them. As their blood feeds the ground, I honor them. And then, it is done. I ease them out. I pray for their spirit so that it passes to where its journey continues. I ask their soul to be a guardian of our homestead; their presence is always welcome here. Their body is our food—the way our bodies will one day feed others . . . Life continues. *(From the* Modern Farmer *website)* [1]

Increasingly people are turning to "do-it-yourself" (DIY) or "backyard" slaughter—that is, the killing of an animal oneself before consumption—for a way to disconnect from industrial animal farming, to reconnect with a more rural, simple lifestyle, and to go "back to the land." But when the brutality of actually killing an animal is at hand, "spiritual" language, deep, heartfelt reasoning, and even mentions of prayer and spirit are often evoked in the journaling, musings, and writings of the DIY slaughterer.

In many DIY slaughter articles and descriptions, such as the one above, we see a glaring contradiction between the employment of spiritual language to make killing seem compassionate or benevolent and the brutality of the violent act that the DIY practitioner (DIYer) engages in. Notice how the quote uses terms of "love," "gratitude," "comfort," "pray," "ease," "spirit," etc. When we see these words on their own, it is hard to imagine that they are from a passage describing the violence of killing someone. The animal being comforted and appreciated in the above quote before having her throat cut is referred to as "it," not him or her. This is another way to separate the reality that this is a sentient individual.

This type of spiritual language employed by DIYers is problematic for two reasons: (1) psychologically, it demonstrates spiritual bypass, and (2) ethically, it is a form of manipulation. Thus, I will show how bypass can be understood as a form of self-manipulation, of one's own ability to perceive the truth (i.e., "spiritual bypass"), and as a form of manipulation of others as well.

While what I discuss in this chapter will be specific to DIY slaughter, the model of spiritual bypass and manipulation that I describe can be extended to anyone using spiritual jargon to dismiss the reality of killing animals for one's own selfish purposes.

Spiritual Bypass

John Welwood, a prominent psychologist who was known for integrating psychological and spiritual concepts, coined the term "spiritual bypass" to refer to a "widespread tendency to use spiritual ideas and practices to sidestep or avoid facing unresolved emotional issues, psychological wounds, and unfinished developmental tasks."[2] Since then, the term "spiritual bypass" is generally taken by psychotherapists to refer to ways that people use an appeal to spirituality to rationalize their avoidance of dealing with their own psychological issues.

However, in the field of ethics and theology (or "theo-ethics"), the connotative range of the term "spiritual bypass" has been broadened to include how people appeal to spirituality to justify unethical behavior or a lack of care for things that are "this-worldly," including (but not limited to) animals and the environment. By this, they use spirituality to "bypass" a sense of ethical responsibility for social justice and other interpersonal issues (herein, I consider animals to be "persons" because of their right to "personhood").

Most articulations of spirituality across cultures involve some emphasis on the pursuit of higher truths, values, and virtues. Spiritual bypass, on the other hand, is a form of self-deception rather than an honest pursuit of these higher purposes. If, then, spirituality is concerned with a revelation of truth, and bypass is a form of self-deception, then spiritual bypass is completely at odds with genuine spirituality.

SPIRITUAL DOUBLESPEAK:
BYPASSING THE REALITY OF EXPLOITATION

Language cannot change the fact that killing to fulfill one's own ends is antithetical to love.* But language can be used to deceive oneself into thinking that violence is spiritual and loving, as a kind of "spiritual doublespeak."

In the opening passage, the terms employed are not accurate descriptions of the act of killing. The terms "love," "gratitude," "comfort," "pray," "ease," and "spirit," falsely convey an attitude of care rather than the truth of exploitation. I use the term "exploitation" herein to mean "asserting one's own selfish desires at the expense of the needs and desires of another." And the desire of any animal, regardless of species, is to live a full life, have babies, experience another summer of sunshine, and live to old age. These terms would not be expressed when harvesting potatoes, these utterances occur because the DIYer knows there is something very different between picking peapods and slitting throats. Care and exploitation of a sentient animal are diametrically opposed to each other—one cannot simultaneously exploit and care for another at the same time in the same action. Killing cannot be *both* exploitation and care, and since it is clearly the former, it can never be the latter.

---

* In this piece, I will be leaving aside the possible exception where eating meat is done for survival, because such a situation is extremely rare in a society with modern agriculture and commerce where food choices often, but not always, allow for one to survive with equal availability and economically on non-animal foods.

When one kills an animal, they take that animal's most valued treasure—her life. The hegemony of the butcher is apparent. The slaughterer completely overpowers the agency of the animal and dominates the animal's ability to choose life over death. The more accurate description of this process would therefore use the language of exploitation, domination, and power. Terms like "love" are diametrically opposed since love can more accurately be considered a profound act of giving rather than a selfish act of taking an animal's very life, and loving relationships are characterized by equality between consenting individuals, rather than hegemony, force, and violence.

By using spiritual language, the killer is not being honest about the reality of the situation and is *bypassing* their rational faculties by not examining the act for what it is. Further, the killer is *bypassing* their affective (i.e., "emotional") faculties by allowing their deeper need to feel love and care to be expressed in a wholly inappropriate way—in an act of violence. Mistaking violence for love indicates some deeper psychological issues,* which we can see in human interpersonal relationships as much as in interspecies ones. Instead of addressing these issues, the DIYer is "bypassing" them by using the euphemisms of spiritual language.

Spiritual Bypass as a "Self-Confirmation" Bias

Understood socially and ethically, at the heart of the issue of spiritual bypass is what might be related to a "self-confirmation bias." In the natural and social sciences, a self-confirmation bias is understood as a

---

* It is an important disclaimer that I'm speaking as a theologian and an ethicist here, not as a psychologist. Thus, when I say "psychological issues," I don't mean in the sense of some clinical pathology. Rather, I mean this in terms of the intersection of theology, ethics, and psychology—that is, one has "psychological issues" when one has positive feelings about and/or "bypasses" hurting others, in the sense that this is problematic for one's psychology as a philosophical axiom. This is to say that in terms of our psychological makeup, it is philosophically undesirable to mistake violence for love, and to commit a violent act while thinking that one is gaining the benefit of a loving relationship. I take this as a belief that does not require justification in relationship to other ideas, and that, as an axiom, it is self-evident. Further, I will also be using the term "spiritual bypass" from the perspective of a trained theologian, so that any language that I use that seems psychological is coming from the intersection of psychology and theology, rather than from the perspective of a trained psychologist.

means of self-deception where a person tends to see what they want to see, or what they expect to see, and will do so even if it is contrary to the empirical data. Hence the need for double-blind, controlled, peer-reviewed scientific studies to mitigate the otherwise inevitable self-interest, or self-confirmation bias, on the part of researchers.

If we were to use conventional spiritual language to describe the self-confirmation bias, we might see that it is related to what spiritualists* call the "ego," or that part of us that is so entrenched with the drama of worldly life that we become selfish and pursue temporary material pleasures, instead of what is spiritually "good" for ourselves and others. (I'm using the word "ego" here in terms of its conventional spiritual usage, related to Sanskrit terms like ahamkāra, asmitā, manas, etc., rather than in the psychological, largely Freudian, sense.) The ego then rationalizes to justify doing what we desire rather than what is spiritual or good, thereby confirming what we want, instead of honestly understanding a situation or course of action.

Psychotherapist and author Mariana Caplan writes that in authentic spiritual practice, "the ego simultaneously experiences the possibility of authentic transformation as a literal death threat."[3] The result is that, "in its great intelligence, the ego co-opts the language and concepts of truth and transformation to ensure that this transformation does not happen, but it does so in the name of truth" by employing spiritual language as a defense mechanism to rationalize actions that are harmful to one's spiritual, emotional, and psychological well-being.

The power of the ego is such that it can even distort spiritual teachings to become a means of selfish pursuits. Thus, in spiritual terms, spiritual bypass, as a form of a self-confirmation bias, is when one's ego appropriates spirituality towards one's selfish ends, employing spirituality as a means to justify selfish pursuits, and even objectifying (i.e., "treating as a mere object") spirituality itself, as an object of consumption rather than a subject of meaningful, personal transformation.

---

*   Used loosely, as in "people who are spiritually oriented." This term is needed because of the current discourse around being "spiritual but not religious" creates a blind spot if we were to just say "religious people." "Spiritualists," as I use it, is meant as "those who consider themselves spiritual."

Spiritual Bypass and Ego Driven Pseudo-Spirituality

Instead of becoming more spiritual, when the ego appropriates spirituality for its own selfish ends, it leads to a kind of pseudo-spirituality, thereby making the bypasser more of a performer than a genuine spiritual aspirant. This pretense of spirituality causes one to go through the motions of spirituality without sacrificing any of one's selfish urges. This is relevant because spirituality throughout the world's religious traditions tends to involve some degree of a movement away from selfish desires and egoism. With an ego-appropriated spirituality, one becomes more self-centered rather than less self-centered—as would be the process of genuine spirituality.

Spiritual bypass as a form of self-confirmation bias, where spiritual language becomes an instrument of one's selfish pursuit rather than a means of overcoming self-centered egoism, is prolific in DIY language. For example:

> . . . [a nearby herbalist] raises sheep for milk and meat, and when she slaughters them, she has a whole ritual: she sings to them and straddles them like she's riding them and then cuts their throat. She calls it 'giving death.' I haven't seen her do it, but she says they're always calm and accepting of their fate. She's very clear that it's a gift.

Such DIY language is an example of an ego-centered distortion of spirituality. The tone of the article is spiritual, and the most extreme act of taking—that is, taking a life—is twisted to being described as "giving." This is a failure on the part of the butcher to recognize the act for what it is—the most intense form of domination one can engage in for the sake of taking for oneself what is not theirs to take, and what is not "given" in any meaningful sense of the term. This type of self-deception is characteristic of spiritual bypass—that is, using spiritual language as a defense mechanism to not acknowledge the real, hurtful consequences of one's selfish, ego-driven action.

Here another trope of spiritual bypass is invoked:

> Inside the space of silence, I think, I could stand to die here. Here, in this pasture, under these mountains, this sky. If, when my time comes, someone lays me down in green grass and soothes my body,

and someone I love then lovingly cuts my throat, and my blood runs into the grass and fertilizes the soil, and my body is used for food and necessity, I could handle that.[4]

It is an act of extreme self-deception where violence becomes perceived as "loving," and selfishness is perceived as "caring." It is especially hard to imagine that one would be so peaceful and accepting in the case of being murdered—especially if that murder was at the hands of "someone I love." Actually, when one is murdered or otherwise becomes a victim of violence at the hands of a loved one, the fact that that person (supposedly) "loves" them does not lessen the quality of violence—it increases the degree of violence of that action because the (arguably) worst act of emotional violence, betrayal of the trust of a loved one, is added to the act of physical violence. The scene that is depicted here sounds more like euthanasia that is granting the wish of the person who is dying, not like a situation where one's life is being taken against their will, which would be the case for animal slaughter. If there really was some "love" between the killer and the victim, this situation would be a horrible confluence of both physical and emotional abuse.[5]

Such depictions are an act of self-deception and are a "bypassing" of the reality of the situation without addressing the truth that if someone really does require love and care to progress spiritually, then killing another being certainly does not qualify as fulfilling that need. Rather than freeing the DIYer from egocentricity, one's ego distorts spirituality for selfish ends—the ends of enjoying and consuming flesh and other byproducts of animal abuse.

Premature Transcendence

In the religions of the world, there is often a tension between transcendence and immanence. Transcendence, or the transcendental, deals with that which is "spiritual" or "beyond the mundane, material life." In many religions, the realization of the transcendental reality is the source of moving beyond the suffering inherent in worldly existence such as survival, old age, disease, death, loss, etc. Immanence, on the other hand, deals with how we find the divine and the sacred within the loss, pain, and difficulties of our lives in this world. The problem arises when those who are spiritually inclined claim to have achieved a spiritual state that is "beyond," or "transcendental to" the suffering of this world, and therefore feel that they are above the accountability of their worldly actions.

Welwood describes a process of "premature transcendence," whereby one employs spiritual language in a way that implies that, due to their "spirituality," they are above the consequences of their actions in the material world. For Welwood, as a psychologist, this takes the form of denying one's humanness and using "absolute truth to disparage or dismiss relative human needs, feelings, psychological problems, relational difficulties, and developmental defects." He notes that this is an "occupational hazard" of the spiritual path, in that spirituality does involve a vision of "going beyond" our worldly situations.[6] But we must not use the transcendental emphasis of spirituality to devalue the world and the suffering that is experienced by others.

When applying spiritual bypass to the ethics of DIY slaughter, the "occupational hazard" of engaging in "premature transcendence" is that the slaughterer dismisses the empirical truth regarding the experience of the animal victim—and pretends to be spiritually advanced beyond the actual questionable morality of the situation. This becomes a psychological issue when the killer becomes dismissive of their conscience and the compassionate and caring aspects of their psychology. "Premature transcendence" is on display when the DIYer portrays the inherently violent act as "transcendental" in a way that dismisses the very real and worldly experience of the animal victims. For example:

> [So and so] feels such compassion for a bird before he kills it, he said, that . . . kosher slaughter has become something of an esoteric experience for him. 'I decided I needed to do this myself,' he explained of his decision to learn the ancient ritual. 'Not only to have an alternative to the economy of the slaughter of animals en masse, but also to have it as a spiritual practice.'[7]

The "occupational hazard" of spiritual bypass in DIY slaughter uses the language of spiritual transcendence to "rise above" the violence that is being committed. This has the effect of making the slaughterer feel as if they have made peace with an action that cannot be described as "peaceful" by any stretch of the term. The needs of the animal are dismissed and denied, and the needs of our own psychology to live a peaceful life are likewise ignored in favor of pretending that an action is peaceful and therefore spiritual. In reality, the act of killing a sensitive, sentient being is always violent, and therefore at odds with the very spiritual values that the DIY slaughterer professes.

I'm not making a value judgment about how these rituals operated in premodern cultures, and I'm open to the possibility that when food choices were restricted in premodern times, killing animals for food may have been necessary for survival. Therefore, the best-case scenario may have been to ritualize the slaughter to inspire a sense of deep regret for what may have been, at one time in the distant past, a necessary act. However, that does not describe the current state of modern Western society where eating animals is almost never done out of necessity. If one is choosing a luxury item such as meat, eggs, and dairy, one is not reluctantly making a necessary choice, so ritualized slaughter is no longer done in the same spirit as it was done in the past. This is a central argument for many vegan organizations associated with various faiths.

Bypass can lead to a split between the transcendent (the "spiritual" that is beyond worldly life) and the immanent (the "spiritual" that can be found within worldly life) in such a way that removes one's spirituality from our this-world, lived experiences. Spirituality is bypassed when we value the transcendental *at the expense of* the material, at the expense of this world.

Further, when spirituality is removed from this world in favor of an exclusive focus on transcendence, it loses its social relevance. If we use spiritual language to disconnect from other living beings around us, rather than to connect with them, the value of such so-called "spirituality" can be called into question. When the focus on transcendence favors the transcendental at the expense of the embodied, the result may be a devaluation of other embodied beings. If this devaluation is taken to the extreme, then such so-called spirituality can devalue others to the point of being not only indifferent to suffering, but also indifferent to one's complicity in violence and even serve as a "justification" for one's violent actions. At this point, spirituality is weaponized as a tool for violence rather than employed for the betterment of ourselves and others. The potential danger of such bypassing is that one not only consciously dismisses the real, violent consequences of one's actions, but one also exposes oneself to subconscious effects. If one uses spiritual language to dismiss one's capacity to express compassion towards the animal victim, it is possible that one will be more likely to dismiss their compassionate expressions elsewhere, and this will have a debilitating effect on one's ability to express and feel compassion in general. This could potentially have a deleterious effect on all relationships. By their own admission, compassion is supposedly part of the spiritual ethos of the DIY slaughter movement, yet it arguably cripples this capacity that it purports to value.

When a focus on the transcendent eclipses an accurate perception of the real experiences of animals who are being killed, then what appears to be lofty and "spiritual" is really bypassing one's basic perceptual capacities, bypassing one's ability to transcend and move beyond the disconnection between self and others through compassion, and bypassing the deeper question of how the DIYer could so blatantly mistake violence for love.

COMPENSATORY IDENTITY; DEFICIENT IDENTITY

Welwood compares a *compensatory identity* that covers up and defends against an underlying *deficient identity*. A "deficient identity" is when one feels bad about oneself, as in "not good enough, or basically lacking." The idea is that when one is engaged in spiritual bypass, one is using one's spiritual practice "in the service of denial and defense"[8] rather than to be a means of personal transformation. One is "compensating" for one's deficiencies rather than addressing those deficiencies.

It is hard to imagine a form of spirituality that does not require personal transformation. Spiritual traditions generally involve an emphasis on a call to be a better person, rather than to be in denial and defensive of one's deficiencies. Denial of one's deficiencies is at odds with an honest, and therefore effective, approach to spirituality.

In the case of DIY spiritualism, spiritually inflated language is used to compensate for a lack of actual spiritual virtue, such as compassion and caring. Evidenced by their language, DIYers often do not directly address the issue of violence (in this case, killing an animal). Rather, spiritual language is used to bypass and ignore the issue altogether by framing the act of killing as if it is some kind of expression of compassion and love, something that supposedly transcends the empirical facts of the situation. The empirical facts—the suffering and killing of the animal—is completely overlooked, completely *bypassed*, and the need to be compassionate rather than violent is betrayed by the language that falsely professes to be so.

We can see that these DIYers actually express a genuine need to be compassionate and loving, but the spiritual language instead enables them to be violent in place of being loving. They use spiritual language to compensate for this deficiency:

> In my work, I have watched many animals pass. In my classes, people ask me sometimes how to ensure that it will go well. I've even had people ask me if there is a way to make it easier. Of course, the discussion flows into humane slaughter regulations and stories of individual experiences with various methods. But I am always sure to mention one thing: It is never easy. It isn't supposed to be.[9]

I take statements like this to be genuine. I've read enough of these entries to know that the DIYers legitimately suffer and grieve, sometimes quite intensely, in the process. Again, there is an awareness that killing animals is very different than picking tomatoes, thus the need for soothing language and rationalization. The act of killing a sentient animal betrays a deeper human need: to be loving rather than violent. Their trauma is a result of working against the need for love and connection, and that need is psychologically bypassed by framing the act of killing as a spiritual one. Their actions here certainly suggest some distortion in how love is expressed. Therefore, the spiritual language used by DIYers seems to be compensating for this deficiency in their capacity to express love and care in a healthy way, by mistaking violence for what domestic animals truly need—protection, nurturing, caring, etc. It is further compensating for the fact that their actions are deficient with regard to the deeper human need to show love and sensitivity for others.

DIS-INTEGRATION VS. HOLISM

"Holism" is a concept that infuses the world's religious traditions, and even more secular forms of spirituality (such as with European Romanticism, for example). This is the idea that our suffering results from having a fragmented view of ourselves and our relationship to the whole of reality—a perennial sense of "incompleteness." By this, spirituality often involves a re-integration of our own psychological/emotional/embodied capacities with each other, and with the entirety of reality—a divine "whole"—so that we move from feeling incomplete to becoming fully complete. In short, "holism" is the spiritual process of feeling complete, feeling whole. By "holism," spiritual practitioners (both within traditional world religions, and in other non-traditional spiritual movements) resist the compartmentalization, and therefore neglect, of our psychological, emotional, and embodied needs, and the fragmentation of ourselves from the systems of reality in the form of selfishness, egoism, etc.

This type of fragmentation is evident in DIY spiritual bypassing. When one bypasses the reality of one's violent actions, the violent action itself is compartmentalized in a way that "remains uninterested with our overall functioning"[10] of one's being. It seems that the DIYers genuinely aspire to be spiritual and compassionate, but this aspiration remains in a separate compartment from one's actual actions in a way that is cognitively dissonant. When one is compartmentalizing like this, we should not be surprised if one's spiritual aspirations towards values like compassion fail to manifest in other aspects of their lives. After all, we become what we practice, and compassion takes practice. And so does violence.

When one's desire to be compassionate and spiritual is sufficiently contradicted by the act of killing, each aspect of one's identity is compartmentalized and fragmented. A disintegration remains between words, aspirations, and actions, and the result is a disharmonious relationship among them, rather than the harmony—the holism—that one would expect from a truly spiritual way of life. The need for integration of one's thoughts, actions, and deeds, as well as for having a sense of integration with a larger, higher reality is a common spiritual impulse in most traditions of holism. Holism is contradicted when there is disharmony between words and deeds, for example when spiritual language of "compassion" is used to justify killing.

Further, spiritual holism can refer to a unified relationship with others in a way that creates harmony. This type of holism is contradicted when one serves one's own interests at the expense of another. For example, when one kills for one's own desire for meat, but presents the violent act as if it is in the interests of the animal.

The sense of harmony and integration, rather than disintegration, is a common theme in spiritual traditions across the world. Some DIYers pick up on this holistic theme:

> The Cycles of Life [slaughter] class . . . is about life and awareness, holistic-dynamism, and inevitable change. It is about the synergy of life and death, a baffling collusion of opposites that humans have struggled to grasp physically and spiritually since the dawn of our species.[11]

Most vegans have heard the "cycle of life" argument where one uses the language of spiritual bypass to make a pretense at a spiritual integration with the "whole" of reality and harmonizing life and death by actively participating in killing (either as a consumer or as a butcher). The implication in phrases like this is that if one is *not* involved with killing, then one is disintegrated from the spiritual holism of nature. This is a fairly straightforward "naturalistic fallacy," that is, just because something occurs in nature doesn't mean that we should model our morality after that behavior. It is unclear how the fact of death and killing in nature would imply that we *should* kill any more than the fact of infanticide or forced copulation in nature implies that we *should* engage in these acts. There are numerous herbivore and omnivore animals (which we are) who are part of the "circle of life" but consume a plant-only diet. We have taken ourselves out of the circle as a prey species—since we have the choice, ability, and capacity, why not choose to compassionately engage in the circle of life on a plant-rich, vegan diet?

Those who seek to express compassion and love through the act of killing are disintegrated since they have compartmentalized their empathetic, caring, and loving nature so that they can engage in an act that is very much against these basic human needs. This leads to a further disintegration of one's words, thoughts, and actions, which is evidenced by the contradiction between the very nurturing language employed and the action being incorrectly described as such. Falsehood is being expounded as spiritual truth.

If spirituality is to accurately reflect holism in a way that doesn't require one to disintegrate and compartmentalize, then our actions should be consistent with our words. Holism, understood as achieving the state of being spiritually "whole," isn't about *dis*integrating one's spiritual experience from the worldly. True spiritual holism would require an integration of our needs and those of others, and the act of killing is the opposite of these. Therefore, killing is *not* an act of spiritual holism—rather it is an act of profound disintegration, disjunction, isolation, and alienation.

SELF-AGGRANDIZEMENT

Another means of self-deception associated with spiritual bypassing is a type of self-aggrandizement symptomatic of an "inflated sense of [one's] own realization."[12] In the DIY movement, the claims that one is somehow facilitating the spiritual journey of the animal victim by taking his life exhibits such an "inflated sense" of one's spiritual capacities. For example:

> I pray for their spirit so that it passes to where its journey continues. I ask their soul to be a guardian of our homestead; their presence is always welcome here.[13]

> "The two-day workshop will begin by getting to know the animal". . . . Then, "there is some ceremony around the death process." Students will pray together before the sacrifice, and then the sheep is fed water, an offering for it to take into the next life.[14]

While the validity of a spiritual truth claim cannot be reduced to its falsifiability (i.e., cannot be proven to be "true" or "false" with absolute certainty), it is important to understand that in many ways spiritual concepts allow for a significant degree of uncertainty about the mystery of higher truth based on our limited capacities to know that which is unlimited—the divine "whole," perhaps. This is why it is sometimes said that "faith is the opposite of certainty."[15]

Before an action that is motivated by spirituality is taken, the aspirant would do well to consider their own limited capacities to know, and act with appropriate humility, *especially* if there is the risk that another being will be hurt by one's actions that are spiritually motivated. Thus, humility is essential to spiritual epistemology ("how we know truth") and the arrogance of self-aggrandizement and an inflated sense of one's own spiritual capabilities are contrary to spiritual practice.

With regard to the question if a DIY practitioner does in fact somehow help "guide" the animal victim in some spiritual capacity, we can ask, is there a reasonable possibility that this claim may be wrong? It is safer to err on the side of compassion rather than self-inflation and self-aggrandizement—safer for our own expression of our spiritual actions and safer for the well-being of the animals.

When such self-aggrandizement happens in religious communities, the result is often disastrous, and often ends in scandal when a religious leader with an "inflated sense of realization" uses self-aggrandizement to bypass the need to develop self-critical aspects of themselves. The effects are frequently devastating when spiritual leaders then use the power of their inflated sense of importance to hurt their followers, exploiting them for their own ends, resulting in spiritual abuse.

This same pattern of inflated sense of spiritual realization is similar to what DIYers express when they have an aggrandized sense of their own capacitates to spiritually transform others (animals). But, if they are wrong, they enact violence (slaughter) rather than actual care for the animals who are in a dependent relationship with them. This pattern of abuse is sadly familiar amongst spiritual leaders who inflate their own abilities to "transcend" the hurtful and sometimes violent actions that they inflict.

Caplan refers to this as "the phenomenon of spiritual mediocrity, which occurs when unprepared individuals prematurely place themselves, or are placed in, positions of power they are not equipped to handle." She associates this with "manipulation" where "dysfunction is instituted within a spiritual group, often rationalized with spiritual, or dharmic, terminology."[16] When a person claims to be able to kill, not only with impunity, but with a divine mandate of "guiding" the victim on their spiritual journey, the pattern is dangerously similar to other examples where self-aggrandizement leads to spiritual abuse. Given that an animal is certainly not a willing participant, wants to live and not die, and is therefore victimized in acts that are described in "spiritual" terms, the designation of DIY spiritual slaughter as "spiritual abuse" or perhaps "spiritual animal abuse" is appropriate.

MANIPULATION, BYPASS, AND DOUBLESPEAK

World Religions in general tend to value epistemological modes (ways of knowing truth) that are transrational, that is, beyond the limits of what can be known rationally alone, such as affective (emotional) states (e.g., "love of God," etc.) and the lived experience of being a practitioner. However, transrational ("beyond the rational") ways of knowing can become highly problematic when they become *irrational*, that is, there are glaring contradictions between what one is experiencing and how one employs the logic to understand—even *justify*—what "spiritual" practices and experiences one engages in.

Transrationalism is the employment of reason to show that which is beyond the purview of logic; irrationality is when a proposition or an action is rationally incoherent or contradictory. This is the basic theological problem with using spiritual language embellished with strained definitions of terms like "compassion" or "care" and then engaging in actions that are completely at odds with the values used to justify them. It is just bad theology when one's spiritual actions and beliefs are irrational rather than transrational.

The result is a sort of spiritual "doublespeak" whereby spiritual language is used to obscure the inherently violent nature of the act of taking an animal's life. Unlike political doublespeak (the original meaning of the term coined by George Orwell) which is intended to deceive others, spiritual doublespeak is employed to deceive oneself as well as others. Spiritual doublespeak seeks to fashion the butcher into the caregiver, the murderer into the savior, and it allows the perpetrator to bypass the cognitive dissonance, philosophical contradiction, and irrational and untenable theology that lies within the executioner's being. This is one of the reasons why those who are not personally invested in animal killing find these statements to be so profoundly disturbing—it just seems to be an example of audacious dishonesty.

CONCLUSION: AN OPEN LETTER TO DIYERS

While this chapter takes the form of a somewhat biting critique of DIYers, I don't mean to dehumanize such practitioners by reducing their entire identity to what I feel is perhaps the worst element—namely, the propensity to enact violence against the most vulnerable beings who depend on them and are looking to them for compassion and care, and instead receive violence and pain. I have tried my best to be charitable in my assumptions even about their spiritual intentions and realizations.

For example, it is quite possible that a DIY slaughterer could have had some genuine spiritual realization but could still be engaged in acts that I have argued are completely contradictory to sincere spiritual development. The human psyche is immensely complex, and there are multiple channels of development whereby a person can be highly advanced in one capacity, and relatively undeveloped in others.[17] It is unrealistic to expect that any given person, even a spiritually advanced one, would be highly developed in all areas of human capacities.

So I will end this chapter with a plea to the DIYers, rather than a tone of condemnation. I hope that such practitioners can hear that my critique is in good faith and is made in the hopes that if the DIYer is genuine about spiritual development, they will examine all acts of violence to animals as contrary to one's higher, spiritual progress. I hope that they will see the act of killing as a profound act of disintegration, rather than some type of holistic integration. I ask them to consider that spiritual transcendence must not be attained *at the expense* of another, but in harmony with the divine immanence within all beings—animals included.

Further, I pray that they might consider that it is critical that any of us who are on the spiritual path do not bypass by employing spirituality as a means of reinforcing, rather than attenuating, our egotistical tendency toward self-centeredness and unnecessary acts of violence. If genuine spirituality is to be weaponized, it should be a weapon yielded *against* domination and oppression, rather than being co-opted and appropriated as an instrument in the service of self-delusion, manipulation, and violence.

Cogen Bohanec holds a Ph.D. in "Historical and Cultural Studies of Religion" from the Graduate Theological Union (GTU) in Berkeley, where his research emphasized comparative dharmic traditions and the philosophy of religion. He also has an M.A. in Buddhist Studies from the Institute of Buddhist Studies at GTU. Dr. Bohanec currently holds the position of Associate Professor in Jain Studies at Arihanta Academy. He has previously taught South Asian Culture & Religions and Sanskrit language at the GTU, and Asian Humanities, World Religions, and Classical Humanities at American River College in Sacramento. He is the co-author of *The Ultimate Betrayal: Is There Happy Meat?* with his wife Hope Bohanec, with whom he has collaborated in the animal rights movement for two decades.

18

USING THE DEEPER DIMENSIONS OF JAIN AHIṂSĀ TO SHED LIGHT ON DAIRY'S HUMANE HOAX

by Christopher Jain Miller, Ph.D.

"If Jainism does not define Veganism, Veganism will define Jainism."—**Dr. Jasvant Modi**, Jain Center of Southern California

*A**hiṃsā*, or non-harming, is a Sanskrit term that is all too familiar within transnational veganism.[1] While this Sanskrit word is directly translated as non-harming, the concept can be thought of more as a dynamic, active compassion. We find the term "ahimsa" used by prominent vegan organizations, such as The Vegan Society,[2] on the t-shirts and necklaces of vegan activists, and the term is often invoked by vegans all around the world to explain the core reason behind their dietary praxis and lifestyle. This should come as no surprise, since Western cultures and the vegan movement itself have continually found inspiration in the South Asian dharma traditions expressing this universal virtue for more than 2,000 years.[3] And though promoted across a number of South Asian philosophical traditions, including Buddhist and Hindu Dharmas, no other tradition has expressed, promoted, and practiced *ahiṃsā* as earnestly as the Jains.*

---

* Jain Dharma is one of the major Indian religions along with Buddhist and Hindu Dharma.

The word "Jain" denotes someone who is a follower of the "Jinas," or conquerors. Despite the potentially violent implications of the word "conqueror," the Jain tradition uses this word to refer to their twenty-four enlightened teachers known as *tīrthaṇkaras* ("bridge-makers") who have, one after the other throughout Jain history, conquered not others, but rather themselves through the perfection of *ahiṃsā*. They have "conquered," or eliminated, all of their passions, desires, egotistical inclinations, and, ultimately, their karma. In doing so, these inspirational spiritual leaders have built a bridge and modeled to others the necessary ethical behavior that is required to cross over from the world of suffering to the world of absolute freedom.

This chapter has two purposes within the broader scope of this volume. First, I will outline three critical aspects of Jain *ahiṃsā* philosophy that speak directly to the humane hoax. These are the three categories of harm known as 1) direct harm *done by someone (kṛta)*; 2) indirect harm *done for someone (kārita)*; and 3) harm *allowed around someone that one permits* by not intervening or trying to prevent it *(anumata)*. All three of these forms of harm—*kṛta, kārita,* and *anumata*—have significant and too-often-overlooked *kārmic* consequences in Jain philosophy. Though not limited to the Jain tradition and found in other dharma traditions, these constitute a central practical imperative for Jains that forms the basis of their intricate and unique karma philosophy that is found in no other tradition.

Next, in light of Jain *kārmic* philosophy, the second purpose of this chapter is to motivate non-vegan Jains to make a transition to veganism. I certainly do not limit this aspiration to the Jain community and do also hope that the chapter will provide some tools from the Jain tradition to encourage anyone inspired to move from a vegetarian or carnivorous lifestyle to a vegan one in light of the manifold animal rights, environmental, human health, and social justice issues involved in the farming of animals.

The Humane Hoax in Contemporary Dharma Traditions

I do not want to romanticize too much here. As an ethnographer by training, I always find it best to start where we are rather than where we ideally want to be. That is to say, by first acknowledging the dietary and cultural realities of contemporary Jains worldwide, we can then decide how to apply the virtue of *ahiṃsā* in an effective and powerful way. Indeed, as of the writing of this chapter, most Jains worldwide today remain lacto-vegetarian, despite the well-documented violence of the dairy industry.[4] Vegans within and outside the Jain community find it shocking that the vast majority of Jains are not vegan, given the Jains' paramount commitment to the virtue of *ahiṃsā*. I have myself been at the center of many debates within the Jain community in which a small minority of vegan Jains from various backgrounds and organizations are continually trying to convince the Jain community at large to transition toward a vegan lifestyle.[5]

The arguments that non-vegan Jains make against veganism vary widely and often overlap with the common justifications that non-vegans make in our global society at large. Indeed, one of the common Jain arguments against veganism that I regularly encounter *is* the humane hoax, which, when considering dairy, amounts to a collective misconception that suggests that milk can somehow still be taken from mother cows for human consumption with little to no violence because it is produced organically or with some other "humane" label. These production methods still cause immense harm because the calves are still taken away from the mother cow at birth, the male calves are sold to be slaughtered for meat, and the mother cow goes to her own brutal death in just a few short months or years.

Within dharma traditions—and often invoked as an example of humane dairy by Jains themselves—there are also non-industrial, caring cow shelters (*gośāla*).[6] The milk produced at these *gośāla*s is often referred to as *ahiṃsā* milk. Despite the good intentions of supposedly humane forms of dairy production within contemporary Hindu organizations that run these *gośāla*s, one will be hard-pressed to actually find one anywhere in the world that is able to completely eliminate the harm that dairy cows and their offspring experience. These organizations, nevertheless, often espouse that they are able to produce dairy harm-free, and use euphemistic theological language based in Vaiṣṇava-cow devotion and protectionism, which suggests that their dairy operations maintain mutually beneficial relations between humans and mother cows. To my knowledge, none of these organizations eliminate all harm to dairy cows, and thus instead perpetuate the humane hoax for the privileged middle- and upper-class patrons who fund their costly operations. Furthermore, even if one were to find a *gośāla* that eliminates all harm, the ability to scale up the operations to a level that would serve all of those who currently consume milk around the world would be made prohibitive by the tremendous costs, land, and other resource usage necessary to keep all cows, male and female, alive for their natural lifespans. It would also certainly exacerbate the climate crisis. To scale up production to feed the world is an impossible endeavor.

The Jain tradition offers some important philosophical principles for holding ourselves and others accountable in light of the hidden violence in dairy. I hope that more Jains who are not yet vegan will take more seriously these principles of their own tradition and liberate themselves from the cognitive dissonance once they have seen through the hoax that asserts milk can be produced humanely. As the epigraph to this chapter insists, if Jains do not proactively define veganism according to their own principles, "Veganism will define Jainism."[7] Instead, I suggest that Jains worldwide now take the opportunity to once again seize their status as the global torchbearers of applied *ahiṃsā* by practicing and promoting a vegan lifestyle of minimal harm for others to emulate.

KṚTA, KĀRITA, AND ANUMATA: THREE DIMENSIONS OF JAIN AHIṂSĀ

Jain karma theory is unique and complex,[8] though there are some core dimensions of this theory that are foundational and powerful for understanding the extent to which one must, for their own spiritual welfare, perfect the virtue of *ahiṃsā* in order to eliminate their karma.

A good starting place for understanding the roots of Jain karma theory is in the ancient Jain text known as the *Ācārāṅga Sūtra* (ca. 300 BCE). Here we find Sudharman, the disciple of Mahāvīra ("Great Hero," ca. 499–427 BCE, the 24th *tīrthaṅkara* who is thought to have been a contemporary of the Buddha), repeating his master's spiritual directives with regards to *ahiṃsā* and the avoidance of injury to all living beings.

This central teaching acknowledges that not only humans, but even the smallest particle of earth, has a soul (*jīva*).[9]

> Now the violent one who employs weapons or instruments that cause harm—even when they are one's own internal conditions[10]—(upon even the tiniest of elemental beings) becomes one who lacks the wisdom of spiritual insight.[11](1.1.1.31) On the other hand, one who desires *not* to use such mechanisms of harm (upon even the tiniest of elemental beings) develops wisdom and spiritual insight.[12](1.1.1.32) Having attained such insight, a wise person should never allow for any instrument of harm, internally or externally, against (even the tiniest) beings in the earth, neither should they cause others to do so, nor should they approve of the engagement of anything, internally or externally, that causes harm.[13](1.1.1.32)

What I would like to focus on at the moment is the fact that *ahiṃsā* involves three indispensable categories. First, "*a wise person should never allow for any instrument of harm, internally or externally, against (even the tiniest) beings in the earth.*" Second, "*neither should they cause others to do so.*" And third, "*nor should they approve of the engagement of anything, internally or externally, that causes harm.*" The meaning of these three categories of *ahiṃsā* are developed and become abundantly clear when we look at later, more systematic Jain karma theories.

For example, in the classical *Tattvārtha Sūtra* (ca. 450 CE), the first systematic rendering of Jain philosophy that is authoritative in all sects of the Jain tradition all the way into the present, author Umāsvāti describes something akin to the *Ācārāṅga Sūtra*'s three categories using the terms *kṛta*, *kārita*, and *anumata*. (Tatia 2004, 6.9)[14] These three categories are intended to help a spiritual aspirant understand what causes the inflow (*āsrava*) of new karma, which in Jainism is an actual material substance to be avoided, from binding to their *jīva* as a result of violence inflicted upon the world.

Kṛta, which literally translates as "done," corresponds to the *Ācārāṅga Sūtra*'s instruction that "a wise person should never allow for any instrument of harm, internally or externally, against (even the tiniest) beings in the earth" towards the environment or animals in a direct way. According to this teaching, one who performs direct acts of violence toward any living being will attract toward their soul a plethora of bad karma that is difficult to eliminate. Forms of violence, such as killing an animal while hunting, fishing, or slaughtering an animal to be butchered, will also result in a future rebirth wherein the perpetrator who has performed such an act of harm will necessarily experience the same pain and violence to their own bodies as a result. These are forms of violence that most modern consumers easily avoid by the ease of obtaining already-slaughtered or extracted animal flesh and secretions such as dairy from grocery stores, farmers markets, butchers, delis, etc. Recognizing this social fact long ago, the Jain tradition necessarily emphasized two further categories of harm that nevertheless retain serious kārmic implications.

Thus Umāsvāti's enumeration of the final two categories of harm in the *Tattvārtha Sūtra*, "*kārita*" and "*anumata*." *Kārita*, a strengthened form of the aforementioned noun "*kṛta*," is intended to convey violence that is "*caused to be* done"[15] rather than done by one's self, and therefore captures the *Ācārāṅga Sūtra*'s aforementioned teaching that a person should not "*approve of the engagement of anything, internally or externally, that causes harm.*" Here we have harm that is, as my colleague Jonathan Dickstein often conveys, "mercenarial."[16] Rather than directly carry out harm against farmed animals, for example, those who participate in *kārita* forms of violence quite literally *cause* the harm to be done *for them* by consuming the animal flesh and secretions from nonhuman animals that someone else killed or violently extracted on their behalf (and thus also increased demand for this harmful process to repeat itself). As Dickstein emphasizes, those who engage these mercenaries of animal husbandry to perform this harm are "equally, or perhaps even more responsible, for the pain and death inflicted."[17]

This brings us, finally, to "*anumata*," which translates literally as "approved" or "allowed." *Anumata* comes from the prefix "*anu*" plus the verbal root "*man*" which together mean "to approve" or "to permit."[18] Within the context of Jain *karma* theory, *anumata* quite literally means that someone "approves" or "permits" violence to happen around them without intervening, calling it out, or trying to stop it. *Anumata* therefore captures the *Ācārāṅga Sūtra*'s aforementioned teaching that a person should not *"approve of the engagement of anything, internally or externally, that causes harm."* In ancient India, this might have referred to someone who saw animals or people being harmed or killed without doing anything about it. From the Jain perspective, even the act of non-intervention has negative *kārmic* consequences for the unwilling passive observer. And indeed, as I will discuss in the next section, dairy farming, whether big or small, constitutes one of the most widely permitted forms of harm on Earth.

CONTEMPLATING DAIRY:
APPLICATIONS OF KṚTA, KĀRITA, AND ANUMATA

The vast majority of dairy that is consumed anywhere by anyone, including Jains, involves not only significant harm to the earth[19] and to human bodies,[20] but also causes substantial harm and the eventual killing of mother dairy cows (and their children) from whom the milk is stolen.[21] Acknowledging this, the U.K.-based organization Jain Vegans hosts an annual campaign that asks members of the Jain community— who habitually avoid other edibles such as root vegetables* for *ahiṃsā* reasons[22]—to consider also giving up dairy. They do this every year during the auspicious festival of Paryūṣaṇ during which, among other things, Jains worldwide ask for forgiveness for all the suffering they may have caused any living being over the course of the prior year and, in repentance, perform various austerities, such as fasting and giving up certain types of food to burn off any karma that may have clung to their soul as a result.

During the campaign, Jain Vegans point out four specific noteworthy benefits of giving up dairy. First, Jains will avoid the well-known harm to farmed dairy cows. As Jain Vegans' website points out, female cows are forcefully impregnated, their newborn calves are routinely stolen (the males are slaughtered or raised for meat and females are raised to produce more milk), the cows suffer from various ailments and infections, and the mother cows are slaughtered at a young age. Second, Jains who give up dairy will avoid harm to the environment. Among other things, "Dairy production," as Jain Vegans' website reminds fellow Jains, "makes a significant contribution to global greenhouse gas emissions."

---

* Some Jains avoid vegetables in which the harvesting causes the death of the plant.

Third, Jains who give up dairy will avoid dairy's contribution to human sickness and disease, including lactose-intolerance, heart disease, and some forms of cancer. And finally, fourth, Jains will also develop "self-control" over their passions and attachments, which is a basic and necessary practice in Jain Dharma that has the benefit of eliminating karma from the spiritual aspirant's soul.[23]

Even though they do not explicitly say so, Jain Vegans are, in other words, effectively pointing toward the *kārita* ("caused to be done") category of harm that fellow lacto-vegetarian community members indirectly and routinely participate in through their consumption of dairy. At the same time, Jain Vegans are also performing something akin to the *kārmic* duty, which requires that harm be prevented through some form of intervention. In disapproving of the harm in dairy and pointing out some of the universal and structural forms of harm involved in all dairy operations, they themselves thus avoid the *kārmic* consequences of *anumata* (harm that is "permitted" due to one's unwillingness to call it out) while also encouraging their fellow community members to practice their ethical obligations in a more effective manner as they take the time during Paryūṣaṇ to reflect on their Jain spiritual path.

CONCLUSION:
EXPANDING OUR USE OF KṚTA, KĀRITA, AND ANUMATA

The intentions behind the *kṛta*, *kārita*, and *anumata* categories of harm are of course not unfamiliar to most vegans, and in fact reflect a vegan's most basic logical decision-making process regarding what is appropriate to routinely buy, eat, and consume. These three ancient concepts can obviously also be extended to understand the humane hoax connected with other non-vegan foods such as eggs and honey (both generally restricted in Jainism).

Even more, as most vegans will acknowledge, certain vegan foods are still connected with unnecessary and unjust forms of violence to animals, humans, and the earth. Whether we are concerned about the inequity of the child and slave labor often involved in producing the supposedly "fair trade" cacao used to make our vegan chocolate,[24] or the (mostly) women's burned and scarred hands that peeled the acidic shell from our cashews for our "sustainable" vegan cheese,[25] or the baby monkey stolen from his mother and enslaved in the coconut trade so we can have dairy-free coconut yogurt,[26] applying the three categories of *kṛta*, *kārita*, and *anumata* can help us discern whether or not engaging in these or any other particular form of vegan consumption—dietary or otherwise—is actually ethical. Thus, Jain dharma offers both Jains and non-Jains, as well as vegans and future vegans alike, an incredibly useful framework for evaluating the extent to which they are inflicting direct harm, enabling indirect harm, or simply not doing their part to call out the manifold, unnecessary harms driven by the supposedly "humane" forms of food consumption that continue to operate all around us. And for Jains in particular, the consideration of *kṛta*, *kārita*, and *anumata* has direct *kārmic* consequences for the liberation of the soul.

Micchāmi dukkadaṁ. I apologize if my words or perspectives shared here have caused any unforeseen harm.

Christopher Jain Miller completed his Ph.D. in the Study of Religion at the University of California, Davis. He is the co-founder and chief academic officer of Arihanta Academy. His current research focuses on applied Jain dharma, as well as the ways in which yoga practices are translated into contemporary transnational yoga communities. He is the author of a number of articles and book chapters concerned with Jain dharma, the history and practice of modern yoga, yoga and politics, and yoga philosophy, and he is a co-editor of the volume *Beacons of Dharma: Spiritual Exemplars for the Modern Age.* Dr. Miller lectures internationally on Jain and Yoga topics, is a certified continuing education provider for Yoga Alliance, and works closely with the global Jain Vegan Initiative to promote a vegan lifestyle in light of the Jain principles of non-violence, compassion, and karma.

CONCLUSION

"My hope is to leave the world a bit better than when I got here."—**Jim Henson**

A s the editor of this volume, I'm compelled to express how compiling this book was not only a labor of love, it was cathartic. The authors have successfully and insightfully explored this issue in such depth that there can be no denying the inescapable conclusion—animal agriculture is inherently cruel—irrespective of the label, the size of the farm, or the procedures and practices.

It's encouraging to see what I started a decade ago with the book *The Ultimate Betrayal: Is There Happy Meat?* expanding into what has now finally gained the attention of so many in the animal activist community. I hope that in this book we have successfully exposed the labels, debunked the lies, dismantled the falsehoods, and unmasked the misrepresentations and fabrications of an industry in its death throes—an industry desperately trying to reassure the cautious consumer that it is possible to slit the throat of animals and call the product humane.

As I mentioned in the introduction, even though I speak out strongly against the humane hoax, I think that it is a hopeful sign; a step in the right direction. Evidenced by the consumer attraction to humane labeling, we are collectively acknowledging that animal suffering is important and demanding that farmed animals be treated humanely. More and more consumers seek out products that are allegedly kinder toward animals and the planet. I think that the industry doesn't see it yet, but they are shooting themselves in the foot by spinning a story of "humane" animal farming—because it can't be done. I'm not saying that it's difficult or expensive, I'm saying *it's impossible.* How can killing a young animal who doesn't want to die ever be done humanely? The truth will come out.

As I elaborate in my book *The Ultimate Betrayal*, killing is the worst transgression one can ever do to another sentient being. It is by far worse than tight confinement, painful body procedures, separating families (all of which are almost always still present in "humane" farming). But to kill—to take someone's life—is the worst thing that one can do to another. Our judicial system and animal welfare laws regarding companion animals reflect this. As the deep emotional lives of farmed animals are revealed, they cannot remain exempt from this inescapable, logical conclusion forever. Compassion toward farmed animals is part of our evolution to a just and civil society. The killing of young animals cannot be avoided to sell profitable animal products, no matter the label. The reality is that meat, dairy, and eggs from animals can never be humane, there can never be "happy meat," and to claim these lies on labels and in marketing is a humane hoax.

I hope that we have shown in this volume that labels can either clarify or obscure, and language can either illuminate reality or rationalize the unjustifiable. While shopping at a natural foods store recently, I saw a chocolate bar proudly announcing on the label that it was made with "grass-fed" milk. I wondered what the manufacturer wanted me to believe about the lives of the cows whose milk contributed to the production of this product. Did they want me to know that these cows were happy? That the product had less environmental impact? That the product was healthier? The answers to these questions are all implied, but ultimately, what does the label really mean? It means that the cows were fed grass for some portion of their lives—nothing more. It reminded me of how deeply manipulative a label can be, how many insinuations and suggestions are assumed from just one or two words, and how easily influenced consumers are by manipulative marketing.

Selling products has always been a game of emotional manipulation, not of presenting facts. As the truth emerges about their common and universally cruel practices, the animal agriculture industry has lately been making course corrections like a ship maneuvering to avoid a storm. It's always astonishing to me when someone points a finger at animal advocates and tells us not to manipulate them or their children. The massive amounts of food and product marketing that surrounds everyone on flashy billboards, in colorful ads, on multimillion-dollar commercials, in popular magazines, on the street, in schools, in our places of work—nearly everywhere we might lazily cast our gaze in our day-to-day lives—is the true manipulation, all competing for our attention and dollars. Every single person in our society is bombarded with these misleading ads for products hundreds of times more frequently than they will ever be exposed to the vegan message. What is the industry's motive for control of your emotions? Their motive is money. Their objective is to generate a profit and make shareholders rich. What is an animal advocate's motive? To create a compassionate, loving world where all can live free of suffering. So I ask you, who is doing the true manipulating?

But I am hopeful. The whole confused cacophony of the humane hoax labeling and hand-wringing over animal welfare standards is because *people care.* People care about animals and they care about a livable planet. A worldwide shift to veganism is a survival imperative. When it comes to climate disruption, the polar ice caps are melting faster than our global governments are moving on the crisis. Greenwashing makes it easy to appease the potential for public opprobrium. We want to feel better about the situation, we want to be soothed into believing that our consumption choices are actually helping the crisis. We want to be able to do the same things, eat the same foods, and trust the industry to make the changes necessary to "do it better."

But we can't trust chicken or dairy producers to reform their own businesses any more then we can trust the fossil fuel industry to do the right thing and stop drilling for oil. Self-regulation never works. Bold changes must be made by consumers, by governmental bodies, to create true change. We have to embrace the urgency and realize that we cannot just "reform" these industries. There are some industries that are so destructive, so cruel and damaging, that they are unreformable and need to be dismantled and replaced. We cannot rely on the farmers, ranchers, suppliers, marketers, and retailers to make these critical changes. It's up to us, on a grassroots level—on a personal level—to make the changes necessary for survival. Going vegan is the least we can do. If the consumers lead, the leaders will follow.

Compiling, writing, editing, and creating this anthology has been an incredible amount of labor for all who have given of themselves to lend their voices to this critical issue. Eighteen authors and numerous editors spent countless hours to publish this book. Make it worth our while. Please use this book. Give copies to friends and colleagues, give it to advocates who educate and present, pull quotes and make memes, suggest it for a book club, utilize it in creative ways and help to expose the humane hoax in all its forms. I have hope that we will see a day when no animal suffers at human hands. Help move us toward that day, and never lose hope that we will get there. Thank you for your compassion.

Hope Bohanec
author, activist, podcaster
Executive Director, Compassionate Living

ACKNOWLEDGEMENTS

I would like to thank Jean Harte for her invaluable assistance with content editing and copyediting of this book, as well as her formatting skills for the preparation of the manuscript.

I would like to thank the following people for their support: Cogen Bohanec, Deborah Blum, Ashley Capps, Ray Cooper, Pat Huey, Wade Spital, Veda Stram, Alastor Van Kleeck, Aja and Sil Vossler, Miriam Wald, and Russ and Melanie Walker. The work that I do for animals is hard. It hurts my heart. Your love, care, and encouragement make it easier to bear and helps me beyond words.

NOTES

Introduction: The Humane Hoax:
Animal Industry's Labels and Lies

1. "Egg Industry Facts and Stats," United Egg Producers, accessed June 8, 2022, https://unitedegg.com/wp-content/uploads/2019/05/Facts-and-Stats-Summary.pdf.
2. Saulius Šimčikas, "Is the Percentage of Vegetarians and Vegans in the U.S. Increasing?," Animal Charity Evaluators, August 16, 2018, https://animalcharityevaluators.org/blog/is-the-percentage-of-vegetarians-and-vegans-in-the-u-s-increasing/.
3. Vasile Stanescu, "Guest Post: Response to the Claim that Only 2% (or Less) of People in the United States Are Vegetarian," Critical Animal, July 1, 2019, http://www.criticalanimal.com/2019/07/guest-post-response-to-claim-that-only.html.
4. Jacy Reese Anthis, "Animals, Food, and Technology (AFT) Survey 2017," Sentience Institute, updated March 17, 2021, https://www.sentienceinstitute.org/animal-farming-attitudes-survey-2017.
5. Ibid.
6. Robert Grillo, *Farm to Fable: The Fictions of Our Animal Consuming Culture* (Boston: Vegan Publishers, 2016), 67.
7. "Butterball to Earn American Humane Certified™ Program Recognition for Third Consecutive Year," Butterball Foodservice, April 20, 2017, https://www.butterballfoodservice.com/press-releases/butterball-to-earn-american-humane-certified-program-recognition-for-third-consecutive-year/.
8. Jacy Reese, *The End of Animal Farming* (Boston: Beacon Press, 2018), 111.
9. Staff Writer, North Denver Star, "Urban Farming Can Turn an Idyllic Pastime into Unwelcome Burden," August 27, 2014, cited in United Poultry Concerns, August 28, 2014, https://northdenvernews.com/keeping-chickens-can-unwanted-surprises/; and MACC Chicken Workgroup, "Standards of Care for Chickens," Chicken Run Rescue Recommendations, May 6, 2009, http://www.brittonclouse.com/chickenrunrescue/STANDARDS%20OF%20CARE%208309.pdf.

10. Nicky Stone, "Common Diseases of Backyard Poultry," Agriculture Victoria, July 2007, https://apo.org.au/sites/default/files/resource-files/2007-07/apo-nid57074_0.htm; and Jacqueline P. Jacob, Henry R. Wilson, Richard D. Miles, et al., "Factors Affecting Egg Production in Backyard Chicken Flocks," University of Florida IFAS Extension, accessed June 8, 2022, https://edis.ifas.ufl.edu/pdf/PS/PS02900.pdf.

11. Ashley Capps, "Grass-Fed Beef Means Much More Methane," A Well-Fed World, accessed June 8, 2022, https://awellfedworld.org/issues/climate-issues/grass-fed-beef/.
See also original full study: Matthew N. Hayek and Rachael D. Garrett, "Nationwide Shift to Grass-Fed Beef Requires Larger Cattle Population," Environmental Research Letters 13, no. 8 (July 2018), https://iopscience.iop.org/article/10.1088/1748-9326/aad401.

12. Charlotte Price Persson, "Fences Are Disrupting African Wildlife on an Unprecedented Scale," Science Nordic, January 26, 2017, https://sciencenordic.com/animals-archaeology-denmark/fences-are-disrupting-african-wildlife-on-an-unprecedented-scale/1441998.

13. John Carter, Allison Jones, Mary O'Brien, et al., "Holistic Management: Misinformation on the Science of Grazed Ecosystems," Hindawi: International Journal of Biodiversity (April 2014), https://doi.org/10.1155/2014/163431; David D. Briske, Andrew J. Ash, Justin D. Derner, et al., "Commentary: A Critical Assessment of the Policy Endorsement for Holistic Management," Agricultural Systems 125 (March 2014): 50–53, https://doi.org/10.1016/j.agsy.2013.12.001.

14. Ibid.

15. Mic the Vegan, "Allan Savory's 5 Big Lies–Debunked," January 20, 2016, video, 08:28, https://www.youtube.com/watch?v=_EDpuQMpyYw.

16. Robert Goodland and Jeff Anhang, "Livestock and Climate Change: What if the Key Actors in Climate Change Are Cows, Pigs, and Chickens?," World Watch (November/December 2009), https://awellfedworld.org/wp-content/uploads/Livestock-Climate-Change-Anhang-Goodland.pdf.

17. Linda Tyler, "Animal Tracker 2019: Methods & Overview," Faunalytics, June 12, 2019, https://faunalytics.org/animal-tracker-2019-methods-overview/; Linda Tyler, "Animal Tracker 2019: Contradictions in Public Opinion," Faunalytics, July 24, 2019, https://faunalytics.org/animal-tracker-2019-contradictions-in-public-opinion/.

Chapter 1: A Pig Called Silver

1. Rodale Institute, "Webinar: Hog Management in a Pastured System," October 16, 2019, video, 1:04:55, https://www.youtube.com/watch?v=h8IMPjIjLr4.

2. "Hogs & Pork," Economic Research Service, U.S. Department of Agriculture, last modified August 20, 2019, https://www.ers.usda.gov/topics/animal-products/hogs-pork/.

3. Ibid.

4. "Sector at a Glance," Economic Research Service, U.S. Department of Agriculture, last modified November 29, 2021, https://www.ers.usda.gov/topics/animal-products/cattle-beef/sector-at-a-glance/.

5. "United States Hog Inventory Down 2%," National Agricultural Statistics Service, U.S. Department of Agriculture, June 24, 2021, https://www.nass.usda.gov/Newsroom/printable/2021/06-24-2021.pdf.

6. Ben Putnam, Jacob Hickman, Prathamesh Bandekar, et al., "A Retrospective Assessment of US Pork Production: 1960 to 2015. Final Report," Pork Checkoff and University of Arkansas, July 7, 2018, https://docplayer.net/213311363-A-retrospective-assessment-of-us-pork-production-1960-to-2015.html.

7. "Food System Primer: Industrialization of Agriculture," Johns Hopkins Center for a Livable Future, accessed September 10, 2021, https://www.foodsystemprimer.org/food-production/industrialization-of-agriculture/.

8. Marta E. Alonso, Jose R. Gonzalez-Montana, and Juan M. Lomillos, "Consumers' Concerns and Perceptions of Farm Animal Welfare," Animals 10, no. 3 (March 2020): 385, https://doi.org/10.3390/ani10030385.

9. "Consumer Perceptions of Farm Animal Welfare," Animal Welfare Institute, accessed June 8, 2022, https://awionline.org/sites/default/files/uploads/documents/fa-consumer_perceptionsoffarmwelfare_-112511.pdf.

10. Ibid.

11. Putnam, Hickman, Bandekar, et al., "A Retrospective Assessment of US Pork Production."

12. Nina G.G. Domingo, Srinidhi Balasubramanian, Sumil K. Thakrar, et al., "Air Quality-Related Health Damages of Food," PNAS 118, no. 20 (May 18, 2021), https://doi.org/10.1073/pnas.2013637118; Carrie E. Givens, Dana W. Kolpin, Mark A. Borchardt, et al., "Detection of Hepatitis E Virus and Other Livestock-Related Pathogens in Iowa Streams," Science of the Total Environment 566-567 (October 1, 2016): 1042–1051, https://doi.org/10.1016/j.scitotenv.2016.05.123.

13. Fengxia Yang, Bingjun Han, Yanru Gu, et al., "Swine Liquid Manure: A Hotspot of Mobile Genetic Elements and Antibiotic Resistance Genes," Scientific Reports 10, no. 1 (September 14, 2020): 1507, https://doi.org/10.1038/s41598-020-72149-6.

14. Domingo, Balasubramanian, Thakrar, et al., "Air Quality-Related Health Damages of Food."

15. Givens, Kolpin, Borchardt, et al., "Detection of Hepatitis E Virus and Other Livestock-Related Pathogens in Iowa Streams"; Qichun Yang, Hanqin

Tian, Xia Li, et al., "Spatiotemporal Patterns of Livestock Manure Nutrient Production in the United States from 1930 to 2012," Science of the Total Environment 541 (January 15, 2016): 1592–1602, https://doi.org/10.1016/j.scitotenv.2015.10.044.

16. Alonso, Gonzalez-Montana, and Lomillos, "Consumers' Concerns and Perceptions of Farm Animal Welfare."

17. "Pig Farming | What is a Pastured Pig?," Pasture Raised on Open Fields (PROOF), accessed June 8, 2022, https://www.proof.net.au/free-range-pork.

18. Margot Hale and Linda Coffey, "Tipsheet: Organic Pig Production," National Center for Appropriate Technology, July 2015, https://www.ams.usda.gov/sites/default/files/media/Organic%20Pig%20Production_FINAL.pdf.

19. Rodale Institute, Shelby Dukes, "Pastured Pork Production," YouTube video, 1:04:55, March 29, 2018, https://www.youtube.com/watch?v=bjr6pEloLQo.

20. Denise Amann, "An Introduction to Mobile Slaughter Units," United States Department of Agriculture, February 21, 2017, https://www.usda.gov/media/blog/2010/08/30/introduction-mobile-slaughter-units.

21. "Our Family Farmers," Niman Ranch, accessed September 7, 2021, https://www.nimanranch.com/raised-with-care/our-family-farmers/.

22. "Pastured Pork," Rodale Institute, accessed September 6, 2021, https://rodaleinstitute.org/why-organic/organic-farming-practices/livestock-management/pastured-pork/.

23. Ibid.

24. Kristina Lindgren, Stefan Gunnarsson, Johan Hoglund, et al., "Nematode Parasite Eggs in Pasture Soils and Pigs on Organic Farms in Sweden," Organic Agriculture 10 (2020): 289–300, https://doi.org/10.1007/s13165-019-00273-3.

25. Rodale Institute, "Pastured Pork."

26. "Pigs: Home on the Range?," Oregon State University, accessed September 12, 2021, https://extension.oregonstate.edu/animals-livestock/swine/pigs-home-range.

27. Bob Comis, "I Raise Pigs on Annual Pasture Crops. Am I Farming Sustainably?," Grist, March 26, 2011, https://grist.org/sustainable-farming/2011-03-25-i-raise-pigs-on-annual-pasture-crops-am-i-farming-sustainably/.

28. Ibid.

29. Alessandra Nardina Trícia Rigo Monteiro, Aurélie Wilfart, Valerio Joe Utzeri, et al., "Environmental Impacts of Pig Production Systems Using European Local Breeds: The Contribution of Carbon Sequestration and Emission from Grazing," Journal of Cleaner Production 237 (November 10, 2019): 117843, https://doi.org/10.1016/j.jclepro.2019.117843.

30. Caixan Tang, Chandrakumara Weligama, and Peter Sale, "Subsurface Soil Acidification in Farming Systems: Its Possible Causes and Management Options," in *Molecular Environmental Soil Science*, eds. Jianming Xu and Donald L. Sparks (Dordrecht: Springer, 2013): 389–412, https://doi.org/10.1007/978-94-007-4177-5_13.

31. Monteiro, Wilfart, Utzeri, et al., "Environmental Impacts of Pig Production Systems Using European Local Breeds."

32. Niels Halberg, John E. Hermansen, Ib Sillebak Kristensen, et al., "Impact of Organic Pig Production Systems on CO_2 Emissions, C Sequestration, and Nitrate Pollution," Agronomy for Sustainable Development 30 (2010): 721–731, https://doi.org/10.1051/agro/2010006.

33. John Arbuckle and Holly Arbuckle, "Fatty Acid Comparisons of Grain and Forage-Fed Pork," Practical Farmers of Iowa, April 25, 2019, https://practicalfarmers.org/research/fatty-acid-comparisons-of-grain-and-forage-fed-pork/.

34. Derris D. Burnett, Jerrad F. Legako, Kelsey J. Phelps, et al., "Biology, Strategies, and Fresh Meat Consequences of Manipulating the Fatty Acid Composition of Meat," Journal of Animal Science 98, no. 2, (February 2020), https://doi.org/10.1093/jas/skaa033; Michel Bonneau and Bénédicte Lebret, "Production Systems and Influence on Eating Quality of Pork," Meat Science 84, no. 2 (February 2010): 293–300, https://doi.org/10.1016/j.meatsci.2009.03.013.

35. Cristina Alfaia, Paula A. Lopes, Marta Madeira, et al., "Current Feeding Strategies to Improve Pork Intramuscular Fat Content and Its Nutritional Quality," Advances in Food and Nutrition Research 89 (2019): 53–94, https://doi.org/10.1016/bs.afnr.2019.03.006; Dolores Ayuso, Ana González, Francisco Peña, et al., "Changes in Adipose Cells of *Longissimus Dorsi* Muscle in Iberian Pigs Raised Under Extensive Conditions," Agrarian Sciences 90, no. 1 (January–March 2018), https://doi.org/10.1590/0001-3765201820150567.

36. Amin A. Nanji and Samuel W. French, "Relationship Between Pork Consumption and Cirrhosis," The Lancet 325, no. 8430 (March 23, 1985): 681–683, https://doi.org/10.1016/S0140-6736(85)91338-8; Kathryn E. Bradbury, Neil Murphy, and Timothy J. Key, "Diet and Colorectal Cancer in UK Biobank: A Prospective Study," International Journal of Epidemiology 49, no. 1 (February 2020): 246–258, https://doi.org/10.1093/ije/dyz064; M.H. Rouhani, A. Salehi-Abargouei, P.J. Surkan, et al., "Is There a Relationship Between Red or Processed Meat Intake and Obesity? A Systematic Review and Meta-Analysis of Observational Studies," Obesity Reviews 15, no. 9 (September 2014): 740–748, https://doi.org/10.1111/obr.12172.

37. Yan Zheng, Yanping Li, Ambika Satija, et al., "Association of Changed in Red Meat Consumption with Total and Cause-Specific Mortality Among US Women and Men: Two Prospective Cohort Studies," BMJ 365 (June 12, 2019), https://doi.org/10.1136/bmj.l2110; Sabine Rohrmann, Kim Overvad, H. Bas Bueno-de-Mesquita, et al., "Meat Consumption and Mortality – Results from the European Prospective Investigation into Cancer and Nutrition," BMC Medicine 11, no. 63 (March 7, 2013), https://doi.org/10.1186/1741-7015-11-63.

38. Doris S.M. Chan, Rosa Lau, Dagfinn Aune, et al., "Red and Processed Meat and Colorectal Cancer Incidence: Meta-Analysis of Prospective Studies," PLoS One 6, no. 6 (June 6, 2011), https://doi.org/10.1371/journal.pone.0020456; Susanna C. Larsson and Alicja Wolk, "Meat Consumption and Risk of Colorectal Cancer: A Meta-Analysis of Prospective Studies," International Journal of Cancer 119, no. 11 (December 1, 2006): 2657–2664, https://doi.org/10.1002/ijc.22170; Xiaodong Xu, Enda Yu, Xianhua Gao, et al., "Red and Processed Meat Intake and Risk of Colorectal Adenomas: A Meta-Analysis of Observational Studies," International Journal of Cancer 132, no. 2 (January 15, 2013): 437–448, https://doi.org/10.1002/ijc.27625; Alicja Wolk. "Potential Health Hazards of Eating Red Meat," Journal of Internal Medicine 281, no. 2 (February 2017): 106–122, https://doi.org/10.1111/joim.12543; Satu Mannisto, Jukka Kontto, Merja Kataja-Tuomola, et al., "High Processed Meat Consumption Is a Risk Factor of Type 2 Diabetes in the Alpha-Tocopherol, Beta-Carotene Cancer Prevention Study," British Journal of Nutrition 103, no. 12 (June 28, 2010): 1817–1822, https://doi.org/10.1017/S0007114510000073.

39. "Organic, Pasture-Raised Meats," Elmwood Stock Farm, accessed June 8, 2022, https://elmwoodstockfarm.com/products/organic-pasture-raised-meats/.

40. "Fresh Pork," Niman Ranch, accessed June 8, 2022, https://www.nimanranch.com/our-meats/fresh-pork/.

41. "Heritage Pork," White Oak Pastures, accessed June 8, 2022, https://whiteoakpastures.com/collections/pastured-pork.

42. "Truly Pastured Pork," Cairncrest Farm, accessed June 8, 2022, https://cairncrestfarm.com/pastured-pork/.

43. Ibid.

44. Déborah Temple, Xavier Manteca, Antonio Velarde, et al., "Assessment of Animal Welfare Through Behavioural Parameters in Iberian Pigs in Intensive and Extensive Conditions," Applied Animal Behaviour Science 131, no. 1–2 (April 2011): 29–39, https://doi.org/10.1016/j.applanim.2011.01.013.

45. Déborah Temple, V. Courboulay, Xavier Manteca, et al., "The Welfare of Growing Pigs in Five Different Production Systems: Assessment of Feeding

and Housing," Animal 6, no. 4 (2012): 656–667, https://doi.org/10.1017/S1751731111001868.

46. Maxime Delsart, Françoise Pol, Barbara Dufour, et al., "Pig Farming in Alternative Systems: Strengths and Challenges in Terms of Animal Welfare, Biosecurity, Animal Health, and Pork Safety," Agriculture 10, no. 7 (July 2, 2020): 261, https://doi.org/10.3390/agriculture10070261.

47. Silvana Pietrosemoli and Clara Tang, "Animal Welfare and Production Challenges Associated with Pasture Pig Systems: A Review," Agriculture 10, no. 6 (June 11, 2020): 223, https://doi.org/10.3390/agriculture10060223.

48. Ibid.

49. Ibid.

50. "Welfare Implications of Swine Castration," American Veterinary Medical Association, May 25, 2013, https://www.avma.org/resources-tools/literature-reviews/welfare-implications-swine-castration.

51. "Welfare Implications of Teeth Clipping, Tail Docking and Permanent Identification of Piglets," American Veterinary Medical Association, July 15, 2014, https://www.avma.org/resources-tools/literature-reviews/welfare-implications-teeth-clipping-tail-docking-and-permanent-identification-piglets.

52. Ibid.

53. Ibid.

54. Pietrosemoli and Tang, "Animal Welfare and Production Challenges Associated with Pasture Pig Systems."

55. Jean-Loup Rault, Donald C. Lay Jr., and Jeremy N. Marchant-Forde, "Castration Induced Pain in Pigs and Other Livestock," Applied Animal Behaviour Science 135, no. 3 (December 15, 2011): 214–225, https://doi.org/10.1016/j.applanim.2011.10.017.

56. Pietrosemoli and Tang, "Animal Welfare and Production Challenges Associated with Pasture Pig Systems."

57. Ibid.

58. M.J. Hötzel, L.C.P. Machado Filho, R. Irgang, et al., "Short-Term Behavioural Effects of Weaning Age in Outdoor-Reared Piglets," Animal 4, no. 1 (2010): 102–107, https://doi.org/10.1017/S1751731109990875.

59. Inonge Reimert, Stephanie Fong, T. Bas Rodenburg, et al., "Emotional States and Emotional Contagion in Pigs After Exposure to a Positive and Negative Treatment," Applied Animal Behavior Science 193 (August 2017): 37–42, https://doi.org/10.1016/j.applanim.2017.03.009.

60. "Twenty-Eight Hour Law," USDA National Agricultural Library, accessed June 8, 2022, https://www.nal.usda.gov/animal-health-and-welfare/twenty-eight-hour-law#:~:text=Twenty%2DEight%20Hour%20Law%20%2D%20Current,the%20law%20by%20issuing%20regulations.

61. Fiona C. Rioja-Lang, Jennifer A. Brown, Egan J. Brockhoff, et al., "A Review of Swine Transportation Research on Priority Welfare Issues: A Canadian Perspective," Frontiers in Veterinary Science 6 (February 22, 2019): 36, https://doi.org/10.3389/fvets.2019.00036.

62. Ibid.

63. EFSA Panel on Animal Health and Welfare (AHAW), Søren Saxmose Nielsen, Julio Alvarez, et al., "Welfare of Pigs at Slaughter," EFSA Journal 18, no. 6 (June 17, 2020), https://doi.org/10.2903/j.efsa.2020.6148.

64. Jeannine Schweihofer, "An Inside Look at Pork Processing," Michigan State University Extension, January 23, 2014, https://www.canr.msu.edu/news/an_inside_look_at_pork_processing.

65. Ibid.

66. AHAW, Nielsen, Alvarez, et al., "Welfare of Pigs at Slaughter."

67. Ibid; People for the Ethical Treatment of Animals (PETA) reported on a USDA inspection violation report that documented an improperly stunned and bled pig being dumped alive into scalding water. Although the report was linked in PETA's news release, it has since been removed from the USDA website.

68. AHAW, Nielsen, Alvarez, et al., "Welfare of Pigs at Slaughter."

69. Silvana and Tang, "Animal Welfare and Production Challenges Associated with Pasture Pig Systems."

70. M.B.M. Bracke, "Review of Wallowing in Pigs: Description of the Behaviour and Its Motivational Basis," Applied Animal Behaviour Science 132, no. 1–2 (June 2011): 1–13, https://doi.org/10.1016/j.applanim.2011.01.002.

71. Pietrosemoli and Tang, "Animal Welfare and Production Challenges Associated with Pasture Pig Systems."

72. Ibid.

73. Dragan R. Milicevic, Milijan Jovanovic, Verica B. Juric, et al., "Toxicological Assessment of Toxic Element Residues in Swine Kidney and Its Role in Public Health Risk Assessment," International Journal of Environmental Research and Public Health 6, no. 12 (December 8, 2009): 3127–3142, https://doi.org/10.3390/ijerph6123127.

74. Pietrosemoli and Tang, "Animal Welfare and Production Challenges Associated with Pasture Pig Systems."

75. Ibid.

76. Ibid.

77. Ibid; I.B. Griffiths and R.G. Douglas, "Photodermatitis in Pigs Exposed to Parsley (Petroselinum Crispum)," Veterinary Record 146, no. 3 (January 15, 2000): 73–74, https://doi.org/10.1136/vr.146.3.73.

78. Pietrosemoli and Tang, "Animal Welfare and Production Challenges Associated with Pasture Pig Systems."

79. Patricia A. Fleming, Shannon J. Dundas, Yvonne Y. W. Lau, et al., "Predation by Red Foxes (*Vulpes Vulpes*) at an Outdoor Piggery," Animals 6, no. 10 (October 8, 2016): 60, https://doi.org/10.3390/ani6100060.

80. Pietrosemoli and Tang, "Animal Welfare and Production Challenges Associated with Pasture Pig Systems."

81. Ibid.

82. Fleming, Dundas, Lau, et al., "Predation by Red Foxes (*Vulpes Vulpes*) at an Outdoor Piggery."

83. Pietrosemoli and Tang, "Animal Welfare and Production Challenges Associated with Pasture Pig Systems."

84. Eric R. Burrough, "Intestinal Salmonellosis in Pigs," Merck Veterinary Manual, last modified September 2021, https://www.merckvetmanual.com/digestive-system/intestinal-diseases-in-pigs/intestinal-salmonellosis-in-pigs.

85. Eric Burrough, Samantha Terhorst, Orhan Sahin, et al., "Prevalence of Campylobacter spp. Relative to Other Enteric Pathogens in Grow–Finish Pigs with Diarrhea," Anaerobe 22 (August 23, 2013): 111–114, https://doi.org/10.1016/j.anaerobe.2013.06.004.

86. Pietrosemoli and Tang, "Animal Welfare and Production Challenges Associated with Pasture Pig Systems."

87. Ibid.

88. Helena Mejer and Allan Roepstorff, "Long-Term Survival of Ascaris Suum and Trichuris Suis Eggs in Relation to Pasture Management," Proceedings of the 23rd International Conference of the World Association for the Advancement of Veterinary Parasitology (2011): 113, http://orgprints.org/20004.

89. Rodale Institute, "Webinar: Hog Management in a Pastured System."

90. Ibid.

91. Ibid.

92. Rodale Institute, "Pastured Pork."

93. Ibid.

94. Rodale Institute, Shelby Dukes. "Pastured Pork Production," video, 1:00:23, March 29, 2018, https://www.youtube.com/watch?v=bjr6pEloLQo.

95. Rodale Institute, "Pastured Pork."

96. Robert Grillo, "Why Rare or Heritage Breed Farming Is not Conservation," Free From Harm, May 9, 2018, https://freefromharm.org/common-justifications-for-eating-animals/rare-heritage-breed/.

97. "Conservation Priority List," The Livestock Conservancy, accessed June 8, 2022, https://livestockconservancy.org/heritage-breeds/conservation-priority-list/.

98. Ibid.

99. "Choctaw," The Livestock Conservancy, accessed September 6, 2021, https://livestockconservancy.org/heritage-breeds/heritage-breeds-list/choctaw-hog/.

100. Ibid.

101. "10 Things that Might Surprise You About the Wild World of Heritage Pork," Food Republic, accessed September 9, 2021, https://www.foodrepublic.com/2014/12/11/10-things-that-might-surprise-you-about-the-wild-world-of-heritage-pork/.

102. Lori Marino and Christina M. Colvin, "Thinking Pigs: A Comparative Review of Cognition, Emotion, and Personality in *Sus domesticus,*" International Journal of Comparative Psychology 28 (2015), https://www.wellbeingintlstudiesrepository.org/cgi/viewcontent.cgi?article=1042&context=acwp_asie.

103. Ibid.

104. Ibid.

105. Reimert, Fong, Rodenburg, et al., "Emotional States and Emotional Contagion in Pigs After Exposure to a Positive and Negative Treatment."

106. James McWilliams, "Loving Animals to Death," The American Scholar, March 11, 2014, https://theamericanscholar.org/loving-animals-to-death/.

Chapter 2: The Terrible Truths of Backyard Chicken Farming

1. "Male–Female Ratio in Day Old Chicks," Poultry Performance Plus, accessed June 8, 2022, https://poultryperformanceplus.com/information-database/incubation/302-male-female-ratio-in-day-old-chicks#:~:text=In%20birds%2C%20the%20gender%20of,or%20female%20is%2050%2F50.

2. See, for example, Tove Danovich, "America Stress-Bought All the Baby Chickens," *New York Times*, March 28, 2020, https://www.nytimes.com/2020/03/28/style/chicken-eggs-coronavirus.html.

3. "Thousands of Chicks Shipped to Farmers Using the U.S. Postal Service Arrive Dead," *CBS News*, August 20, 2020, https://www.cbsnews.com/news/chicks-usps-pingree-dead-maine-farmers/.

4. "Finding a New Home for a Chicken," Chicken Run Rescue, accessed June 8, 2022, http://www.chickenrunrescue.org/Finding-a-New-Home-for-a-Chicken.

5. "About Chickens," Humane Society International, May 2014, https://www.hsi.org/wp-content/uploads/assets/pdfs/about_chickens.pdf.

6. Jerry Adler and Andrew Lawler, "How the Chicken Conquered the World," *Smithsonian Magazine,* June 2012, https://www.smithsonianmag.com/history/how-the-chicken-conquered-the-world-87583657/.

7. Rockwell Schwartz, "Eggs: The Leading Cause of Chicken Cancer that Nobody Talks About," *HuffPost*, last modified September 1, 2017, https://www.huffpost.com/entry/eggs-the-leading-cause-of-cancer-nobody-talks-about_b_59a0b5c5e4b0d0ef9f1c13df.

8. Patricia A. Johnson and James R. Giles, "The Hen as a Model of Ovarian Cancer," Nature Reviews Cancer 13, no. 6 (May 16, 2013): 432–436, http://dx.doi.org/10.1038/nrc3535.

Chapter 3: Murder, She Wrote

1. My use of the term "legitimation crisis" here is adapted broadly from Jürgen Habermas in *Legitimation Crisis* (Boston: Beacon Press, 1975).
2. Whole Foods developed its first "Animal Compassionate Standards" in 2005. The company later partnered with the Humane Society of the United States to create the Global Animal Partnership (GAP), a certification process based on "acceptable" levels of violence and cruelty against farmed animals. The GAP and the HSUS partnered with animal farmers and ranchers, promoting "humane" exploitation and killing of animals as the supposed "alternative" to the factory farming system. "Humane Myth in the Media: Advocacy-Industry Collaboration: Deconstructing the Myth," https://www.humanemyth.org/mediabase/1009.htm. Accessed Aug. 29, 2022.
3. Carol Adams, *The Sexual Politics of Meat* (Boston: Beacon Press, 1990).
4. Lily McCaulou, *The Call of the Mild: Learning to Hunt My Own Dinner* (New York: Grand Central Publishing, 2012), 238.
5. Virginia Woolf, *Three Guineas* (London: The Hogarth Press, 1938, 1968), 13-14. Quoted in Carol Adams, *The Sexual Politics of Meat* (Boston: Beacon Press, 1990), 123.
6. Betty Friedan, *The Feminine Mystique* (New York: W.W. Norton & Company, 1963), 15–21.
7. Camas Davis, *Killing It: An Education* (New York: Penguin, 2019).
8. Jenna Woginrich, *Barnheart: The Incurable Longing for a Farm of One's Own* (North Adams, MA: Storey Publishing, 2011).
9. Jenna Woginrich, *One Woman Farm: My Life Shared with Pigs, Chickens, Goats, and a Fine Fiddle* (North Adams, MA: Storey Publishing, 2013), 45.
10. Ibid.
11. Jessie Knadler, *Rurally Screwed: A Memoir of Losing Myself for Love* (New York: Berkley/Penguin, 2013).
12. Suzanne McMinn, *Chickens in the Road: An Adventure in Ordinary Splendor* (Harper & Row, 2013), 127, 165.
13. Kristin Kimball, *The Dirty Life: A Memoir of Farming, Food, and Love* (New York: Scribner, 2010), 4.
14. Woginrich, *One Woman Farm*, 80.
15. Kimball, *The Dirty Life*, 92.
16. McMinn, *Chickens in the Road*.
17. Woginrich, *One Woman Farm*, 119.

18. Josh Kilmer-Purcell, *The Bucolic Plague: How Two Manhattanites Became Gentlemen Farmers* (New York: Harper, 2011).

19. Barbara Kingsolver, *Animal, Vegetable, Miracle: A Year of Food Life* (New York: Harper 2017), 223.

20. Ibid.

21. Kingsolver, *Animal, Vegetable, Miracle*, 93.

22. Catherine Friend, *Hit by a Farm: How I Learned to Stop Worrying and Love the Barn* (New York: Marlowe & Co, 2006), 27.

23. Woginrich, *One Woman Farm*, 111.

24. Ellen Stimson, *Mud Season: How One Woman's Dream of Moving to Vermont, Raising Children, Chickens and Sheep, and Running the Old Country Store Pretty Much Led to One Calamity After Another* (Woodstock, VT: Countryman Press, 2013), 163, 165.

25. Friend, *Hit by a Farm*, 113.

26. McMinn, *Chickens in the Road*, 116.

27. Friend, *Hit by a Farm*, 217.

28. Friend, *Sheepish: Two Women, Fifty Sheep, and Enough Wool to Save the Planet,* (Boston: Da Capo Press, 2011), 72.

29. Woginrich, *Barnheart*, 102.

30. Friend, *Sheepish*, 76.

31. Woginrich, *One Woman Farm*, 109.

32. McMinn, *Chickens in the Road*, 156.

33. Jenna Woginrich, *Made from Scratch: Discovering the Pleasures of a Handmade Life* (North Adams, MA: Storey Publishing, 2008), 119.

34. Susan McCorkindale, *500 Acres and No Place to Hide: More Confessions of a Counterfeit Farm Girl* (New York: Berkely/Penguin, 2011), 300.

35. Friend, *Sheepish*, 90.

36. McMinn, *Chickens in the Road*, 156.

37. Kingsolver, *Animal, Vegetable, Miracle*, 89.

38. Novella Carpenter, *Farm City: The Education of an Urban Farmer* (New York: Penguin Books, 2010), 92.

39. Friend, *Hit by a Farm*, 153.

40. Carpenter, *Farm City*, 194.

41. Ibid, 224.

42. James Baldwin, *Notes from a Native Son* (Boston: Beacon Press, 1951), 14.

43. Gabrielle Hamilton, *Blood, Bones and Butter: The Inadvertent Education of a Reluctant Chef* (New York: Random House, 2012), 19.

44. Kimball, *The Dirty Life*, 128.

45. McMinn, *Chickens in the Road*, 223.

46. Friend, *Sheepish*, 8.

47. McMinn, *Chickens in the Road*, 87.

48. McCaulou, *The Call of the Mild*, 112, 114, 185.

49. Lierre Keith, *The Vegetarian Myth* (Crescent City, CA: Flashpoint, 2009), 5, 79.

50. Carpenter, *Farm City*, 94.

51. Ibid, 245–246.

52. Ibid, 76.

53. Ibid, 158.

54. Friend, *Sheepish*, 4.

55. Ibid, 68.

56. Woginrich, *One Woman Farm*, 93.

57. Alex D. Ketchum, "Feminist Restaurant Management," in *The SAGE Encyclopedia of Food Issues*, ed. Ken Albala (New York: SAGE, 2015), 1205-1206.

58. Christine Lennon, "Why Vegetarians Are Eating Meat," *Food & Wine*, last modified June 26, 2017, https://www.foodandwine.com/special-diets/vegetarian/why-vegetarians-are-eating-meat.

59. Adrienne Rich, "Toward a Woman-Centered University," in *On Lies, Secrets, and Silence* (New York: W.W. Norton & Company, 1979), 133, 130.

60. In her 2018 bestseller, *Killing It*, Camas Davis singles out Adams' *Sexual Politics of Meat* for ridicule, as an example of her supposed earlier "naivete" as a young vegetarian when she was in college and was supposedly enamored with Adams' book.

61. Susan Faludi, *Backlash: The Undeclared War Against American Women* (New York: Crown, 1991), 1.

62. Kimball, *The Dirty Life*, 22.

63. Kim Severson, "Young Idols with Cleavers Rule the Stage," *New York Times*, July 7, 2009, https://www.nytimes.com/2009/07/08/dining/08butch.html.

64. Friend, *Hit by a Farm*, 13, 171–172.

65. Susan McCorkindale, *500 Acres and No Place to Hide* (New York: Penguin, 2011), 308.

66. "Animal Welfare," Tyson Foods, accessed June 9, 2022, https://www.tysonfoods.com/animal-welfare-viewpoint#:~:text=For%20us%2C%20proper%20animal%20handling,animals%20at%20our%20processing%20plants.

67. Judith Capper, "Do Moms Have Instant Beef Credibility?," Bovidiva, November 14, 2013, https://bovidiva.com/2013/11/14/do-moms-have-instant-beef-credibility/.

68. Alex Lockwood, "Why Aren't More Men Vegan?," Plant Based News, February 21, 2018, https://plantbasednews.org/opinion/why-arent-more-men-vegan/; Melanie Radzicki McManus, "Why 79 Percent of American Vegans are Women," HowStuffWorks, accessed June 9, 2022, https://recipes.howstuffworks.com/why-79-percent-u-s-vegans-are-women.htm.

Chapter 5: Reinforcing Rationalizations and a Rooster

1. Kurt Snibbe, "California Farms Produce a Lot of Food—but What and How Much Might Surprise You," The Orange County Register, last modified August 20, 2019, https://www.ocregister.com/2017/07/27/california-farms-produce-a-lot-of-food-but-what-and-how-much-might-surprise-you/.
2. M. Shahbandeh, "Top dairy producing states in the U.S. based on number of milkcowsfrom2014to2018(in1,000s)*," Statista,August9,2019,https://www.statista.com/statistics/194962/top-10-us-states-by-number-of-milk-cows/.
3. "Animal Welfare: Issues and Opportunities in the Meat, Poultry, and Egg Markets in the U.S.," Packaged Facts, April 10, 2017, https://www.packagedfacts.com/Animal-Welfare-Meat-10771767/.
4. Ibid.
5. Karen Davis, "Interspecies Sexual Assault: A Moral Perspective," United Poultry Concerns, June 13, 2017, https://upc-online.org/turkeys/170613_interspecies_sexual_assault-a_moral_perspective.html.
6. Josh Gabbatiss, "Meat and Dairy Companies to Surpass Oil Industry as World's Biggest Polluters, Report Finds," Independent, July 18, 2018, https://www.independent.co.uk/climate-change/news/meat-dairy-industry-greenhouse-gas-emissions-fossil-fuels-oil-pollution-iatp-grain-a8451871.html.
7. Melanie Joy, Why We Love Dogs, Eat Pigs, and Wear Cows, (Newburyport, MA: Red Wheel/Weiser, 2009).
8. Robert Grillo, Farm to Fable: The Fictions of Our Animal Consuming Culture, (Boston: Vegan Publishers, 2016), 66.
9. Barnes V. Tillamook, "Challenging Tillamook's Deceptive Advertising," Animal Legal Defense Fund, last modified June 16, 2021, https://aldf.org/case/challenging-tillamooks-deceptive-advertising/.

Chapter 7: Greenwashing a Bloody Business:
The Planet Can't Survive "Sustainable" Animal Farming

1. J. Poore and T. Nemecek, "Reducing Food's Environmental Impacts Through Producers and Consumers," Science 360, no. 6392 (June 1, 2018): 987–992, https://doi.org/10.1126/science.aaq0216.
2. Philip K. Thornton, Mario T. Herrero, and Polly J. Ericksen, "Livestock and Climate Change," International Livestock Research Institute, November 2011, https://cgspace.cgiar.org/handle/10568/10601.
3. "Livestock and Landscapes," Food and Agriculture Organization of the United Nations, 2013, https://www.fao.org/publications/card/en/c/18055fac-a807-528e-8be2-d3146a095f7d/.

4. Kelly Anthis and Jacy Reese Anthis, "Global Farmed & Factory Farmed Animals Estimates," Sentience Institute, last modified February 21, 2019, https://www.sentienceinstitute.org/global-animal-farming-estimates.

5. Kenneth J. Thomson, "World Agriculture: Towards 2015/2030: An FAO Perspective," Land Use Policy 20, no. 4 (October 2003): 375, https://doi.org/10.1016/S0264-8377(03)00047-4.

6. Nicholas Bowles, Samuel Alexander, and Michalis Hadjikakou, "The Livestock Sector and Planetary Boundaries: A 'Limits to Growth' Perspective with Dietary Implications," Ecological Economics 160 (June 2019): 128–136, https://doi.org/10.1016/j.ecolecon.2019.01.033.

7. Jacy Reese, "There's No Such Thing as Humane Meat or Eggs. Stop Kidding Yourself," *The Guardian*, November 16, 2018, https://www.theguardian.com/food/2018/nov/16/theres-no-such-thing-as-humane-meat-or-eggs-stop-kidding-yourself.

8. Jan Dutkiewicz, "The Climate Activists Who Dismiss Meat Consumption Are Wrong," *The New Republic*, August 31, 2020, https://newrepublic.com/article/159153/climate-change-dismiss-meat-emissions-wrong.

9. Josh Gabbatiss, "In-Depth Q&A: What Does the Global Shift in Diets Mean for Climate Change?" CarbonBrief, September 15, 2020, https://www.carbonbrief.org/in-depth-qa-what-does-the-global-shift-in-diets-mean-for-climate-change/.

10. Lorraine Boissoneault, "What Really Turned the Sahara Desert from a Green Oasis into a Wasteland?" *Smithsonian Magazine*, March 24, 2017, https://www.smithsonianmag.com/science-nature/what-really-turned-sahara-desert-green-oasis-wasteland-180962668/; David K. Wright, "Humans as Agents in the Termination of the African Humid Period," Frontiers in Earth Science (January 26, 2017), https://doi.org/10.3389/feart.2017.00004.

11. Karl-Heinz Erb, Thomas Kastner, Christoph Plutzar, et al., "Unexpectedly Large Impact of Forest Management and Grazing on Global Vegetation Biomass," Nature 553 (January 4, 2018): 73–76, https://doi.org/10.1038/nature25138.

12. Eric Guiry, Fiona Beglane, Paul Szpak, et al., "Anthropogenic Changes to the Holocene Nitrogen Cycle in Ireland," Science Advances 4, no. 6 (June 13, 2018), https://doi.org/10.1126/sciadv.aas9383.

13. Alfred W. Crosby Jr., *The Columbian Exchange: Biological and Cultural Consequences of 1492* (Westport, CT: Greenwood Publishing Group, 1972).

14. Jim Mason, *An Unnatural Order: Roots of Our Destruction of Nature* (New York: Simon & Schuster, 1993).

15. Benjamin S. Arbuckle, "The Rise of Cattle Cultures in Bronze Age Anatolia," Journal of Eastern Mediterranean Archaeology & Heritage Studies 2, no. 4 (2014): 277–297, https://doi.org/10.5325/jeasmedarcherstu.2.4.0277.

16. Hayley G. Brazier, "*Cattle Colonialism: An Environmental History of the Conquest of California and Hawai'i*, by John Ryan Fischer," review of *Cattle Colonialism: An Environmental History of the Conquest of California and Hawai'i*, by John Ryan Fischer, Native American and Indigenous Studies 3, no. 2 (2016): 138–139, https://muse.jhu.edu/article/641387.

17. Virginia DeJohn Anderson, *Creatures of Empire: How Domestic Animals Transformed Early America* (Oxford, U.K.: Oxford University Press, 2004).

18. Percy Bysshe Shelley, *A Vindication of Natural Diet* (London: Smith & Davy, 1813).

19. Dave Merrill and Lauren Leatherby, "Here's How America Uses Its Land," *Bloomberg*, July 31, 2018, https://www.bloomberg.com/graphics/2018-us-land-use/.

20. "Land Use in Australia—At a Glance," Australian Collaborative Land Use and Management Program (ACLUMP), accessed June 13, 2022, https://www.awe.gov.au/sites/default/files/abares/aclump/documents/Land_use_in_Australia_at_a_glance_2006.pdf.

21. Mathilde Cohen, "Animal Colonialism: The Case of Milk," American Journal of International Law Unbound 111 (September 18, 2017): 267–271, https://doi.org/10.1017/aju.2017.66.

22. Vasile Stanescu, "Selling Eden: Environmentalism, Local Meat, and the Postcommodity Fetish," American Behavioral Scientist 63, no. 8 (February 28, 2019): 1120–1136, https://doi.org/10.1177/0002764219830462.

23. Carol J. Adams, *The Sexual Politics of Meat: A Feminist-Vegetarian Critical Theory* (New York: Continuum International Publishing Group, 1990).

24. Aph Ko and Syl Ko, *Aphro-ism: Essays on Pop Culture, Feminism, and Black Veganism from Two Sisters* (New York: Lantern Publishing & Media, 2017).

25. Christopher Sebastian, "They Want to Take Away Your Hamburgers: Animal Exploitation and White Nationalism," Christopher Sebastian, last modified March 27, 2020, https://www.christophersebastian.info/post/they-want-to-take-away-your-hamburgers-animal-exploitation-and-white-nationalism.

26. Margaret Robinson, "Veganism and Mi'kmaq Legends," The Canadian Journal of Native Studies, https://www.academia.edu/47222545/Veganism_and_Mikmaq_legends.

27. Sarah DeWeerdt, "Is Local Food Better?," World Watch Magazine 22, no. 3 (May/June 2009), https://impactbioenergy.com/wp-content/uploads/2017/01/local-food-article.pdf.

28. Hannah Ritchie, "You Want to Reduce the Carbon Footprint of Your Food? Focus on What You Eat, not Whether Your Food Is Local," Our World in Data, January 24, 2020, https://ourworldindata.org/food-choice-vs-eating-local.

29. Vilma Sandström, Hugo Valin, Tamás Krisztin, et al., "The Role of Trade in the Greenhouse Gas Footprints of EU Diets," Global Food Security 19 (December 2018): 48–55, https://doi.org/10.1016/j.gfs.2018.08.007.

30. Ian Johnston, "What McDonald's Doesn't Want You to Know About Its 'British' Beef," *Independent*, May 18, 2017, https://www.independent.co.uk/climate-change/news/mcdonald-s-beef-burgers-amazon-rainforest-deforestation-cargill-bunge-a7741541.html.

31. Baylen J. Linnekin, *Biting the Hands that Feed Us: How Fewer, Smarter Laws Would Make Our Food System More Sustainable* (Washington, D.C.: Island Press, 2016).

32. Michael Corkery and David Yaffe-Bellany, "The Food Chain's Weakest Link: Slaughterhouses," *The New York Times*, April 18, 2020, https://www.nytimes.com/2020/04/18/business/coronavirus-meat-slaughterhouses.html.

33. James McWilliams, "Support Industrial Slaughterhouses," Pacific Standard, last modified June 14, 2017, https://psmag.com/social-justice/support-industrial-slaughterhouses-local-meat-76120.

34. Deena Shanker, "Most Grass-Fed Beef Labeled 'Product of U.S.A.' Is Imported," *Bloomberg*, May 23, 2019, https://www.bloomberg.com/news/articles/2019-05-23/most-grass-fed-beef-labeled-product-of-u-s-a-is-imported#xj4y7vzkg.

35. Jason Beaubien, "Why There's So Much Beef Being Sent Between the U.S. And Mexico," *NPR*, November 28, 2018, https://www.npr.org/2018/11/28/671675948/why-theres-so-much-beef-being-sent-between-the-u-s-and-mexico.

36. Julie E. Kurtz, Peter B. Woodbury, Zia U. Ahmed, et al., "Mapping U.S. Food System Localization Potential: The Impact of Diet on Foodsheds," Environmental Science and Technology 54, no. 19 (September 14, 2020): 12434–12446, https://doi.org/10.1021/acs.est.9b07582.

37. Miles McEvoy, "Organic 101: What the USDA Organic Label Means," U.S. Department of Agriculture, March 13, 2019, https://www.usda.gov/media/blog/2012/03/22/organic-101-what-usda-organic-label-means.

38. Verena Seufert, Navin Ramankutty and Jonathan Foley, "Comparing the Yields of Organic and Conventional Agriculture," Nature 485 (May 10, 2012), https://doi.org/10.1038/nature11069.

39. Karl-Ludwig Schweisfurth, "Organic: A Climate Saviour?" FoodWatch, accessed June 13, 2022, https://www.foodwatch.org/fileadmin/foodwatch_international/campaigns/climate/foodwatch_report_on_the_greenhouse_effect_of_farming_05_2009.pdf.

40. Maximilian Pieper, Amelie Michalke, and Tobias Gaugler, "Calculation of External Climate Costs for Food Highlights Inadequate Pricing of Animal Products," Nature Communications 11, no. 6117 (December 15, 2020), https://doi.org/10.1038/s41467-020-19474-6.

41. George Monbiot, "I've Converted to Veganism to Reduce My Impact on the Living World," *The Guardian*, August 9, 2016, https://www.theguardian.com/commentisfree/2016/aug/09/vegan-corrupt-food-system-meat-dairy.

42. John Carter, Allison Jones, Mary O'Brien, et al., "Holistic Management: Misinformation on the Science of Grazed Ecosystems," International Journal of Biodiversity (April 23, 2014), https://doi.org/10.1155/2014/163431.

43. Matthew N. Hayek and Rachael Garrett, "Nationwide Shift to Grass-Fed Beef Requires Larger Cattle Population," Environmental Research Letters 13, no. 8 (July 25, 2018), https://doi.org/10.1088/1748-9326/aad401.

44. Maria Chiorando, "Study Branding Cow's Milk Better than Soy 'Makes No Sense,' Says Scientist," Plant Based News, August 18, 2020, https://plantbasednews.org/news/study-cows-milk-better-than-soy-no-sense/.

45. Sarah Flack, "Dairy Farming Without Grain," On Pasture, November 17, 2014, https://onpasture.com/2014/11/17/dairy-farming-without-grain/.

46. Susan Kerr, "Pigs: Home on the Range?," Oregon State University, 2015, https://smallfarms.oregonstate.edu/pigs-home-range.

47. James Hermes, "Feeding Pastured Poultry," Oregon State University, 2008, https://smallfarms.oregonstate.edu/feeding-pastured-poultry.

48. Mike Badger, "Latest Greenwashing Craze: Pasturewashing Poultry," Pastured Poultry Talk, April 4, 2019, https://pasturedpoultrytalk.com/2019/04/04/latest-greenwashing-craze-pasturewashing-poultry-ppt083/.

49. Laurie Neverman, "Why We Won't Be Raising Heritage Meat Chickens Next Year," Common Sense Home, accessed June 13, 2022, https://commonsensehome.com/heritage-meat-chickens/.

50. Robert Grillo, *Farm to Fable: The Fictions of Our Animal-Consuming Culture* (Boston: Vegan Publishers, 2016).

51. Thornton, Herrero, and Ericksen, "Livestock and Climate Change."

52. Oliver Lazarus, Sonali McDermid, and Jennifer Jacquet, "The Climate Responsibilities of Industrial Meat and Dairy Producers," Climatic Change 165, no. 30 (March 25, 2021), https://doi.org/10.1007/s10584-021-03047-7.

53. Tim Searchinger, Craig Hanson, Janet Ranganathan, et al., "Creating a Sustainable Food Future: A Menu of Solutions to Sustainably Feed More than 9 Billion People by 2050," World Resources Institute, July 19, 2019, https://www.wri.org/research/creating-sustainable-food-future.

54. Penn State, "Seaweed Feed Additive Cuts Livestock Methane but Poses Questions," ScienceDaily, June 17, 2019, https://www.sciencedaily.com/releases/2019/06/190617164642.htm#:~:text=Seaweed%20feed%20additive%20cuts%20livestock%20methane%20but%20poses%20questions,-Date%3A%20June%2017&text=Summary%3A,strategy%20to%20battle%20climate%20change.

55. Fred Pearce, "Grass-Fed Beef Is Bad for the Planet and Causes Climate Change," New Scientist, October 3, 2017, https://www.newscientist.com/article/2149220-grass-fed-beef-is-bad-for-the-planet-and-causes-climate-change.

56. Carrie Hribar, "Understanding Concentrated Animal Feeding Operations and Their Impact on Communities," National Association of Local Boards of Health, 2010, https://www.cdc.gov/nceh/ehs/docs/understanding_cafos_nalboh.pdf.

57. "False Promises and Hidden Impacts of Dairy Digesters," Center for Food Safety, April 24, 2019, https://www.centerforfoodsafety.org/fact-sheets/5576/false-promises-and-hidden-impacts-of-dairy-digesters.

58. Carter, Jones, O'Brien, et al., "Holistic Management."

59. Tara Garnett, Cécile Godde, Adrian Muller, et al., "Grazed and Confused? Ruminating on Cattle, Grazing Systems, Methane, Nitrous Oxide, the Soil Carbon Sequestration Question—and What It All Means for Greenhouse Gas Emissions," Food Climate Research Network, October 3, 2017, https://www.oxfordmartin.ox.ac.uk/downloads/reports/fcrn_gnc_report.pdf.

60. Jonathan Foley, "The Other Inconvenient Truth: The Crisis in Global Land Use," Yale Environment 360, October 5, 2009, https://e360.yale.edu/features/the_other_inconvenient_truth_the_crisis_in_global_land_use.

61. Poore and Nemecek, "Reducing Food's Environmental Impacts Through Producers and Consumers."

62. Andrew Wasley and Alexandra Heal, "Walmart Selling Beef from Firm Linked to Amazon Deforestation," *The Guardian*, February 13, 2021, https://www.theguardian.com/environment/2021/feb/13/walmart-selling-beef-from-firm-linked-to-amazon-deforestation.

63. Dom Phillips, "Meat Company Faces Heat over 'Cattle Laundering' in Amazon Supply Chain," *The Guardian*, February 20, 2020, https://www.theguardian.com/environment/2020/feb/20/meat-company-faces-heat-over-cattle-laundering-in-amazon-supply-chain.

64. "U.S. Forest Facts and Historical Trends," U.S. Department of Agriculture Forest Service, September 2001, https://www.fia.fs.fed.us/library/brochures/docs/2000/ForestFactsMetric.pdf.

65. B. H. Green, "Agricultural Intensification and the Loss of Habitat, Species and Amenity in British Grasslands: A Review of Historical Change and Assessment of Future Prospects," Grass and Forage Science 45, no. 4 (December 1990): 365–372, https://doi.org/10.1111/j.1365-2494.1990.tb01961.x.

66. "Grade A Choice? Solutions for Deforestation-Free Meat," Union of Concerned Scientists, June 10, 2012, https://www.ucsusa.org/resources/grade-choice#:~:text=of%20meat%20production.-,Grade%20A%20Choice%3F,impacts%20of%20the%20meat%20industry.

67. Robin Wall Kimmerer and Frank Kanawha Lake, "The Role of Indigenous Burning in Land Management," Journal of Forestry, November 2001, https://static1.squarespace.com/static/57b62cb1ebbd1a48387a40ef/t/6142 7901fab4f40448e1f71c/1631746306507/LANDMGMT.pdf.

68. Rattan Lal, "Managing Soils and Ecosystems for Mitigating Anthropogenic Carbon Emissions and Advancing Global Food Security," BioScience 60, no. 9 (October 1, 2010): 708–721, https://doi.org/10.1525/bio.2010.60.9.8.

69. Helen Harwatt, Joan Sabaté, Gidon Eshel, et al., "Substituting Beans for Beef as a Contribution Toward US Climate Change Targets," Climatic Change 143 (May 11, 2017): 261–270, https://doi.org/10.1007/s10584-017-1969-1.

70. Garnett, Godde, Muller, et al., "Grazed and Confused?"

71. EstherShantil, "But Veganism Isn't that Sustainable," Vegan Rebuttals, August 13, 2016, https://veganrebuttals.wordpress.com/2016/08/13/but-veganism-isnt-that-sustainable/.

72. L. H. MacDaniels and Arthur S. Lieberman, "Tree Crops: A Neglected Source of Food and Forage from Marginal Lands," BioScience 29, no. 3 (March 1, 1979): 173–175, https://doi.org/10.2307/1307798.

73. Christian J. Peters, Jamie Picardy, Amelia F. Darrouzet-Nardi, et al., "Carrying Capacity of U.S. Agricultural Land: Ten Diet Scenarios," Elementa: Science of the Anthropocene 4 (July 22, 2016), https://doi.org/10.12952/journal.elementa.000116.

74. Mesfin M. Mekonnen and Arjen Y. Hoekstra, "National Water Footprint Accounts: The Green, Blue and Grey Water Footprint of Production and Consumption," Daugherty Water for Food Global Institute, May 2011, https://digitalcommons.unl.edu/cgi/viewcontent.cgi?article=1077&context=wffdocs.

75. Mesfin M. Mekonnen and Arjen Y. Hoekstra, "A Global Assessment of the Water Footprint of Farm Animal Products," Ecosystems 15 (January 24, 2012): 401–415, https://doi.org/10.1007/s10021-011-9517-8.

76. Michael F. Jacobson and Center for Science in the Public Interest, Six Arguments for a Greener Diet: How a Plant-based Diet Could Save Your Health and the Environment (Washington DC: Center for Science in the Public Interest, 2006).

77. "More meat threatens the planet," Greenpeace, accessed, June 14, 2022, https://www.greenpeace.org/usa/sustainable-agriculture/issues/meat/#:~:text=Industrial%20livestock%20agriculture%E2%80%94raising%20cows,in%20Figueir%C3%B3polis%20d%C2%B4Oeste.

78. "Clean Water Crisis Facts and Information," National Geographic, accessed June 14, 2022, https://www.nationalgeographic.com/environment/article/freshwater-crisis#:~:text=By%202025%2C%20an%20estimated%201.8,%2C%20growth%2C%20and%20climate%20change.

79. Rabobank, "Rabobank Beef Quarterly Q2 2018: Production Continuing to Grow, but Supply Pressure Starting to Mount," PerishableNews.com, May 24, 2018, https://www.perishablenews.com/meatpoultry/rabobank-beef-quarterly-q2-2018-production-continuing-to-grow-but-supply-pressure-starting-to-mount/.

80. Food & Water Watch, "Ocean Desalination No Solution to Water Shortages," Common Dreams, February 4, 2009, https://www.commondreams.org/newswire/2009/02/04/ocean-desalination-no-solution-water-shortages.

81. Janet Ranganathan and Richard Waite, "Sustainable Diets: What You Need to Know in 12 Charts," World Resources Institute, April 20, 2016, https://www.wri.org/insights/sustainable-diets-what-you-need-know-12-charts.

82. M. Berners-Lee, C. Kennelly, R. Watson, et al., "Current Global Food Production Is Sufficient to Meet Human Nutritional Needs in 2050 Provided There Is Radical Societal Adaptation," Elementa: Science of the Anthropocene 6 (July 18, 2018), https://doi.org/10.1525/elementa.310.

83. Sarah Rizvi, Chris Pagnutti, Evan Fraser, et al., "Global Land Use Implications of Dietary Trends," PLOS One 13, no. 10 (October 3, 2018), https://doi.org/10.1371/journal.pone.0205312.

84. Alon Shepon, Gidon Eshel, Elad Noor, et al., "The Opportunity Cost of Animal-Based Diets Exceeds All Food Losses," Proceedings of the National Academy of Sciences 115, no. 15 (March 26, 2018): 3804–3809, https://doi.org/10.1073/pnas.1713820115.

85. Peter Alexander, Calum Brown, Almut Arneth, et al., "Losses, Inefficiencies and Waste in the Global Food System," Agricultural Systems 153 (May 2017): 190–200, https://doi.org/10.1016/j.agsy.2017.01.014.

86. Christine Costello, Esma Birisci, and Ronald G. McGarvey, "Food Waste in Campus Dining Operations: Inventory of Pre- and Post-Consumer Mass by Food Category, and Estimation of Embodied Greenhouse Gas Emissions," Renewable Agriculture and Food Systems 31, no. 3 (June 1, 2016): 191–201, https://doi.org/10.1017/S1742170515000071.

87. Food and Agriculture Organization, *Dimensions of Need: An Atlas of Food and Agriculture* (Rome, Italy: Food and Agriculture Organization of the United Nations, 1995).

88. Anne Mottet, Cees de Haan, Alessandra Falcucci, et al., "Livestock: On Our Plates or Eating at our Table? A New Analysis of the Feed/Food Debate," Global Food Security 14 (September 2017): 1–8, https://doi.org/10.1016/j.gfs.2017.01.001.

89. Poore and Nemecek, "Reducing Food's Environmental Impacts Through Producers and Consumers."

90. Lauren Manning, "Only a Small % of What Cattle Eat is Grain. 86% Comes from Materials Humans Don't Eat," Sacred Cow, September 10, 2019, https://www.sacredcow.info/blog/qz6pi6cvjowjhxsh4dqgldogiznou6#:~:text=eat%20is%20grain.-,86%25%20comes%20from%20materials%20humans%20don't%20eat.,13%25%20of%20global%20livestock%20feed.

91. Elin Röös, Mikaela Patel, Johanna Spånberg, et al., "Limiting Livestock Production to Pasture and By-Products in a Search for Sustainable Diets," Food Policy 58 (January 2016): 1-13, https://doi.org/10.1016/j.foodpol.2015.10.008.

92. "We Can Feed 9.7 Billion by Growing Crops for Humans, Not Animals," Global Agriculture, July 26, 2018, https://www.globalagriculture.org/whats-new/news/en/33321.html.

93. Gerardo Ceballos, Paul R. Ehrlich, and Rodolfo Dirzo, "Biological Annihilation via the Ongoing Sixth Mass Extinction Signaled by Vertebrate Population Losses and Declines," Proceedings of the National Academy of Sciences 114, no. 30 (July 25, 2017), https://doi.org/10.1073/pnas.1704949114.

94. Brian Machovina, Kenneth J Feeley, and William J Ripple, "Biodiversity Conservation: The Key Is Reducing Meat Consumption," Science of the Total Environment 536 (December 1, 2015): 419–431, https://doi.org/10.1016/j.scitotenv.2015.07.022.

95. "Appetite for Destruction," World Wildlife Fund, October 2017, https://www.wwf.org.uk/sites/default/files/2017-11/WWF_AppetiteForDestruction_Full_Report_Web_0.pdf.

96. David R. Williams, Michael Clark, Graeme M. Buchanan, et al., "Proactive Conservation to Prevent Habitat Losses to Agricultural Expansion", Nature Sustainability 4 (April 2021): 314–322, https://doi.org/10.1038/s41893-020-00656-5; Tim G. Benton, Carling Bieg, Helen Harwatt, et al., "Food System Impacts on Biodiversity Loss: Three Levers for Food System Transformation in Support of Nature," Chatham House (February 3, 2021), https://doi.org/10.13140/RG.2.2.34045.28640; Jenny Splitter, "The Way We Eat Could Lead to Habitat Loss for 17,000 Species by 2050," Vox, February 18, 2021, https://www.vox.com/future-perfect/22287498/meat-wildlife-biodiversity-species-plantbased.

97. Yinon M. Bar-On, Rob Phillips, and Ron Milo, "The Biomass Distribution on Earth," Proceedings of the National Academy of Sciences 115, no. 25 (May 21, 2018): 6506–6511, https://doi.org/10.1073/pnas.1711842115.

98. Rachael Bale, "This Government Program's Job Is to Kill Wildlife," National Geographic, February 12, 2016, https://www.nationalgeographic.com/animals/article/160212-Wildlife-Services-predator-control-livestock-trapping-hunting.

99. Testimony of Erik Molva, Federal Lands Subcommittee Hearing, July 9, 2018.

100. "Protecting Point Reyes Tule Elk," Center for Biological Diversity, accessed June 14, 2022, https://www.biologicaldiversity.org/campaigns/ protecting_Point_Reyes_elk/index.html#:~:text=The%20Center%20 is%20working%20to,habitats%20at%20the%20national%20seashore.; "Cows and Elk by the Numbers: How the National Park Service Prioritizes Commercial Cattle Grazing Over Tule Elk Protection on Your Public Lands at Point Reyes National Seashore," Center for Biological Diversity, accessed June 14, 2022, https://www.biologicaldiversity.org/campaigns/protecting_ Point_Reyes_elk/pdfs/CowsAndElkByTheNumbers.pdf.

101. Erik Molvar, "Livestock Industry's Campaign to Get Rid of Wild Horses Is a Scam to Cheat the Taxpayers," The Wildlife News, December 4, 2020, https://www.thewildlifenews.com/2020/12/04/livestock-industrys-campaign-to-get-rid-of-wild-horses-is-a-scam-to-cheat-the-taxpayers/.

102. Erik Molvar, "Trump Administration Calls Wild Horses Biggest Threat to Public Lands—Here Are the Real Threats," *The Hill*, October 12, 2019, https://thehill.com/opinion/energy-environment/465538-trump-administration-calls-wild-horses-biggest-threat-to-public/.

103. Travis Bruner, "Grazing Leads to Blazing," The Wildlife News, August 21, 2015, https://www.thewildlifenews.com/2015/08/21/grazing-leads-to-blazing/.

104. George Wuerthner, "How Livestock Differs from Wildlife," The Wildlife News, August 31, 2020, https://www.thewildlifenews.com/2020/08/31/ how-livestock-differs-from-wildlife/.

105. Will Anderson, *This Is Hope: Green Vegans and the New Human Ecology* (Earth Books, 2013).

106. Joy Manning, "Is There Such a Thing as Humanely Raised Veal?" Edible Communities, May 7, 2019, https://www.ediblecommunities.com/stories/ is-there-such-a-thing-as-humanely-raised-veal/.

107. Derrell S. Peel, "Dairy Influence on Beef Markets," Drovers, June 24, 2016, https://www.drovers.com/markets/dairy-influence-beef-markets.

108. Joey Carbstrong, "The Only Dairy Farm I Will Ever Drink Milk From," January 15, 2021, 13:38, https://www.facebook.com/ watch/?v=1608196066039317.

109. William Gildea, "Why Do Environmentalists Disagree About Food?" The Ecologist, March 26, 2019, https://theecologist.org/2019/mar/26/ why-do-environmentalists-disagree-about-food.

110. Tim Searchinger, Craig Hanson, Janet Ranganathan, et al., "Creating a Sustainable Food Future: A Menu of Solutions to Sustainably Feed More than 10 Billion People by 2050," World Resources Institute, July 19, 2019, https://www.wri.org/research/creating-sustainable-food-future.

111. Shepon, Eshel, Noor, et al., "The Opportunity Cost of Animal-Based Diets Exceeds All Food Losses."

112. Karen Kaplan, "Going Vegan, America Could Feed an Additional 390 Million People, Study Suggests," Phys.org, March 28, 2018, https://phys. org/news/2018-03-vegan-america-additional-million-people.html.

113. Carys E. Bennett, Richard Thomas, Mark Williams, et al.," The Broiler Chicken as a Signal of a Human Reconfigured Biosphere," Royal Society Open Science 5, no. 12 (December 12, 2018), https://doi.org/10.1098/ rsos.180325.

114. Olivia Norfolk, "Keeping Honeybees Doesn't Save Bees—or the Environment," *The Conversation*, September 12, 2018, https://theconversation. com/keeping-honeybees-doesnt-save-bees-or-the-environment-102931.

115. Krisy Gashler, "Native Bees Are Better Pollinators, More Plentiful than Honeybees, Finds Entomologist," Cornell Chronicle, October 24, 2011, https:// news.cornell.edu/stories/2011/10/native-bees-are-better-pollinators-honeybees.

116. Jonas Geldmann and Juan P. González-Varo, "Conserving Honey Bees Does Not Help Wildlife," Science 359, no. 6374 (January 26, 2018): 392–393, https://doi.org/10.1126/science.aar2269.

117. Daniel Rubinoff, "Bees Gone Wild: Feral Honeybees Pose a Danger to Native Bees and the Ecosystems that Depend on Them," Scientific American, January 16, 2018, https://blogs.scientificamerican.com/observations/bees-gone-wild/.

118. Charles A. Stock, Jasmin G. John, Ryan R. Rykaczewski, et al., "Reconciling Fisheries Catch and Ocean Productivity," Proceedings of the National Academy of Sciences 114, no. 8 (January 23, 2017), https://doi.org/10.1073/ pnas.1610238114.

119. Daniel Zwerdling and Margot Williams, "Is Sustainable-Labeled Seafood Really Sustainable?," *NPR*, February 11, 2013, https://www.npr. org/2013/02/11/171376509/is-sustainable-labeled-seafood-really-sustainable.

120. L. Lebreton, B. Slat, F. Ferrari, et al., "Evidence that the Great Pacific Garbage Patch Is Rapidly Accumulating Plastic," Scientific Reports 8, no. 4666 (March 22, 2018), https://doi.org/10.1038/s41598-018-22939-w; "Ghost Gear: The Abandoned Fishing Nets Haunting Our Oceans," Greenpeace, November 6, 2019, https://www.greenpeace.org/aotearoa/ publication/ghost-gear-the-abandoned-fishing-nets-haunting-our-oceans/.

121. "Factory Fish Farming," Food and Water Watch, February 1, 2013 (archived, accessed December 5, 2021), https://web.archive.org/web/20201206162248/ https://www.foodandwaterwatch.org/insight/factory-fish-farming.

122. Jillian P. Fry, Nicholas A. Mailloux, David C. Love, et al., "Feed Conversion Efficiency in Aquaculture: Do We Measure It Correctly?," Environmental Research Letters 13, no. 2 (February 6, 2018), https://doi. org/10.1088/1748-9326/aaa273.

Chapter 8: Grazing vs. the Planet:
The Failed Attempt to Greenwash Animal Farming

1. Henning Steinfeld, Pierre Gerber, Tom D. Wassenaar, et al., "Livestock's Long Shadow: Environmental Issues and Options," Food & Agriculture Organization, 2006, https://www.fao.org/3/a0701e/a0701e.pdf.
2. Christopher L. Weber and H. Scott Matthews, "Food-Miles and the Relative Climate Impacts of Food Choices in the United States," Environmental Science & Technology 42, no. 10 (2008): 3508–3513, https://doi.org/10.1021/es702969f.
3. Amin Kassam, Theodor Friedrich, Francis Shaxson, et al., "The Spread of Conservation Agriculture: Justification, Sustainability and Uptake," International Journal of Agricultural Sustainability 7, no. 4 (2009): 292–320, https://doi.org/10.3763/ijas.2009.0477.
4. Helen Harwatt, William J. Ripple, Abhishek Chaudhary, et al., "Scientists Call For Renewed Paris Pledges to Transform Agriculture," The Lancet Planetary Health 4, no. 1 (January 1, 2020): E9-E10, https://doi.org/10.1016/S2542-5196(19)30245-1.
5. GRAIN and the Institute for Agriculture and Trade Policy (IATP), "Emissions Impossible: How Big Meat and Dairy Are Heating Up the Planet," GRAIN, July 18, 2018, https://grain.org/article/entries/5976-emissions-impossible-how-big-meat-and-dairy-are-heating-up-the-planet.
6. Vera Röös and Pete Ritchie, "Bonus: Why Isn't Food on the COP Agenda? (Part 1)," Table, 2021, https://tabledebates.org/podcast/episode17.
7. Tara Garnett, Cécile Godde, Adrian Muller, et al., "Grazed and Confused? Ruminating on Cattle, Grazing Systems, Methane, Nitrous Oxide, the Soil Carbon Sequestration Question—and What It All Means for Greenhouse Gas Emissions," Food Climate Research Network, October 3, 2017, https://www.oxfordmartin.ox.ac.uk/downloads/reports/fcrn_gnc_report.pdf.
8. Ibid.
9. Atul K. Jain, Prasanth Meiyappan, Yang Song, et al., "CO_2 Emissions from Land-Use Change Affected More by Nitrogen Cycle, than by the Choice of Land-Cover Data," Global Change Biology 19, no. 9 (September 2013): 2893–2906, https://doi.org/10.1111/gcb.12207.
10. Julie Wolf, Ghassem R. Asrar, and Tristram O. West, "Revised Methane Emissions Factors and Spatially Distributed Annual Carbon Fluxes for Global Livestock," Carbon Balance and Management 12, no. 16 (September 29, 2017), https://doi.org/10.1186/s13021-017-0084-y.
11. Matthew N. Hayek and Rachel D. Garrett, "Nationwide Shift to Grass-Fed Beef Requires Larger Cattle Population," Environmental Research Letters 13, no. 8 (July 25, 2018), https://doi.org/10.1088/1748-9326/aad401.

12. Gunnar Myhre, Drew Shindell, François-Marie Bréon, et al., "Anthropogenic and Natural Radiative Forcing," in *Climate Change 2013: The Physical Science Basis*, eds. Thomas F. Stocker, Dahe Qin, Gian-Kasper Plattner, et al. (Cambridge, U.K.: Cambridge University Press, 2014): 711–712.

13. Steinfeld, Gerber, Wassenaar, et al., "Livestock's Long Shadow."

14. Emily S. Cassidy, Paul C. West, James S. Gerber, et al., "Redefining Agricultural Yields: From Tonnes to People Nourished per Hectare," Environmental Research Letters 8, no. 3 (August 1, 2013), https://doi.org/10.1088/1748-9326/8/3/034015.

15. Yinon M. Bar-On, Rob Phillips, and Ron Milo, "The Biomass Distribution on Earth," Proceedings of the National Academy of Sciences 115, no. 25 (May 21, 2018): 6506–6511, https://doi.org/10.1073/pnas.1711842115.

16. Hayek and Garrett, "Nationwide Shift to Grass-Fed Beef Requires Larger Cattle Population."

17. William J. Ripple, Pete Smith, Helmut Haberl, et al., "Ruminants, Climate Change and Climate Policy," Nature Climate Change 4 (January 2014): 2–5, https://doi.org/10.1038/nclimate2081.

18. Hayek and Garrett, "Nationwide Shift to Grass-Fed Beef Requires Larger Cattle Population."

19. Matthew N. Hayek, Helen Harwatt, William J. Ripple, et al., "The Carbon Opportunity Cost of Animal-Sourced Food Production on Land," Nature Sustainability 4 (January 2021): 21–24, https://doi.org/10.1038/s41893-020-00603-4.

20. Timothy D. Searchinger, Stefan Wirsenius, Tim Beringer, et al., "Assessing the Efficiency of Changes in Land Use for Mitigating Climate Change," Nature 564 (December 13, 2018): 249–253, https://doi.org/10.1038/s41586-018-0757-z.

21. Hayek, Harwatt, Ripple, et al., "The Carbon Opportunity Cost of Animal-Sourced Food Production on Land."

22. Robin S. Reid, K.A. Galvin, and R.S. Kruska, "Global significance of Extensive Grazing Lands and Pastoral Societies: An Introduction," in *Fragmentation in Semi-Arid and Arid Landscapes*, eds. Kathleen A. Galvin, Robin S. Reid, Roy H. Behnke, Jr., et al. (New York: Springer, 2010), 1–24.

23. J. Poore and T. Nemecek, "Reducing Food's Environmental Impacts Through Producers and Consumers," Science 360, no. 6392 (June 1, 2018): 987–992, https://doi.org/10.1126/science.aaq0216.

24. Cassidy, West, Gerber, et al., "Redefining Agricultural Yields."

25. Mariko Thorbecke and Jon Dettling, "Carbon Footprint Evaluation of Regenerative Grazing at White Oak Pastures: Results Presentation," Quantis, February 25, 2019, https://blog.whiteoakpastures.com/hubfs/WOP-LCA-Quantis-2019.pdf.

26. "Bottled Water Shown to Have Lightest Environmental Footprint among Packaged Drinks, New Study Finds," PR Newswire, February 4, 2010, https://www.prnewswire.com/news-releases/bottled-water-shown-to-have-lightest-environmental-footprint-among-packaged-drinks-new-study-finds-83566932.html#:~:text=4%20%2FPRNewswire%2F%20%2D%2D%20A%20new,has%20the%20lightest%20environmental%20footprint.

27. NPT Staff, "Bottled Water Industry Urges National Park Service to Permit Bottled-Water Sales in Parks," National Parks Traveler, April 24, 2015, https://www.nationalparkstraveler.org/2015/04/bottled-water-industry-urges-national-park-service-permit-bottled-water-sales-parks26528.

28. Jason E. Rowntree, Paige L. Stanley, Isabella C. F. Maciel, et al., "Another Industry Attempt to Greenwash Beef," Plant Based Data, January 13, 2021, https://plantbaseddata.medium.com/the-failed-attempt-to-greenwash-beef-7dfca9d74333.

29. Allan Savory, "How to Fight Desertification and Reverse Climate Change," TED, March 4, 2013, video, 22:03, https://www.ted.com/talks/allan_savory_how_to_fight_desertification_and_reverse_climate_change?language=en.

30. Valérie Masson-Delmotte, Panmao Zhai, Hans-Otto Pörtner, et al., *Climate Change and Land: An IPCC Special Report on Climate Change, Desertification, Land Degradation, Sustainable Land Management, Food Security, and Greenhouse Gas Fluxes in Terrestrial Ecosystems* (Intergovernmental Panel on Climate Change, 2019).

31. John Carter, Allison Jones, Mary O'Brien, et al., "Holistic Management: Misinformation on the Science of Grazed Ecosystems," International Journal of Biodiversity (April 23, 2014), https://doi.org/10.1155/2014/163431.

32. Tim Searchinger, Craig Hanson, Janet Ranganathan, et al., "Creating a Sustainable Food Future: A Menu of Solutions to Sustainably Feed More than 10 Billion People by 2050," World Resources Institute, July 19, 2019, https://www.wri.org/research/creating-sustainable-food-future.

33. Donald Sawyer, Beto Mesquita, Bruno Coutinho, et al., "Ecosystem Profile: Cerrado Biodiversity Hotspot," Critical Ecosystem Partnership Fund, last modified February 2017, https://www.cepf.net/sites/default/files/cerrado-ecosystem-profile-en-updated.pdf.

34. "Building a Farmer-Led Movement for a Better Food System," Transfarmation, accessed June 14, 2022, https://thetransfarmationproject.org/.

35. "'Advocates for the Farmer, Families, Their Land & the Planet,'" Rancher Advocacy Program, accessed June 14, 2022, https://rancheradvocacy.org/.

36. "Biocyclic Vegan Agriculture: Organic Farming Based on Ethical and Sustainability Principles," Biocyclic Vegan International, accessed June 14, 2022, https://www.biocyclic-vegan.org/.

37. Paul Hawken, *Drawdown: The Most Comprehensive Plan Ever Proposed to Reverse Global Warming* (New York: Penguin Books. 2017).

Chapter 9: New and Improved?:
Deconstructing the Narrative of So-Called Better Meat

1. Diana Rogers, "Film Update!," Sustainable Dish, August 11, 2019, https://sustainabledish.com/film-update/.
2. James McWilliams, "Beyond Manure: The Future of Veganic Farming," Free from Harm, December 7, 2012, https://freefromharm.org/sustainable-agriculture/beyond-manure-the-future-of-veganic-farming/.
3. Ashley Capps, "It's Time to Replace Slaughterhouses with Greenhouses," Free from Harm, December 13, 2018, https://freefromharm.org/common-justifications-for-eating-animals/marginal-lands/.
4. Madeleine Howell and Gareth May, "The Hidden Cruelty of the Cashew Industry—and the Other Fashionable Foods that Aren't as Virtuous as They Appear," The Telegraph, April 4, 2019, https://www.telegraph.co.uk/food-and-drink/news/healthy-foods-that-are-ruining-the-environment/.
5. Veganic agriculture is organic farming of plant food without any animal inputs—no manure, blood, bone, or feather meal.
6. Capps, "It's Time to Replace Slaughterhouses with Greenhouses."
7. Marco Springmann, H. Charles J. Godfray, Mike Rayner, et al., "Analysis and Valuation of the Health and Climate Change Cobenefits of Dietary Change," Proceedings of the National Academy of Sciences 113, no. 15 (March 21, 2016): 4146–4151, https://doi.org/10.1073/pnas.1523119113.
8. "Livestock a Major Threat to the Environment—Remedies Urgently Needed," The Pig Site, December 5, 2006, https://www.thepigsite.com/news/2006/12/livestock-a-major-threat-to-environment-remedies-urgently-needed-1.
9. Helen Harwatt, Joan Sabaté, Gidon Eshel, et al., "Substituting Beans for Beef as a Contribution Toward US Climate Change Targets," Climatic Change 143 (May 11, 2017): 261–270, https://doi.org/10.1007/s10584-017-1969-1.
10. Sujatha Bergen, "Less Beef, Less Carbon," Natural Resources Defense Council, March 22, 2017, https://www.nrdc.org/experts/sujatha-jahagirdar/less-beef-less-carbon.
11. Steve Boyan, "How Our Food Choices Can Help Save the Environment," EarthSave, accessed June 14, 2022, https://www.earthsave.org/environment/foodchoices.htm.
12. "U.S. Could Feed 800 Million People with Grain that Livestock Eat, Cornell Ecologist Advises Animal Scientists," Cornell Chronicle, August 7, 1997, https://news.cornell.edu/stories/1997/08/us-could-feed-800-million-people-grain-livestock-eat#:~:text=%22If%20all%20the%20grain%20currently,24%2D26%20meeting%20of%20the.

13. "The Nutrition Source: Protein," Harvard T.H. Chan School of Public Health, accessed June 14, 2022, https://www.hsph.harvard.edu/nutritionsource/what-should-you-eat/protein/#:~:text=Choose%20fish%2C%20poultry%2C%20beans%2C,white%20rice%20and%20white%20bread).

14. Kate Good, "5 Ways Factory Farming Is Killing the Environment," One Green Planet, accessed June 14, 2022, https://www.onegreenplanet.org/animalsandnature/factory-farming-is-killing-the-environment/.

15. "Soybeans," Union of Concerned Scientists, October 9, 2015, https://www.ucsusa.org/resources/soybeans.

16. Philip K. Thornton, Mario T. Herrero, and Polly J. Ericksen, "Livestock and Climate Change," International Livestock Research Institute, November 2011, https://cgspace.cgiar.org/handle/10568/10601.

17. Alon Shepon, Gidon Eshel, Elad Noor, et al., "The Opportunity Cost of Animal-Based Diets Exceeds All Food Losses," Proceedings of the National Academy of Sciences 115, no. 15 (March 26, 2018): 3804–3809, https://doi.org/10.1073/pnas.1713820115.

18. Ibid.

19. Mesfin M. Mekonnen and Arjen Y. Hoekstra, "Four Billion People Facing Severe Water Scarcity," Science Advances 2, no. 2 (Feburary 12, 2016), https://doi.org/10.1126/sciadv.1500323.

20. Virginia Morell, "Meat-Eaters May Speed Worldwide Species Extinction, Study Warns," Science, August 11, 2015, https://www.science.org/content/article/meat-eaters-may-speed-worldwide-species-extinction-study-warns.

21. Kelsey Gee, "America's Dairy Farmers Dump 43 Million Gallons of Excess Milk," *The Wall Street Journal*, October 12, 2016, https://www.wsj.com/articles/americas-dairy-farmers-dump-43-million-gallons-of-excess-milk-1476284353.

22. Michael Pollan, "The Intelligent Plant," *The New Yorker*, December 15, 2013, https://www.newyorker.com/magazine/2013/12/23/the-intelligent-plant.

23. "Should Communication Between Pea Plants Raise Tough Issues for Vegetarians?," Say What, Michael Pollan?, May 1, 2012, https://saywhatmichaelpollan.wordpress.com/tag/plants/.

24. David Robinson Simon, "Can Animal Foods Be Produced Sustainably? (Part Two—Organic Follies)," Meatonomic$: The Bizarre Economics of Meat and Dairy, September 3, 2013, https://meatonomics.com/2013/09/03/can-animal-foods-be-produced-sustainably-part-two-organic-follies/.

25. Mark Middleton, "Number of Animals Killed to Produce One Million Calories in Eight Food Categories," Animal Visuals, October 12, 2009, https://animalvisuals.org/docs/animalvisuals_1millioncalories3.pdf.

26. Ibid.

27. VegSource, "Man or Beast: Who's Good, Who's Evil? – Jeffrey Masson, PhD," January 27, 2014, video, 13:44, https://www.youtube.com/watch?v=cF-dV4v7W1I. .

28. Sherry Colb, *Mind If I Order the Cheeseburger?: And Other Questions People Ask Vegans* (New York: Lantern Publishing & Media, 2013), 139.

Chapter 10: A Fox Guarding the Henhouse: Can Animal Agriculture Reform Itself?

1. "Chickens Deserve Better," The Humane League United Kingdom, accessed June 14, 2022, https://thehumaneleague.org.uk/Chickens-deserve-better.

2. Jackie Linden, "Deep Pectoral Myopathy (Green Muscle Disease) in Broilers," The Poultry Site, June 2, 2014, https://www.thepoultrysite.com/articles/deep-pectoral-myopathy-green-muscle-disease-in-broilers; Marina Hosotani, Takeshi Kawasaki, Yasuhiro Hasegawa, et al., "Physiological and Pathological Mitochondrial Clearance Is Related to Pectoralis Major Muscle Pathogenesis in Broilers with Wooden Breast Syndrome," Frontiers in Physiology 11 (June 16, 2020), https://doi.org/10.3389/fphys.2020.00579; Jean E. Sander, "Sudden Death Syndrome of Broiler Chickens," MSD Veterinary Manual, last modified October 2019, https://www.msdvetmanual.com/en-au/poultry/sudden-death-syndrome-of-broiler-chickens/sudden-death-syndrome-of-broiler-chickens.

3. Christine Nicol, "Feather Pecking and Cannibalism," Debeaking, Science Direct, 2018, https://www.sciencedirect.com/topics/agricultural-and-biological-sciences/debeaking.

4. Karen Victor and Antoni Barnard, "Slaughtering for a Living: A Hermeneutic Phenomenological Perspective on the Well-being of Slaughterhouse Employees," International Journal of Qualitative Studies in Health and Well-being 11, no. 1 (April 20, 2016), https://doi.org/10.3402/qhw.v11.30266.

5. "Confessions of a Slaughterhouse Worker," *BBC News*, January 6, 2020, https://www.bbc.com/news/stories-50986683.

6. Anna Pippus, "Meet the Former Slaughterhouse Worker Who Became an Animal Rights Activist," *HuffPost*, last modified December 6, 2017, https://www.huffpost.com/entry/meet-the-former-slaughter_b_10199262.

7. Amy J. Fitzgerald, Linda Kalof, and Thomas Dietz, "Slaughterhouses and Increased Crime Rates: An Empirical Analysis of the Spillover From 'The Jungle' Into the Surrounding Community," Organization & Environment 22, no. 2 (June 2, 2009), https://doi.org/10.1177/1086026609338164.

8. Jennifer Dillard, "A Slaughterhouse Nightmare: Psychological Harm Suffered by Slaughterhouse Employees and the Possibility of Redress

through Legal Reform," Georgetown Journal on Poverty Law & Policy (September 24, 2007), https://ssrn.com/abstract=1016401.

9. Sandra Laville, "Shocking State of English Rivers Revealed as All of Them Fail Pollution Tests," *The Guardian*, September 17, 2020, https://www.theguardian.com/environment/2020/sep/17/rivers-in-england-fail -pollution-tests-due-to-sewage-and-chemicals.

10. J. Poore and T. Nemecek, "Reducing Food's Environmental Impacts Through Producers and Consumers," Science 360, no. 6392 (June 1, 2018): 987–992, https://doi.org/10.1126/science.aaq0216.

11. Matthew Chalmers, "Mangroves: How Shrimp Farming and Sea Level Rise Are Threatening These Vital Ecosystems," Sentient Media, March 5, 2021, https://sentientmedia.org/mangroves/.

12. "Upton Sinclair Quotes," Brainy Quote, accessed June 14, 2022, https://www.brainyquote.com/authors/upton-sinclair-quotes.

13. Mark Koba, "Meet the '4%': Small Number of Farms Dominates US," *CNBC*, May 6, 2014, https://www.cnbc.com/2014/05/06/state-of-american-farming-big-producers-dominate-food-production.html.

14. David Yaffe-Bellany, "The New Makers of Plant-Based Meat? Big Meat Companies," *The New York Times*, October 14, 2019, https://www.nytimes.com/2019/10/14/business/the-new-makers-of-plant-based-meat-big-meat-companies.html.

15. Sentient Media, "Veganism is More than Just a Fad," April 28, 2021, http://sentientmedia.org/increase-in-veganism/.

16. "The Regenerative Ranching Racket," Unpopular Science, April 19, 2021, https://medium.com/@unpopularscience/the-regenerative-ranching-racket-fe6cce917a42.

17. Gosia Wozniacka, "Can Regenerative Agriculture Reverse Climate Change? Big Food Is Banking on It," *NBC News*, October 29, 2019, https://www.nbcnews.com/news/us-news/can-regenerative-agriculture-reverse-climate-change-big-food-banking-it-n1072941.

18. Ken E. Giller, Renske Hijbeek, Jens Andersson, et al., "Regenerative Agriculture: An Agronomic Perspective," Outlook on Agriculture 50, no. 1 (2021), https://doi.org/10.1177/0030727021998063.

19. Nathalie Pettorelli, Philip A. Stephens, Jos Barlow, et al., "Making Rewilding Fit for Policy," Journal of Applied Ecology 55, no. 3 (May 2018): 1114–1125, https://doi.org/10.1111/1365-2664.13082.

20. James McWilliams, "All Sizzle and No Steak," Slate, April 22, 2013, https://slate.com/human-interest/2013/04/allan-savorys-ted-talk-is-wrong-and-the-benefits-of-holistic-grazing-have-been-debunked.html.

21. "Is Grass-Fed Beef Good or Bad for the Climate?" University of Oxford News & Events, October 3, 2017, https://www.ox.ac.uk/news/2017-10-03-grass-fed-beef-good-or-bad-climate#:~:text=Explaining%20the%20key%20 takeaways%20from,problem%2C%20as%20are%20all%20livestock.

22. "From Thomas Jefferson to George Washington, 14 August 1787," Founders Online, accessed June 14, 2022, https://founders.archives.gov/documents/ Jefferson/01-12-02-0040.

23. Matthew Zampa, "First-Ever Cruelty Investigation into an Organic Dairy Farm," Sentient Media, July 26, 2019, https://sentientmedia.org/ cruelty-investigation-organic-dairy-farm/.

24. "Mastitis," Zoetis United States, accessed October 21, 2021, https://www. zoetisus.com/conditions/dairy/mastitis.aspx#:~:text=It%20may%20 be%20accompanied%20by,in%20the%20most%20severe%20cases.

25. "Is Red Tractor High Welfare?," Farms Not Factories, September 4, 2020, https://farmsnotfactories.org/articles/is-red-tractor-high-welfare.

26. "The Policy," Better Chicken Commitment, accessed June 14, 2022, https:// betterchickencommitment.com/en/policy/.

27. "Polluted Runoff: Nonpoint Source (NPS) Pollution," United States Environmental Protection Agency, last modified May 31, 2022, https:// www.epa.gov/nps.

28. Austyn Gaffney, "How the Dairy Industry Is Fouling the Drinking Water of These Wisconsinites," NRDC, March 6, 2019, https://www.nrdc.org/ stories/how-dairy-industry-fouling-drinking-water-these-wisconsinites.

29. Mary H. Ward, Rena R. Jones, Jean D. Brender, et al., "Drinking Water Nitrate and Human Health: An Updated Review," International Journal of Environmental Research and Public Health 15, no. 7 (July 23, 2018): 1557, https://doi.org/10.3390/ijerph15071557.

Chapter 11: The Ethical Vegetarian Myth

1. Derrick Jensen, *The Myth of Human Supremacy* (New York: Seven Stories Press, 2016).

2. Sailesh Rao, *Animal Agriculture Is Immoral* (Phoenix: Climate Healers Publications, 2020).

3. Valérie Masson-Delmotte, Panmao Zhai, Hans-Otto Pörtner, et al., *Climate Change and Land: An IPCC Special Report on Climate Change, Desertification, Land Degradation, Sustainable Land Management, Food Security, and Greenhouse Gas Fluxes in Terrestrial Ecosystems* (Intergovernmental Panel on Climate Change, 2019).

4. Sailesh Rao, "Animal Agriculture is the Leading Cause of Climate Change," Journal of Ecological Society 32–33 (April 1, 2021): 155-167, https://doi. org/10.54081/JES.027/13.

5. Lindsay Wilson, "The Carbon Footprint of 5 Diets Compared," Shrink That Footprint, 2015, https://shrinkthatfootprint.com/food-carbon-footprint-diet/.

6. Christian. J. Peters, Jamie Picardy, Amelia. F. Darrouzet-Nardi, et al., "Carrying Capacity of US Agricultural Land: Ten Diet Scenarios," Elementa: Science of the Anthropocene 4 (July 22, 2016), https://doi.org/10.12952/journal.elementa.000116.

7. J. Poore and T. Nemecek, "Reducing Food's Environmental Impacts Through Producers and Consumers," Science 360, no. 6392 (June 1, 2018): 987–992, https://doi.org/10.1126/science.aaq0216.

8. Yinon M. Bar-On, Rob Phillips, and Ron Milo, "The Biomass Distribution on Earth," Proceedings of the National Academy of Sciences 115, no. 25 (May 21, 2018): 6506–6511, https://doi.org/10.1073/pnas.1711842115.

9. T.W. Crowther, H.B. Glick, K.R. Covey, et al., "Mapping Tree Density at a Global Scale," Nature 525 (September 2, 2015): 201–205, https://doi.org/10.1038/nature14967.

10. "'The Lifestyle Carbon Dividend'," Compassionate Spirit, accessed June 14, 2022, https://compassionatespirit.com/wpblog/2016/02/22/the-lifestyle-carbon-dividend/.

11. Hannah Ritchie and Max Roser, "Meat and Dairy Production," Our World in Data, last modified November 2019, https://ourworldindata.org/meat-production.

12. Kees Klein Goldewijk, Arthur Beusen, G. Van Drecht, et al. "The HYDE 3.1 Spatially Explicit Database of Human Induced Global Land-Use Change over the Past 12,000 Years," Global Ecology and Biogeography 20, no. 1, (September 11, 2010): 73–86, https://doi.org/10.1111/j.1466-8238.2010.00587.x.

13. Phillipe Ciais, Christoper Sabine, Govindasamy Bala, et al., "Carbon and Other Biogeochemical Cycles," in *Climate Change 2013: The Physical Science Basis*, eds. Thomas F. Stocker, Dahe Qin, Gian-Kasper Plattner, et al. (New York: Cambridge University Press, 2014).

14. Ritchie and Roser, "Meat and Dairy Production."

15. Michel Greger, "Eggs vs. Cigarettes in Atherosclerosis," Nutrition Facts 12 (March 11, 2013), https://nutritionfacts.org/video/eggs-vs-cigarettes-in-atherosclerosis/.

16. Sherry Colb, *Mind If I Order the Cheeseburger?: And Other Questions People Ask Vegans* (New York: Lantern Publishing & Media, 2013), 46–47.

17. Katrina Fox, "Why Compassion is Essential to Social Justice," in *Circles of Compassion: Essays Connecting Issues of Justice*, ed. Will Tuttle (Danvers, MA: Vegan Publishers, 2014), 44.

18. Carmen M. Cusack, "Feminism and Husbandry: Drawing the Fine Line Between Mine and Bovine," Journal for Critical Animal Studies 11, no. 1 (2013): 24–45, https://faunalytics.org/wp-content/uploads/2015/05/Citation2336_Feminism%20and%20Husbandry%20-%20Drawing%20the%20Fine%20Line%20Between%20Mine%20and%20Bovine.pdf.

19. Poore and Nemecek, "Reducing Food's Environmental Impacts Through Producers and Consumers."

20. Anastassia M. Makarieva, Victor G. Gorshkov, and Bai-Lian Li, "Precipitation on Land Versus Distance from the Ocean: Evidence for a Forest Pump of Atmospheric Moisture," Ecological Complexity 6, no. 3, (September 2009): 302–307, https://doi.org/10.1016/j.ecocom.2008.11.004.

21. Bar-On, Phillips, and Milo, "The Biomass Distribution on Earth," 6506–6511.

Chapter 12: Corrupting the Language of Animal Welfare

1. Lindsay Chichester, "Meat Labeling Terms—What Do They Mean? Part 2: Organic, All-Natural, and Naturally Raised," University of Nebraska–Lincoln, March 1, 2014, https://newsroom.unl.edu/announce/beef/3039/17310.

2. Aurora Paulsen, "The Humane Labeling Of Animal-Based Food Products: A Working Overview," 2010, https://law.lclark.edu/live/files/6702-humane-labeling-standards. In using the term "humane labeling," this overview refers to labeling on animal-based food products that impacts, or appears to impact, current farm animal husbandry standards.

3. Daniel Vernick, "3 Billion Animals Harmed by Australia's Fires," World Wildlife Fund, July 28, 2020, https://www.worldwildlife.org/stories/3-billion-animals-harmed-by-australia-s-fires.

4. Grace Hussain, "How Many Animals Are Killed for Food Every Day?," Sentient Media, December 17, 2021, https://sentientmedia.org/how-many-animals-are-killed-for-food-every-day/#:~:text=How%20Many%20Animals%20Are%20Killed%20Each%20Day%3F,jumps%20to%20over%20150%20million.

5. Arran Stibbe, "Language, Power and the Social Construction of Animals," Society & Animals 2, no. 9 (January 1, 2001): 145–161, https://doi.org/10.1163/156853001753639251.

6. Ibid; Sven Gins, "Everything but the Squeal: The Politics of Porcinity in the Livre des Propriétés des Choses," Religions 12, no. 4, (April 8, 2021), https://doi.org/10.3390/rel12040260; Cary Williams, "The Framing of Animal Cruelty by Animal Advocacy Organizations," The Honors College at the University of Maine 91, (May 2012), https://digitalcommons.library.umaine.edu/honors/91.

7. Nguyen Toan Tran, Stéphanie Baggio, Angela Dawson, et al., "Words Matter: A Call for Humanizing and Respectful Language to Describe People Who Experience Incarceration," BMC International Health and Human Rights 18, no. 41 (November 16, 2018), https://doi.org/10.1186/s12914-018-0180-4.

8. Arran Stibbe, *Animals Erased: Discourse, Ecology and Reconnection with the Natural World* (Middleton, CT: Wesleyan University Press, 2012); Stibbe, "Language, Power and the Social Construction of Animals," 145–161.

9. Ibid.

10. Williams, "The Framing of Animal Cruelty by Animal Advocacy Organizations."

11. Stibbe, *Animals Erased.*

12. Mara Miele, "Killing Animals for Food: How Science, Religion and Technologies Affect the Public Debate About Religious Slaughter," Food Ethics 1 (June 2016): 47–60, https://doi.org/10.1007/s41055-016-0004-y; Animal Welfare Institute, "Label Confusion 2.0: How the USDA Allows Producers to Use 'Humane' and 'Sustainable' Claims on Meat Packages and Deceive Consumers," September 2019, https://awionline.org/sites/default/files/publication/digital_download/19%20Label%20Confusion%20Report%20FINAL%20WEB%20II.pdf; C. Victor Spain, Daisy Freund, Heather Mohan-Gibbons, et al., "Are They Buying It? United States Consumers' Changing Attitudes toward More Humanely Raised Meat, Eggs, and Dairy," Animals 8, no. 8 (July 25, 2018), https://doi.org/10.3390/ani8080128.

13. "Certified Animal Welfare Approved by AGW Food Label," A Greener World, accessed June 15, 2022, https://agreenerworld.org/certifications/animal-welfare-approved/.

14. Hope Bohanec, *The Ultimate Betrayal Is There Happy Meat?* (Bloomington, IN: iUniverse, 2013).

15. Spain, Freund, Mohan-Gibbons, et al., "Are They Buying It?"

16. Ibid.

17. Caitlin A. Ceryes and Christopher D. Heaney, "'Ag-Gag'" Laws: Evolution, Resurgence, and Public Health Implications," New Solutions 28, no. 4 (2019): 664–682, https://doi.org/10.1177/1048291118808788; Stibbe, "Language, Power and the Social Construction of Animals;" Williams, "The Framing of Animal Cruelty by Animal Advocacy Organizations."

18. Joe Loria, "Study: 60 Percent of All Mammals Are Farmed Animals," Mercy For Animals, May 31, 2018, https://mercyforanimals.org/blog/study-60-percent-of-all-mammals-are-farmed/.

19. Stibbe, "Language, Power and the Social Construction of Animals," 145–161.

20. Spain, Freund, Mohan-Gibbons, et al., "Are They Buying It?"

21. Hussain, "How Many Animals Are Killed for Food Every Day?"

Chapter 13: Kindred Spirits or Commodified Objects?: Disconnection and Perception in the Humane Hoax

1. Jim Mason, *An Unnatural Order: Uncovering the Roots of Our Domination of Nature and Each Other* (New York: Simon & Schuster, 1993), 116–117.

2. Michael Mountain, "About Earth in Transition," Earth in Transition, accessed June 15, 2022, https://www.earthintransition.org/about-earth-in-transition-2/.

3. Simon Shuchat, "Deceptive Advertising by Animal Products Industry Fools Consumers; Advocates Fight Back," Their Turn, December 29, 2016, https://theirturn.net/2016/08/09/deceptive-advertising-animal-agriculture/.

4. Timothy Pachirat, *Every Twelve Seconds: Industrialized Slaughter and the Politics of Sight* (New Haven: Yale University Press, 2011), 9.

Chapter 14: "Humane Eggs" and "Happy Wings": A Look Beyond the Labels

1. Jennifer Chait, "What Does 'Free Range' Really Mean?" The Balance Small Business, last modified November 6, 2019, https://www.thebalancesmb.com/what-does-free-range-really-mean-2538247.

2. United Poultry Concerns, "The End of Hens: Inside a 'Spent Hen' Slaughterhouse." Poultry Press Vol. 4, No. 4 (Spring 2015). https://www.upc-online.org/pp/spring2015/spent_hen_slaughterhouse.html.

3. U.S. Department of Agriculture, National Organic Program. https://www.ams.usda.gov/about-ams/programs-offices/national-organic-program.

4. See, for example, U.S. Department of Agricultural Marketing Service, "Confinement of Organic Poultry due to risk of Avian Influenza," April 3, 2017. https://www.ams.usda.gov/content/confinement-organic-poultry-due-risk-avian-influenza.

5. United Poultry Concerns, "The Rougher They Look, The Better They Lay," December 30, 2014. https://www.upc-online.org/freerange/141230_the_rougher_they_look_the_better_they_lay.html. First published in Poultry Press Vol. 2, No. 4 (Fall 1992), 4-5. https://www.upc-online.org/pp/2.4PoultryPress-Fall1992.pdf.

6. Sauder's Eggs: Family-Owned Egg Wholesaling Business, accessed June 15, 2022, https://www.saudereggs.com/.

7. United Poultry Concerns, "Home on the Range," Poultry Press Vol. 2, No. 2 (Spring 1992), 4. http://www.upc-online.org/pp/2.2PoultryPress-Spring1992.pdf.

8. Aaron Lee, "Nelson Farm Putting Eggs on Its Plate," Nelson County Times, April 16, 2008. https://www.newsadvance.com/nelson_county_times/news/nelson-farm-putting-eggs-on-its-plate/article_ea06bac0-d612-5973-9962-b5bb4d4ffc96.html.

9. United Poultry Concerns, "Black Eagle Farm: Story of an Organic Egg Scam," Poultry Press, Vol. 20, No. 3 (Winter 2010). http://www.upc-online.org/pp/winter2010/black_eagle.html.

10. United Poultry Concerns, "Black Eagle: An Organic Egg Farm Revisited," Poultry Press Vol. 21, No. 4 (Winter 2011-2012). http://www.upc-online.org/pp/winter2011/black_eagle_revisited.html.

11. Ibid.

12. Laura Reiley, "The Organic Food Industry is Booming, and That May Be Bad for Consumers," The Washington Post, March 14, 2019. https://www.washingtonpost.com/business/2019/03/14/organic-food-industry-is-booming-that-may-be-bad-consumers/?utm_term=.8cdec384aebd&wpisrc=nl_rainbow&wpmm=1.

13. Oliver Milman, "Free-range Eggs Producer Accused of Deceiving US Consumers," The Guardian, March 7, 2019. https://www.theguardian.com/us-news/2019/mar/07/nellies-free-range-eggs-lawsuit-packaging.

14. Tom Philpott, "What Does 'Cage-Free' Even Mean?" Mother Jones, January 14, 2015. http://www.motherjones.com/tom-philpott/2015/01/you-cant-produce-eggs-industrial-scale-without-breaking-few-hens.

15. Harriet Schleifer, "Images of Death and Life: Food Animal Production and the Vegetarian Option," in In Defense of Animals, ed. Peter Singer (New York: Basil Blackwell Inc., 1985), 70.

16. United Poultry Concerns, "ASPCA Helps Poultry Producer Expand His Business," Poultry Press Vol. 22, No. 2 (Summer-Fall 2012). http://www.upc-online.org/pp/summer2012/aspca_helps_poultry_producer_expand.html.

17. Marc Bekoff, "Baby Chicks Used as Packing Filler," Psychology Today, April 23, 2012. https://www.psychologytoday.com/us/blog/animal-emotions/201204/baby-chicks-used-packing-filler. Reposted by United Poultry Concerns in "Hatcheries Ship Baby Roosters as Packing Material," April 23, 2012. http://www.upc-online.org/backyard/120423hatcheries_ship_chicks_as_packing.html.

18. Terry Gross, "Food Writer Becomes a Butcher to Better Understand the Value of Meat," Fresh Air, July 24, 2018. https://www.npr.org/programs/fresh-air/2018/07/24/631748681.

19. Earl W. Benjamin and Howard C. Pierce, *Marketing Poultry Products* (New York: John Wiley & Sons, 1937), 139. See also Benjamin, George C. Watson, *Farm Poultry: A Popular Sketch of Domestic Fowls for the Farmer and Amateur,* 3rd edition. Rural Science Series. (New York, Macmillan, 1901.) Cited in Karen Davis, *More Than a Meal: The Turkey in History, Myth, Ritual, and Reality* (New York: Lantern Books, 2001), 64-65.

20. Virgil Butler, Excerpted from Press Conference organized by People for the Ethical Treatment of Animals in Little Rock, Arkansas, February 19, 2003. See also Virgil Butler, "Clarification of Stunner Usage," The Cyperactivist, May 27, 2004. In this post, he writes: "every chicken is bled out while still sentient. They hang there and look at you while they are bleeding. You can definitely tell that they know what is going on. Sometimes if they are not completely immobilized by the stunner (which happens frequently), they will try to hide their head from you by sticking it under the wing of the chicken next to them. https://www.upc-online.org/slaughter/91104stunner.htm.

21. Steve Striffler, *Chicken: The Dangerous Transformation of America's Favorite Food* (New Haven: Yale University Press, 2005), 156.

22. Striffler, *Chicken*, 168.

23. Peter Singer and Jim Mason, *The Way We Eat: Why Our Food Choices Matter* (Rodale 2006), 104.

24. Christine Morrissey, "Photo Essay: Paying the Price for 'Pampered' Poultry," Satya September 2006, 38-39. Quoted in Karen Davis, Prisoned Chickens, Poisoned Eggs: An Inside Look at the Modern Poultry Industry (Summertown, TN: Book Publishing Company, 2009), 168.

25. For example, the U.S. Department of Agriculture's Animal and Plant Health Inspection Service (APHIS), since February 2022 "has been in a costly battle with avian influenza, reported Food Safety News, June 1, 2022. "With an emergency $793 million transfer from the agency's Commodity Credit Corporation, APHIS has eradicated more than 40 million birds from 372 flocks in 38 states." https://www.foodsafetynews.com/2022/06/aphis-turns-attention-to-swine-fever-after-months-of-battling-avian-flu/?utm_source=Food+Safety+News&utm_campaign=dc59fcef43-RSS_EMAIL_CAMPAIGN&utm_medium=email&utm_term=0_f46cc10150-dc59fcef43-40430175.

26. Jaclyn Cosgrove, "To Stop a Virus, California Has Euthanized More Than 1.2 Million Birds. Is It Reckless or Necessary?" Los Angeles Times, June 7, 2019. https://www.latimes.com/local/lanow/la-me-ln-virulent-newcastle-disease-outbreak-in-southern-california-20190607-story.html.

27. Law Office of Chad D. Morgan, Attorney for Plaintiff, Save Our Birds vs. Dr. Annette Jones, CA Dept of Food and Agriculture, Defendants, Complaint for Injunctive Relief, May 28, 2019. http://www.chadmorgan.com/wp-content/uploads/2019/05/Save-Our-Birds-v.-Jones-Complaint.pdf?fbclid=IwAR2PZo1NgjihotQ-LStBEB-ECleT8QTufi_udQlkgNlUVPoKMlde8-cY_PM.

28. Elizabeth Henderson, "Organic Farms Are Under Attack From Agribusiness, Weakened Standards," Truthout - Independent

Media Institute, March 17. 2019. https://truthout.org/articles/organic-farms-are-under-attack-from-agribusiness-weakened-standards.

29. Bruce Webster, et al., "Update on Hen Disposition." Paper presented at the 1996 International Poultry Exposition Egg Program (Atlanta, GA), January 25, 1996, 5. See Karen Davis, Prisoned Chickens, Poisoned Eggs (note 24 above), 80: "Before going to slaughter, laying hens are deprived of food for an average of four days to 'provide a modest net return to help pay for the costs of hen disposition. . . . The greatest benefit of fasting occurs on the third day. In this scenario, fasting a flock provides as much as 3.6 cents extra per hen that can be put against the cost of flock removal'" (Webster).

30. Gina Warren, "The Chicken Project," Orion Magazine, June 2015. https://orionmagazine.org/article/the-chicken-project.

Chapter 15: Humane Myths and Media: The Reproduction of Speciesism in Mainstream U.S. News

1. On the myth of nonhuman animal "consent" to exploitation, see Matthew Cole, "Getting 'Green' Beef: Anti-Vegan Rhetoric and the Legitimizing of Eco-Friendly Oppression," in *Critical Animal and Media Studies*, eds. Núria Almiron, Matthew Cole, and Carrie P. Freeman (New York: Routledge, 2016), 113; Jonathan Safran Foer, *Eating Animals* (New York: Little Brown and Company, 2009), 99–101; Robert Grillo, *Farm to Fable* (Danvers, MA: Vegan Publishers, 2016), 24–27; and Vasile Stănescu, "New Weapons: 'Humane Farming,' Biopolitics, and the Post-Commodity Fetish," in *Animal Oppression and Capitalism*, ed. David Nibert (Santa Barbara, CA: Praeger, 2017), 121–123.

2. Vesanto Melina, Winston Craig, and Susan Levin, "Position of the Academy of Nutrition and Dietetics: Vegetarian Diets," Journal of the Academy of Nutrition and Dietetics 116, no. 12 (December 1, 2016): 1970–1980, https://doi.org/10.1016/j.jand.2016.09.025.

3. For an overview of the major proposed definitions of *speciesism* since its inception in the 1970s, see Joan Dunayer, *Speciesism* (Deerwood, MD: Ryce, 2004), 1–5. For an elaboration of this sociological and economic description of speciesism, see David Nibert, *Animal Rights/Human Rights: Entanglements of Oppression and Liberation* (Lanham, MD: Rowman & Littlefield, 2002).

4. "Public Radio Finances," *NPR*, accessed June 15, 2022, https://www.npr.org/about-npr/178660742/public-radio-finances#nprrevenues.

5. On the pro-establishment orientation of media, see Noam Chomsky, *Manufacturing Consent* (New York: Pantheon Books, 2002); and Robert McChesney, *Rich Media, Poor Democracy* (New York: The New Press, 2015). On speciesism in media, see John Sorenson, *Constructing Ecoterrorism:*

Capitalism, Speciesism and Animal Rights (Black Point, Nova Scotia: Fernwood Books, 2016); David Nibert, *Animal Oppression and Human Violence* (New York: Columbia University Press, 2013); and Núria Almiron, Matthew Cole, and Carrie P. Freeman, *Critical Animal and Media Studies* (New York: Routledge, 2016).

6. Stănescu, "New Weapons."

7. Carol J. Adams, *The Sexual Politics of Meat* (London: Continuum, 2000), 14.

8. Kate Stewart and Matthew Cole, "The Conceptual Separation of Food and Animals in Childhood," Food, Culture & Society 12, no. 4 (2009), https://doi.org/10.2752/175174409X456746. Helpful in illuminating this further is Kate Stewart and Matthew Cole's theorization of two intersecting spectrums in cultural representations of nonhuman animals: 1) the degree to which the represented animals are objectified (rather than given subjectivity as individuals with moral value); and 2) the degree to which they are hidden (as opposed to being made visible to many people). Using this conceptual mapping, we can say that animals in "humane" farming rhetoric are made to appear more visible, but they are no less objectified as in conventional farming.

9. Karen Davis, "The Disengagement of Journalistic Discourse about Nonhuman Animals: An Analysis," in *Critical Animal Studies: Toward Trans-Species Social Justice*, eds. Atsuko Matsuoka and John Sorenson (London: Rowman & Littlefield, 2018), 73.

10. On the use of the impersonal pronoun "it" for nonhuman animals, see Joan Dunayer, *Animal Equality: Language and Liberation* (Deerwood, MD: Ryce Publishing, 2001), 149–153; and Carrie P. Freeman and Debra Merskin, "Respectful Representation: An Animal Issues Style Guide for All Media Practitioners," in *Critical Animal and Media Studies*, eds Núria Almiron, Matthew Cole, and Carrie P. Freeman (New York: Routledge, 2016), 213.

11. Lindgren Johnson and Susan Thomas, "Interview with Carol J. Adams," Journal for Critical Animal Studies 11, no. 1 (2013): 120.

12. Ibid, 122.

13. Ibid.

14. Terry Gross, "Food Writer Becomes a Butcher to Learn the Value of Meat," *NPR*, July 24, 2018, https://www.npr.org/sections/thesalt/2018/07/24/631845582/food-writer-becomes-a-butcher-to-better-understand-the-value-of-meat#:~:text=Press-,Food%20Writer%20Becomes%20A%20Butcher%20To%20Better%20Understand%20The%20Value,Her%20memoir%20is%20Killing%20it.

15. Ibid.

16. Vasile Stănescu, "'Green' Eggs and Ham? The Myth of Sustainable Meat and the Danger of the Local," Journal for Critical Animal Studies 8, No. 1/2 (2010), https://www.criticalanimalstudies.org/wp-content/uploads/2009/09/2-JCAS-Vol-VIII-Issue-I-and-II-2010-Essay-GREEN-EGGS-AND-HAM-pp-8-32.pdf.

17. Gross, "Food Writer Becomes a Butcher to Learn the Value of Meat."

18. Ibid.

19. Hope Bohanec, *The Ultimate Betrayal: Is There Happy Meat?* (Bloomington, IN: iUniverse, 2013), 136.

20. Gross, "Food Writer Becomes a Butcher to Learn the Value of Meat."

21. Camas Davis, *Killing It: An Education* (New York: Penguin Press, 2018), 7.

22. Ibid, 7–8.

23. Lisa A. Barca, "The Agency Factor: Neoliberal Configurations of Risk in New Discourse on the Steubenville, Ohio Rape Case," Critical Discourse Studies 15, no. 3 (June 2018): 265–284, https://doi.org/10.1080/17405904.2017.1408476.

24. Davis, *Killing It*, 10.

25. Compassionate Living, "John Sanbonmatsu: 'Lady Macbeth at the Rotisserie'," February 7, 2019, video, 54:10, https://www.youtube.com/watch?v=OFObmTqE0Fo.

26. Gross, "Food Writer Becomes a Butcher to Learn the Value of Meat."

27. Ibid.

28. Ibid.

29. Ibid.

30. Bohanec, *The Ultimate Betrayal*.

31. A corrective to Camas Davis's anecdotal and unscientific beliefs about chickens is available through a wealth of recent scholarly literature on their highly complex cognition, emotions, and social behavior. See for example Lori Marino, "Thinking Chickens: A Review of Cognition, Emotion, and Behavior in the Domestic Chicken," Animal Cognition 20, no. 2 (March 2017): 127–147, https://doi.org/10.1007/s10071-016-1064-4; Carolynn L. Smith and Sarah L. Zielinski, "The Startling Intelligence of the Common Chicken," Scientific American, February 1, 2014, https://www.scientificamerican.com/article/the-startling-intelligence-of-the-common-chicken/; Lesley J. Rogers, "Chickens' Brains, Like Ours, Are Lateralized," Animal Sentience 17, no. 3, (2017), https://doi.org/10.51291/2377-7478.1216; Carolynn L. Smith, "The Chicken Challenge: What Contemporary Studies of Fowl Mean for Science and Ethics," Between the Species 15, no. 1 (August 2012): 75–102, https://doi.org/10.15368/bts.2012v15n1.4; Rosa Rugani, Lucia Regolin, and Giorgio Vallortigara, "Imprinted Numbers: Newborn Chicks' Sensitivity to Number vs. Continuous Extent of Objects They Have

Been Reared with," *Developmental Science* 13, no. 5 (September 2010): 790–797, https://doi.org/10.1111/j.1467-7687.2009.00936.x; and Robert Grillo, "Chicken Behavior: An Overview of Recent Science," Free from Harm, February 7, 2014, https://freefromharm.org/chicken-behavior-an-overview-of-recent-science/. Mainstream press articles include Fiona Macrae, "Can Chickens REALLY Be Cleverer than a Toddler? Studies Suggest Animals Can Master Numeracy and Basic Engineering," *The Daily Mail*, last modified June 19, 2013, https://www.dailymail.co.uk/sciencetech/article-2344198/Chickens-smarter-human-toddlers-Studies-suggest-animals-master-numeracy-basic-engineering.html.

32. Johnson and Thomas, "Interview with Carol J. Adams."

33. The piece appeared in *The New York Times* through T-Brand Studio, whose website announces: "We create and distribute insightful brand content and experiences that shape opinion;" "T Brand Studio is the brand marketing unit of *The New York Times*;" "We create content and experiences that spark imagination and influence the most influential audiences around the world;" "We take a journalistic approach to crafting brand stories."

34. John Stauber and Sheldon Rampton, *Toxic Sludge Is Good For You: Lies, Damn Lies and the Public Relations Industry* (Monroe, ME: Common Courage Press, 2002), 179–196.

35. "Changing the Face of the Dairy Industry," *The New York Times*, accessed June 15, 2022, https://www.nytimes.com/paidpost/land-o-lakes/changing-the-face-of-the-dairy-industry.html.

36. Ibid.

37. Ibid.

38. Sune Borkfelt, Sara Kondrup, Helena Röcklinsberg, et al., "Closer to Nature? A Critical Discussion of the Marketing of 'Ethical' Animal Products," Journal of Agricultural and Environmental Ethics 28 (December 2015): 1053–1073, https://doi.org/10.1007/s10806-015-9577-4.

39. Sorenson, *Constructing Ecoterrorism*, 322.

40. Jana Canavan, "'Happy Cow' Welfarist Ideology and the Swedish 'Milk Crisis': A Crisis of Romanticized Oppression," in *Animal Oppression and Capitalism* 1, ed. David Nibert (Westport, CT: Praeger, 2017), 47.

41. *The New York Times*, "Changing the Face of the Dairy Industry."

42. Mary Trachsel, "The Presence of 'Pork' and the Absence of Pigs: Changing Stories of People and Pigs in Iowa," in *Animal Oppression and Capitalism*, ed. David Nibert, (Westport, CT: Praeger, 2017), 91–92.

43. *The New York Times*, "Changing the Face of the Dairy Industry."

44. See Stănescu, "'Green' Eggs and Ham?"

45. VCU Brandcenter, "Maggie Rose–She-I-O," August 24, 2018, video, 2:46, https://www.youtube.com/watch?v=PzFctkAH4Jk.

46. *The New York Times*, "Changing the Face of the Dairy Industry."
47. Corey Wrenn, "Toward a Vegan Feminist Theory of the State," in *Animal Oppression and Capitalism* 2, ed. David Nibert (Westport, CT: Praeger, 2017), 212.
48. Ibid.
49. Lauren Steussy, "Would You Pay $200 for a Designer Thanksgiving Turkey?" New York Post, November 14, 2018, https://nypost.com/2018/11/14/would-you-pay-200-for-a-designer-thanksgiving-turkey/.
50. "Understanding Labels & Loopholes," Humane Facts, accessed June 15, 2022, https://humanefacts.org/labels-loopholes/.
51. Bohanec, *The Ultimate Betrayal*, 82.
52. Grillo, *Farm to Fable*, 50.
53. Steussy, "Would You Pay $200 for a Designer Thanksgiving Turkey?"
54. UChanel, "Moving Beyond Fast Food Nation," August 14, 2007, video, 01:29:14, https://www.youtube.com/watch?v=UfO4TwrUqZM.
55. Robert Grillo, "Why Rare or Heritage Breed Farming Is Not Conservation," Free from Harm, May 9, 2018, https://freefromharm.org/common-justifications-for-eating-animals/rare-heritage-breed/#:~:text=As%20for%20the%20issue%20of,for%20them%20to%20go%20extinct.
56. Steussy, "Would You Pay $200 for a Designer Thanksgiving Turkey?"
57. Canavan, "'Happy Cow' Welfarist Ideology and the Swedish 'Milk Crisis'", 47.
58. Karen Davis, *More than a Meal: The Turkey in History, Myth, Ritual, and Reality* (New York: Lantern Publishing & Media, 2001).
59. Steussy, "Would You Pay $200 for a Designer Thanksgiving Turkey?"
60. Cole, "Getting 'Green' Beef," 109–110, 112–113.
61. John Sanbonmatsu, "Capitalism and Speciesism," in *Animal Oppression and Capitalism* 2, ed. David Nibert (Westport, CT: Praeger, 2017), 17–24.
62. Ibid.
63. Sune Borkfelt, Sara V. Kondrup, and Mickey Gjerris, "Closer to Nature: The Ethics of 'Green' Representations in Animal Product Management," in *The Ethics of Consumption: The Citizen, the Market, and the Law*, eds. Helena Röcklinsberg and Per Sandin (Wageningen, Netherlands: Wageningen Academic Publishers, June 2013), 1068.
64. Ibid.
65. Alastor Van Kleeck, "The Inescapable Speciesism of 'Progressive' Media," Striving with Systems, February 27, 2016, https://strivingwithsystems.com/2016/02/27/the-inescapable-speciesism-of-progressive-media/; John Sorenson, "Constructing Extremists, Rejecting Compassion: Ideological Attacks on Animal Advocacy from Right and Left," in *Critical Theory and Animal Liberation*, ed. John Sanbonmatsu (Lanham, MD: Rowman & Littlefield, 2011), 219–238.

66. Quoted in Freeman and Merskin, "Respectful Representation," 205.
67. "The Cambridge Declaration on Consciousness," Francis Crick Memorial Conference, Cambridge, U.K., July 7, 2012, https://fcmconference.org/img/CambridgeDeclarationOnConsciousness.pdf.

Chapter 16: Modern Foodie Culture: A Celebration of Violence

1. Abraham Hayward, *The Art of Dining: Or, Gastronomy and Gastronomers* (London: John Murray, 1852), 112.
2. Schwartz Media, "Food Fighters: AA Gill and Anthony Bourdain in Conversation," May 3, 2013, video, 49:54, https://www.youtube.com/watch?v=F2tjvTmbEVw.
3. Ludwig Wittgenstein, *Philosophical Investigations* (New York: Macmillan, 1953).
4. Susan Wolf, "The Ethics of Being a Foodie" in *The Oxford Handbook of Food Ethics*, eds. Anne Barnhill, Mark Budolfson, and Tyler Doggett (Oxford: Oxford University Press, 2018), 727–728.
5. Jacy Reese Anthis, "Animals, Food, and Technology (AFT) Survey 2017," Sentience Institute, November 20, 2017, https://www.sentienceinstitute.org/animal-farming-attitudes-survey-2017.
6. Marlene C. Onwezen and Cor N. van der Weele, "When Indifference Is Ambivalence: Strategic Ignorance about Meat Consumption," Food Quality and Preference 52 (September 2016): 96–105, https://doi.org/10.1016/j.foodqual.2016.04.001.
7. Ibid.
8. Jared Piazza, Matthew B. Ruby, Steve Loughnan, et al., "Rationalizing Meat Consumption. The 4Ns," Appetite 91 (August 1, 2015): 114–128, https://doi.org/10.1016/j.appet.2015.04.011.
9. Julie Powell, *Julie and Julia: 365 Days, 524 Recipes, 1 Tiny Apartment Kitchen.* (Little, Brown and Company, 2005), 194.
10. B. R. Myers, "Hard to Swallow," *The Atlantic*, September 2007, https://www.theatlantic.com/magazine/archive/2007/09/hard-to-swallow/306123/.
11. Carol J. Adams, *The Sexual Politics of Meat* (Boston: Beacon Press, 1990).
12. Gabrielle Hamilton, *Blood, Bones & Butter: The Inadvertent Education of a Reluctant Chef* (New York: Random House, 2011), 104–105.
13. Justin McCurry, "Live Shrimp Covered in Ants, Anyone? Noma's Japanese Restaurant Serves Up a Rare Treat," *The Guardian*, January 29, 2015, https://www.theguardian.com/world/2015/jan/29/twitching-live-shrimp-covered-ants-dish-noma-restaurant-japan.
14. Dana Goodyear, *Anything That Moves: Renegade Chefs, Fearless Eaters, and the Making of a New American Food Culture* (New York: Riverhead Books, 2013), 15.
15. Elsa Newman, Telephone Interview, March 15, 2015.
16. B. R. Myers, "The Moral Crusade Against Foodies," *The Atlantic*, March 2011.

17. Schwartz Media, "Food Fighters."

18. Hope Bohanec, *The Ultimate Betrayal: Is There Happy Meat?* (Bloomington, IN: iUniverse, 2013); Vasile Stănescu, "'Green' Eggs and Ham? The Myth of Sustainable Meat and the Danger of the Local," Journal for Critical Animal Studies 8, No. 1/2 (2010), https://www.criticalanimalstudies.org/wp-content/uploads/2009/09/2-JCAS-Vol-VIII-Issue-I-and-II-2010-Essay-GREEN-EGGS-AND-HAM-pp-8-32.pdf.

19. Kathryn Gillespie, "How Happy Is Your Meat? Confronting (Dis) connectedness in the 'Alternative' Meat Industry," The Brock Review 12, no. 1 (2011): 100–128, https://doi.org/10.26522/br.v12i1.326.

20. Adams, *The Sexual Politics of Meat*; Lori Gruen, *Ethics and Animals: An Introduction* (Cambridge: Cambridge University Press, 2011); Compassionate Living, "John Sanbonmatsu: 'Lady Macbeth at the Rotisserie'," February 7, 2019, video, 54:10, https://www.youtube.com/watch?v=OFObmTqE0Fo; Vialles Noilie, *Animal to Edible* (Cambridge: Cambridge University Press, 1994).

21. Robert Grillo, "Eating Animals and the Illusion of Personal Choice," Free From Harm, August 15, 2012, https://freefromharm.org/animal-products-and-psychology/five-reasons-why-meat-eating-cannot-be-considered-a-personal-choice/.

22. P.J. Gerber, H. Steinfeld, B. Henderson, et al., "Tackling Climate Change Through Livestock: A Global Assessment of Emissions and Mitigation Opportunities," Food and Agriculture Organization of the United Nations, 2013, https://www.fao.org/3/i3437e/i3437e.pdf; Javier Mateo-Sagasta, Sara Marjani Zadeh, Hugh Turral, et al., "Water Pollution from Agriculture: A Global Review," Food and Agriculture Organization of the United Nations and the International Water Management Institute, 2017, https://www.fao.org/3/i7754e/i7754e.pdf.

23. David R. Simon, *Meatonomics: How the Rigged Economics of Meat and Dairy Make You Consume Too Much—and How to Eat Better, Live Longer, and Spend Smarter* (Newburyport, MA: Conari Press, 2013); Tony Weis, *The Ecological Hoofprint: The Global Burden of Industrial Livestock* (London: Zed Books, 2013).

24. Samantha Lycett, Florian Duchatel, and Paul Digard, "A Brief History of Bird Flu," Philosophical Transactions of the Royal Society B: Biological Sciences 374 (May 6, 2019), https://doi.org/10.1098/rstb.2018.0257; Mike Davis, "The Swine Flu Crisis Lays Bare the Meat Industry's Monstrous Power," *The Guardian*, April 27, 2009, https://www.theguardian.com/commentisfree/2009/apr/27/swine-flu-mexico-health; Jason Lusk and John D. Anderson, "Economic Impacts of COVID-19 on Food and Agricultural Markets," CAST Commentary, 2020, https://www.cast-science.org/publication/economic-impacts-of-covid-19-on-food-and-agricultural-markets/; Kendra

Coulter, "Coronavirus Shows We Must Get Serious about the Well-Being of Animals," The Conversation, May 24, 2020, https://theconversation.com/coronavirus-shows-we-must-get-serious-about-the-well-being-of-animals-138872.

Chapter 17: Honor Killing:
Spiritual Bypass and False Faith in Do-It-Yourself Slaughter

1. Erica Alvey, "Farm Confessional: I Slaughtered an Animal I Truly Loved," Modern Farmer, November 13, 2015, https://modernfarmer.com/2015/11/farm-confessional-i-slaughtered-an-animal-i-truly-loved/.

2. Tina Fossella and John Welwood, "Human Nature, Buddha Nature: An Interview with John Welwood by Tina Fossella," Tricycle: The Buddhist Review, 2011, http://translatedby.com/you/human-nature-buddha-nature-an-interview-with-john-welwood-by-tina-fossella/original/.

3. Mariana Caplan, Eyes Wide Open: Cultivating Discernment on the Spiritual Path (Boulder: Sounds True, 2009), 116.

4. Meredith Leigh and Jean-Martin Fortier, The Ethical Meat Handbook (Gabriola, BC: New Society Publishers, 2015).

5. For a more in depth rendering of the relationship of betrayal to violence in animal agriculture, see Hope Bohanec, The Ultimate Betrayal: Is There Happy Meat? (Bloomington, IN: iUniverse, 2013).

6. Fossella and Welwood, "Human Nature, Buddha Nature."

7. "Ethical Slaughter and Butchery Summer Course," BeginningFarmers.org, April 24, 2017, https://www.beginningfarmers.org/ethical-slaughter-butchery-course/.

8. Fossella and Welwood, "Human Nature, Buddha Nature."

9. Leigh and Fortier, The Ethical Meat Handbook, 84.

10. Fossella and Welwood, "Human Nature, Buddha Nature."

11. Ashley Capps, "Dear Asheville: Your 'Humane Slaughter' Instructors Are Not Your Victims," Free From Harm, November 3, 2017, https://freefromharm.org/animal-rights/humane-slaughter-instructors-are-not-victims/.

12. Caplan, Eyes Wide Open, 125.

13. Alvey, "Farm Confessional."

14. Aiyanna Sezak-Blatt, "Sacred Sacrifice: Upcoming Workshop Embraces Conscious Butchering Practices," Mountain Xpress, October 7, 2015, https://mountainx.com/food/sacred-sacrifice-upcoming-workshop-embraces-conscious-butchering-practices/.

15. "The opposite of faith is not doubt, but certainty. Certainty is missing the point entirely," Anne Lamott, *Plan B: Further Thoughts on Faith* (New York: Riverhead Books, 2006). Also, "Doubt is not the opposite of faith; it is an element of faith," Paul Tillich, *Systematic Theology* 2 (Chicago: University of Chicago Press, 1975).
16. Caplan, *Eyes Wide Open*.
17. Ibid, 126.

Chapter 18: Using the Deeper Dimensions of Jain Ahiṃsā to Shed Light on Dairy's Humane Hoax

1. Christopher Jain Miller and Jonathan Dickstein, "Jain Veganism: Ancient Wisdom, New Opportunities," Religions 12, no. 7, (2021), https://doi.org/10.3390/rel12070512.
2. American Vegan Society, accessed June 15, 2022, https://americanvegan.org/.
3. Tristram Stuart, *The Bloodless Revolution: A Cultural History of Vegetarianism from 1600 to Modern Times* (New York: W.W. Norton & Company, 2006).
4. Lacto-vegetarian refers to someone who does not eat meat and eggs, though still consumes dairy.
5. Miller and Dickstein, "Jain Veganism."
6. Hope Bohanec, "The Humane Hoax: Factory Farming vs. Alternative Farming," The Humane Hoax Project, accessed June 15, 2022, https://humanehoax.org/the-humane-hoax-factory-farming-vs-alternative-farming/.
7. Dr. Jasvant Modi, former president of the Jain Center of Southern California, in email correspondence with the author on August 12, 2021.
8. Kristi L. Wiley, "Karman and Liberation" and "Karman and Saṃsāra," in *Brill's Encyclopedia of Jainism*, eds. John E. Cort, Paul Dundas, Knut A. Jacobsen, et al. (Leiden, Netherlands: Brill, 2020).
9. I would like to pay special thanks to Cogen Bohanec for translating this section of the *Ācārāṅga Sūtra* on my request (August 23, 2021). See the notes that follow.
10. Note from translator (Cogen Bohanec): All of these terms are glossed from *satthaṃ* (Sanskrit *śastra*). This is how Yuvācārya Mahāprajña glosses the term, citing "the *Niryukti* (the earliest commentary) on the Āyāro" (Mahāprajña 1981, 18–19). *Ācārāṅga Sūtra of Ācārya Tulsī*, 1981. "Jain Canonical Text Series," Yuvācārya Mahāprajña, Delhi: Goyal Offset.
11. *Ācārāṅga Sūtra* 1.1.1.31: *ettha satthaṃ samārambhamāṇassa icchete ārambhā apariṇṇātā bhavaṃti* || 31 || "Now (ettha) the [violent *vihiṃsai*, from 1.1.1.27] one who

desires (icchaete) to use (*samārambhamānassa*) a weapons or instruments that cause harm even when they are one's own internal conditions that can be used as weapons (*sattham*, Sanskrit *śastra*) [upon even the tiniest of elemental beings, from previous verses] becomes one who lacks the wisdom of spiritual insight (*aparinnātā*, Sanskrit: aparijñātā)."

12. Ibid. 1.1.1.32: *ettha sattham asamārambhamānassa icchete ārambhā parinnātā bhavamti || 32 ||* "On the other hand (*ettha*) one who desires (*icchete*) not to use (*asamārambhamānassa*) weapons or other such instruments that cause harm such as one's own internal conditions (*sattham*) [upon even the tiniest of elemental beings] develops (wisdom and spiritual insight (*parinnātā*, Sanskrit *parijñātā*)."

13. Ibid. 1.1.1.33: *Tam parinnāya mehāvī neva sayam pudhavi − sattham samārambhejjā, nevannehim pudhavi − sattham samārambhāvejjā, nevanne pudhavi − sattham samārambhamte samanujānejjā ||33||* "Having attained such insight (tam parinnāya), a wise person should never allow for any instrument of harm, internally or externally (sattam), against [even the tiniest] beings in the earth (*mehāvī neva sayam pudhavi − sattham samārambhejjā, nevannehim pudhavi* −), neither should they cause others to do so (*sattham samārambhāvejjā, nevanne pudhavi*), nor should they approve of the engagement of anything, internally or externally, that causes harm (*sattham samārambhamte samanujānejjā*)."

14. Nathmal Tatia, *Tattvārtha Sūtra: That Which Is* (New Haven: Yale University Press, 2011).

15. Monier Williams, *Monier-Williams Sanskrit–English Dictionary* (Oxford: The Clarendon Press, 1899), 274.

16. See Dickstein's article about this issue within the modern yoga communities: Jonathan Dickstein, "Yoga Communities Must Live the Fight Against Factory Farming," Medium, April 17, 2020, https://jonathandickstein.medium.com/yoga-communities-must-live-the-fight-against-factory-farming-7130c1a6ff9a.

17. Ibid.

18. Williams, *Monier-Williams Sanskrit–English Dictionary*, 36.

19. Olivia Petter, "Veganism Is 'Single Biggest Way' to Reduce Our Environmental Impact, Study Finds," *The Independent*, September 24, 2020, https://www.independent.co.uk/life-style/health-and-families/veganism-environmental-impact-planet-reduced-plant-based-diet-humans-study-a8378631.html.

20. "Plant-Based Foods Are Good for Both Health and the Environment," University of Oxford News & Events, October 29, 2019, https://www.ox.ac.uk/news/2019-10-29-plant-based-foods-are-good-both-health-and-environment#:~:text=New%20analysis%20by%20researchers%20from,low%20impact%20on%20the%20environment.

21. "The Dairy Industry," The Vegan Society, https://www.vegansociety.com/go-vegan/why-go-vegan/dairy-industry.

22. Among other things, Jains believe that root vegetables contain countless living organisms attached to them that will be harmed if the root vegetable is uprooted (which also kills the whole plant).

23. "In light of the violence in milk production, we invite Jains to consider giving up dairy this Paryushana.

24. "Transparency in the Chocolate Industry," Food Empowerment Project, https://foodispower.org/human-labor-slavery/transparency/.

25. Zoe Drewett, "Women in India Pay the Price for Cashew Nut Demand as Vegan Diets Rise," Metro, April 4, 2019, https://metro.co.uk/2019/04/04/women-india-pay-price-cashew-nut-demand-vegan-diets-rise-9110415/.

26. Jane Fryer, "Did Slave Monkeys Pick Your Coconuts? With Casual Brutality, Baby Macaques Are Snatched from their Mothers, Chained and Forced to Harvest Up to 1,000 Coconuts a Day—All to Feed the West's Addiction for This Oh-So Trendy Delicacy," Daily Mail, July 8, 2020, https://www.dailymail.co.uk/news/article-8503765/Macaques-snatched-mothers-chained-forced-harvest-1-000-coconuts-day.html.

ABOUT THE EDITOR

HOPE BOHANEC has been active in animal protection and environmental activism for thirty years and has published the book *The Ultimate Betrayal: Is There Happy Meat?* She is the Executive Director of Compassionate Living and the host of the Hope for the Animals Podcast. Hope co-founded the Humane Hoax Project, the Ahimsa Living Project, and has organized numerous online and in-person events including the Humane Hoax Online Conference, the Humane Hoax Chicken Webinar, and the Sonoma County VegFest. Over the last three decades, Hope has worked for the national non-profits United Poultry Concerns and In Defense of Animals and has contributed chapters to two anthologies.

ABOUT THE PUBLISHER

LANTERN PUBLISHING & MEDIA was founded in 2020 to follow and expand on the legacy of Lantern Books—a publishing company started in 1999 on the principles of living with a greater depth and commitment to the preservation of the natural world. Like its predecessor, Lantern Publishing & Media produces books on animal advocacy, veganism, religion, social justice, humane education, psychology, family therapy, and recovery. Lantern is dedicated to printing in the United States on recycled paper and saving resources in our day-to-day operations. Our titles are also available as ebooks and audiobooks.

To catch up on Lantern's publishing program, visit us at www.lanternpm.org.

facebook.com/lanternpm
twitter.com/lanternpm
instagram.com/lanternpm